AESTHETICA

CREATIVE WRITING AWARD 2026

WIN £5000 & PUBLICATION

SUBMIT YOUR POETRY | FICTION

DEADLINE 31 AUGUST 2026

aestheticamagazine.com/creativewriting

GRANTA

12 Addison Avenue, London W11 4QR | email: editorial@granta.com
To subscribe visit subscribe.granta.com, or call +44 (0)1371 851873

ISSUE 175: SPRING 2026

EDITOR	Thomas Meaney
MD & DEPUTY EDITOR	Luke Neima
SENIOR EDITOR	Josie Mitchell
MANAGING EDITOR	Tom Bolger
ASSOCIATE DESIGN DIRECTOR	Daniela Silva
ASSOCIATE EDITOR	Brodie Crellin
EDITORIAL ASSISTANT	Aea Varfis-van Warmelo
PHOTOGRAPHY EDITOR	Max Ferguson
SPECIAL PROJECTS	Janique Vigier
CONSULTING EDITOR	Morten Høi Jensen
COMMERCIAL DIRECTOR	Noel Murphy
OPERATIONS & SUBSCRIPTIONS	Sam Lachter
MARKETING	Simon Heafield
PUBLICITY	publicity@granta.com
CONTRACTS	Isabella Depiazzi
ADVERTISING	Renata Molina-Lopes, Renata.Molina-Lopes@granta.com
FINANCE	Thomas Smith
SALES	Rosie Morgan
IT SUPPORT	Ravi Dhir
PRODUCTION & DESIGN DIRECTOR	Sarah Wasley
PROOFS	Katherine Fry, Jessica Kelly, Jess Porter, Will Rees, Francisco Vilhena
CONTRIBUTING EDITORS	Anne Carson, Michael Hofmann, A.M. Homes, Rahmane Idrissa, Karan Mahajan, Leo Robson
PUBLISHER	Sigrid Rausing

p.6 Quote from *Knut Hamsun Remembers America*, translated and edited by Richard Nelson Current, published by University of Missouri Press; p.171–181 'Backwoods Fable' is an excerpt from the novel *Låŋtdievvá* (North Sámi) / *Planterhaug* (Norwegian) by Sigbjørn Skåden. Special thanks to Simen V. Gonsholt, Karolina Ramqvist, Damion Searls.

This selection copyright © 2026 Granta Trust.

Granta (ISSN 173231 USPS 508) is published four times a year by Granta Trust, 12 Addison Avenue, London, W11 4QR, UK.

Airfreight and mailing in the USA by agent named World Container Inc., 150–15, 183rd Street, Jamaica, NY 11413, USA.

Periodicals postage paid at Brooklyn, NY 11256.

Postmaster: Send address changes to *Granta*, ESco, Trinity House, Sculpins Lane, Wethersfield, Braintree, CM7 4AY, UK.

Subscription records are maintained at *Granta*, c/o ESco Business Services Ltd, Wethersfield, Essex, CM7 4AY, UK.

Air Business Ltd is acting as our mailing agent.

The manufacturer's authorised representative in the EU for product safety is Authorised Rep Compliance Ltd, 71 Lower Baggot Street, Dublin D02 P593, Ireland (arccompliance.com)

Granta is printed and bound in Italy by Legoprint. This magazine is printed on paper that fulfils the criteria for 'Paper for permanent document' according to ISO 9706 and the American Library Standard ANSI/NIZO Z39.48-1992 and has been certified by the Forest Stewardship Council® (FSC®). *Granta* is indexed in the American Humanities Index.

ISBN 978-1-909-889-80-4

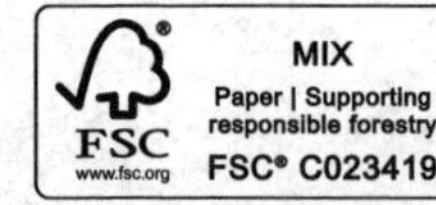

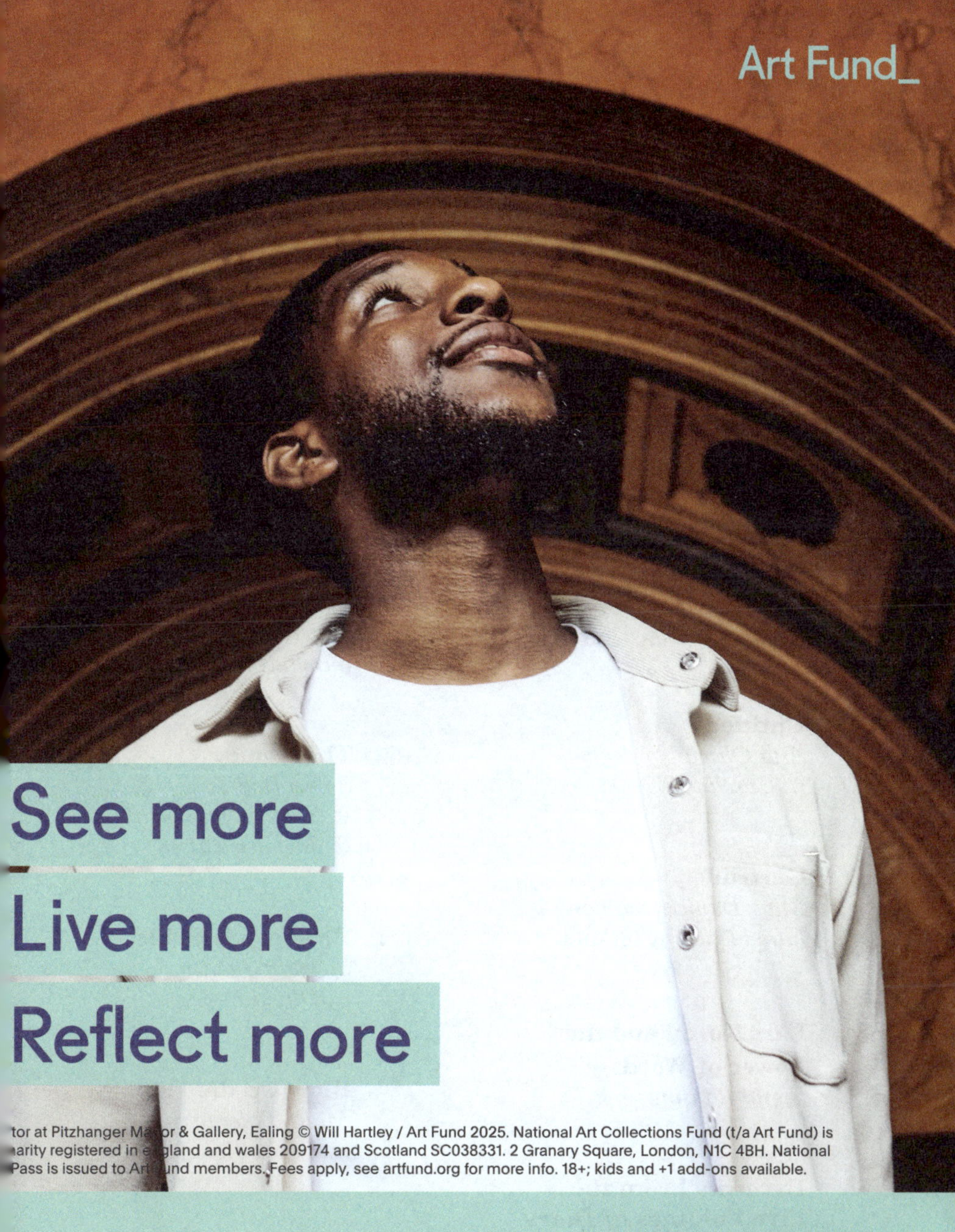
Art Fund_
See more
Live more
Reflect more
tor at Pitzhanger Ma r & Gallery, Ealing © Will Hartley / Art Fund 2025. National Art Collections Fund (t/a Art Fund) is
arity registered in e gland and wales 209174 and Scotland SC038331. 2 Granary Square, London, N1C 4BH. National
Pass is issued to Ar und members. Fees apply, see artfund.org for more info. 18+; kids and +1 add-ons available.
njoy free or half price entry
100s of museums and galleries
iscover more, visit ArtFund.org
National Art Pass_

CONTENTS

We live up here in the hills that rise like a second story over other European lands. Now and then the din carries up from down below, from the noisy, lively, lusty world.

– Knut Hamsun, 21 January 1885

Independent People?

1

Alfred Nobel made his fortune with the nitroglycerin-based explosive known as dynamite, but his dream was to be a poet. He wrote verse in moleskin notebooks, sketched out plays, and, shortly before his death in 1896, completed a four-act tragedy set in Renaissance Rome about a woman who murders her rapist father. When it came to style, Nobel was a Romantic of a simple sort. He believed writers should lift readers up and show the will of the individual triumphing over adversity. His favorite writer of his day was the now largely forgotten poet Viktor Rydberg, an ardent progressive and idealist. When Nobel left instructions for the literary prize that bears his name, he stipulated the honor should go to 'outstanding work in an ideal direction'. He almost certainly had in mind the direction of Rydberg. For many years, the Swedish Academy abided by Nobel's wishes, and awarded the Prize to writers who would likewise be forgotten.

In Nobel's time there was another poet who raged in the opposite direction. He followed his thoughts to the darkest recesses of his mind, and confronted the concrete reality of his age, including the inventions of Nobel himself. In 1883, August Strindberg – whom Nobel did not care for – wrote 'Folkupplagan', an ode to the dynamite used in assassination attempts on the Russian Tsar ('Nobel, we rarely hear your name praised!'). When it became clear – after more than a decade of being passed over by the Swedish Academy – that Strindberg would never win the Nobel Prize, more than 20,000 people across Sweden contributed to funding an anti-Nobel Prize, which Strindberg declined. Since the beginning, the most stubborn spirits of modern Scandinavian literature have pitted themselves against the lures of respectability and prestige. The sweeter irony would have to wait another century, when Nobel's play *Nemesis* was performed at Strindberg's Intimate Theater in Stockholm to unanimously negative reviews.

What sets Scandinavian literature apart from the rest of European literature? Why, at its best, does its fiction seem to pack in more force, pound for pound?

If one had to sum up the reasons in a word, it would be: *lateness*.

Christianity arrived *late* in the lands of the north. When it did come, starting in the ninth century, it had less luck uprooting pagan beliefs and practices. Unlike on the European mainland, where pagan epics were Christianized, or left to molder in libraries, early Christian leaders in Scandinavia did not suppress the Viking sagas and cosmologies. Valhalla was not emptied of its gods. The result was a store chest that modern writers from Sigrid Undset to Halldór Laxness could draw upon. They did not need to fawn over Homer and Virgil, epics from another world; they had their own.

Scandinavia was also *late* to de-Christianize. The strict Lutheran Pietism that covered the region stressed the rigorous examination of one's soul and the redemptive power of faith. But when Pietism began to thaw in the nineteenth century, it left behind strange specimens in its wake: people with faith, in a world without God, fighting to extract meaning from nothingness. The condition was not unique to Scandinavia, but the most significant diagnosis of it was. A young Dane in Copenhagen – Søren Kierkegaard – was among the first to see how the emerging secular order was, in fact, a disaster. The project of providing rational justifications for moral life had failed. Instead, radical commitment – leaps of faith – had to be called upon to do the work reason could not shoulder. Scandinavian literature is full of characters in this predicament: maniacs who curse a God they know doesn't exist, farmers who would rather worship sheep than saints, and outcasts, like Pär Lagerkvist's Barabbas, who are stunned by their own numbness in the face of transcendence.

Aftershocks of the collapse of Pietism are still there in Scandinavian literature. Characteristically, its greatest writers distrust abstraction and analysis – the operations of reason itself. Kierkegaard liked to joke that Hegel's philosophical treatises, which feature Reason as their hero, would have been extraordinary if he had only thought of them as novels. Laxness deplored the 'novel of ideas' as the wrong road for art: 'With this method the writer does not try to build from the material he has in front of him, but rather tries to analyze and criticize it, to conceal it, and never set his eyes again on any edifying central power.' Lars Norén's way of mocking abstraction was to have a character on the verge of sleeping with his mother analyze his social position with reference to the theories of Pierre Bourdieu.

Scandinavia was *late* to industrialize, *late* to shed its peasantry, and *late* to develop the historical motor known as the bourgeoisie. One aspect of Henrik Ibsen that never fails to astonish is how he approaches this class as if for the first time. His characters are almost exclusively professionals: shipbuilders, accountants, printers, architects, developers, financiers. The kind of social critique Ibsen pioneered is still alive in Scandinavian literature today – it continues to mark the work of young Scandinavian playwrights, like Kathrine Nedrejord and Fredrik Brattberg, and traces of it are visible in writers as different as Vigdis Hjorth and Jonas Eika. For Ibsen, the modern world that professes freedom and progress is built on repression and illusion. In making his characters so archetypal, in exposing the hypocrisies of bourgeois life so baldly, Ibsen made his work much more universal – and exportable – than most. Before she left the Shanghai stage to marry Mao Zedong and join the Communists, Jiang Qing played Nora in *A Doll's House*.

Even after Denmark, Sweden and Norway pulled apart from one another and, by the early twentieth century, had settled into nation states, 'Scandinavia' remained a coherent social world. Its cultural and political headquarters were in Copenhagen, where most publishers were located. It was not uncommon for writers as far away as Iceland, such as Gunnar Gunnarsson, to write in Danish. Scandinavian writers translated one another and produced each other's plays. All the while, each developed a distinctive modern literature. In Denmark, Henrik Pontoppidan brought the young-man-from-the-provinces *Bildungsroman* to its apogee, while Tove Ditlevsen introduced a new kind of working-class writing. In Sweden, writers from Hjalmar Söderberg (his revival in English will come) all the way to Stig Dagerman honed a tradition of psychological portraiture. In Norway, a country without a native nobility, writers became a kind of aristocracy, with more of a license to experiment. Their greatest aesthetic innovations were grounded in their suspicion of the 'novelistic'. 'Truth is neither objectivity nor the balanced view,' Knut Hamsun wrote, 'truth is a *selfless subjectivity*.' This use of the self as a battered observation deck finds an echo in Karl Ove Knausgård. When the protagonist of *My Struggle* looks at the paintings he most admires, he focuses on 'a distance between reality and the portrayal of reality', believing 'it was doubtless in this interlying space where it "happened", where it appeared, whatever it was I saw, when the world seemed to step forward from the world.'

2

For those on the outside, Scandinavia can appear to be a near-mythical land. In the 1930s, when Europe was turning toward the Right, Social Democratic parties established their dominance in Sweden and Norway. Two centuries of Lutheran *husförhör* – household examinations to test the ability of people to read the small catechism – paved the way for worker education. The secret of the Social Democratic triumph, however, was the canny placating of farmers, who in the rest of Europe often joined the ranks of fascism. Meanwhile, the urban commercial classes reached a compromise with the proletariat: workers could live better than their peers on the continent as long as they forswore revolutionary programs. Franklin Roosevelt looked at this 'middle way' with envy. Steering clear of the Manichaeanism of the Cold War, Sweden in particular followed a 'neutral' line that inoculated its citizens from mass hysteria. In figures like Rudolf Meidner, Olof Palme, and Dag Hammarskjöld, the largest state in Scandinavia seemed to be helmed by dignified sages, determined to do good everywhere from Kiruna to the Congo.

But Scandinavia's aloofness from the wider West has always been something of an illusion. There may be no better example than Palme himself, who, while he posed for the cameras with Castro and compared the American bombing of Hanoi to Guernica, facilitated covert defense agreements with the CIA and NATO. 'For God's sake make sure that our military cooperation with the Americans continues now that I'm messing with their government,' he told his defense ministers at the height of the Vietnam War. More significant for Swedish culture was Palme's authorization of the surveillance of his New Left opposition. The failure of the Social Democrats to incorporate those radicalized in the 1960s and 70s more effectively into government meant that they concentrated in the cultural sphere. This separation has had benefits and drawbacks: a more autonomous culture industry but also a more hermetic one.

What is the real legacy of the Social Democratic achievement? It is true that Swedes and Norwegians still have greater labor protections, and more hours of paid leave, than elsewhere in the West. But their special position has eroded since the 1970s. Once upon a time, Social Democratic parties in Scandinavia devised mechanisms such as wage-earner funds, corporate taxes used to buy shares in companies for trade unions, with the idea that they would eventually own their workplaces. This never came to pass. Instead, a later generation of Social Democratic leaders increased their faith in the market. Unthinkable in the 1970s, by some measures Sweden today has the highest wealth inequality in all of Europe. The Swedish Right, in the form of the Sweden Democrats, has made gains by presenting itself as the defender of the welfare state, borrowing the old Social Democratic rhetoric of the *Folkhemmet* – 'the people's home' – while advertising its appetite to diminish unions.

Many of the leaps in living conditions in Sweden and Norway originated in wildcat strikes and agitation from the militant trade unionists. All the while, Social Democrats spared no energy in containing, marginalizing, and repressing formations to their left. In 1951, as part of Norway's headlong plunge into NATO, the ruling Labour Party launched 'Operation Asphalt'. Claiming to be concerned about Communist spies visiting the graves in Norway of the thousands of Soviet POWs whom the Germans had captured during Operation Barbarossa, the Labour Party went to the trouble of digging up the burial grounds. Among the interred were Communist Norwegian Resistance fighters. Their remains were shipped to an anonymous mass grave on the island of Tjøtta, with orders for the naval transport carrying the rotted corpses to fire warning shots at protestors in the port. In the 1970s, instead of a resource-curse, Norway experienced a resource-kiss, with the discovery of offshore oil, the profits of which were channeled into distributive funds enjoyed by much of the population. But there was never any real chance for using these funds to purchase portions of the productive economy by the people. Instead, what Terje Tvedt has dubbed 'the humanitarian-political complex' took hold, with hundreds of thousands of Norwegians anesthetized into NGO work.

But in very few ways is Scandinavia still synonymous with humanitarian goodwill. In 2016, Denmark passed the so-called 'jewelry law', which authorized seizing the valuables of asylum seekers entering the country. The country's current humanitarian-in-chief, Mette Frederiksen, has set the bar higher, aiming for a 'zero' refugee policy. She advocates the self-deportation of Syrians back to the US-European-Israeli-brokered chaos in the Middle East. 'It's what I would have done,' she said. So unintegrated has Sweden become that it now has its own party for minority voters from immigrant backgrounds, *Partiet Nyans* (the Nuance Party), which won three municipal seats in the 2022 election. The integrative success of some of the larger Scandinavian cities can be contrasted to a town like Stavanger, the oil capital of Norway, where, around the harbor at night, migrant youth sell themselves for the price of a cocktail.

The situation of the Indigenous Sámi is more paradoxical. Their position as punished people spanning the northern reaches of Norway, Sweden, and Finland began to change in the late 1980s, as they received increased autonomy, and acknowledgment from Nordic states of the gruesome sterilization campaigns waged against them through the mid-twentieth century. Today there are significant efforts to bridge the communities and languages of the north via the the Saami Council. But the entry of the Sámi into wider Scandinavian culture often takes unfortunate forms. Artists have had to manifest their nativeness in pre-scripted ways. The performance reached an apotheosis this year in the Tate Modern's Turbine Hall, where the Hyundai Motor Company funded Máret Ánne Sara's attempt to redeem the museum's past as an oil-fired power station by draping its interior with the pelts of Arctic animals. Reindeer-washing, in a word.

The Arctic north is not the only under-examined region in Nordic literature. In much of its fiction 'America' functions as the void where characters find themselves after they are swept off the stage of a novel, typically to chase their fortune. Knut Hamsun first tried to make his name as a travel correspondent in the US only to wind up lecturing in Midwestern town halls and minding pigs in Minneapolis. He developed a disgust with the modern world, of which he took America to be a grisly preview. 'A mulatto stud-farm,' he called it. Starting off as an anarchist – he wore a ribbon to commemorate the Haymarket Massacre in Chicago – he found his ideological home in Nazism ('I am German'), convinced that Hitler would put an end to vampiric English commercial values. The other great Nordic literary reaction to America came from the Left. Halldór Laxness was a Communist who moved to Los Angeles, where he tried to write for the screen. His view of US society was the opposite of Hamsun's. 'I am like a black man in America!' he declared in solidarity after listening to the singer Roland Hayes in Oakland.

Laxness did everything he could to distance himself from the dark star of Hamsun's genius. Nevertheless, both believed their countries should stand apart from the rest of the world. Hamsun was worried that Norway would become a country like Switzerland: a land of waiters, resorts, and rest cures. Laxness was likewise preoccupied with infringements on his country's sovereignty. He devoted *The Atom Station* to the drama of Iceland's entry into NATO, which yielded the largest street protest in the country's history. In the novel, a young serving woman from the north overhears the Reykjavík notables selling out the nation. The difference between Hamsun and Laxness was in the fineness of their irony. In Laxness's *Independent People*, Bjartur of Summerhouses works himself to the bone to keep his farm out of debt and under his own command, but all the while he is dependent on the most cosmopolitan of commodities: coffee.

3

The Scandinavia issue of *Granta* was marked by an overflow of material. We avoided some things: historical dress-rehearsal fiction, fantasias of the deep Scandinavian past; stories of quiet, contemplative people performing daily routines; and what Hans Magnus Enzensberger once dubbed social democratic literature: 'well-meaning opinions, a respectable and decidedly antifascist and democratic attitude . . . harmless aesthetics'. We were delighted by how much of the fiction, poetry, and photography seized us.

Helle Helle is a celebrated author in her native Denmark, though her work has only recently begun to gain wider attention in English. The six stories that appear here, adeptly translated by Martin Aitken, are drawn from her collections *Rester* and *Biler og dyr*, longtime fixtures on Danish school syllabi. The stories, set in small towns on the rural margins, introduce the familiar yet off-kilter domestic encounters that characterize her disquieting fiction. Olga Ravn is one of the most dexterous Danish writers, having written sci-fi, poetry, Gothic fiction, and, most recently, an adaptation for the stage of Tove Ditlevsen's *Copenhagen Trilogy*. Her work has concentrated on the body as a site of contestation between the self and the external world. In Ravn's story for this issue, also translated by Aitken, a woman's difficult second birth is eased by the 'High Priestess', a tarot card made manifest – perched atop her shoulder – and giving guidance.

Malte Tellerup, a former elite handball player, is known for writing about youthful characters on the outskirts of society. His work is marked by an interest in nature, either his native Fyn, or in his second novel *Hedeselskabet*, the West Jutland heaths. In 'Blow Up the Factory', translated by Denise Rose Hansen, he attends to the first stirrings of an unfolding eco-activist plot, which requires an enormous amount of fertilizer. Solvej Balle has made her name in the Anglosphere with

On the Calculation of Volume, a set of seven linked novels about Tara Selter, an antiquarian bookseller who finds herself repeatedly living through the same day. In 'The Aviary', translated by Sophia Hersi Smith and Jennifer Russell, Balle turns her attention to childhood in an unsettling story of a brother and sister's excitement when a stranger comes to stay. Jonas Eika is the author of the exceptional collection of stories *After the Sun*. In 'The Forest Kindergartners', part of a novel still underway, translated here by Sherilyn Hellberg, Eika sets the action in the wake of the 2022 Danish 'Act on Parental Responsibility', as two parents come to terms with the nowness that is a newborn and struggle to prioritize politics, pleasure, and care.

The playwright, poet, and novelist Jon Fosse hardly needs any introduction. No writer of our time is more in tune with the repetitive power of words, and the incantatory possibilities of prose that becomes a fluid in which all characters are held, rather than a substance that divides them. In 'Vaim Hotel', an excerpt from his forthcoming novel, Fosse's fine shifts of attention come to the fore, as does his gift for comedy, rendered here in Damion Searls's supple translation. In 'The Good Person of Sandvika', Vigdis Hjorth returns to the magazine with a story set in a local pub, where the writer quietly observes the other regulars. Her fellow drinkers sink pints, escalate from beers to whiskeys, and although the clientele keep mostly to themselves, the narrator develops a one-sided intimacy with those around her. In charismatic prose, translated by Charlotte Barslund, Hjorth not only examines the underside of social spaces but also the ethics of interference.

Kyrre Andreassen could perhaps be described as a recovering dirty realist. The author of one of the most beloved recent Norwegian novels, *Ikke mennesker jeg kan regne med* (*Not People I Can Depend On*), he is an expert at crafting original characters and satirizing social democratic pieties. Andreassen's 'Furthermore, I Consider that Carthage Must Be Destroyed' – translated by Lucy Moffatt – is a roving monologue from Krister, an electrician forced into a career change by a workplace injury. Krister rolls his eyes at the constrictions of politeness, at his wife's desire for an Italian-style pergola in their snowy garden, at the superciliousness of his son's schoolteachers, and at how susceptible he is to participating in everything he hates. Swerving the reification of Indigeneity, we are pleased to present Sigbjørn Skåden's 'Backwoods Fable', translated by Olivia Lasky from both the Northern Sámi and Norwegian. In a noir tale with overtones from James Joyce's *Ulysses*, a police inspector's evening is interrupted by ominous visions.

Finland, like Iceland, may not be formally part of Scandinavia, but it is bound up with it historically. In the Finnish novelist Pirkko Saisio's 'Ioseb', an excerpt from *Suliko* translated by Aleksi Koponen, the future Joseph Stalin, aged ten, meets a local priest in the Georgian town of Gori as he prepares to leave home and enter the town's school of theology – the first stage of a clerical education that would precede his political formation.

In two brief, forthright poems, Audun Mortensen, who has just turned forty, assesses whether any childishness remains in his life. It is still there, revealing itself in his sullenness, inattentiveness, apathy, envy, all confessed with Mortensen's gift of conjuring emotion from monotony. Søren Ulrik Thomsen formed part of the Danish generation of so-called Eighties poets inspired by the punk scene. His debut, *City Slang*, was a restless evocation of the nightscapes of Copenhagen, Hamburg, and Amsterdam. Thomsen, a few decades ahead of Mortensen, also confronts age in a sequence of poems inspired by Charles Bukowski's 'The Worst And The Best', translated by Patrick Phillips. The poet and novelist Asta Olivia Nordenhof has been a force in Danish literature since her twenties, and is now known for her ongoing septology *Scandinavian Star*. In 'Untitled', translated by Caroline Waight, Nordenhof considers the absurdity of consumer reviews in two registers, in some of the most point-blank poetry we encountered. Ingela Strandberg, whose selected poems *Granta* will publish in English next year, in a collection translated by Sigrid Rausing, is revered by Swedish readers for her startling capacity to make landscapes breathe with life. The Icelandic Sunna

Dís Másdóttir's poems – translated by Esja Alyssa Matich and Larissa Kyzer – send up the received image of an Icelandic poet, all while packing each line with raw detail. Since his debut with *Sakte dans ut av brennende hus* (*A Slow Dance Out of a Burning House*), Espen Stueland has become the great Norwegian poet and essayist of dissection. He shows here in his 'Dummy Genealogy', translated by Ingvild Burkey, that he continues to write with a scalpel.

On our art front, Maja Daniels enters into the wake of the Swedish witch trials in Älvdalen; Stephen Gill takes us on the school run and absorbs the seasons of Skåne; Ikram Abdulkadir captures the spontaneity of Malmö on the move; and Inuuteq Storch uses archival photos by his parents to subvert ethnographic depictions of Greenland. We also showcase recent paintings by Mamma Andersson, in whose work the natural world appears like a sublime ruin.

In our nonfiction in this issue, we feature a condensed excerpt from the Finnish writer Eeva Kilpi's *Naisen päiväkirja* (*A Woman's Diary*), which records the year 1978 from spring to autumn, in entries shaped by motherhood, the challenge of writing, and periods of depression. Now ninety-eight and long recognized in Finland, Kilpi remains a central figure in Finnish letters. Our selection focuses on her June entries written after she retreats to a cabin in Piskola to work on her next book, in a section translated by Mia Spangenberg.

In 2008, a book was published in Sweden that caused a scandal. Lars Norén's 1,680-page diary – *En dramatikers dagbok* – which he retrospectively called a novel, heaped venom on his fellow directors and actors, and recounted his life in unsparing detail. A typical entry:

> I was sitting watching a worthless Harrison Ford movie when I suddenly got a bad bout of stomach cramp. Went to the lavatory. Shit on my shorts. Mainly blood. A significant amount. I cleaned up, washed my clothes, hung them up to dry, packed my rucksack, shoved in cigarettes, glasses, book, money. Phoned the emergency room at Danderyds Hospital, but the nurse who

> answered said she didn't think I needed to come in. She said the blood might be the result of an inflammation which I've got because I frequently need to go to the lavatory. She told me to wait and see. Fell asleep late. Restless. Woke at 7 this morning. Beautiful outside. Calm, minus 14 degrees celsius. Sun. Went shopping at Rimi. Sat and read between cramps. Called Charly and said that unfortunately I couldn't make it. Went out to buy cigarettes. Slept two hours. Spoke for a while with Masja and Linda. Slept again. I love the current silence. Don't know if I can travel to Gotland. Will have to see if there is more blood tonight.

It says something that a younger generation of Scandinavian writers read a passage like this and saw possibilities for their art. In Knausgård's six-novel cycle, *My Struggle*, the accounting is more solemn, almost Lutheran in its austerity, but no less exhaustive. The whole profane existence of the novelist is laid out for sacred inspection. We present, for the first time in English, a selection of Norén's diaries in a haunting translation by our in-house Swede, Sigrid Rausing. 'There's space for everything in Norén's writing, from the trivial to the profound,' Rausing writes. 'He records it all, typing and smoking compulsively in bare rooms.'

Finally, this issue includes an essay by Knausgård about the Norwegian novelist and poet Tarjei Vesaas, who, in two recent Penguin reissues, is now enjoying the attention in English he never received in his lifetime. There are certain advantages to being Scandinavian, Knausgård reminds us, not least of which is being able to read its literature in the original. In 'A Strange Bird's Cry', he considers several of the themes that bind this issue together: repetition, silence, hatred, care, despair, renewal. 'Literature,' Knausgård writes, 'is the place where the other reality, the one that takes place between people, animals, things and places, and which cannot be seen but is invisible, literature is the place where all this takes shape.' ■

TM

FROM THE **WINNER** OF THE NOBEL PRIZE IN LITERATURE

WHAT ARE WE **GIVEN**, AND WHAT DO WE HAVE TO **TAKE** FOR OURSELVES?

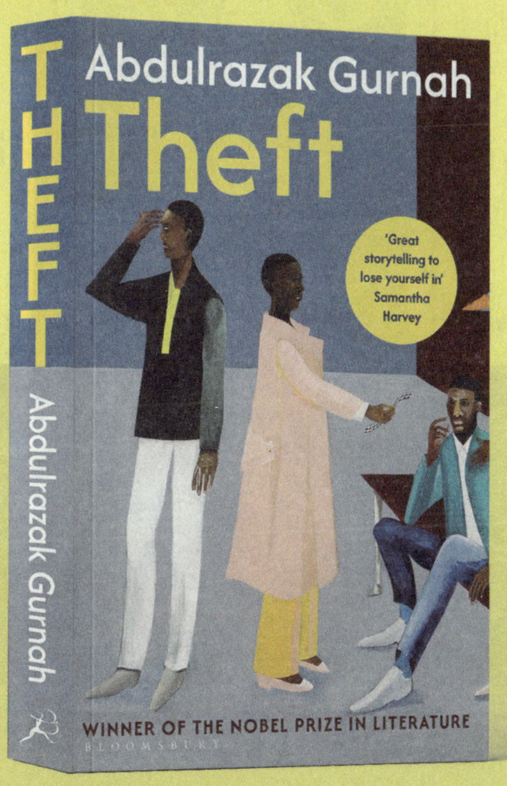

'A poignant portrait of love, friendship and betrayal' GUARDIAN

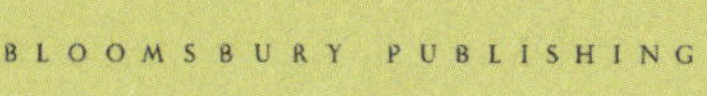

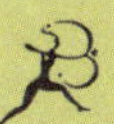

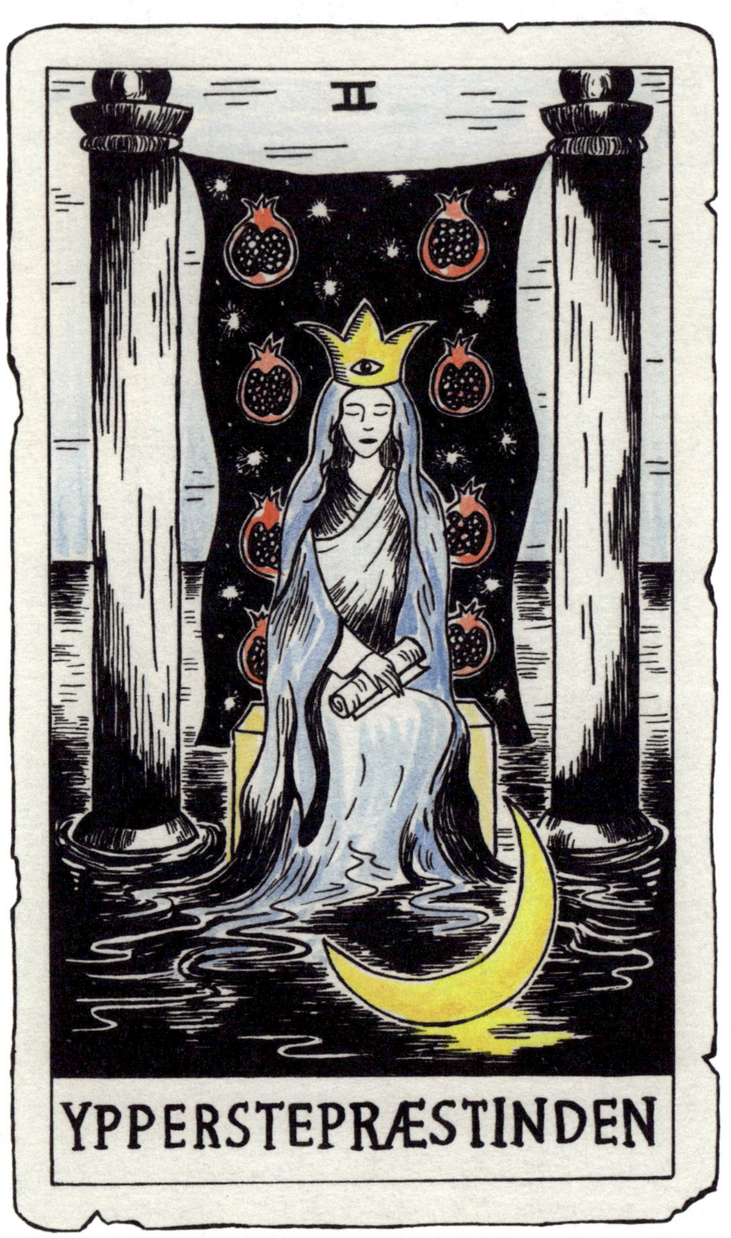

PERNILLE GREGERSEN

THE HIGH PRIESTESS

Olga Ravn

TRANSLATED FROM THE DANISH BY MARTIN AITKEN

As a child, to the puzzlement of those around me, I developed an interest in tarot cards. When at first they gave me horse-themed playing cards, I considered it an insult. As soon as I was old enough, I took the S-train and bought myself a beginner's set from The Bookshop of the Unknown. It was a simple yellow box containing a deck of playing cards and a blue book about how to read them. In time, I became familiar with every card. One in particular fascinated me. The High Priestess. It showed a woman seated between two pillars, in her lap she held a scroll. Her bright blue headscarf, cape and dress ran together as one. A slender yellow crescent moon rested at her feet. On her head was a crown, behind her a drape patterned with pomegranates. There was something mesmerising about the drape, it drew you in, and beyond it lay the suggestion of a horizon or the sea, a wonderful darkness.

I mention it now, because this figure visited me when I was about to give birth to my second child. I had not used the tarot cards in years, other than perhaps as a party trick on New Year's Eve. It was evening and the contractions were doing their work. I had told my husband early that morning that we should drive to the hospital, but when the midwife there had examined me they sent us home again, I was no more than two centimetres dilated. Miraculously,

February was awash with golden light, and the frost came together with the warm sunshine to fill the firmament with eddies of mist. We had borrowed the neighbour's car. At 3 p.m. we drove to the hospital again, this time I was certain the baby would come, but I was only three centimetres dilated and was sent home once more.

My father-in-law had arrived at the flat to babysit the eldest and was surprised to see us back already. I couldn't understand it, my first child had come quickly, but now I could no longer read my body, my womb, my muscles, and there were new signals too that I was unable to decode. I focused intently on each contraction.

'How long have they been going on?' my father-in-law asked.

'Since this morning,' someone replied.

Evening came, it was 6 p.m. My father-in-law's presence was becoming a problem. I wanted to be naked. I was too self-conscious to surrender fully to the contractions with him there. I asked him to leave and come back later. My husband was very embarrassed, but when a woman is giving birth, there is no room for manners.

The child was put to bed. You should sleep too, I told my husband. The contractions kept coming, the uterus tightening and hardening, but still there was no regularity to it. Soon everyone was sleeping. The city too, seen through the windows, switched off its lights; midnight approached. I watched a drunken man in the street fumble to pull out his penis and urinate into the wire fence, over the blackberries and the bittersweet nightshade. But it was a phantasm, for it was winter, the soil was bare. I looked up at a shelf, and there was the old box with the tarot cards in it. I picked a card. It was the High Priestess. There was a fleeting smile. I tidied up, I packed a bag. Alternately, I paced the flat or lay on my side in bed next to my sleeping husband, rising again whenever it hurt too much to stay there. I asked myself continually whether I should wake him up, whether now was the time to go to the hospital, whether we should phone my father-in-law again. All the time, the stupid thought kept coming back to me that I no longer knew my own body, that I had to be constantly on the lookout for signs that would indicate my current condition. That was when I noticed her. I saw her, though not with my eyes, because she was directly behind my left shoulder. The High Priestess.

'What shall I do?' I asked her.

'Wait,' she said.

I waited a while. The contractions continued. It started hurting in a new way.

'What shall I do?' I asked.

'Wait,' she said.

I waited some more.

'What shall I do?' I asked.

'Now you can wake him,' she said.

I woke my husband and told him it was time. We phoned, left the flat, etc.

Now the city was a night-city. We drove through it. It was excruciating to be sitting in the car. I said nothing. She was on my shoulder.

In the examining room I could hardly bear to lie on my back.

'You're four centimetres dilated,' a hospital staff member said. I have no idea if she was a midwife or who she was. I didn't see her face, and never saw her again, but I remember blurting out in disbelief: 'Four centimetres?'

I started crying.

'Would you please just admit me?'

She was still on my left shoulder, attentive but silent.

'All right, I'll call a midwife who can take you to a delivery room.'

Unable to look up, I had to cling to the wall. All the way along the corridor I saw nothing but the floor and the midwife's bare feet in a pair of blue flip-flops. I hated her so fiercely for those flip-flops.

'I'm ready for some laughing gas now,' I said, my eyes still fixed on the floor.

'We don't have laughing gas here,' she said.

She was exactly the kind of unbearable person who sings Disney songs when drunk.

'Why not?' my husband asked.

'For environmental reasons.'

The flip-flop midwife stroked my arm. Apparently, I was now lying down.

'Please stop stroking my arm,' I said.

She stepped away.

But soon she was there again, stroking away.

'Stop touching me,' I hissed, the High Priestess on my shoulder.

'I think you should go,' I said.

'But I can't go, not when you're in such a state.'

'Go!'

Oh, the startled brown eyes of that flip-floppy girl we wished never to see again. I pulled my husband towards me and rattled: 'Get me another midwife.'

He nodded and went away, and came back with another. She introduced herself politely and I saw that her hair was in dreadlocks even though she was white. She would have to do. I myself could do no more. I shat the bed.

'Let me have a look at you,' the new midwife said.

I tried to turn onto my back, but it was no use, it hurt too much.

'I can't,' I groaned.

'Try again after the next contraction,' the new midwife said.

'Can I?' I silently asked the High Priestess.

'No,' she replied.

'I can't,' I said out loud.

'OK,' the new midwife said, 'I can see you're in some discomfort.'

'I want an epidural,' I said.

'Are you sure?' the new midwife said.

'Yes,' the High Priestess said.

'Yes,' I said.

And there were fingernails scraping across a yellow porous wall of stone, there was a ravine, a possible fall, beneath me danger, a sea of pain or a valley of cold fire, unseen but sensed.

'I want an epidural,' I said again.

'I'll fetch my superior,' the new midwife said.

When the ward midwife appeared, I was standing naked up against the wall. They got me back onto the bed, my legs started shaking violently. They examined me.

'You're seven centimetres dilated.'

'I want an epidural,' I said.

'Hmm,' the ward midwife said. 'Why not move around for an hour first?'

'An hour?' I screeched.

The High Priestess shook her head.

'Do I need an epidural?' I asked in my mind, directing the question towards my left shoulder where still she sat.

'Yes,' she said.

'I need that epidural, now,' I said out loud.

'OK, we'll send for a doctor,' the ward midwife said.

The doctor came. The epidural was administered and it was good. I ate a slice of toast. I could lie on my back. I smiled, looked around me, and, as if for the first time, noticed my husband. I'd forgotten he was there. Then the urge came over me to push, and I said so.

'OK,' the new midwife said. She had been sitting in the corner, writing in my patient record. Now she came over and examined me.

'You're almost ready, but don't push yet.'

With the epidural I was in control, I lifted my chin and gasped between contractions, without pushing.

At some point in time, although time did not exist, the new midwife said: 'Try getting down on all fours,' and so that was what I did, on the bed.

'Now try pushing,' she said, and I did that too.

I kept on pushing.

'Now the head is out,' she said.

And with the next contraction he was delivered.

Then came the placenta.

Then there was a shift handover.

I was happy. The High Priestess on my shoulder nodded

approvingly. I stood up, blood ran down my leg and stained my sock, I laughed with surprise.

'What a plump little one you are,' I said, and kissed the child.

He was the spitting image of my father-in-law.

He latched on hard, and in the days that followed we worked together to help the milk come in. The High Priestess sat on my left shoulder, her small feet dangled in their small blue shoes, she had not left me since the moment she first appeared in the flat. During the night, in the hours before the milk came in, I was furious with my husband because he wanted – no, I can no longer remember. What I do remember is locking myself in the bathroom on the ward and weeping with rage, that feeling of melting away from oneself, like paper dissolving in water, and as I cry I keep repeating out loud: 'What am I going to do? What am I going to do?' And the High Priestess on my shoulder, replying: 'You must relax.' And me raising my voice to answer her: 'But I can't.' And then I stop, realising that I've been speaking out loud to myself, or rather to a voice on my shoulder, and it scares me, I say to her: 'It's time for you to go.' And this she accepts, but she says too: 'Until we meet again.' And there was no metallic laughter, no pears fell happily from the tree into the wet grass, no nails were hammered into petals, there was nothing so tender as flesh or the frayed edge of the unbridled cloth, no deep blue velvet under careful silk, no, there was linoleum, latex, paper, glue. Loneliness and understanding, a footstep in snow, and the creak it made. I was a human being. ■

Cormorant

A Cultural History of Greed and Prejudice

Gordon McMullan

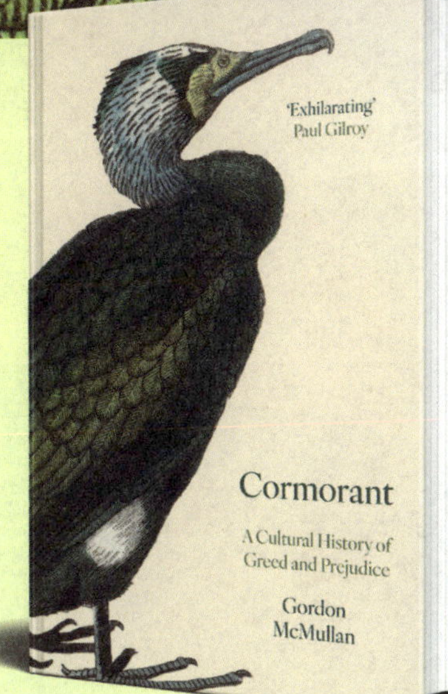

'This is one of the most original, stylish and memorable works of cultural criticism I have read in a long time.'

Sir Jonathan Bate, Regents Professor of Literature and Foundation Professor of Environmental Humanities at Arizona State University, and author of *The Song of the Earth*

'A fascinating, wide-ranging, spiky, cultural and biological biography of "pretty much nobody's favourite bird".'

Tim Birkhead, author of *The Great Auk*

'A brilliant portrait of the cormorant, and a story about historical bias and colonial extraction.'

Bénédicte Boisseron, Professor of Afroamerican and African Studies, The University of Michigan

'This exhilarating cultural ecology presents human and animal in truly complex relation.'

Paul Gilroy, Emeritus Professor of the Humanities at University College London

www.cambridge.org/cormorant

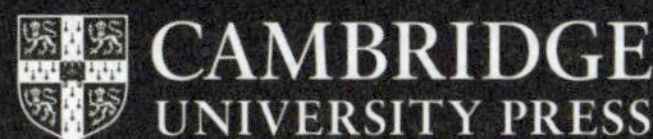

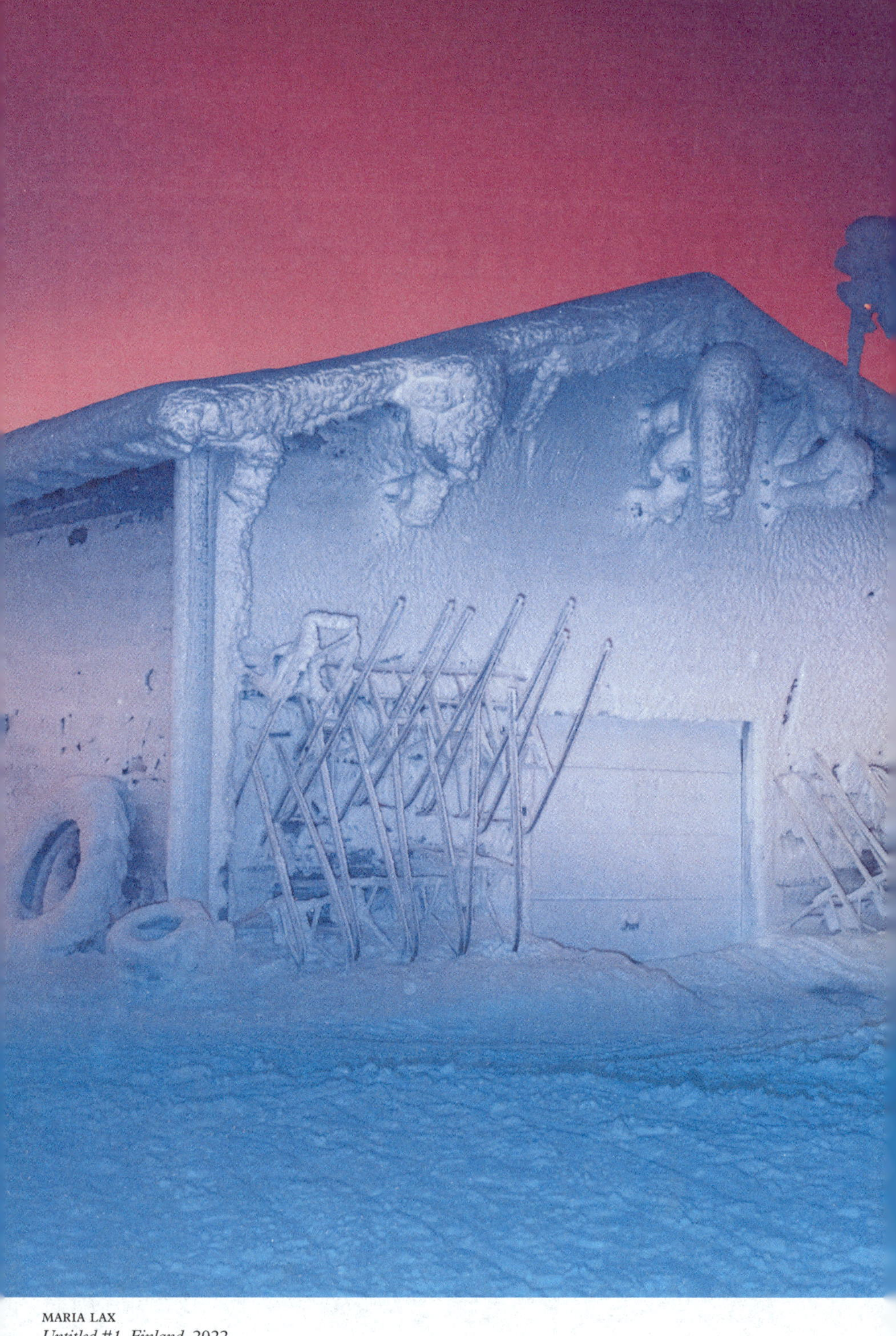

MARIA LAX
Untitled #1, Finland, 2022

SIX STORIES

Helle Helle

TRANSLATED FROM THE DANISH BY MARTIN AITKEN

SOMETIME THAT SPRING

Sometime that spring, during the period when I was writing my thesis, I got into the habit of walking down to the harbour every day after lunch. I would sit and smoke on a bench there, watching the sailing crowd as they came in and went ashore to buy provisions on the quay. When the weather was fine I would take off my coat to enjoy the sunshine on my arms. Mostly though it was cloudy, at least that's how I remember it.

One of the last times I went there, a woman sat down beside me. I took her to be a tourist; I'd certainly never seen her before. She leaned across and asked me for a light, I handed her a box of matches, which she kept.

We sat smoking as we looked out on the harbour. A couple came with their small boy to feed the seagulls, but the boy wouldn't let go of the bread he was holding, the seagulls wheeled above his head. Then the father held the boy's arms tight behind his back, the mother prised the bread from his hands and tossed it into the water. The boy threw himself to the ground, his parents called for him to come. He didn't move. They began to walk away, without looking back. The boy was lying face down and was quite still.

When his parents were some distance away on the far side of the harbour, the woman beside me began to speak.

'I'm sitting here wondering when the boy's going to feel frightened and run after his parents,' she said.

'That's what I'm thinking too,' I said.

'Looks like I've time for another cigarette before anything happens,' she said.

I took out my cigarettes too and asked for a light; she struck a match for me and put the box back in her pocket.

'They're a long way from him now,' she said. 'It'll be a form of upbringing, I shouldn't wonder.'

'People have their different ways,' I said.

'All the same, I'm going to help that boy find his parents again once he gets up.'

The parents had by then disappeared from view behind some sheds. The boy was still lying there without moving.

'What if something's the matter with him?' the woman said. 'He hasn't moved.'

'I'm sure they know their son,' I said. 'He's probably done this before.'

'And I'm sitting here smoking,' the woman said.

'Yes, it's a bad habit,' I said.

'I want to tell you something,' the woman said. 'It means nothing now, my daughter's grown into a happy and well-adjusted person. But before she was even two months old she was left on her own for three days in her cot. My pride was to blame for her lying there all that time. She could have died. Babies can't survive very long without fluids.'

'What happened?' I asked.

'To be frank with you, after the birth I developed a strong craving for cigarettes. Doubtless it was hormonal, but whatever the reason was, all I did from the day I came home from the maternity unit was sit and smoke. I smoked whenever my daughter slept. I'd rock her to and fro in the carrycot, and when she fell asleep I'd put her in the bedroom and close the door. Then I'd sit in the living room and chain-smoke, lighting one cigarette from the tip of the other. I don't know what I thought about. The future, most likely, and my money situation. I lived on my own and hardly saw anyone, apart from my daughter of course, but she was so little. She slept most of the time. Babies really do need their sleep. I couldn't myself, I'd just sit and smoke, and once every four hours when my daughter woke, I'd stub my cigarette out and warm a bottle for her. I was unable to breastfeed her unfortunately; my milk was bad. It was dark in colour and far too runny, and soon it stopped altogether. But they do say that bottle-fed children are just as healthy as others, and my daughter's never had anything wrong with her. So fortunately, my breasts didn't swell up either during the three days I was away from her. My leg certainly did though.'

'What was wrong with your leg?' I asked.

'They never did find out. It wasn't broken or anything. Which was what I'd thought as I lay there screaming in the middle of the road. I'd gone to buy cigarettes. Normally I'd be stocked up, knowing that I couldn't just pop out to buy a packet whenever I liked. I had my daughter to look after. But then one afternoon I discovered I'd run out. I didn't know what to do with myself, I was stuffing myself with chocolate, staring at the television. Nothing helped. I had to smoke, I had to go out and get some cigarettes.

'I was hit by a green car, I remember it clearly. A very green car, and me lying in the road. There was no blood or anything, but an ambulance came. And I was taken into hospital.'

'Didn't you tell anyone that your daughter was at home?'

'No. I didn't, that's just it. I think I would have done, if I'd known they were going to keep me in for three days. They X-rayed me straight away and nothing was broken, so I assumed they'd be sending me home. But they gave me a hospital gown to wear and put me in a bed to keep me under observation. My leg was terribly swollen, but I lied and said it really didn't hurt. I wanted to get home as quickly as I could.'

'Why didn't you tell anyone then?'

'I was embarrassed. It was as simple as that. I was too ashamed to admit that I'd left her in the flat. I should have been mindful of the risk involved in crossing a busy road. And quite apart from that, cigarettes are a very poor excuse for leaving a baby alone. And then I fell asleep. It's terrible, I know, but I actually fell asleep. You must remember that I hadn't had a proper night's sleep in nearly two months and almost never rested during the day, because I always had to have another cigarette. I slept and I slept. By the time I woke up, twenty-four hours had gone and my leg was still very painful. I asked for some painkillers under the pretext of having a headache. I shouldn't have done that. They said they were going to have to keep me in for another day, in case I'd suffered a concussion. I insisted that I wanted to go home. They asked if there was anyone there to look after me, which of course there wasn't. So they had to keep me in.'

'And still you told them nothing?'

'No, it was far too late by then. What kind of mother sits in a hospital bed with tea and toast while her daughter is probably screaming with hunger at home?'

'Weren't you afraid she would die?'

'Very afraid. But I reassured myself that she was a strong baby, and that her high birth weight would see her through. As I said, there was the matter of fluids, but I tried not to dwell on that.'

'There were other ways she could have been harmed.'

'You mean psychologically? Yes, that's right. I've been told that an infant that age can give up life very quickly if deprived of physical contact. Luckily I didn't know that at the time. I was just grateful she was so little that she wouldn't be able to remember anything about it. And would never be able to tell anyone.'

'Was that important to you?'

'Of course it was. I didn't want anyone to find out. And they didn't.'

'And you returned home after three days?'

'Yes. The swelling in my leg went down on day three, by which time I'd saved up a number of painkillers. I took them all at once, and was able to leave the hospital without showing too much discomfort. My leg was still painful, you understand.'

'So you just got up and left?'

'No, no. It was all by the book. I discharged myself with the consultant's approval, on the condition that I came back for a check-up the following week.'

'And then you went home to your daughter.'

'Yes.'

'Was she screaming?'

'She wasn't making a sound. She was lying in her cot, wet and soiled. I bathed her, rubbed baby oil into her skin, dressed her in clean clothes and settled her into the bed beside me.'

'So she hadn't become sick.'

'No, thank goodness. I realised as well that she wouldn't be able to cope with too much milk all at once. It would have ruined her stomach. So I increased her feed gradually, and by the next day she was on her normal amount.'

'Have you ever told your daughter what happened?'

'Let me answer that by asking you a question. Is your mother alive?'

'Yes.'

'Has she told you everything that happened to you before you were old enough to remember?'

'Of course not. It wouldn't be possible to recount everything in full.'

'Exactly. We choose what to pass on to our children and what to leave out.'

'And you chose to leave this story out.'

'I judged that it would do far more harm to tell it than to keep it to myself.'

'And what about your leg?'

'I got used to it hurting. But of course I still went for weekly check-ups for a while.'

'Did you leave your daughter at home again?'

'She'd passed the test, you could say. But I did stop smoking for a number of years. I gave my daughter everything she needed, and today she's a happy person. She doesn't know that she was left on her own. It's a different thing altogether with that boy over there.'

She jerked her head in his direction, he was still lying face down on the ground.

'He's old enough to remember. Perhaps he'll never forgive his parents.'

She got to her feet and drew her scarf around her neck, dipped into her pocket for her gloves and put them on.

'In any case, I'm going to help him,' she said.

'You've still got my matches.'

'Sorry. Here you are,' she said, and handed me the box.

I watched her go over to the boy and crouch in front of him. She may have spoken to him, I don't know. But the boy turned quickly and kicked her hard in the stomach, causing her to fall over backwards. Then he jumped up and ran off in the same direction his parents had gone.

She was still on her back when I walked away. ■

MORE COFFEE

It's me who sees him first. He's sitting over by the carport. He's wearing something green, like a hunter would wear. He's sitting in the old garden chair, comfortably reclined. He rubs his hands up and down his thighs. The sun's coming up.

'Martin. There's a man sitting by the carport,' I say.

Martin turns round with his coffee mug in his hand. He looks out the window, turns back, sets his mug down. He reaches for a slice of bread.

'Is it Ole Hansen?' I say.

Martin nods. And shakes his head. And nods again.

'Yes. It's Ole Hansen,' he says then.

'What do you think he wants?'

'He won't know that himself.'

Martin places two slices of cheese on his bread. He takes a bite and chews, brushes some crumbs from his sweater.

'Should I go out with some coffee for him?' I say.

'No, you shouldn't. You shouldn't go out at all today.'

'No.'

I spread some honey on my crispbread.

'Do you think there's something wrong with him?' I say.

'No more than usual.'

Martin knows what he's talking about; he works at the council offices. Almost daily Ole Hansen comes and sits in their canteen, even though he's got no business there. He sits and rubs his hands up and down his thighs. His trousers are worn thin with all that rubbing. He's not stupid. He used to be an ear, nose and throat specialist. But then he contracted a virus that affected his brain, and around that same time he lost his only son. No one comes through that sort of thing unscathed, that's why they let him sit in the canteen. He doesn't talk to anyone, he just sits there. After he's sat for a while, he gets up and leaves.

'Why do you think he's come to our house?' I say.

'It's random. He's been round to some of the others too.'

'Has he?'

'Yes. He's done it with Allan. And with Ursula. And someone from the benefits office as well.'

'How does he get your addresses?'

'He doesn't. He just mooches around.'

'It's so sad for him.'

'Yes.'

Martin goes to the bathroom to brush his teeth. I can hear him in there. I stay at the table and look down the garden. The trees are bare, you can see right through the hedge. Some sparrows settle on the bird table.

I send Ole Hansen a nod. He doesn't respond, he probably can't see me from there.

Martin sits on the stairs and does up his shoelaces. There's a smell of toothpaste about him.

'Anyway, I'll get him to move on now,' Martin says.

'How?'

'I'll just tell him to leave, and he'll leave.'

'It doesn't bother me if he wants to sit there.'

Martin looks up.

'We can't have him sitting in our garden if you're going to be on your own here, it stands to reason.'

'I'm not scared of him.'

'You've no need to be. I just don't want him here, that's all.'

He gets up and puts on his coat.

'I hope you start feeling better,' he says, and pecks me on the cheek.

I close the door behind him. I stand at the pane and watch him go down the garden path to where Ole Hansen is sitting. He stops a moment in front of him, one hand in his pocket. Then he goes into the carport, unlocks the car and gets in. He starts the engine. At the same time, Ole Hansen gets up out of the chair. He goes through the carport, alongside the reversing car, he turns right at the pavement and disappears. Martin swings the car out onto the road and turns left. He beeps the horn and gestures to me that Ole Hansen has gone again. I nod.

As soon as Martin's car is out of sight, I step into my wellies. I leave the house, go through the garden and turn right, the same way Ole Hansen went. I can't see him anywhere. I look in all the gardens and driveways, and behind the fence by the cycle path.

He's sitting on a bench outside the scout hut, rubbing his thighs.

I stand still on the pavement.

'Hello, Ole Hansen,' I say, and smile at him. 'My name's Betina. That was my garden you were sitting in just now. I'm married to Martin from the council offices.'

Ole Hansen doesn't respond.

'It's rather cold today, isn't it?' I say. 'I was wondering if you'd like a cup of coffee? I can pop home and bring you one.'

Now he looks at me. He says nothing.

'I'll do that, then. Don't go anywhere.'

I back away along the pavement. I'm still smiling at him.

'Don't go anywhere,' I say again.

I turn and hurry home. I put Martin's old coat on; it's hanging right there in the hall. I put a scarf on too, and a pair of gloves. I pick up the Thermos from the kitchen table and take a mug from the cupboard. I tuck the mug into a pocket and lock the door behind me with my free hand. I walk quickly back to the scout hut.

He's still there.

'Here I am again, with hot coffee,' I say as I go towards him. I set the mug down on the bench and fill it. He's stopped rubbing his thighs now, he takes the mug and drinks. He sits with the mug in both his hands. I stand there with the Thermos.

He blows on the coffee between sips. Steam rises from the mug into his face.

'You like a good walk and a sit-down,' I say.

He doesn't reply; I'm not expecting him to either.

'I work as a lab technician,' I say. 'Only today I'm off sick. I've got a slight cold. Martin thought I should stay at home.'

The ground in front of the bench is covered with rotten leaves. I dig at the leaves with a welly boot.

'Sometimes it's nice to step away from the rush. Especially on a fine day like this.'

I clear my throat and look at Ole Hansen. He puts the mug down on the bench. Immediately, I step fowards.

'More coffee?' I say, a bit cheerier than I meant to.

He springs to his feet and waves me away. He heads left along the pavement, quickly. I scurry after him down the quiet residential road with the Thermos held aloft in front of me.

'What's the matter?' I say. 'Is there anything I can do?'

He strides along. We get to the bottom of the road. Bente's in the garden with a patio brush. She straightens up and says my name; I ignore her. I reach out to Ole Hansen from behind, touch his shoulder.

'Won't you sit down somewhere?' I say. 'We could sit together for a bit.'

He stops and turns towards me. We stand face-to-face, and rather close. He smells of wool. Ever since then I can't help connecting the two things; the smell of wool and what he says.

'Your husband's cheating on you with Ursula Steen,' he says.

He's wearing a thick sweater under his green jacket, I hadn't noticed until now. I wonder if it's hand-knitted, and who knitted it for him if so.

'That's a nice sweater,' I say.

He turns round and walks on. I follow after him. I don't say anything else, I just walk a few metres behind him. We walk past the sports hall and the sugar refinery, all the way into the centre of town and through the narrow streets. He lets himself into a red half-timbered house. It must be where he lives. He shuts the door behind him without saying goodbye, I walk on along the street and up to the square. I walk past the fountain and stop just short of the council offices.

My arm hurts, the arm that's holding the Thermos. I let it hang down by my side and rub the aching muscle. A dribble of coffee runs from the lip of the Thermos, onto the pavement. That's how I stand. ■

ONE CHAIR SHORT

We'll have to cancel, he says, but she tells him that's not an option. It's far too late, the guests are probably already on their way, the candles are on the table and she's got sorbet in the freezer. But the bathroom still has to be cleaned, one of them will have to do it, and then there's the party poppers and her hair that needs setting, it's all over the place, she can't look like this.

He pushes her down onto the sofa. I can't go through with it, he says, it's no use. She pulls his hand away and gets up, tells him he should have thought about that before, they owe people this party. How many times have they sat in the homes of friends and acquaintances, eating their salmon and drinking their champagne? Which reminds her, she needs to go and check on the roast, and in the meantime he can go downstairs to the basement, if he doesn't mind, and bring up the last of the chairs. He says he can't stand it, she tells him it's the least he can do; as far as she's concerned, once he's done that, he can sit and cry on the sofa until the guests arrive.

She stands in the kitchen busily slicing a white loaf. He comes up from the basement and tells her they're one chair short. She tells him that can't be right, she's checked everything, more than once. Sixteen matching plates, sixteen wine glasses, sixteen chairs in all, she's counted them. He says she can go to the basement and see for herself; there genuinely aren't any more chairs, only fifteen in all. She goes down to the basement, then makes a tour of the flat, her heels clacking on the wooden floor, she concedes that he's right. She tells him they'll have to make do.

He starts crying, he props himself against the worktop and starts crying, she stirs a saucepan of dark red gravy and gives it a pinch of salt. He says he almost hates himself, she says that in her world there's no such thing as almost. In her world there's only a dark red gravy and a roast that mustn't be overdone, the candles on the table, and of course the bathroom, she tells him to go and clean it, now.

She can hear him in there as she sets the plates on the table; the running water, the clacking jars. She considers swapping the blue candles for bottle-green ones, decides to stick with blue, lays out the knives and forks, polishes the glasses with a tea towel. The table is resplendent, she lights the candles, straightens a spoon, and goes to the bedroom to set her hair.

He comes in and stands beside her. He tells her he's seen the table and that she's done a lovely job. He says he'll wear his suit. She tells him to be quick about it, and returns to the kitchen. He joins her again once he's got changed, stands at the window and lights a cigarette. She tells him to put it out and crush some ice cubes, she can't do everything herself, she says, and takes the drinks glasses from the cupboard. He asks if he should crush the ice cubes with a hammer; she tells him he can do as he likes.

The kitchen resounds as she stands in the hall and takes off her shoes. She puts them in her bag, ties her boots, shrugs into an overcoat. She returns an umbrella to its hook and goes out the door, bag in hand.

He's put the ice cubes into a plastic bag and stands in the kitchen bashing them hard with the hammer. He opens the bag and scoops up some of the crushed ice with his hand, drops it into a glass. He pours gin and white wine into the glass and lays a slice of lemon on top. He does this sixteen times in all.

Shortly afterwards the doorbell rings. ■

MOBILE

It's approaching midnight and my husband hasn't come home yet. I've watched a programme about dolphins, very moving, while lying on the sofa waiting for him; it's not like him to be late. He had a committee meeting to attend at the county council, something routine, they should have been finished hours ago.

I turn the radiators up, the forecast said down to minus ten tonight.

At a quarter past midnight my husband calls from his mobile phone and says he's had an accident in the car. He doesn't know what happened, the car must have skidded on a bend, he's only just come to and is bleeding from his head, he thinks he may have been sitting like that in the car for more than half an hour.

I almost stop breathing; he reassures me. Nothing serious has happened, his head's a bit sore, that's all, there's nothing to worry about. But the car won't start now, so he wants me to look up the number for roadside assistance. I ask him where he is, he says he's at the edge of some woods. He doesn't know exactly where, but he'll find out before he phones for help.

I hear him open the car door. There's a moment's pause, then he's back on and tells me he can't get up. He's going to sit for a minute and collect himself, then he'll get out of the car and try to figure out where he is. I ask if he really can't remember; he can't.

But he'll call me back shortly.

I sit on the floor in the living room, the television's still on, I've turned the sound down. I find the roadside assistance number in the book and place my finger underneath it, my other hand is on the receiver.

He phones back and says he's still having trouble getting out of the car. It's the strangest thing, he says, because there's no pain at all in his legs, and he can move his toes too, in fact he's wriggling them as he speaks. It's probably the shock, he says, you hear about that. I ask if he's bleeding a lot, he tells me it's stopped. He can see in the mirror that he's got a minor cut on his forehead, that must have been where the blood was coming from.

I ask if he still can't remember which way he went. He can't, but he says there aren't that many possibilities, chances are he took the shortest way home. At any rate, he's come to a halt at the edge of some woods, he can see the lights of a village a few kilometres away, he thinks it's probably ours. In a few minutes he'll have found out where he is, then he'll phone the roadside assistance service and they'll come out and give him a hand. I say he should probably phone for an ambulance as well, he says I really shouldn't worry, there's no need for that kind of help. Then he hangs up again.

I tell myself that at least he can remember our number. And I remind myself that sometimes I too, when I wake up in the morning, find that I can't move, that I'm completely paralysed, and must lie there and check each part of my body in turn, feet, legs, back, before I can get up. Usually it's because of a dream that was so real my body continues to believe it's somewhere else. I wonder if my husband perhaps had a similar dream while he was unconscious, and I think about him now sitting in a car at the edge of some woods with a minor cut on his forehead, waiting to feel steady again.

I call his number, he answers by saying his surname, it encourages me. I ask him what the situation is now, whether he's found out where he is. He says he's got no further in that matter. On the other hand, he's remembered the first-aid kit in the glove compartment, he's in the process of cleaning his wound and intends to put a plaster on it. He asks me if I think he should treat the wound with iodine before doing so. I say yes, he winces.

I ask about his legs, whether he can move them. He's still wriggling his toes, he says. I ask him to check, to try to feel each muscle. He says it actually helps. He thinks he may even be able to get out of the car now, it's just his head that still hurts. I tell him to move cautiously.

We agree that a bang on the head such as he probably received is bound to bring on a headache. I suggest he rings me back once he's out of the car. He says he will.

Things are moving forwards now, I'm certain of it. As soon as he's got some fresh air, everything will be fine. He'll call the roadside assistance and they'll make sure both he and the car are transported home. I decide to phone the out-of-hours doctor as soon as he gets here. It's possible he's concussed, it definitely can't be ruled out that his headache is the result of a concussion.

I go into the bedroom and drape his duvet over the radiator, I want to do everything I can for him, I want to make him tea and give him something to eat, if he feels up to eating, I take some bread rolls out of the freezer and switch the oven on, I put the butter out.

It's a while before he calls back, roughly ten minutes. He's now standing in front of the car, no problem whatsoever, he's moving freely, getting his bearings. As far as he can tell, the car does seem to have skidded on the bend and hit a kind of tree stump, the road is incredibly slippery, he was lucky nothing serious happened.

He can see it's not woods at all where he's come to a halt, just a row of trees along the driveway to a farm. It's all dark up there, they've probably gone to bed. I tell him to go up and ring the doorbell, he's not very keen, he'd rather walk along the road a bit until he comes to a signpost of some sort. I insist he goes up to the farm, eventually he gives in. We agree he's to ring me back after they let him in.

I take some vegetables from the pantry, potatoes and onions, hot soup is good at night. There's some leftover chicken in the fridge, I'll blend the soup and put the meat in last.

I go into the bedroom and turn over the duvet on the radiator, decide to stay home from work in the morning, it could well be very late before I get to bed, and I don't know if I'll be able to sleep or if I'll just be lying there next to my husband, watching his eyelids move as he dreams.

There's no one in at the farm, he says. I say there's always someone in at a farm, they'll have livestock, they can't just go away. My husband says that as far as he can make out they don't have livestock on this farm, the place is far too quiet. And there's definitely no one in at the house, he's knocked on all the doors. I tell him to ring the doorbell, but there is no doorbell, and no name on the door either, there might not even be anyone living there at the moment.

My husband says he'll walk along the road a short way and hope to come across a signpost or something else that might tell him where he is. He's actually not feeling too bad now, he just wants to get home where it's warm. It's freezing cold, he says, and I tell him he's right, the forecast was for heavy frost tonight. I can hear his footsteps as he goes down the driveway again, then we hang up.

I wait five minutes, then ring back. He's walking along the road now, he's out of breath. I'm encouraged by him walking briskly, his headache's better now too, he says. I tell him I'm boiling some vegetables for a soup, that I'm warming his duvet. He can't wait to be under his duvet, he says, what a night; first an unexpectedly long meeting, and now this. I ask how the meeting went. Same as usual, he says. Then I hear a car go past him. I tell him sharply to flag it down; it's too late now, he says. I tell him sharply that this has gone far enough, I'll ring for help myself, he asks how anyone is supposed to come and help him when they don't know where he is. I say it can't be that difficult, they'll just have to drive around and keep an eye out on the roads around the village, I ask again if he's sure he doesn't recognise the place, perhaps he's seen the fields before, or something in the fields, whatever. It's too dark, he says.

I tell him I'm definitely going to ring for help now, maybe they can trace him via his mobile phone, it's hardly inconceivable. He says he doesn't want to make a drama out of it, he's fine, he's going to walk home, it can't be far, he thinks he can already see the church tower. He might just sit down a minute first though and have a rest, not because he's tired, it's just his legs, they're still a bit funny, but that's hardly unnatural. I tell him he mustn't under any circumstance sit down, that he has to keep moving. He must carry on walking, and he must promise me that he'll stop the next car that happens to pass, if any does. He promises. He tells me too that I should go to bed, there's no reason to sit up waiting. I tell him there's no way I can go to sleep yet. But I'll go into the kitchen and blend his soup, and turn his duvet. He thanks me and hangs up.

I press the vegetables through a sieve and pour the soup back into the pot. I wonder whether he'd prefer his soup with or without chicken; meat sits heavily in the stomach, all the more so at bedtime. And he needs to sleep as long as he can; he can't possibly work tomorrow, not after a night like this. Perhaps we could both have a lie-in, perhaps we'll stay in bed the whole day, without answering the phone or going to the door, if anyone should ring the bell. But of course there's the car, which the breakdown service will have to collect; on the other hand, leaving it an extra day won't matter. It can't start anyway, so no one can steal it.

I ring back to ask my husband if he'd prefer his soup with or without chicken. I can't get through; there's no connection at the moment, a voice says. I wonder if my husband could have switched his phone off without thinking about it, that must be it, he'll no doubt realise in a minute and call me back.

He doesn't call, and I still can't get through. I sit on the living-room floor, I'm freezing, I think about the frost outside and the cut on my husband's forehead. I promise myself we'll stay in bed all day tomorrow, that at the most I'll get up and make him some coffee, hot coffee with milk, and I'll bring the television into the bedroom and we'll lie there and not give a thought to the fact that we should have been at work, both of us.

I call his number and call it again, there's no connection. I wander about and stir the soup, turn the duvet, stir the soup again. Then I call my husband's sister. I tell her what's happened. She says she'll ring the emergency services right away. She'll get dressed as well, and go out looking in the car. I ask her to come and pick me up first, I tell her I can't stand to sit here and wait. She says it'll be out of her way if she has to pick me up first, I tell her she's got to take me with her; after all, I've been in contact with my husband and know roughly where he is.

Approximately two kilometres outside the village, somewhere near an empty farmhouse, I tell her once we're in the car. She wants to know what the hell I've been doing, how many hours I've allowed her brother to sit bleeding in the darkness in his car, in this cold weather as well. It's not like that at all, I tell her, I've been wanting to ring for help, but he wouldn't hear of it, and anyway he wasn't bleeding much. It was only a minor cut to his forehead, I tell her. She tosses me a road map and says the least I can do is come up with an idea as to where we should look. I tell her we need to be south of the village.

Under different circumstances I'd ask her to slow down, but I can hardly be so bold now, I have no right to fear for my own life.

She drives down the middle of the road, we keep our eyes peeled on either side, I keep seeing what I don't want to see; my husband's body in a ditch, an outline in the darkness, the mobile phone out of battery.

We've almost done a full loop of the village when I spot the car. We drive up and stop, and it's just as my husband described; the car appears to have skidded while going through the bend and hit a metre-high tree stump head-on.

We drive on up the road, this time very slowly. My husband's sister then pulls in and thrusts a torch at me; we get out. We walk on either side of the road, shining our torches and calling out, but come up empty. We go back to the car and drive a bit further, repeat the procedure. There's nothing, not a trace.

My husband's sister says she'll drive to a phone box and ring the emergency services to hear if they've found him. In the meantime, I can keep searching. I tell her I don't want to be out on the road alone, that I really couldn't bear to look for him here on my own. She doesn't answer me, strides towards the car. I run after her and get in, she drives off.

I wait in the car while she phones. She stands with her back to me in the phone box, one arm held stiffly at her side. I sit wishing she'd move it, drop her shoulder, relax her posture. She puts the receiver down and comes back to the car.

They've found him, she says, he's fine. Then she hits me hard across the face. I understand you, I tell her, meeting her gaze. He's home now, she says, and drives us back.

My husband's sitting in the living room with two ambulance workers. The ambulance workers get to their feet as soon as we come in; everything should be all right now, they say, and leave. My husband's cheeks are red and there's a plaster on his forehead. He's on the sofa with a blanket wrapped around him. I was lucky, he says, I could have been dead. Yes, you could, his sister says, and steps towards him. He places a hand on her arm, reaches out to me with the other. Yes, you could, I tell him, you really could. I nod towards the kitchen, I've got to check on something, I say, and back my way out.

The soup is burnt, it's completely inedible, I'll never get that pot clean. I put it in the bin outside and cover it up with a newspaper. ■

TIMETABLES

He's a married man and the only person I haven't talked to all evening. Nevertheless, around eleven, he asks me to go for a walk with him, right when the party is at its height. He tells me he's been watching me for several hours and is taken by the way my nose lifts up when I laugh.

We walk along the beach, metres apart. I hold my coat closed at the throat with both hands; it's cold, and underneath I'm wearing only a short dress, made of synthetic fabric.

He and his wife have just returned home after four years in Canada. As a biologist he was working on a research project, something about epidemics among birds; she's just completed her thesis and is now looking for work. They've known each other since school, it's a happy marriage.

'I don't usually go for walks at night with women I don't know,' he says, and suggests we go up into the dunes. He takes my hand, and I let him, I'm freezing, the sand is wet and gets in my hair.

Afterwards we sit looking at the sea. I offer him a cigarette, he doesn't smoke. He brushes sand from his jacket, empties his shoes.

'This shouldn't have happened,' he says. 'I've no idea what I'm going to say to her.'

I stick my cigarette in the sand and draw a face around it. He doesn't look.

'She might already have noticed the two of us are missing,' he says. 'She might actually be out looking for us now.'

He gets up and glances around; the beach is deserted.

'I'm afraid I'll have to drive you to the train,' he says. 'I know it's a bit unfair, but it's the only way out.'

I tell him the last train will have gone hours ago, and in any case I don't want to go home yet.

'My marriage is at stake here,' he says. 'I'll tell her you asked me to drive you to the train and that I couldn't say no.'

He pulls me to my feet, I bend down to retrieve my cigarette. We walk back to the house. His car is parked further up the road, he unlocks the door and bundles me into the passenger seat.

'I need to get my bag,' I tell him.

He asks if it's really necessary.

'It's got my keys and money in it,' I tell him. 'I can't leave without it.'

He tells me to hurry in and get it. If his wife sees me, I'm to say I'm feeling unwell.

'Say you've had a migraine all evening and can hardly bear to move,' he says.

'But I've been dancing.'

'That's beside the point.'

There's loud music in the living room, they're singing and clapping in time. His wife appears from out of the kitchen with a bowl of crisps. I grab a handful and find my bag in the hall. I find half a bottle of white wine too, someone's put it down and left it. I take it with me to the car. The engine's idling.

'Here,' I say. 'Have a swig.'

He's not at all interested in drinking now. He pulls away and doesn't turn the headlights on until we reach the main road.

'Did you see my wife?' he asks.

'Yes,' I tell him. 'She gave me some crisps.'

'Did she say anything?'

'No.'

'Are you sure it was her?'

'Yes. She's the one in the green dress, right?'

'Yes. Long hair, with a wave to it. It's quite natural, she doesn't get it permed or anything.'

'I see.'

'But she didn't say anything to you?'

'No.'

'How did she come across?'

'She seemed happy enough.'

'In what way, happy?'

'You know. Smiling, I suppose.'

'You suppose?'

'No, she was smiling.'

'Okay. So chances are she hasn't noticed anything.'

'Probably not.'

'Good.'

He changes gear and turns off the main road. He thinks he remembers that you can take a shortcut to the station by driving through some woods. It's only a couple of kilometres, meaning he can be there and back in around ten minutes, including the time it'll take to see me onto the train. He turns the radio on. I put the bottle to my lips and take a swig of tepid white wine.

'Would you mind not doing that?' he says.

'Why?'

'At least use a plastic cup. There are some in the glove compartment.'

I take a plastic cup, and find a camera there too.

'Put that back,' he says.

On our way through the woods we hit an animal. The car lurches; we pull up and get out. The animal turns out to be a fox, it's bleeding from the mouth. He crouches in front of it and touches its fur. It turns its head and growls at him, he snatches his hand back.

'Bloody hell,' he says.

'Did it bite you?' I ask. I'm standing just behind him.

'No, but nearly.'

The fox is still growling.

'It's suffering,' I say. 'We should put it out of its misery.'

'You're right,' he says, and darts into the woods. He returns with a rock and holds it poised above the fox's head.

'Do it now,' I tell him.

'I don't think this is heavy enough,' he says. 'I don't think it'll die.'

'Then find something bigger.'

'I'm not actually sure I can bring myself to do it.'

'I thought you were a biologist.'

'I am,' he says. 'But this is different.'

I suggest we get back in the car and drive over it again. He doesn't want to do that. He tosses the rock into the ditch.

'My assessment is that it'll be dead within five minutes anyway,' he says.

He gets back in the car. I do likewise, and drink some more white wine.

The last train left more than an hour ago. He stares at the timetable on the wall outside the station building. I try the door of the waiting room; it's locked. Then I sit down on the step and light a cigarette.

'The last one's gone,' he says.

'Yes.'

'That's that, then.'

'Yes.'

We get back in the car again, he asks me to put my cigarette out. I throw it out the window, buckle up.

'I suppose it'd be too much to ask for you to wait here and catch the first train in the morning,' he says.

'Yes,' I say. 'That would be too much to ask.'

'Yes,' he says. 'Of course.'

He starts the car, reverses out onto the road. As we leave the town behind us he glances at his watch; twenty minutes have gone, his schedule isn't holding.

'Bloody trains,' he says. 'Why does everything always have to be so difficult?'

He slams the heel of his hand down on the steering wheel.

'And that bloody fox to boot.'

I suggest we drive back through the woods.

The fox's legs are twitching; some blood has pooled on the road.

'I thought it'd be dead by now,' I say.

'It should be.'

'The least we can do is move it off the road,' I say.

He prods it with the toe of his boot. It growls; he recoils.

'You're welcome to try,' he says.

'It wasn't me who hit it.'

'It ran out in front of me, it's only got itself to blame,' he says.

'Let's just go then,' I say.

We sit for a moment in the car without speaking. He winds the window down and stares at the animal.

'I can't do this,' he says. 'It goes against my professional ethics to leave an animal in such a state.'

'Yes, I imagine it does.'

He turns his head and looks at me.

'What would you say,' he says, 'if I drove you back to the party, picked up a shovel or something, then came back here on my own and killed the fox?'

'That would be a decent thing to do,' I say.

'Would it?'

'Yes.'

'Then that's what we'll do,' he says, and starts the car.

He pulls in a short distance from the house and asks me to get out first. He says he'll wait a minute or two, then go into the garage and see if he can find a suitable implement. He puts a hand on my shoulder.

'Maybe you should go and lie down straight away,' he says.

'I will,' I tell him, and shut the door with a heavy clunk.

A chain dance is taking place in the front garden. I go inside into the kitchen, eat some crisps, pour some wine into a glass. I let the wine sit in my mouth, swill it back and forth between my cheeks before swallowing. I go out into the hall, find the telephone underneath some coats and order a taxi to take me all the way home.

I smoke a cigarette out on the road while I wait. They're still dancing in the garden, arms and glasses lifting into view above the hedge, someone sees me and calls out.

'Come and join us,' they shout, and dance on.

'In a minute, maybe,' I call back, and toss my cigarette away as the taxi turns the corner and comes towards me.

The driver goes the quick way, through the woods. I spot him from a distance in the taxi's headlights; he's sitting on a tree stump holding a shovel, the fox is lying at his feet. His car is parked between two trees. He doesn't see me. ■

A WHIP-ROUND

It's nearly always Jeanette who has to front the money whenever something needs buying. Last year they set up a collection box, only it's not working out. People forget to put the money in every month, meaning she still has to go round collecting from everyone afterwards. There are nineteen of them in their department. So there's always a birthday, a new baby, or some other occasion that calls for flowers or a present.

This time it was a funeral bouquet. One of the secretaries, Edith, had lost her husband. He dropped dead all of a sudden, he wasn't even sixty. They were the kind of couple who still held hands; they never had any children. They travelled abroad several times a year. Edith was always the first to leave the Christmas party or any other festive occasion. I need to be getting home to Erik, she'd say, we're going to the cinema tonight. Or to the theatre, or to Møn. They kept a weekend home on Møn. It was set on a large untamed plot of land that went all the way down to the sea. That was where he dropped dead. She thought he'd stretched out in the grass to watch the birds. She was shaking the rugs on the patio and saw him lying there. She opened the windows to air the rooms, and put the rugs back in place. She prepared two slices of bread and cheese and made the coffee, then carried it all down through the grass. Coffee's here, she was going to say. She would have told him she'd found a mouse's tail under one of the rugs. She wondered what had happened to the mouse; she was going to ask Erik how it might have come about. She carried the bread and cheese on a yellow plate, she walked slowly through the grass.

Jeanette was told all about it by Dorte from HR. They bumped into each other on the stairs. Edith had phoned in and informed Dorte shortly before. She'd sounded remarkably calm; she was in the process of tidying up his papers. The funeral was to take place quietly, it was how he'd always wanted it.

Jeanette had then gone back to the department and told everyone that Edith wouldn't be coming in due to her husband having passed away. She recounted how it had happened. Afterwards, she went down to the florist's. She wasn't sure whether they should send a wreath or a bouquet, but decided on the latter. She paid what it cost and returned to the office; she found it hard to concentrate the rest of the day. Everyone spoke so tenderly to each other. They sat for a long time over lunch. Everything could wait; including money matters.

Edith insisted on returning to work two days after the funeral. She was thin and rather quiet. At the morning meeting she stood up and thanked everyone for the flowers. She was wearing a blue dress. She told them briefly about her plans for the future; she would move into a flat, sell the weekend home, and otherwise devote herself to her job. She requested that no special considerations be made.

After the meeting she went round and shook everyone by the hand. Her hand was cold. Jeanette hadn't known what to say. It didn't seem to matter. Edith smiled at everyone, and afterwards she sat down in front of her computer at her desk by the window in the middle office. She stared at the screen intently all day. Now and then, she reached for a ring binder on the shelf, looked up a name or an address. She muttered quietly to herself, she drummed her fingers against her cheek. She conducted ordinary telephone conversations.

Three weeks later there are still nine of them who haven't paid. Jeanette goes round with the empty collection box and a list of names to cross off. It comes to sixteen-fifty each. She's decided it's the last time she fronts the money for them. After all, it's usually quite a lot, and there's always someone who never gets round to paying.

She visits the different offices. She puts on a cheerful voice, she's mindful of seeming petty or overbearing. Many don't have the right change, and she hasn't got enough to break the larger notes. They decide it'll have to wait in that case. But one of her male colleagues puts his money promptly in the box and touches her hand. They smile at each other. She crosses him off the list with a single cautious stroke.

She's still smiling as she goes through the middle office. Edith looks up from her screen and nods towards the box, which Jeanette is holding in both her hands.

'Are we having another whip-round?' Edith says, and reaches for her bag on the floor.

Jeanette comes to a stop without replying.

'Whose birthday is it this time?'

Edith takes her purse out of her bag and rummages in it.

'I've only got a fifty.'

She holds out the note, her nails are long and varnished. Jeanette has never seen her with nail varnish before. Jeanette thinks: she doesn't know what to do with herself either in the evenings.

She says:

'Edith, you don't need to chip in. It's just something from before.'

'Don't I owe you anything?'

Edith smiles. Jeanette shifts the box into one hand and lets her arm drop.

'I don't think so,' she says, and swallows.

'Are you sure? Have a look at your list, just in case.'

But then luckily the door opens and they both turn their heads. It's a bike courier with a thick brown envelope. Jeanette takes the envelope from him, turns it over in her hands, reads out what it says, and gives it a shake. The courier is taken aback by all the attention being lavished on the envelope.

'I just need a signature,' he says, and Edith signs. ■

Asta Olivia Nordenhof

Untitled

autumn 09 I had sex for money
it's a thing I used to do
but what's unusual here
was the booking that came in

a man whose name and face I don't recall
ordered
something called a lesbian show

I was on duty with anastacia
a wonderful person
who in her tracksuits and with her coarse
tongue was all the things
I wished
I was

well anyway, we did the show
and I lost sight of
the man completely
all I felt was
anastacia

what am I trying to say
I guess I feel like
now and then
in times of hardship
there can still be
pockets of affection

I left the brothel
when I got my first writing grant
I could hardly wrap my head around
the hundred grand in my account

I'd spent so long
in government offices
begging for such basic things
and suddenly the money was just there
no questions asked

*

there's a website
where escorts' clients can review what
they call
their goddesses
I got largely
positive write-ups

beautiful and seems
very innocent
it said
although
one minor niggle
my pussy
could be tighter
you didn't quite

feel like you were
the first

I read these reviews
with a
manic coolness
just like
when I read my
book reviews

who are you
stranger
to come so close to my body
and to decide
my finances
who are you
to adjudicate
my life

*

I'm losing patience
with the concept
of money
why don't we do away with it

try to imagine a world
where we work
together
that's already
how it is
except we're so eager
to act like
somebody got there first
and was the only one

who should get the money
who earned it
who earned
their good reviews
their book tours and high
fees
who has earned
their name
writ large
on the poster

no one has
dear friends
we shared
our lives

and in return
we don't want
money and honour
no
what we really
want
is warmth
and care
and food
so we can share
ourselves again

Translated from the Danish by Caroline Waight

HALF PRICE OFFER

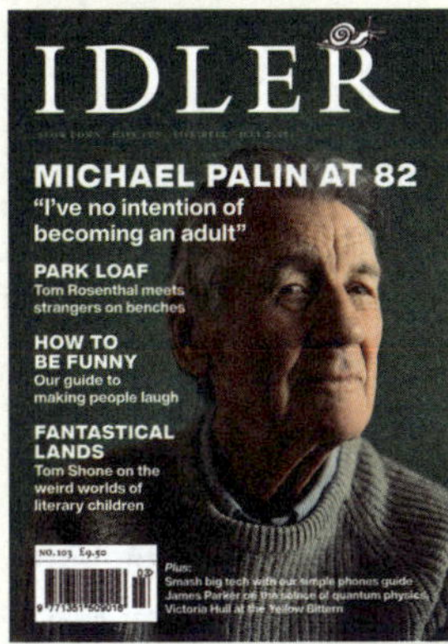

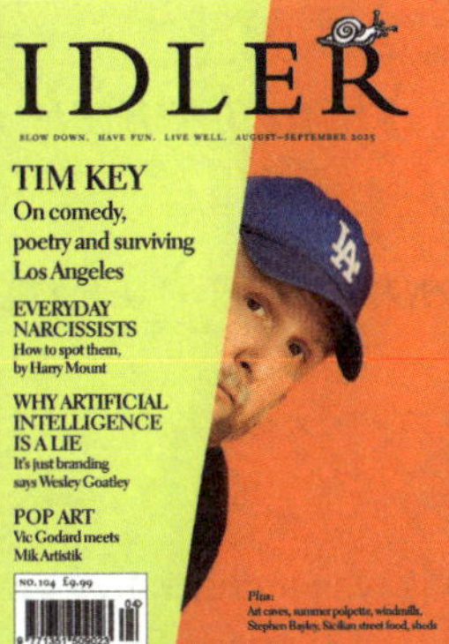

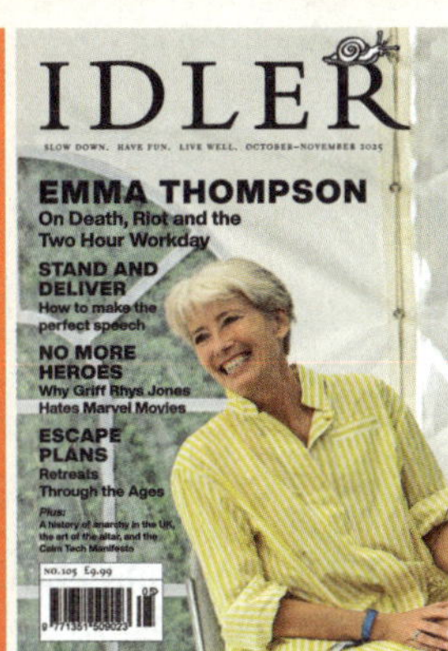

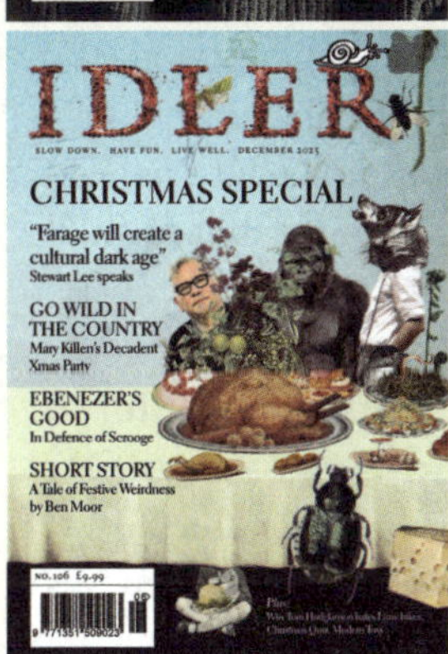

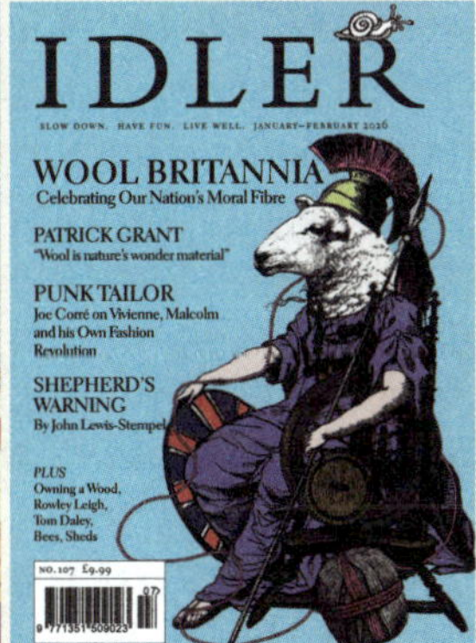

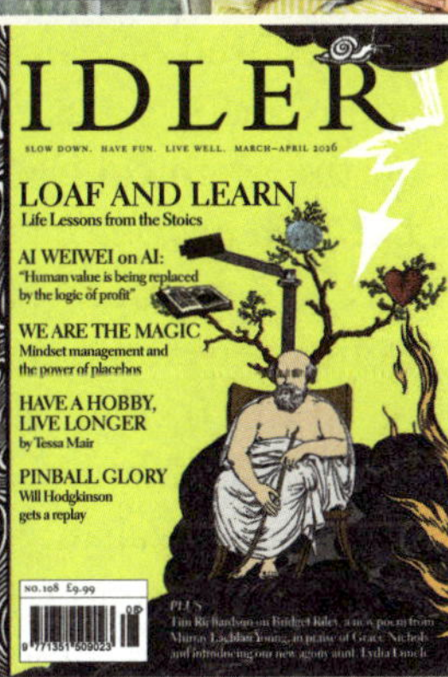

A SIX ISSUE SUBSCRIPTION TO THE IDLER FOR £28.50

HALF SHOP PRICE

PLUS FREE BOOK

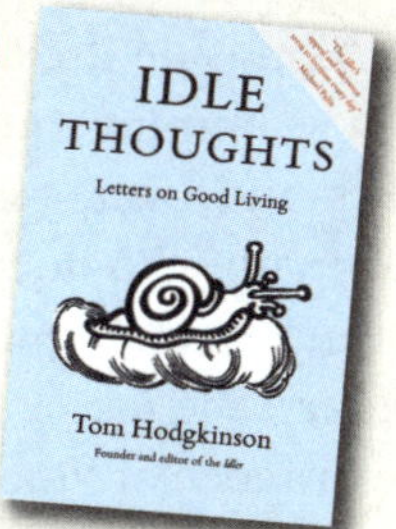

Go to idler.co.uk/join, select PRINT and use code **GRANTA26** or call 01442 820581

SLOW DOWN. HAVE FUN. LIVE WELL.

UK DD offer only. Price will revert to standard £49.95 after six issues. Cancel any time. Non-UK readers: use same code for 20% off.

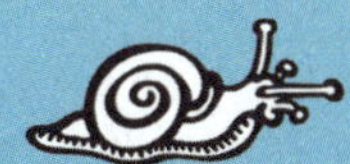

GERTRUD

Maja Daniels

Introduction by Granta

When Maja Daniels was a child, her grandparents in Älvdalen told her the story of Getrud Svendsotter, a twelve-year-old girl accused of walking on water in 1667. Under interrogation, the young shepherdess confessed to sorcery and to dining with the devil on the mythical island of Blåkulla. Her subsequent trial sparked *Det stora oväsendet* ('The Great Uproar'), a witch-hunt that rapidly spread through Sweden. More than three hundred people – mostly women – were executed.

In 2010, Daniels began taking photographs that explored Älvdalen's history and the town's use of the hyper-vernacular language Elfdalian. Spoken by around 3,000 people, it is the closest living language to Old Norse. Her latest project, *Gertrud*, examines the traces the witch trials have left in the region, in particular the female strength and independence she has come to associate with the period.

Alongside dreamlike photographs of contemporary rural life – wild swimming, burning vegetation, grazing animals – are archival, black-and-white prints by Tenn-Lars Persson (1878–1938), a local polymath who documented the landscape and people of Älvdalen. Daniels's analogue photographs employ long exposures to fade colours; she uses Persson's work both to heighten and gnaw away at the distance of time.

'I found Gertrud in the gaze of the girls and women Persson photographed,' Daniels told *Granta*. 'The combined portraits become a vessel that many Gertruds may look back through, across history.' ■

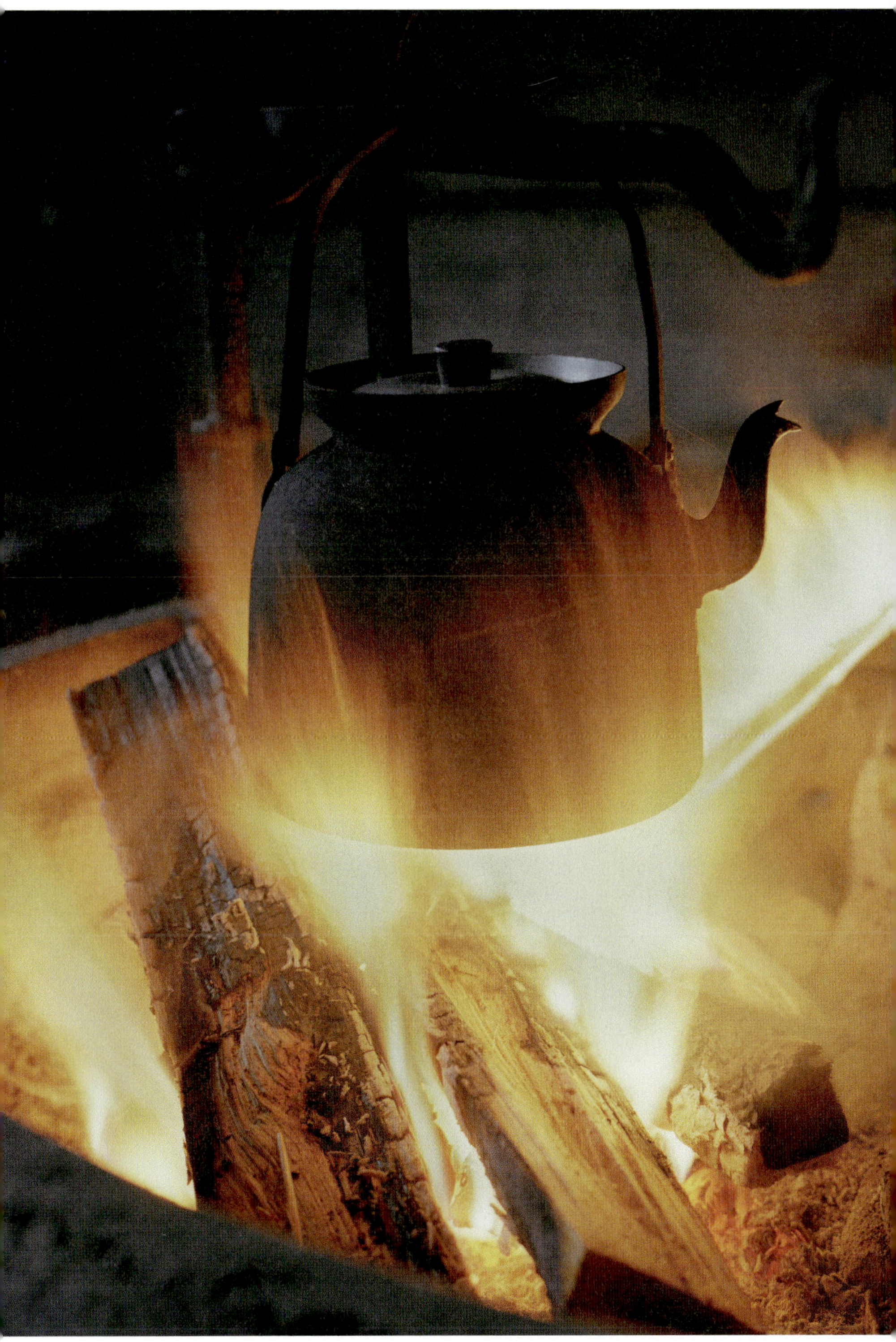

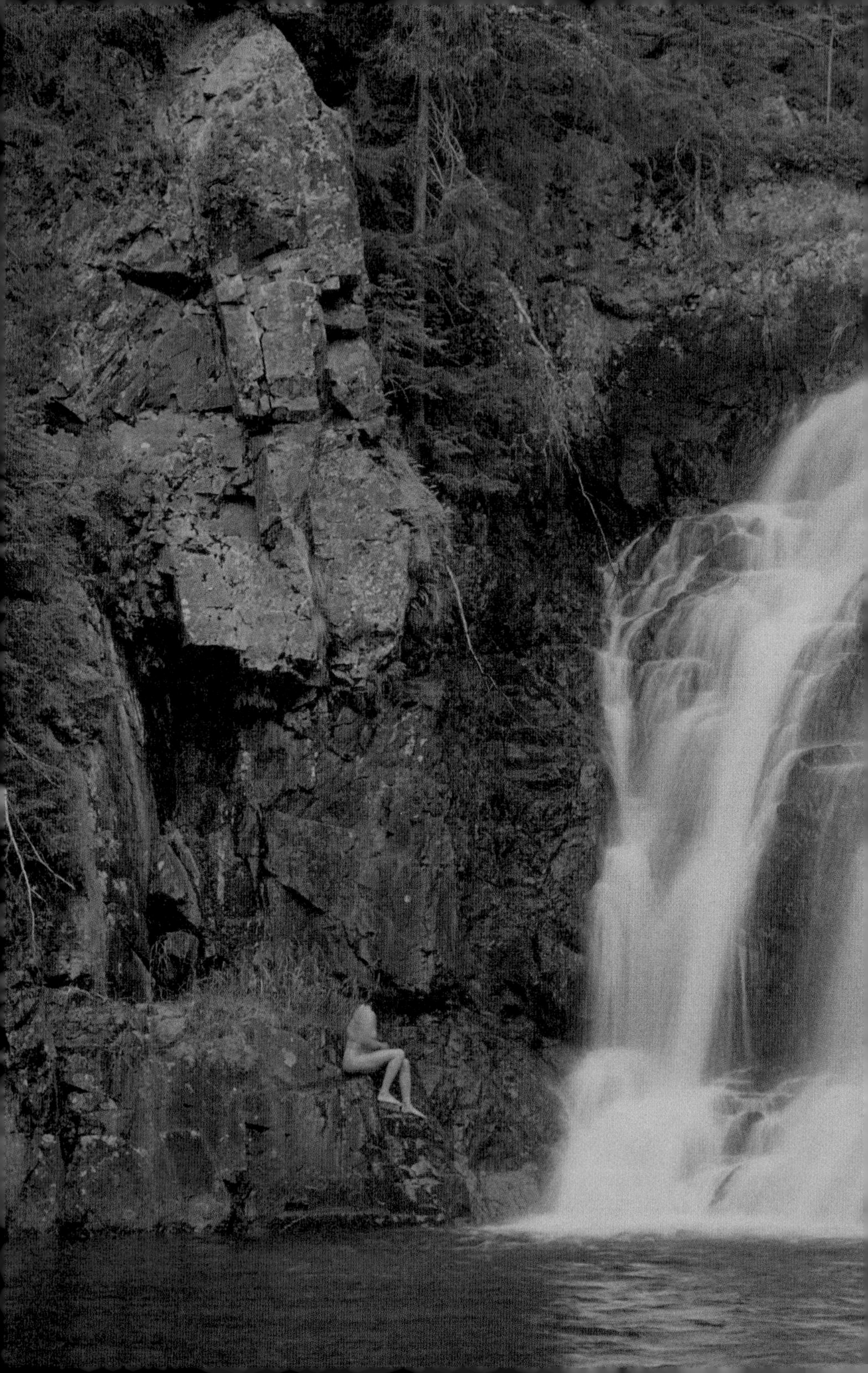

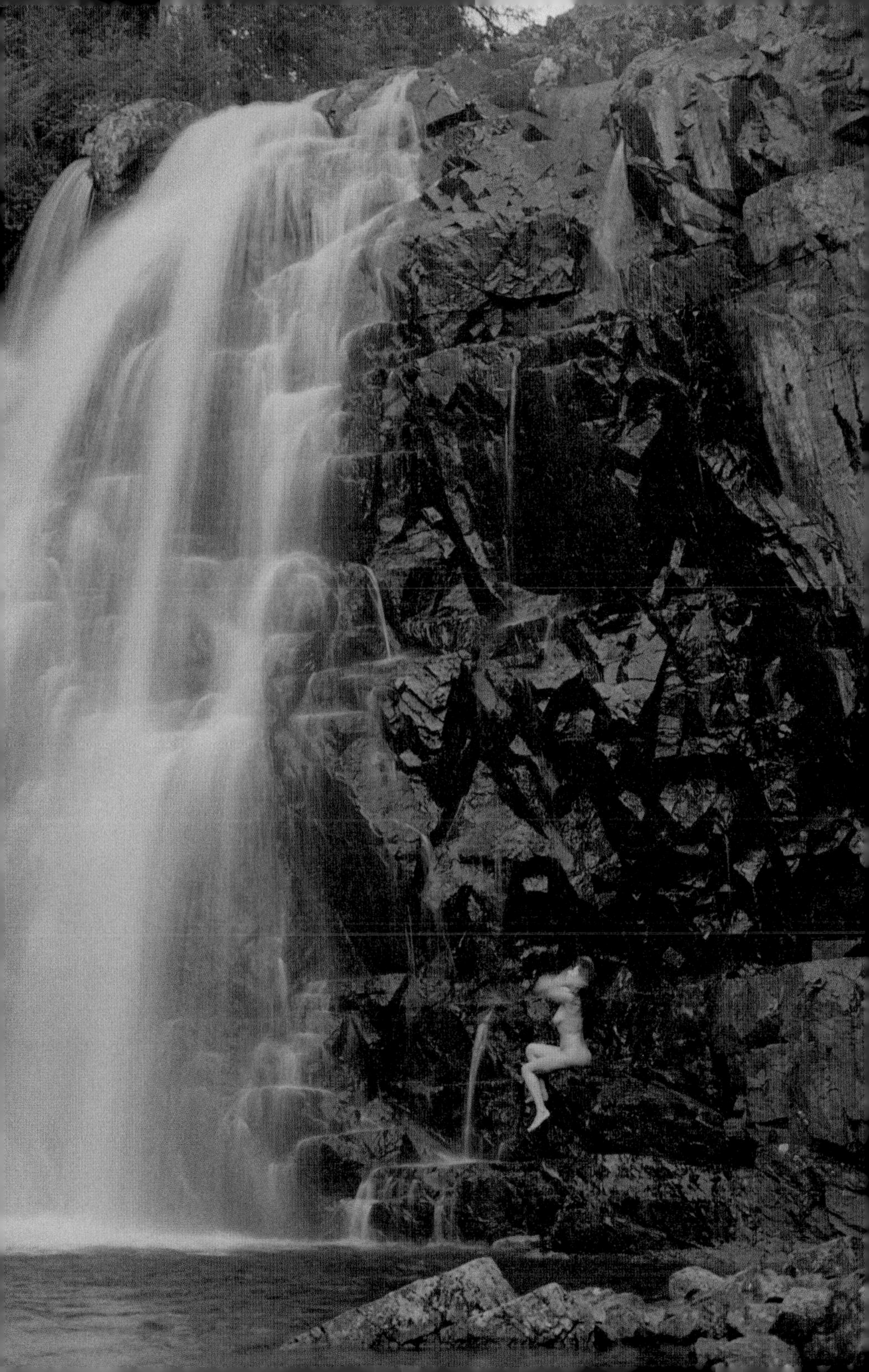

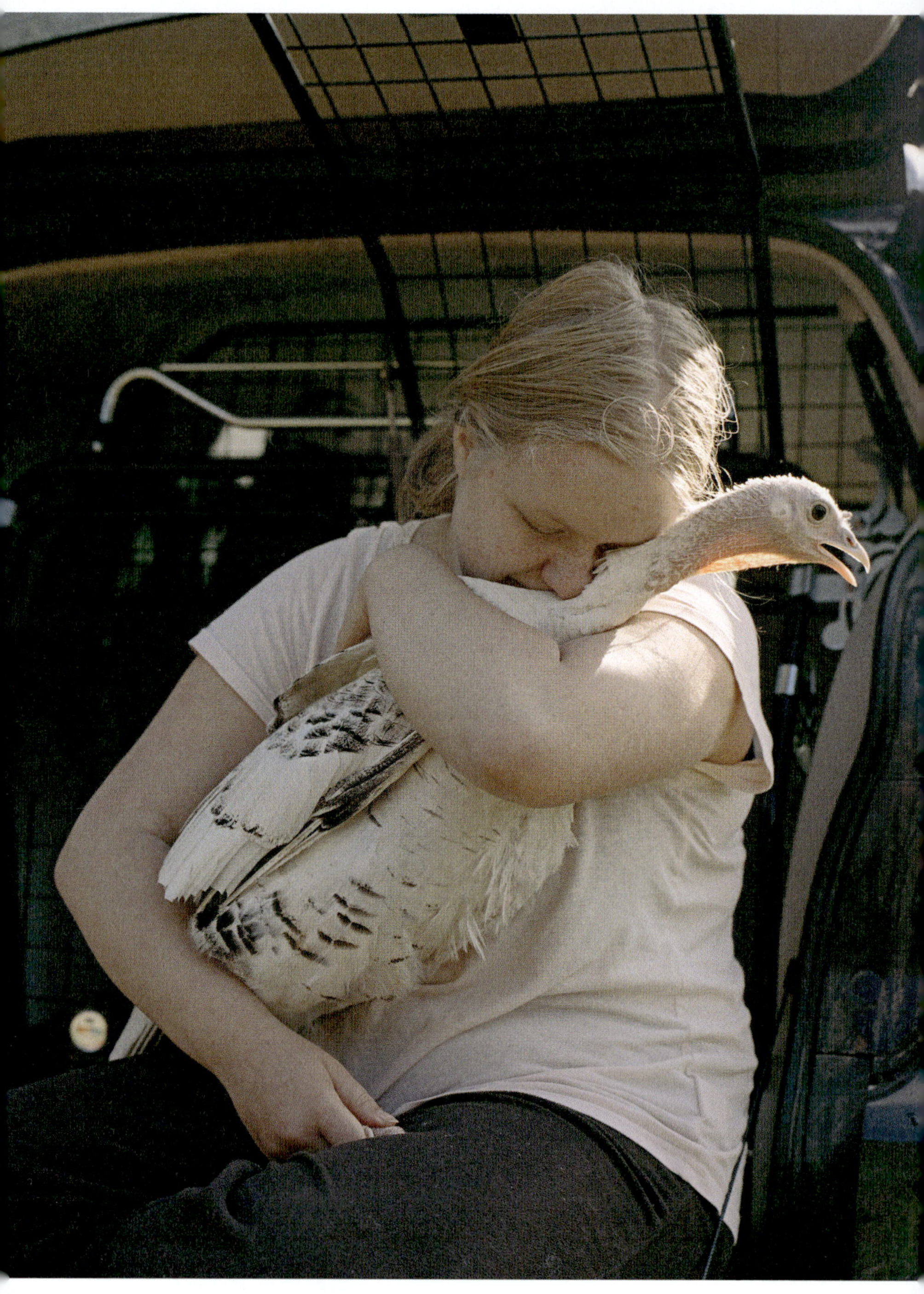

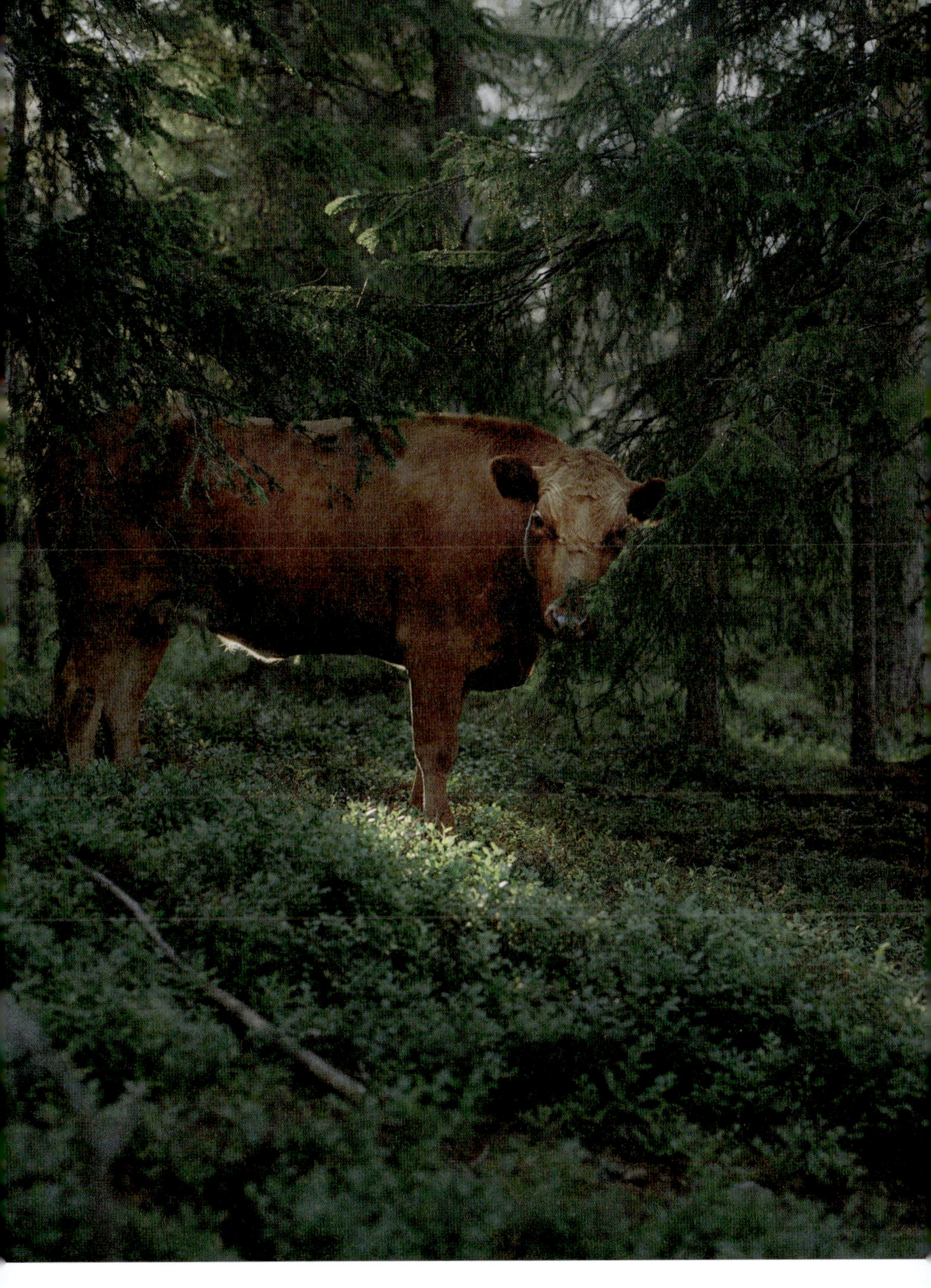

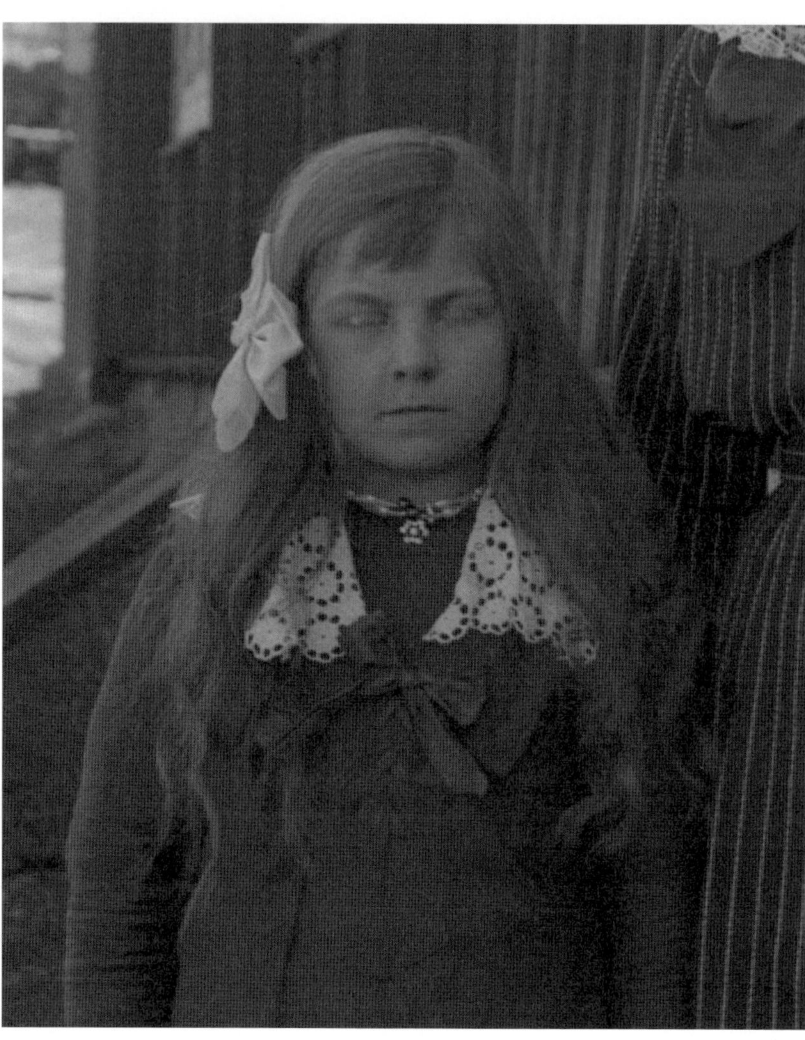

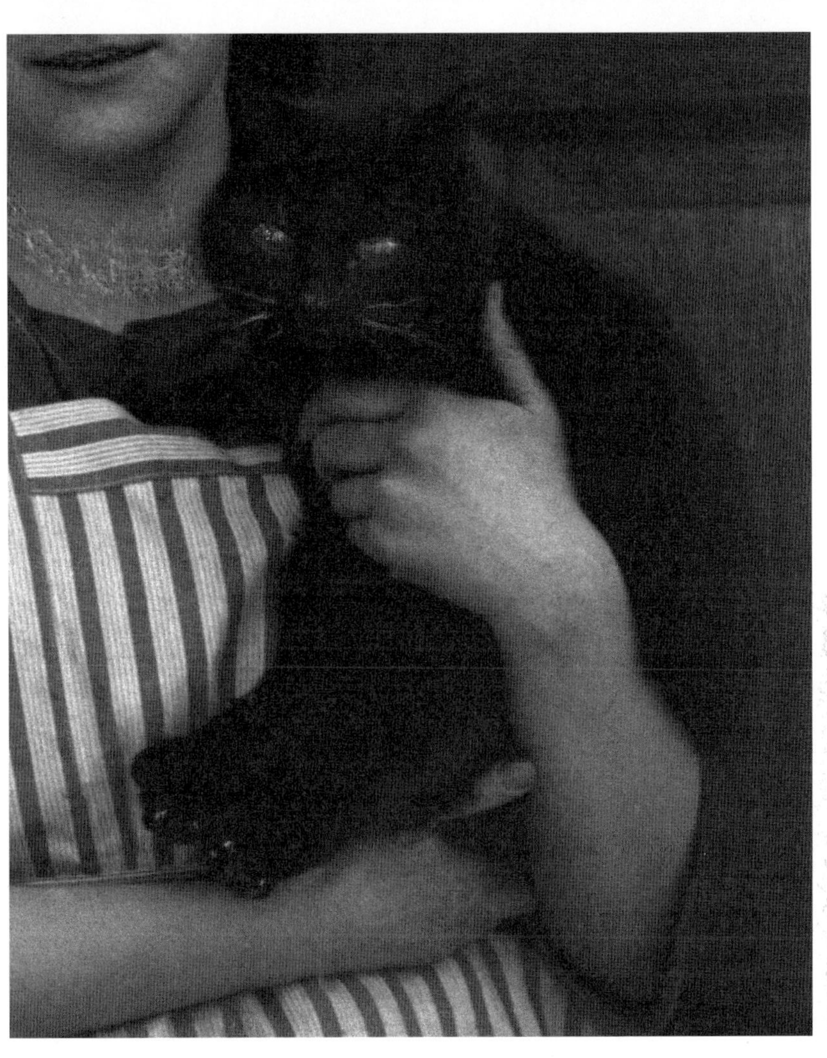

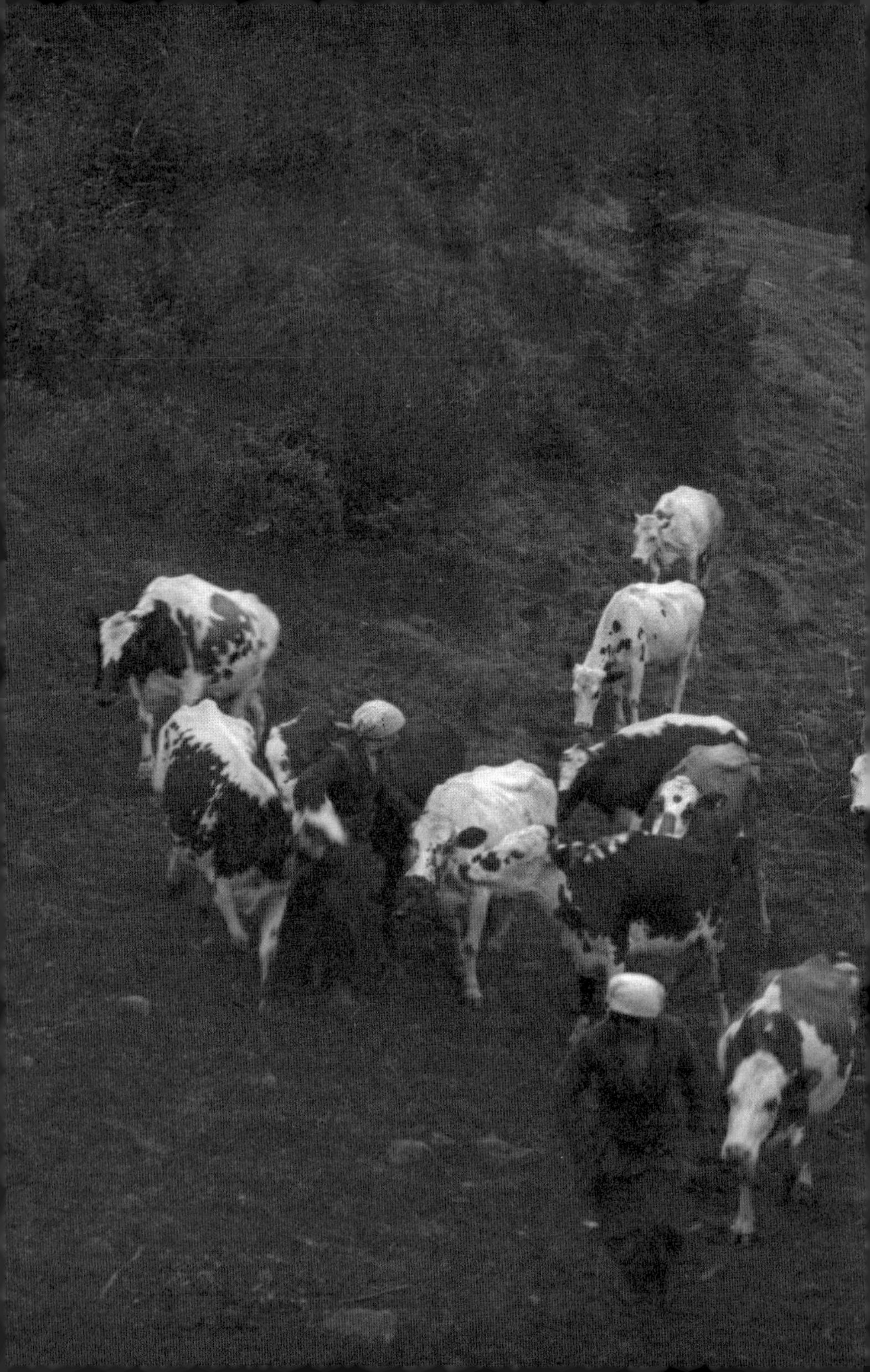

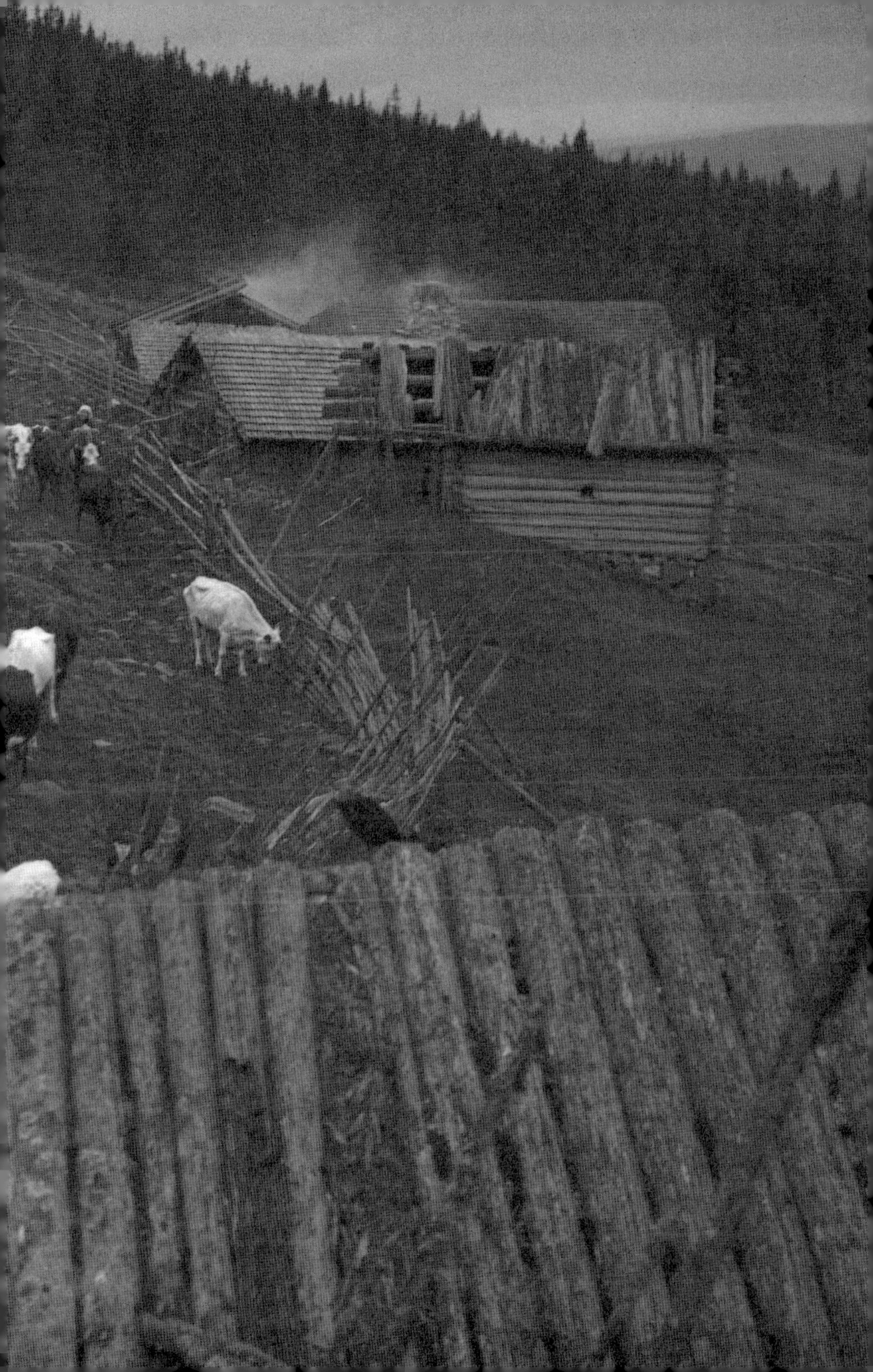

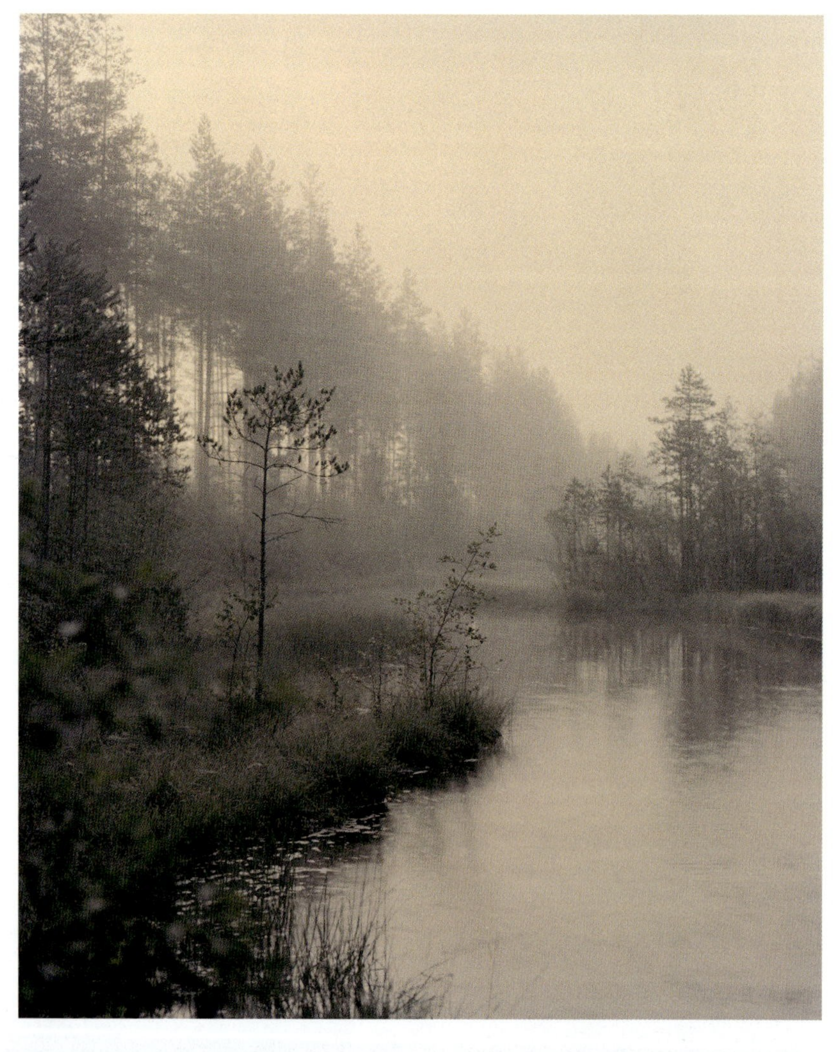

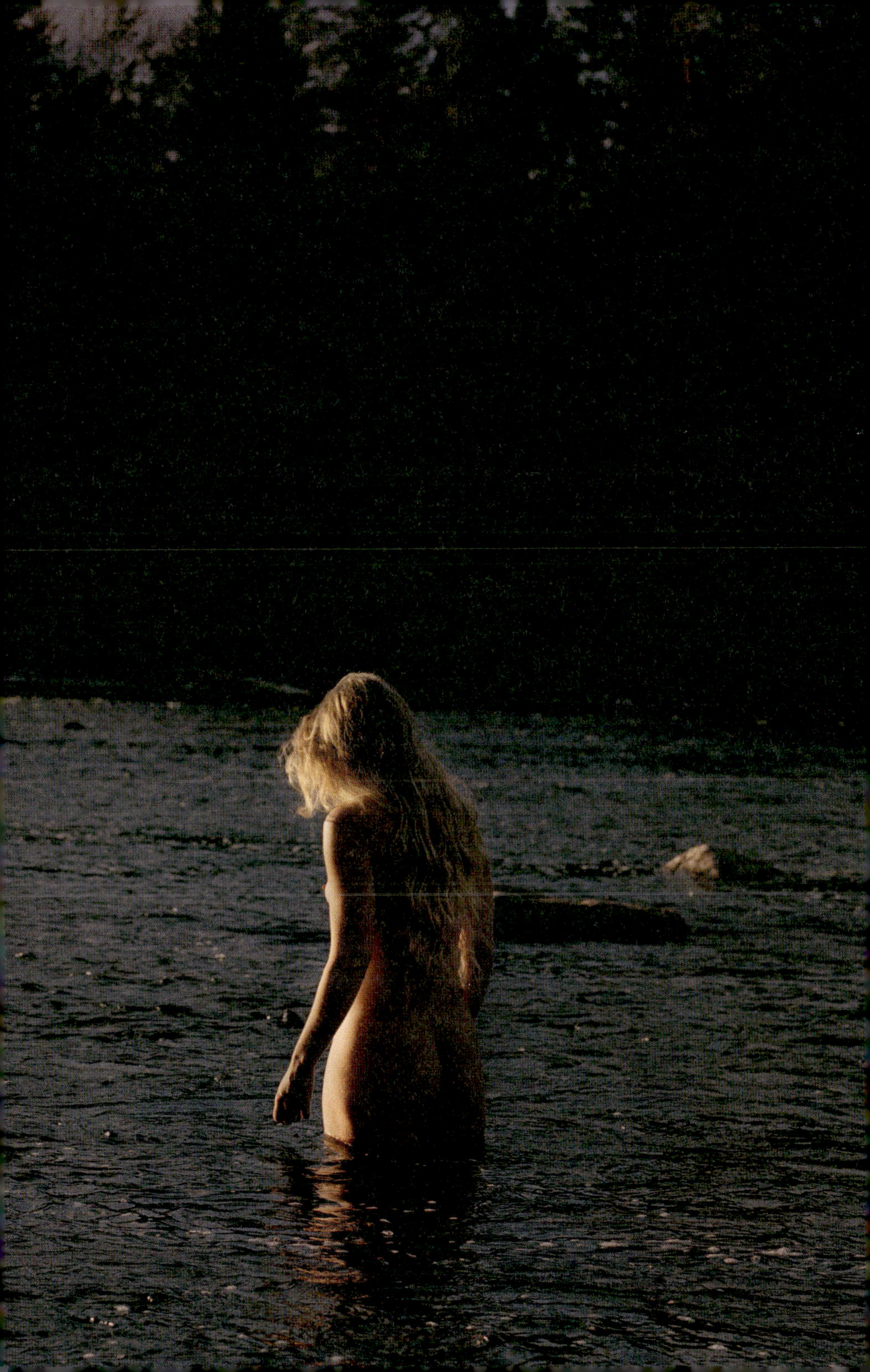

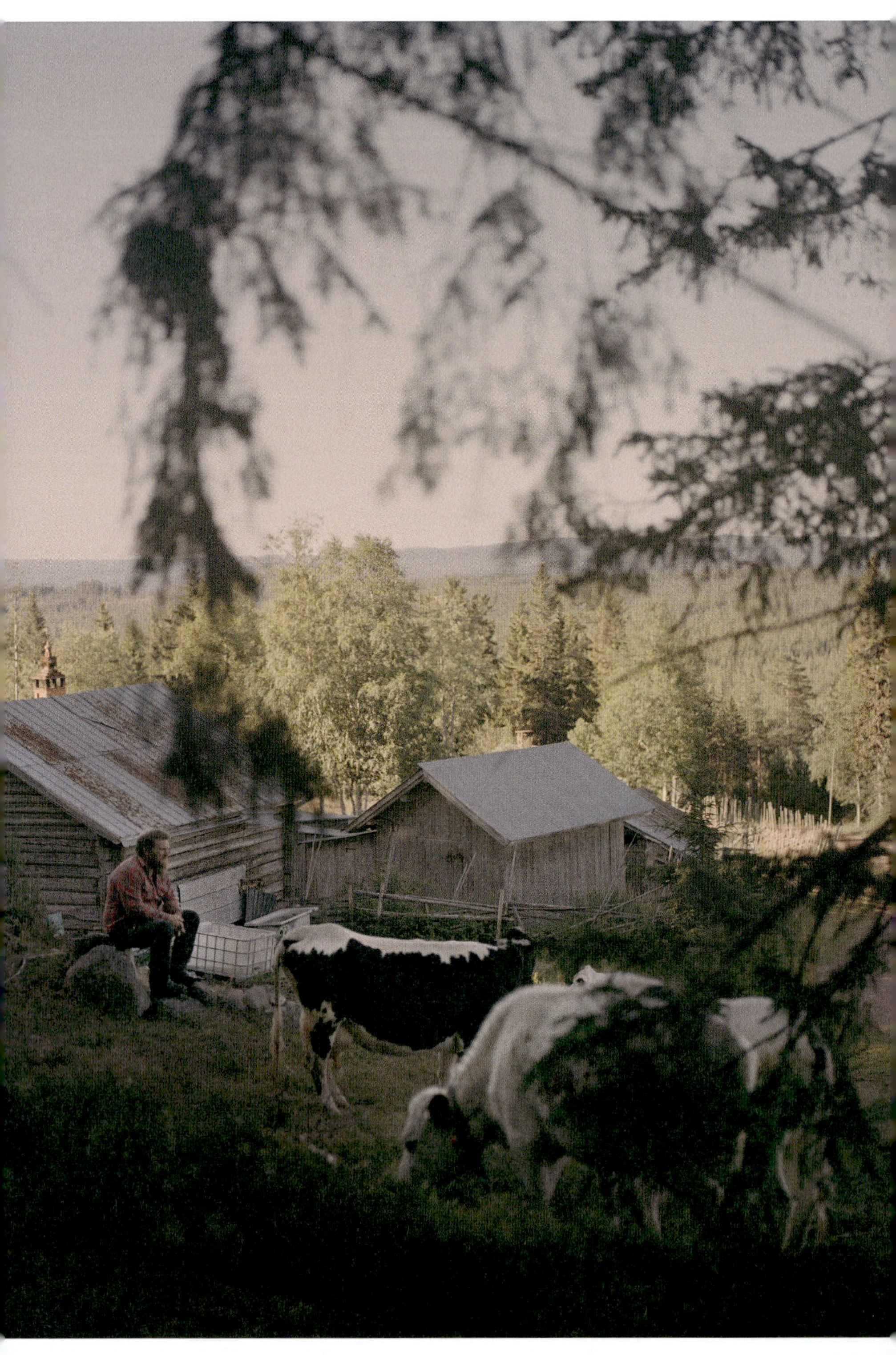

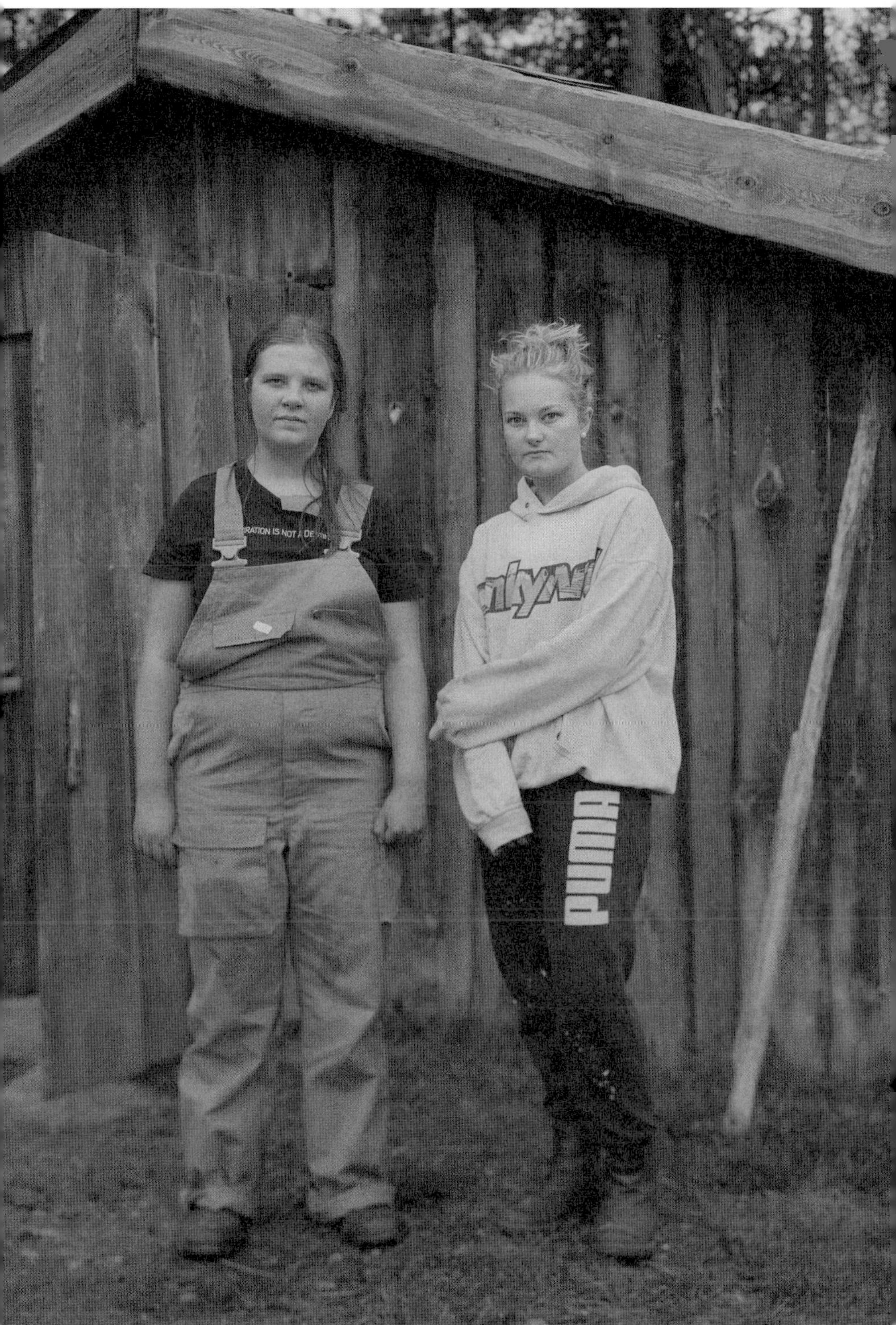
PUMA

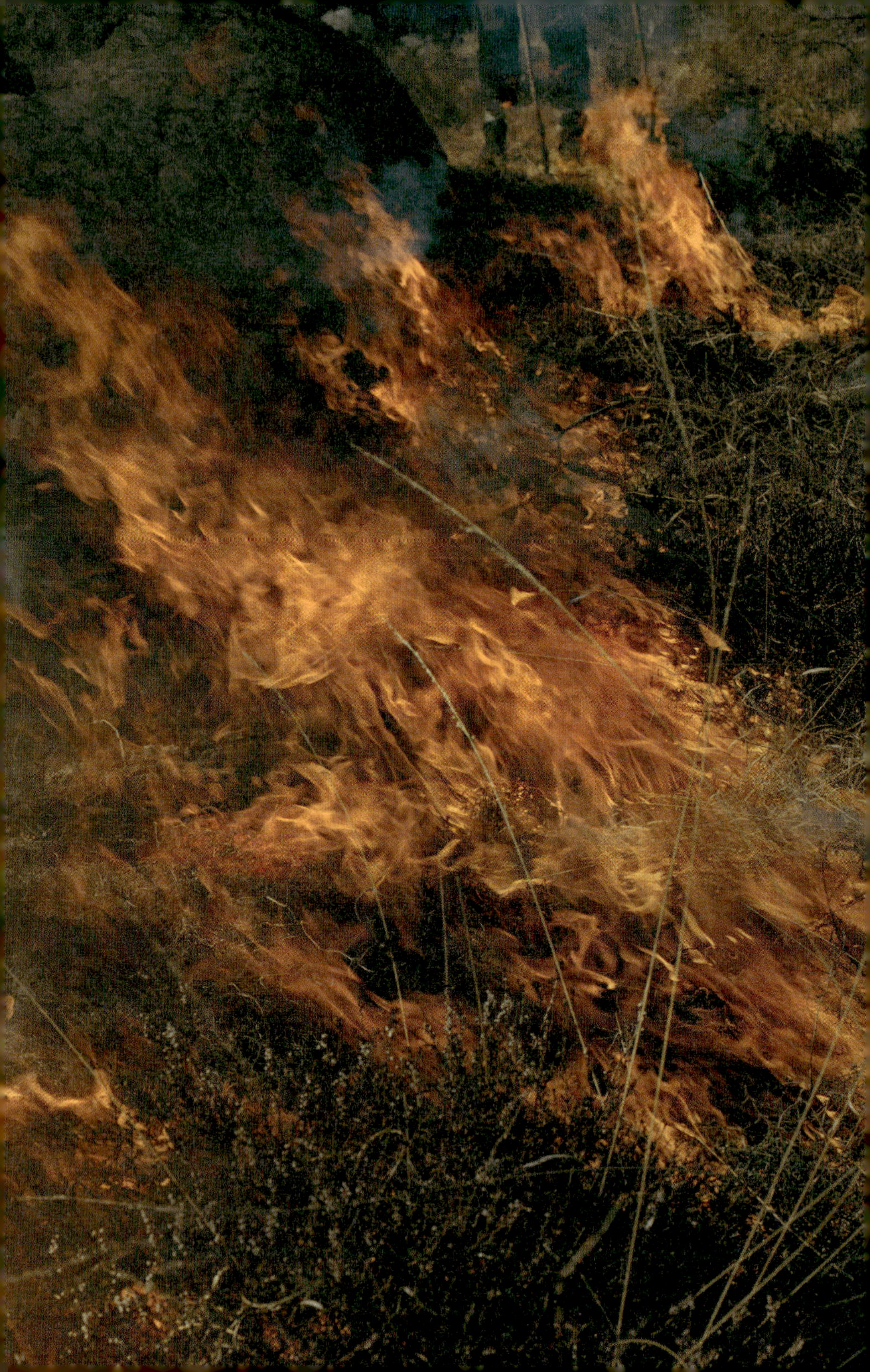

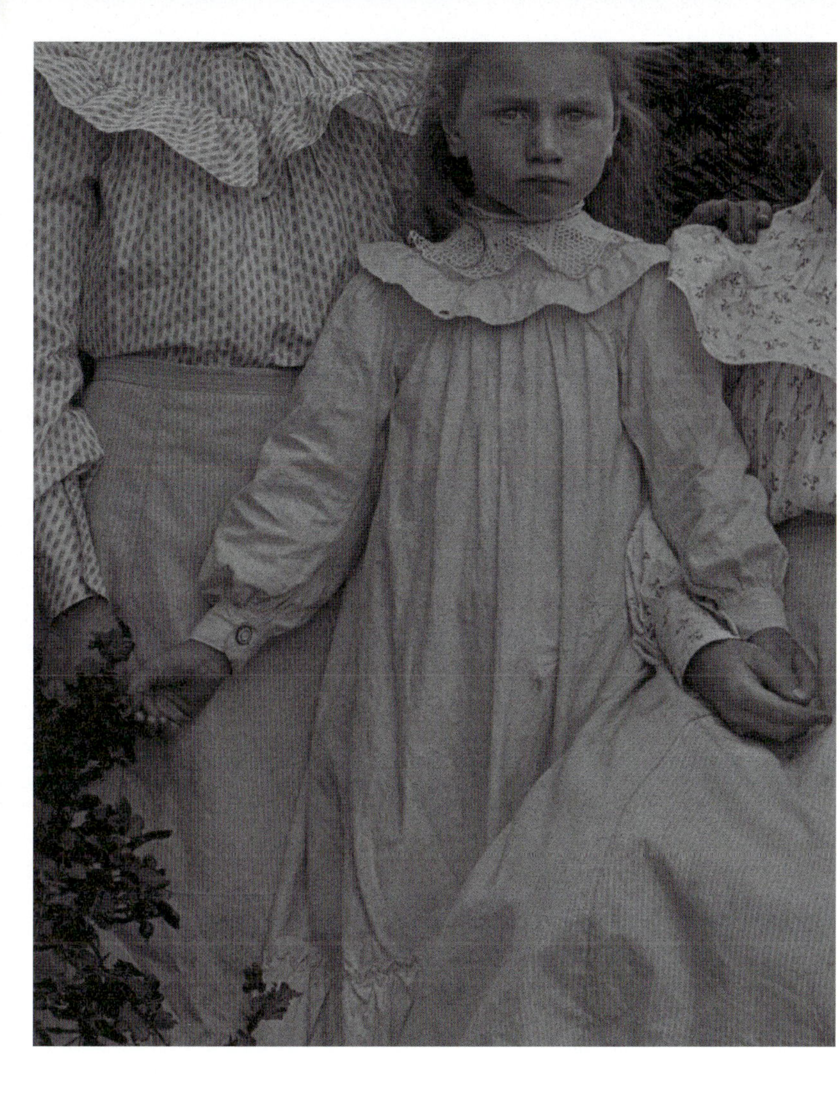

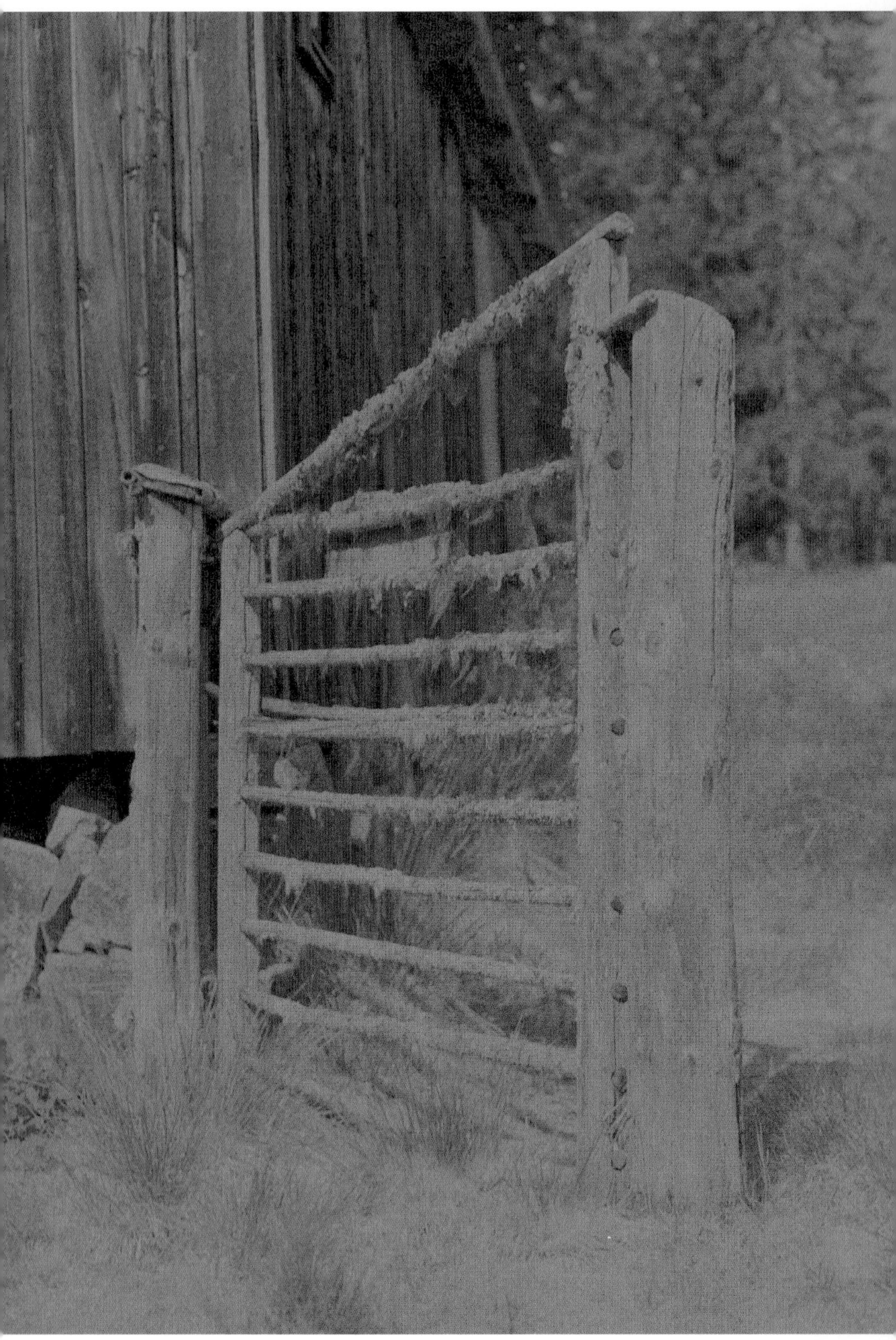

READ MICK

"Mick is doing for Chicago what Joyce did for Dublin."

— Jerry Stahl

"We don't read Betancourt to learn about Mick.
We read him to learn about ourselves."

— Rafael Alvarez

Mick Betancourt

Stories of work, class, and consequence.

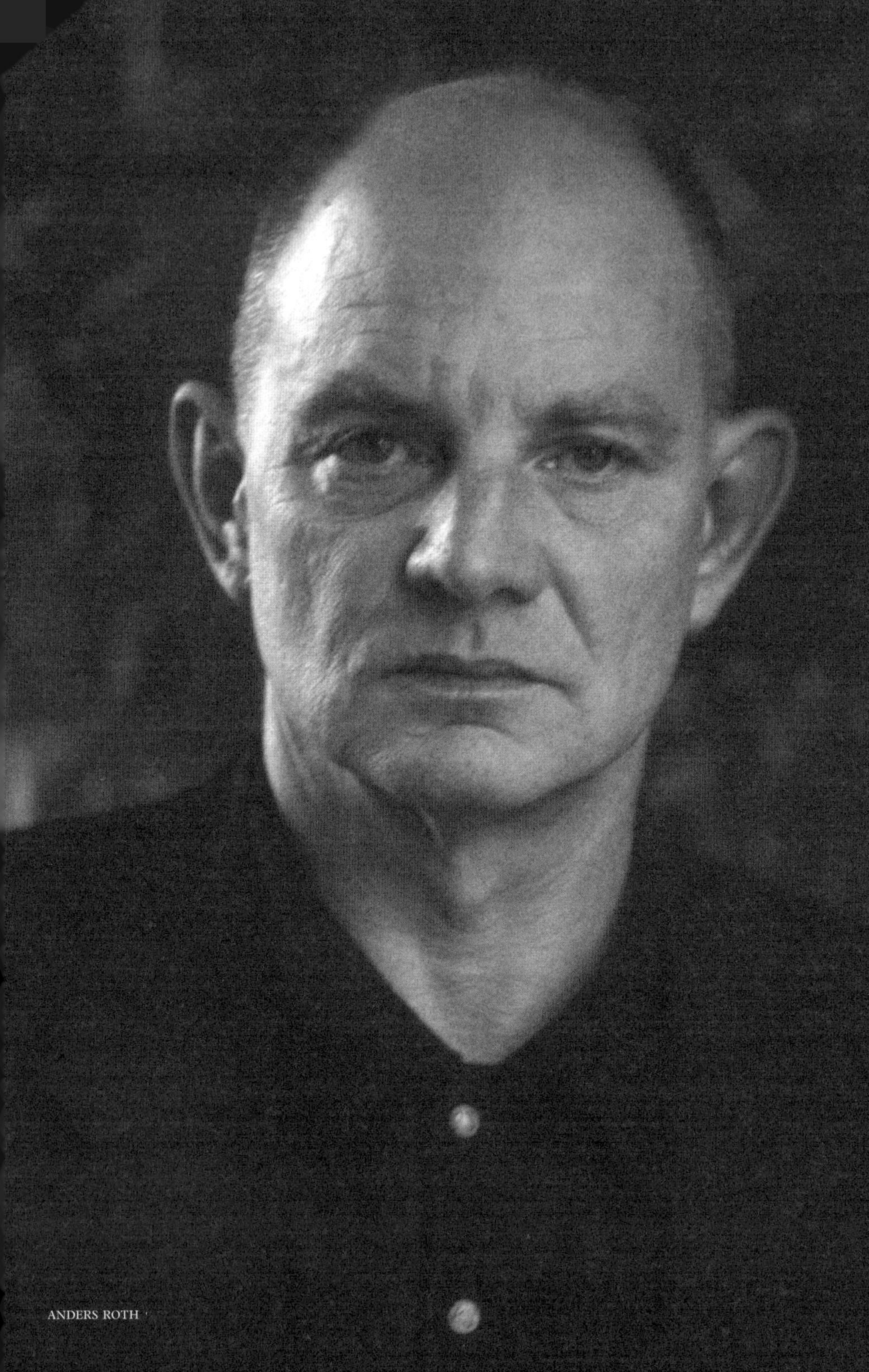
ANDERS ROTH

LARS NORÉN AND THE POWER OF WORDS

Sigrid Rausing

The late playwright and writer Lars Norén was a household name in his native Sweden, and well known in the rest of Scandinavia and Continental Europe. The themes of his plays, only a few of which have been staged in English, reflect a lifelong fascination with outsiders – alcoholics, sex workers, criminals and the insane – but most are family dramas; characters talking past each other, hostile, unheard and misunderstood. Norén, who often directed or co-directed his own work, encouraged the actors to bare themselves onstage, and because the moments of confrontation in the dialogue were so sudden and maybe because people recognised something of their own emotional ambiguity in the text, audiences would often laugh. His collaborator Suzanne Osten noted the laughter and had the idea in the early 1980s of staging the plays like Woody Allen films, but there was always an undertone of bleak tragedy and existential loneliness in the scripts, alongside a profound sense of psychoanalytic doom. The characters, many of them sexualised and hard-drinking beings, seemed to be free-associating onstage. The psychoanalytic idea that there is a gap between what we do and what we say (or even think) we do was always part of it – and what follows from that is the unsettling idea that we don't quite know who we really are. The productions also have somewhat shifting and elusive identities since the playscripts are very long, and were cut and edited for each individual production. Norén's writing, in that sense, was always a work in progress – there is a feeling both in the plays and in his diaries of perpetual renewal held fast by recurring themes.

Norén was born in Stockholm, in 1944. When he was six, his parents leased a small-town hotel in the south, and that is where he grew up. He has often spoken about that hotel as a theatrical set; a space for the enactment and embodiment of class, of rootlessness, alienation and alcoholism. He was exposed to extreme bullying by other boys, and has talked about finding in writing both a refuge and a compulsion to create meaning in a disordered world. He was praised by critics, but cruel tabloid headlines followed him throughout his life, commenting on his appearance, his oddness and – a particularly vicious charge – his 'lying pretentiousness'.

He fought his adversaries with words. The published work alone is monumental: poetry, fiction, more than 150 plays counting shorter pieces, and five volumes of densely printed, unpaginated diaries. Millions of words describing his daily life and routines, never translated into English before. In Sweden, they gained critical acclaim for Norén's distinctive language as well as a degree of notoriety for his barbed comments about fellow members of the cultural elite. But the attempt to write a life by giving ordinary experiences the same space as dramatic events became deeply influential as a way of writing about trauma in all its ambiguity and complexity while earthing the text in domestic detail.

Norén began publishing the diaries after his highly controversial play *7:3*. The idea for the play started when a high-security prisoner asked Norén to run a theatre workshop inside his prison. 'I think it only took him the time between two fags to decide,' the man later said to the journalist Elisabeth Åsbrink, who wrote a meticulously researched book – *Smärtpunkten* – about what then happened. The men, all violent criminals, two of them neo-Nazis, were so-called 7:3'ers, the term coined from the paragraph in the penal code setting out the strictest prison regime. The prisoners wanted to make a play about their experiences and beliefs and Norén made it happen, creating a script with them and directing them onstage. They were all hardened criminals, now performing as themselves in public theatres with minimum oversight. The audience sat in stunned silence as the men revealed their lives and thoughts onstage. One critic who stood up in the middle of a performance to protest against the platforming of neo-Nazi ideology was crudely shouted down by one of the cast members, and it was clear, even then, that a critical boundary between theatre and political reality had been crossed.

The day after the tour finished, one of the prisoners left the theatre, and, together with two other men, robbed a bank. Police followed. The men tried to kill one policeman, then, a little later, blocked a second police vehicle and shot and killed the two policemen in it. The incident brought home the questions Norén had reflected on in abstract terms in all his work – the link between childhood trauma and violence, the role of ideology and the moral responsibility of the auteur.

Now he had to live it. From the time of publication of the diaries, Norén himself was on a metaphorical stage, exposed in all his obsession, desire and despair. The language is intensely private – questions have no question marks and sentences are as long or short as the mood takes him. Each date is one long paragraph, with any breaks in the writing marked with a dash after a full stop.

Towards the end of the last diary – and his own life – Norén reflects on the American woman Lisa Montgomery, who was to be executed in January 2021 for a gruesome murder. She had been brutally sexually abused as a child and murdered a heavily pregnant woman she met online before cutting the baby out of the victim's womb and passing it off as her own. In Norén's mind the implied causation was clear, and he considers whether he can save Montgomery from the death penalty, but he is also working – separately – on a text about her life. Can she be saved? Could the neo-Nazis he worked with twenty years earlier have been saved? The man he visits in Kalmar jail in the first extract below wanted Norén to adopt him, and the deep unease around the question of the limits of responsibility is palpable in the writing. How far is he, or any one of us, responsible for the souls and fates of others? How can young people be saved from experiencing, and then potentially inflicting, acts of unimaginable depravity and violence? What is salvation? To most of us these questions are mercifully hazy. To Norén, the grandson of a Lutheran pastor who had experienced severe psychotic episodes when he was young, they seem to have felt viscerally real.

On rereading the diaries, what strikes me now are the set routines of Norén's life. Certain themes ring through the text with the regularity of church bells. Love for his children is one. Erotic love another. Intense working experiences a third. Gardening at his house on Gotland. Buying clothes – he likes brand names, and Issey Miyake and Comme des Garçons appear on the page with Heidegger, Hannah Arendt, Hegel and Rilke. It's easy to understand the writers and philosophers, but the clothes? Sometime in 2008 he notes: '[…] when I was last in Stockholm a man came up to me and said he's reading my book. You write about what clothes you buy, he said, but you never write about what you are wearing.' It's an important observation. The brand names ground the text (and maybe his mind), but the fantasy and reality of what they did for him was located in the act of buying, not wearing, the clothes.

There's space for everything in Norén's writing, from the trivial to the profound. He records it all, typing and smoking compulsively in bare rooms. I like to think of him gardening on Gotland, saving the lives even of plants he doesn't like, replanting them by the roadside, returning at night to his pristine house (white walls, a few pieces of beautiful furniture). Salvation, again. Harsh, obsessive physical work repaid with order. A hint of the spectre of nothingness, then remembering that night is the mother of day – the title of his best-known play – and that life goes on. He observes himself, notes his moods and terrors, listens to the voices within. He knows that in words he is safe.

The last extract ends where the diary ends. No full stop. The sentence is finished, but it has no end.

Time is eternal, he has written elsewhere, even when it ends.

Lars Norén died of Covid on 26 January 2021. He was seventy-six years old. ■

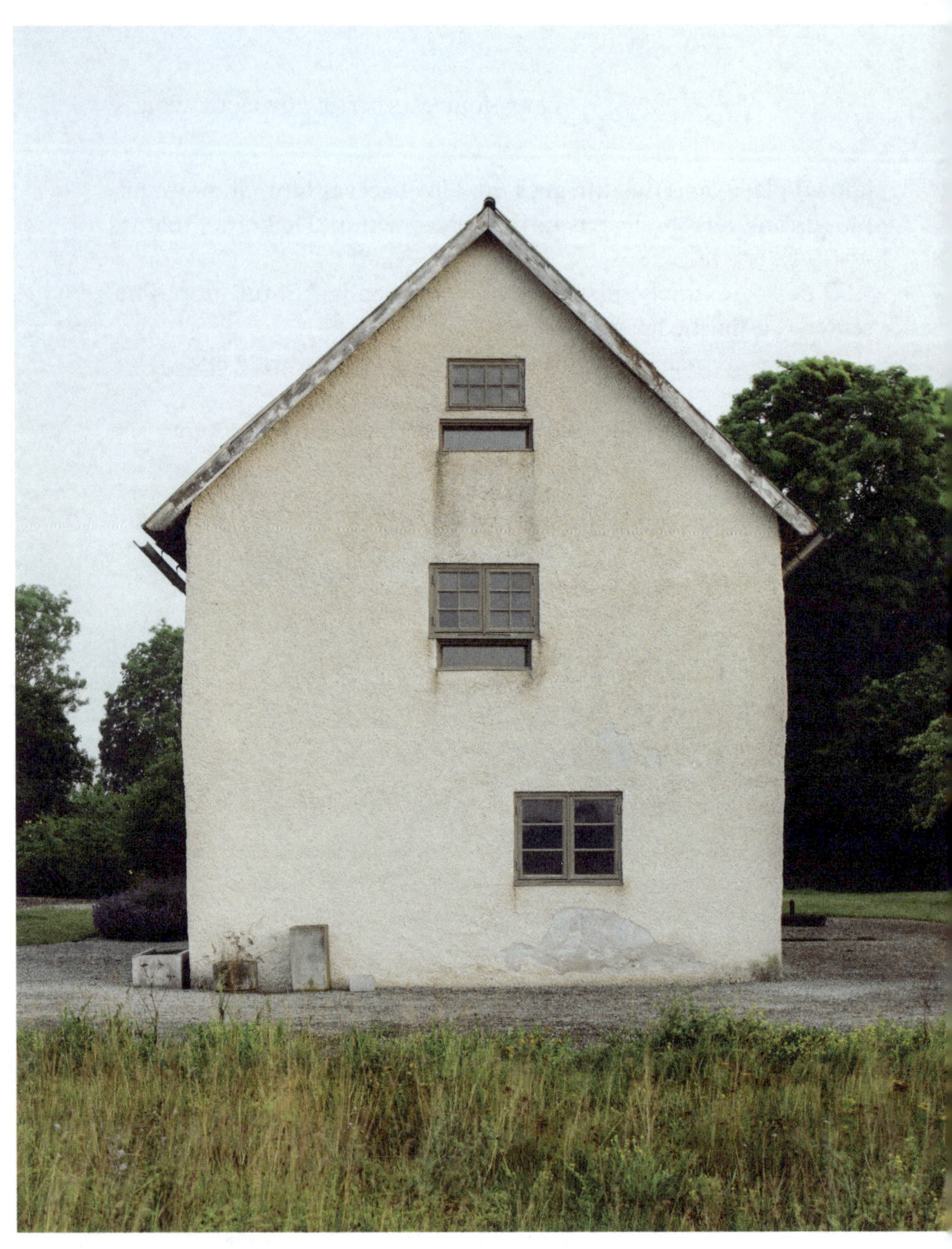

MIKAEL OLSSON
Lars Norén's home on Gotland, 2021

EXCERPTS FROM THE FIVE VOLUMES OF *DIARY OF A PLAYWRIGHT*

Lars Norén

TRANSLATED FROM THE SWEDISH BY SIGRID RAUSING

23 SEPTEMBER 2000, KALMAR PRISON

Got up at half past six. Micha picked me up at eight. Then we drove to Kalmar, 450 kilometres – we only stopped once at a café outside Norrköping and then again in Småland to fill up the car. It was incredibly beautiful. But as soon as you stop and get out of the car you step into a foreign country and an incomprehensible language. Autumn is more serious further south. Micha was speeding, driving between 140 and 150 kilometres an hour, but it was a straight road and almost no traffic, just a German who passed us without seeing that a car in front was turning left, but Micha was able to brake in time. He drives a Volvo, a frighteningly fast car. He loves to drive fast. They only had bad Russian cars in Poland when he was young, and he always dreamt of owning a good car. We talked a lot, and didn't prepare at all for the visit to Kalmar Prison. We got there by 12.30 p.m. and had lunch at a restaurant near the prison, built by a peaceful lake in 1853. There are fifty-three inmates and a permanent staff of some sixty guards. Gunnar and Göran arrived late, a bit stressed – they had driven down from Alvesta. We entered the prison. They rigged up the equipment and a guard brought Mats out. His hair was a bit longer than before, he was pale and you could tell he'd been inside for a while. He gained weight when he was on remand at Kronoberg (no gym) but now he's working out. I don't know if this placement is permanent or if they will try to move him as often as they can. He was in a good mood, not defensive and said he'd been at Kalmar before. One of the guards was a school friend. What do they talk about? They presumably avoid talking about what happened – all prisoners do – or why one of them became a criminal and the other a prison guard. What remains of conversations that avoid an authentic encounter? Which one of them holds the power? The one whose actions can't be predicted. The room we were in was small and we sat very close to each other. It felt as though we pushed Mats up against the wall. Two cameras and Göran, who recorded sound. And then me. I felt uneasy – how could he relax in that space? But I had to tell him that I can't – and that I don't want to – have any contact with him unless he makes a serious effort to tear himself away from Nazism, however deeply rooted it is in him. I told him about our work with Primo Levi and about the survivors I had met a few days earlier, a meeting that had made it even more impossible for me to see Mats socially. I can't mix socially with a terrible disease, an illness one tries not to be contaminated by, I can't even attempt to distinguish between what is Mats and what is Nazism because it's a constant presence in him. It's so repulsive and corrosive that it taints my life. Once we threw up coming out of a rehearsal in Tidaholm, that time when Tony explained why he had become a Nazi. I want Mats to be saved, but I don't have the ability or the tools or the time to do it. We need help. I could see that my words got through to him but what he'll do with them I don't know. I gave him the MS of *If This is a Man* and a CD of Bach's partita for keyboard in C minor played by Martha Argerich. I gave him the most beautiful music I know, played by the greatest pianist of them all. We were there for three hours. By the time we left we were completely exhausted by the tension and concentration. I wish we hadn't brought cameras. – I am not thinking about Mats now, but if criminals are psychopaths, all you can do is give them a sense of safety, a simple and regulated life with proper boundaries. Because punishment is meaningless – crime is a disease. Sick people are not accountable. It's an illness, destroying all sense of responsibility, control, insight, social consequences, guilt, morality. It's a disease, hollowing out the brain. If there is no cure punishment is even more immoral than the crime. – Had coffee in a café near the beach under some great oak trees. Walked by the sea, then we returned. Back in Stockholm by nine. We shared a few glasses of wine and had some mozzarella, pesto and tomatoes. I am lucky to have a friend like Micha. I have many wonderful friends whom I love and trust, at least in so far as I need to trust them. C was having dinner with Karin and a Russian translator. I was invited too but couldn't go. She wants to invite us to Moscow this autumn. Which autumn?

24 SEPTEMBER 2000, STOCKHOLM

The meetings with Mats have left me with some dark thoughts and feelings. I feel like the father I am not when I see him. He wanted me to adopt him. It would be like adopting myself, my most unpredictable self. I want to help him. I want him to get therapy. I know what happened to him, what he was subjected to as a small child. I know his nightmares, his anguish and his pain. If you have seen that you can't unsee it and forget. It's not surprising that he is holding on to Nazism, that hardness and ruthlessness. How can I support someone crying for help I can't give, while at the same time I am also working so hard? As we were driving Micha said that he doesn't know anyone who exposes himself to as much reality as I do. It frightened me. The decisive words in that sentence are 'exposes himself' – not that I experience more reality than anyone else but that I can't stop, say no, turn around. I keep thinking about it. Where are my places of rest? Well, Bryor, the three ruins on Gotland, music, love. The children, running, the stillness, the light, what I see and try to describe. I can't write about what I already know. I am not interested in stories whose endings I know. – Walked around town with C. To Moderna Museet.

Bought a book by Luc Tuymans. Then to Svensk Form. What were we doing there. I hate it. Home. Worked. Oh yes, we made it to the art bookshop at Sergels torg too, where I bought another book, about Tuymans and Mirosław Bałka. Home. Then we went to Cassilis on Valhallavägen and saw Nelly and Peter and Vibeke and had some Greek food. Linda served. She is quick and cheerful, a bit nervous because it was us, but she got this job on her own merit. I don't like to be served by her, I don't want my daughter to serve me, I don't like it. Worked for a long time in the evening.

5 DECEMBER 2001, BERLIN

I was deeply irritated with the actors yesterday. Not Bernd and Barbara, but the others. They were sluggish, uninterested. Isabel can be unbearable. Spoilt. I showed them how much I hated them at that moment. I can't stand Peter Pagel. I wanted to push him up against the wall. He said something and Katja asked if she should translate. No, I said, fuck that. I think I should, she said. But I ignored what he said. I told him he either does what I ask him to do, or he can go home. I was properly angry. Got home by midnight. Couldn't sleep. Felt the same raw rage in the morning. I was cold and determined. The only people I am growing with and learning from are Bernd Stempel and Barbara. We worked on the lighting yesterday. It's okay. I have told them I don't want any light or sound effects. I want pure performance. I am tired of the false seduction music brings. I want to trust the words, the music of the words and the inner music of the actors. The music of the words is enough. I don't want more. But they are still trying to create mysterious spaces and lit-up images. I have told them the place must be dead. The light within them is the same as the light outside. Their body temperature is the same as the temperature of the room. That is hell – the fact that there's no distinction between the inner and the outer. They are nowhere. Not even at point zero. It's just the actors and a few chairs. They move, and the space is as cold and raw as the morgue which awaits them. I got rid of the glasses on their heads. I had wanted them to sit with glasses of water on their heads, knees and hands, but it was no good because they had to get the glasses, fill them with water and then put them in place. Now, they touch a glass and you hear a loud pling, as though all the glasses were breaking. Then they take an invisible glass and sit down with it. That's all. The only light effect I want happens when Emma unscrews a faulty light bulb and puts in a new one and a wonderful light fills the stage. Katja asked me what I will miss about Berlin: You. Everything. And one more thing: To be unknown, not recognised, anonymous. To go wherever I want without others seeing me, looking at me, coming over to greet me. Katja has clear brown eyes and a wary childlike smile. – Talked to Masja today. She said it was precisely that lack of anonymity which worried her. We can't be strangers in Stockholm. Tomorrow Linda arrives. Ilka will pick her up at Tegel because I have to do the evening rehearsal. Then they'll come to the theatre. And after the theatre we'll go and have dinner somewhere. I am not rehearsing in the morning and I have cancelled the evening run-through. They need to rest. They are working hard, like pit ponies. I don't want to show them kindness before they deserve it. I am becoming German. When I am cold, they act better. Strange. Saw a few journalists during the break. The journalist I saw yesterday talked about Hans-Michael Rehberg who was at the table next to ours in the canteen. He has the lead role in *Titus Andronicus* on the big stage and played Frank in the first staging of *Demons* in Stuttgart. The journalist said Rehberg's father was a Nazi, and wrote Nazi plays. Rehberg himself says his father was a very good writer. He hasn't been staged since the end of the war. Today I gave another interview, in the Rheinhardt room. Named after the street outside, Rheinhardtstraße? The journalist told me that when he visited East Berlin in the 90s there were no radiators in the houses. His friends carried buckets of coal from the cellars. We ran through the play in the foyer yesterday. Isabel was lying on the sofa, not interested, languid, as though she had just made love. Ulli got her food and wine.

Katrin is sleepwalking but she is good. She is good, but she could be a hell of a lot better if they didn't exhaust her, working her to death. Mattias (Michael) is very good too. Every day he comes in with a new medical diagnosis predicting death within weeks. We had a photo session today. Talked to Eirik Stubø. He arrives Friday. Ulrika and I will have lunch with him if I have time. I arranged a ticket for him to Marthaler's performance at the Volksbühne on Saturday. Riks Drama are seeing Sarah Kane's *4.48 Psychosis* on Saturday. I can't make it, I have a dress rehearsal. I'll come back in January. Robert asked me yesterday if I had seen them in anything other than *Tristano*. I said no. Masja told me that she felt nauseous again and had an upset stomach when she got home. She is anxious. I saw a very big rat outside the theatre, at dusk. It ran across Oranienburgerstraße almost down to Friedrichstraße. It was as big as Göring but disappeared under a fence at the market square. The journalist today had a thought about something which I now can't remember. Charly was there for the run-through this morning but disappeared as soon as it was finished. That's okay. I want to be alone anyway. I still have the scent of Masja on my fingers. I did some more interviews and wasn't done until half past four. Then I walked home, finally. It was evening by the time I got to Teutoburger Platz. Got some groceries at the usual supermarket on Rosenthalerstraße. Talked to Linda who hadn't received her ticket, which is now waiting for her at Arlanda. When I have time, I think about Masja's body. It stays with me. I long to make my way inside it. Soon I'll be home. I don't want to sleep in the same bed as C. I feel as though I have committed a crime against her. No. We can't sleep in the same bed any longer. It's not possible. I'll move into the study for the time being. She goes to Haverdal on the 15th of December. She will help with the Christmas preparations. I don't know if she has found a flat yet. She says she wants to move out as soon as possible. I should have been firmer from the beginning. It's a waste of time being firm now. It's stupid. It's just mental hygiene, an attempt to wash off my own way of being. I go to the west alone tomorrow, without Charles. I have consumed enough. *Consummatum est.* I want to say goodbye to that part of Berlin. This part I have already started to say goodbye to; I am almost done. I created a hiatus yesterday in the scene between Peter Pagel and Bernd. I asked them to quietly lean in and then attempt to strangle one another. It was an articulation of my state of being. I can't bear to see Pagel toss back the long grey horsehair from his face like a teenage girl one more time. Soon I'll hit him. What is the vulnerable, humiliated place in me that is so provoked by him? I don't know. Find out. I have to be at the theatre at a quarter to six tomorrow morning. First a meeting with Oliver, then soundcheck. Then we are rehearsing a scene transition and after that there's a rehearsal at 7 p.m. Call C. How many people already know – Chatarina, Ulrika, Svein, Gunilla, Chatarina's sister, V, Masja's mother, Charly, G, and some of Masja's friends. How long will it take before a rumour reaches C? I have to talk to her before that happens. – I have just talked to C. She has found a flat. Two rooms and a kitchen at Tulegatan / Surbrunnsgatan. She'll sign the contract tomorrow. 1.9 million SEK. I was incredibly happy. I was happy for twenty minutes, then I asked myself why I was happy and felt sad instead. But it's wonderful. And she'll be quite close to me. She moves the 15th of December. She said it was a bit scary, she's only seen the flat once, last Sunday. Talked to Charly for a long time. He fears going home. He has talked to G who doesn't want him to come home on Saturday. He is going to Örebro Tuesday. So he arrives in Stockholm eleven thirty at night, then he has to leave at eight the next morning. How does he do it? G has her own flat. I will probably be assaulted by memories like an invasion of damp and mould. I have loved C so much and for such a long time. I still love her, but in the past tense. I feel like crying, but I don't have time. We reached a mute point, a cold wall of no language which we couldn't break through. Now I only remember how happy we were; childish and kind, childish and childless. I don't want to hurt her. I don't want her to suffer. I'll be there for her. I want to go home and talk to her. I wish I was home now. I wish there weren't so many nights between us. I can go home on Friday. – Berlin is clear and still tonight. No one can reach me. A monotonous searchlight sweeps the western parts like a lighthouse. The cranes by the side of the dark cupola of the dome are illuminated. Charité is strongly lit. I've already left, even though I am still here. I am going to talk to Robert about Bruno Bettelheim. I want it back. I exchanged him for Wittgenstein but then we'll lose an important connection – abuse. I'm going to read McEwan's *Amsterdam*. I'm going to call Masja to tell her what happened. Barbara is fairy-tale beautiful at a distance. When you get closer you see that she is unhappy and afraid. I saw it the first time. I have so much work left in me – in my inner self. In my houses. In my thoughts. Reine will play me again in *Detaljer* at Dramaten. He is my shadow-actor. But it's not me. It's only some made-up versions of things I have experienced.

6 JULY 2002, GOTLAND

Woke up with a bad headache. It stayed with me the whole day. I think I'm dehydrated, I've hardly drunk any liquid since I arrived. The water tastes off and I am worried about bacteria. Buy a water filter. Cycled to Stenkyrka at half past eight. Back by a quarter to ten. Had breakfast. Went into the garden at a quarter past ten and worked until half past three when the sun was above the left gable of the house. I am trying to take it easier today, but it's difficult. I notice how much hatred I didn't know was in me comes up when I stop thinking. The same inner phrases come up again and again like schizophrenic perseverations and at times I say them out loud in a strong clear voice. I let it be. I notice it and observe myself, but I let it be. I've cleared the raspberry bushes and a bit of the wild meadow. I've started a square limestone wall around the beech tree, where one might sit as a ninety-seven-year-old. Every time I go in that direction I bring a few more stones. I have removed some trees, and cut dead or dying branches. I don't use the word 'perseverations' to lighten the mood with a medical term, the word is a verbal remnant of the terror of schizophrenia I felt when I was young and which I thought I saw in Hill's drawings, too. I have started the planting in front of the raspberry bushes. I have removed whatever I don't like, replanting some in the meadow, though the soil is poor there. But the peonies I can't throw out. Partly because C liked them so much and partly because I find it difficult to throw out living plants. I dug them up and planted them by the road where I won't have to see them. I have moved three shrubs. I am moving another four tomorrow. I have watered the roses with nettle-water. If I go on like this I'll end up collecting seeds and writing out labels. I slept for half an hour this afternoon. I wrote, made some food, tidied up. I've been sad today, permeable and weak. But I love the garden. I forgot to buy drinking water in Stenkyrka. The first pink flowers are beginning to crawl out of the hollyhocks, sticky and damp. The small New Dawn growing behind the rose bush has opened up into two roses. I have a hedgehog in the garden. Every evening it strolls past the kitchen window and around to the right of the house. I drank a glass of R. I ate too much. I went for a walk at dusk and photographed the fields of oats and the meadows and the gathering fog. The sky is white and still. The leaves move so slowly and softly that you hear them more than you can see them.

7 JULY 2002

Rain last night. It woke me up. Slept badly, sat around for several hours in the morning. I went out at half past ten and worked for five hours. I moved the four peonies. They can stay where they are now until next year. It took me almost two hours to replant them. Dig them up, get soil, water them, put the hose down, water again. I sat on the grey stool and smoked and felt pretty good. Then I went down to the raspberries. I took out five or six different yellow plants C had put in. I kept two. They were planted too close together. It looks better now. I don't like yellow plants. I replanted them out on the meadow. I gave them new soil from the abandoned vegetable patch – I am digging it up bit by bit to get rid of the soil. I thought I'd mix in some sand next spring and plant some vegetables and herbs. I have felt a bit dizzy for the last few days. My blood pressure is very low, Helleday asked me to look into it. The medicine lowers it even more. I have boiled some water so at least I have clean liquid. The sun came out around two and it was warm and wonderful. I worked up a sweat and got indescribably dirty since the soil was still wet after last night's rain. I was totally finished and very satisfied when I was done. Sat on the steps for a while. Showered. Made some food. Got potatoes from the vegetable plot and some poor-looking onions. Herbs from the herb garden. Poached cod with egg sauce. Drank two and a half glasses of wine, one glass too many. I got tired and sad. Washed three loads of laundry and the kitchen rug. Hung up the laundry to dry and took it in again. Walked around the land as I do every evening, inspecting what I've done during the day. Photographed dusk. Wrote. *Stilla Vatten* had some amazing moments. The play from prison – well, it's good. I am unhappy tonight. Don't know why. I blame the medicine which has run out. It doesn't help to try to be tougher with myself. Talked to Nelly. They are still in Österlen. Maybe they'll come tomorrow. I must send some money to Linda's account. Allan tomorrow. It's getting warmer but I think the weather has been good. I prefer cool air and rain to heat and drought. One of the reasons I love being here is that it's so far from Sweden, mentally. I get depressed at the thought that it can't last very long. – Don't identify too much with him, Olof Lagercrantz said once when we were talking about Stig Dagerman. Did Olof really understand him when he was still alive? I remember some ruthless reviews he wrote about the new poets, Ekelöf and Lindegren, in the 1930s. Later he became their greatest advocate. But a critic obviously shouldn't be merciful. At least Lagercrantz had the courage to continuously reassess his values, whether literary or political. – I have been busy the whole day. I haven't even had time to go for a run. The roses are tremendous.

19 OCTOBER 2002, STOCKHOLM

I am very happy and very sad at the same time. It's the same thing. I long for her so intensely. I don't call. I don't want to talk any more. I want to live. I don't want my life to be an empty space in time, a void between the hours passing by. I don't want to be on the outside. Yes, I do, but not in this way. So full of love I can't give. Or receive. I look at Bill Jacobson's images. One of the things I like about them is that they don't feel clinical which is something that often disturbs me with other photographers. The other day when I came to Judiska Teatern and she was angry, for a brief moment it was as though she saw straight through me. In the mornings I feel anxiety and regret. My greatest mistake comes to me – the writing of this book. I want to give myself to somebody else. Give myself to somebody else – can I do it? I saw Chatarina at half past ten, had lunch with her at Lydmar. We talked about work, directing, what we want to do in the future, how we can arrange to work together again and so on. Then I met Nelly at Stureplan. I said I'd get her any shoes she wanted. She deserved it. I took her to Paul & friends and showed her some beautiful Prada shoes, easy to walk in, but they didn't have her size. Then we went to NK where she found another pair of Prada shoes with high heels, which I bought for her. After that we went to Pluto in Sturegallerian – Northern Europe's dullest mall and the customers are as dull as the mall. I only go for Hedengrens. It was a cool and beautiful day, harsh sunlight. I talked to Charly briefly. He said he was at Sturehof, and we went in just to give him a hug. Then we left and parted ways. I went shopping at Baronen and longed for A. I nearly called her again. From now on I only want her. I don't know why it's so bloody strong. I think her sensitivity and her hardness are the same thing. The sensitivity under the hard surface is a big thing. I'm going to curl up in bed and think about her. I give up. It's so long since I gave up. Alongside that feeling there are also the hard facts – I'm a dirty old man who has no right to be in love with a woman twenty-four years younger than me. Thirty-four years old and a mother of two. That alone is bad enough.

I can't change it. And of course she's aware of it. I went to lie down. Nature is playing a joke on her. I am not her future. I am cold with love. I weep internally. I hear strange fragments of what she has said to me. I asked if my saying I missed her made her tired. She answered: No . . . I feel the same way. She said: I long for you. I bought the bloody sunglasses. Why, what will I do with them? There is no sun. I think it will be hard to see her tomorrow. I'm worthless. Why doesn't she want to be with me when I am happy and free? I felt like – and acted like – an idiot the few times we met in the presence of others. Not a damn word the whole day. I'm angry with her for making me feel this way, at my age. Serves me right. Now I'm getting a taste of everything I did to others. Serves me right. It's fair. I deserve it. If she wanted to, she'd come. It's ten to six. I saw Gunnar Harding on Birger Jarlsgatan. He said he'd seen *Stilla Vatten* and thought it was one of the best things he'd seen. I hugged him. Now we don't have to be sad that you don't write poetry any more, he said. You are still making poetry. I was enormously happy. In that blissful moment I got my phone out to call her but when I saw her number I didn't. What's the point? What is she thinking? Perhaps she's doing what I've always done. What I did to Masja, what I've always done. I won't go on. I didn't go on. But this love is strong enough to touch. You could lift it up. It actually exists. Where is she in it? It weighs 200 kilos. It's too heavy for me. I saw *Dirty Eyes*. Stefan is incredibly good. And there's no limit to how good he could be, if he gets the chance to develop. He has no boundaries. It's just a matter of reducing, of scraping his expressions bare. But then he'd have to live another life. How many people are actually able to do that? It's not good that he hasn't acted much. But his instruments are unspoilt. There was a letter from a daughter that was very good. I was shaken. Not moved. Shaken. In real life I am in the darkness of love, I am alone, I am cold, I am ill, and she is the one who has made me ill. No, I did it to myself. She woke up this morning with her bra around her neck. Charly said Stefan told him that when he asked how A was. Yes, I want to get out of this darkness but at last I am living, because it's so painful. It's been a long time. After thirteen years Claude Simon published a new novel, *Le Jardin des plantes*. I will buy it when I leave Berlin. We will age together. I will read it on a park bench and it will slowly turn white, the words disappearing, turning pale and indistinct. Fainter. I imagine sitting there holding a volume of obscure voices I suddenly can no longer hear. I listen to the silence. Not the one all around me but the one inside me. I love her. I see a thorn in her eye.

27 SEPTEMBER 2003, PARIS

Saturday. I am alone in the two white rooms. I feel a paralysing sense of my own loneliness tonight, mostly because I don't have the energy to break through it or to think further ahead than this precise moment of emptiness and fatigue. I haven't talked to A since Wednesday. She doesn't call. Nor do I. I feel a sense of hard grief. I don't know what's happening. My ever-present refusal, my perennial act of refusing, is waiting to strike. It's hot again. I want to get out. I am done. My work here is more or less done. Now I have to stay and take care of it, preserve it, give them all love. I know I have another three weeks here at least. I go to Stockholm on Thursday. It will be good to be away for a few days. Then I go to the mountains. Peter Örn came by yesterday. He was part of the rehearsal. Afterwards we went to Bofinger for lobster and oysters, same as last Friday. Strangely enough I happened to walk down all the streets where A and I had walked before. I started packing. I had dinner again with Peter tonight. Same menu as last Saturday. He told me about his younger brother who left his clinical director position and about his stepfather who didn't like him and who was an alcoholic and about his mother with whom he is no longer in touch. Afterwards I thought a lot about my own father. Sometimes I feel his presence, or rather my guilt towards him. A woman is running very fast on the street. Why is she running. Is she trying to catch up with someone. Is she looking for someone, or is she fleeing from someone. A couple are walking in the park, wandering around the gravel paths, stopping by the large sunken fountain. They go to one of the benches, stop, carry on to the next one where there's more light. The woman sits down. The man stands for a while. Then he sits down too, next to her. When I think about my father and his unhappy life it's like observing a sleeping father. It's like watching your own father while he's asleep. When I parted from Peter I went home to read, but I don't remember anything I read. I talked to Nelly. There's a suspect in the murder case, the actual killer or someone else.[1] She says you can follow the perpetrator on the CCTV inside NK. It's shown on the news again and again as if the murder will never take place. The man enters, goes up the escalator, disappears, re-enters, goes to an escalator, ascends, disappears. A big German paedophile ring has been exposed. The Americans don't know if Saddam is dead or alive or both. It rained all day in Stockholm. Ulrika is in Mexico City. Tomorrow she'll go to the opening of *Demons*. Both she and Corinna thought the couple at the Royal Court played too much to Greek tragedy, but that the son was brilliant. I don't know how it went. I have no relationship with English theatre, except for Pinter. But Pinter is the kernel of England. Kafka is channelled straight through him – the theme of the great shadow of the father. The power in the room. Lonely people in a room, and then someone knocks on the door to take them away to visible or invisible extinction. The order. The avoidance of communication, the revelation of weakness. Both of them created a completely new language made up of the language all around them but twisted, disturbed to the point of hallucination. Damp clammy nightmares fill the rooms. Today I worked on the last scenes. The others have not been told about Gérard's secret until now. I wish it was finished already. I feel like I want to die. I live the lives of others, the actors and the roles. Again I feel homeless, unprotected and naked. I want to go home to write. I wonder how I will get out of it, how I will do whatever I want to do without falling into brutal self-

---

[1] In September 2003 Sweden's foreign minister Anna Lindh was stabbed at the department store NK in the centre of Stockholm. She died in hospital the following day.

love. I can take it for another month, I tell myself. P called Thursday morning. He said he had left the set at Galeasen a week before the premiere, that it was his own decision, not stage fright. He said he was close to a nervous breakdown Sunday and saw that he couldn't do it. Now he's going back to what he was doing before, trying to get *Blood* staged in Paris. I have a strong feeling that A has met someone else. It might be for the best. It might. I just want to write. I want to travel to a land of silence. Tomorrow Vibeke arrives. You can't be a guest forever. A filial hallucination before the father who has become a corpse of the powers that be . . . Louis Jouvet is the name I couldn't remember.

4 APRIL 2005, STOCKHOLM

Meeting at 11 a.m. at Bonnier with Harriet and Kristoffer Leandoer. Discussed the diaries. I brought up the defamatory sections in part one. He says most people know about those things anyway. That's an argument, to be sure. He was nice, quick and easy. He told me he had lived in Minsk, where his wife worked for the UN, the year *7:3* was staged. I'm seeing him again next week. Meanwhile he has read the first 40pp and a lawyer is considering potential lawsuits. I went home. I couldn't write. I had an appointment with the therapist on Sigtunagatan at 4.15 p.m. I met A and Julia on the way – Julia was going to be with Nelly while we were in the session. I was clear and unambiguous. I listened, I made an effort to listen. I made an effort to let her finish her sentences. I said that I did not want to have a child. I might come back and write about this later, but right now I can't. I am psychologically exhausted by our relationship. I assume she is too. We were there until 6.15 p.m., then I went home. I said we'd be in touch and I suppose we will. I really did listen to what she said, every word, but I also listened to what I said. I can't do it any more. I wrote when I got home. Got some sushi for me and Nelly on the way home. We had a TV dinner. Nelly had been to a fancy-dress shop owned by one of her friend's dads, where they let Julia borrow a beautiful Chinese coat she's wearing to her costume party on Saturday. Her birthday is on the 12th. Couldn't sleep. Then I listened one more time to everything we had said in that ground-floor back room with three chairs and the little table in the middle. I like the therapist and he's good, but we can only get to the place we need to get to by ourselves. Sometimes I look at him as though he were a stalker in a Tarkovsky movie, and the inner room, which we may never reach, is the place where we relinquish each other.

27 AUGUST 2009, STOCKHOLM

I set off to A's at a quarter to nine. Took a taxi. Still an intense feeling of summer but the air is autumnal. Not too much traffic at Skeppsbron. Got off at Hornsgatan and walked up to Puckeln where I lived for three years in the 1960s, Hornsgatan 52a. I still have bad memories from that time. Went through the door and up the cold staircase, stone steps hollowed out by countless people walking here over the centuries. Rang the doorbell. A opened. Hugged her, and walked into the small bedroom where Sasha was lying on her tummy on the bed. It was as if a great wave of tenderness and joy washed over me and threw me over. She woke up and looked at me wonderingly, but I was not altogether alien to her. She hasn't grown as much as I'd feared, but she will soon be crawling properly. She can already propel herself forward on her hands and feet, moving quickly across the floor. I blew on her tummy as I used to and lifted her up and she recognised that. I blew on A's tummy in the same way, and Sasha thought that was funny. We walked up to the nursery Maria Magdalena at the top of Blecktornstrappan by Bastuparken to leave our application for a place next autumn even though we both feel some doubt about it because it's full of celebrities. But it's a wonderful place, a big yard with old trees and greenery, no traffic, an eighteenth-century house, open and calm. If she gets in it would be a safe place for her, close to home. Then we went to a café at Puckeln. We met A's dad on the way. He had picked up a high chair for Joshua, Åsa's boy, who came from London with Åsa last night. The funeral is at 1 p.m. at Råcksta crematorium chapel. I told him I wasn't going. We stayed for a while at the café and then went home to A's. Sasha was fed. Emm and Julia woke up and all three of them put on black dresses. We parted outside A's door. I went down to Slussen and took a taxi to Stureplan. Bought Carolina Thorell's poetry collection where she writes in one poem that she sees me at the central train station in Brussels, someone, I can't remember who, told me about it, but I didn't look for the poem. Elisabeth's book, *Smärtpunkten*, was on the counter. Publishing date tomorrow. I went home. Paid 500 kronor for a lamp at Plan1, regretted it, will pick it up next week. I read, slept for a while. Got up and wrote, I'm on page 26 of *Dödsmusik*. Conversation about planning the reading of *Oedipus Rex* and *The Oresteia*. Today I'm more interested in *Oedipus*, but tomorrow . . . Talked to Göran Ragnerstam, Ulrika and I are seeing him Sunday 11.30 a.m. at Non Solo. Staffan Roos is ill again and will not be directing my play at Dramaten. Someone called Sara Giese will do it instead. I started proofing the diary yesterday, wrote two pages and will carry on now. I am not adding, I'm cutting – it will take years but I'm not in a hurry. I fly to Gothenburg next Thursday, there's a reading from *The Oresteia* between 2 p.m. and 6 p.m. Friday I have a meeting with Steffen and Lisa who are in charge of the costumes. Then there's another reading Saturday. Monday Ulrika and I will see Emmet, who is coming to Gothenburg to meet us. We will discuss productions and potential collaborations between us and Det Kongelige. – The existential places I have been during this year which soon will be over, no, not have been, these are all places where I still remain – Södra BB where Sasha was born, the weight and mercy of Place [Saint-] Sulpice, Bryor, where I weeded the lavender and the Roman wormwood, the funeral at Skogskyrkogården, the rehearsal room at the Grand Palais, the walks through Paris, through death, poverty – none of it ends, it runs like the water from the hard mouth of the angel in the great sculpted fountain at Saint-Sulpice and it never floods, it maintains the same controlled ecstasy, streaming through my thoughts. To carry Sasha, to kiss A, to see Nelly, see Nelly smile, and then the great absence of Linda. – I talked to Stig Larsson this morning before leaving Bryor. I told him the truth, that I've read his play and was somewhat fascinated by it, the whirlwind of minutiae, the energy, the almost grotesque amount of period detail and manic perseverance but I also said that it would be hard for us to put it on in the next few years, not least because of the homogenous late-middle age of our ensemble – we are prioritising work for the ensemble we have. He said he understood. He also mentioned that he is trying to leave Berit Gullberg's theatre company. He said she doesn't put enough work into the plays. She's getting old, like us. He's met Lotta Neuhauser, he said, whom he believes I know. I talked about a different play, a project he started some years ago at Dramaten, about a group of young immigrant guys from a council estate. I asked him to send it to me and to come and see Ulrika and me in September. This is exactly what we should do – it's our subject, persistent and flexible. We could start working out a timeline for the project, premiering autumn 2011 or spring 2012. He'll get the time to work with actors and non-professionals, and we can start a deeper collaboration with the citizens of the estates. We don't want to create theatre that doesn't leave its mark. He also has a language which might be useful for them and for us. I wish we had the money to commission writers like Stuart MacBride or Pelecanos to write for us and for our young people. We have to find, define and create a space of authenticity between the two extremes, social and existential theatre – as if there were some deep difference between them. – I met the leader of Vänsterpartiet when I left A today. We slowly passed each other on Roslagsgatan, and recognised each other. I said hi and he greeted me back, looking happy and relaxed. I was happy to see him, too. But I suddenly couldn't remember his name . . . His name is Lars, too . . . but I couldn't get any closer than that. I am working on *Oedipus* just to be sure it's not the play I want to put on. I am more interested in the children in *The Oresteia* than in the parents. But Oedipus of course is simultaneously a child and a parent. *The Oresteia* is the first play and Euripides' *The Bacchae* the last in the great century of Greek drama. The scene: a rectangle within a circle. That, and the words, will draw the public into the drama. Nothing else. But the words are in the hands, the feet and the faces, too. The hands open the body. The voice opens and preserves the horror and the beauty of the drama. No – *The Oresteia* for the sake of the children and the Furies. I have to finally understand them. If they fail, if they don't exact revenge, they will be without homeland, without mission, and, in the end, without life. They have one task only – to correct, to mete out justice and to impose restitution in the original sense. I am interested in the punishment. It's already there on Orestes's face, like a divine wound. Orestes is freed by the first democratic court of law, founded by Pallas Athena to solve the unsolvable. And meanwhile Clytemnestra is not rehabilitated and there is no reconciliation. Not only because she is a woman, but also because the murder of a king is the murder of an order, of a divine principle, a moral *summum bonum*, while her own murder is private, individual. We have to keep researching how we depict, how we depict that great historical inequality. I don't know yet. I can't think about it. It was warm tonight, grey and still like a Bobrowski poem. A life darkened by tears. Shall I write more. Do I have a book left in me. I run on my hands, not my feet . . . it says that in *The Eumenides*, if I remember correctly. Plato's state was made real by Hitler. Every new philosophical epoch must read Plato and the others from the starting point of their own historical situation. That is the kernel of philosophy. Heidegger may have been the last person to try to restore the comprehensive Spirit of Being in Hegel's sense, albeit without the metaphysical elements; a Spirit of Being, a phenomenology which didn't make scientific claims but rather attempted to create the room, the idea of the room which existed prior to being, before space itself, the room which must exist to contain being, in which being would take place, to be and being, in the sense of Presence. And presence can be felt only through Time. Time is Being more than Time. He also deepened our knowledge of how history reifies a world, the subject Rilke too got worked up about, and later Munk. How can I get the actors to run on their hands. But I will leave *Oedipus* for now. *Oedipus* is mine. It must wait. I'll start with *The Oresteia*, with the intention of staging all three parts. The last one may be the most important. It initiates our era, and shows us where we have failed. I ought to read Hegel before reading Fichte, Lessing and maybe Mills, but there's not enough time. In some mysterious way they all anticipate each other, describing, with different models of causation, the same *Zeitgeist*. I cut, I adapt *The Oresteia* to make it mine, I begin to work. Göran was too tired this morning to take part in the physical exercises. He wanted to meet for brunch at 11.30 a.m. Ulrika was in a taxi with Kickan when I called, going back to her flat to get a swimsuit for the sea. A said the funeral was beautiful and moving. Now Ture lies there held by his own hands, so small and still that there's space enough in his own working hands. I have proofed four pages of the diary. I don't have anything from August to the middle of October that year. Have pages disappeared. I know I had an enormous amount of work on at that time. I'll just carry on. Was that when I decided to stop writing a diary. I can't find my books on Heidegger. I need them. I need to return to the attempt to experience thinking and thought in a way which predates – as far as possible – all systems of thought and contingent perception. I only have fragments in my memory. It's my only chance to reimagine my past, to place myself within the illusion of the world I lived in before I began to narrate it in accordance with the stories of others. Is that why I feel such a strong need for Greek tragedy, it stays with me. To get there before it. Not possible. Of course not. I can't take away what made me. I can't take away History, not even *Les Demoiselles d'Avignon*, Kafka, the father and the mother, death. I can't abolish death. Death is the snow falling steadily on all things and all people, it falls on what I do every day, wherever I go and whenever I sit down and whoever I talk to I see the snow falling on us, on truth, on the way, on memory, and not least on all the characters who have been me, the man stepping out of all the other men while you look at that which was me and even more at the one who is not yet me. But time is eternal. It's eternal even when it ends. Yes, I know it will take far too long to find *Being and Time* here. I'll go out and buy it. Maybe Rönnells will have it. That too is part of Being. I have been watching *Kulturnyheterna* on TV this week. It's unbearably poor and shallow, a kind of cultural Ikea or Cheap Monday in its banal attempt to reach an already habituated public with something soothing, and in the self-love exhibited by the reporters. It's certainly reciprocated. Yesterday, for example, they spent ten minutes on rapper Ken, good and important I'm sure, while Gunnel Wåhlstrand got barely two minutes. There is smugness in their failure to think independently and seriously, offering us shit instead, a very arrogant conformity. I will say no to any invitation to take part in it.

1 JANUARY 2013, STOCKHOLM

New Year's Day, obviously so. The streets are filled with the detritus of the ebb and flow of last night's dull parties. The stink of guilt and anguish, of fights and arguments changing nothing. I was almost alone shopping at the Co-op with only a few other lonely wretches. I woke up at 10.22 a.m., even though I fell asleep before midnight yesterday. The last thing I remember is Nelly calling from the party at Fröja's wishing me a happy new year. I tried to reach A and Sasha but no one answered. I ate a lobster and a half. Then I lay down reading Adorno on social pain which like all pain carries one message: go! Worked until nine. I had no feeling for the last day of the year and not much feeling for the new year either. I don't see layers of change according to the new year, except some new laws which may not concern me. Today I begin *Rekviem*. How, I don't know. I don't have the energy or the will for it. I started sorting out some boxes of books under my bed and the boxes of Sasha's drawings and photographs which I will pack in the hard suitcases; the books go to the basement or to Gotland divided into what I will read in the near future and what I will never read unless I suffer a serious crisis of identity. What is left is Heidegger, Adorno, Ricœur, Blanchot and Gadamer. That's enough. Talked to A this morning, a warm and happy conversation. I promised to tell her about the potential trip to Paris around January 14th, but I don't believe we can do it. I got to page 561 in the other diary and I'm delivering the pages to Gunilla tomorrow. Got some cod loin from ICA. Talked to Peter too, who called this morning. They've had an intense social life over New Year. Now he's walking along Årstaviken; he said he's collected some of the oldest still-living actors from Dramaten, among them Ingvar Kjellson, Jan-Olof Strandberg, Margaretha Byström and Gunnel Lindblom, who is eighty now, for Chekhov readings at Forum in March. I have made a little list of future work. I'll finish correcting the proofs in January, if I can. Make notes for *Rekviem*. Work on the new diary, this one, the third one. Old age. I don't know if I can give the other diary the title *Pulvis et Umbra*, Dust and Shadow, which is what it is, but they are words that have lost their meaning through overuse. I am happy to read the pages about Sasha's impending birth. The date is getting closer now. I talked to her on the phone this morning and she was clear and precise, grasping for things that were to hand in the room she was in. It was almost like poetry to see how she tries to grasp the ungraspable. She told me dogs are frightened by fireworks and hide under cushions and that they were going over to Mia and Jörgen and Dante and that Dante has no toys – perhaps she meant toys suitable for her age. They were at Lisa Siwe's house yesterday watching the fireworks over Zinkensdamm and Strömmen. I am continuing with Heraclitus and Heidegger tonight. I am reading them in parallel, but I am not reading his Heraclitus seminars yet. Each work flows easily and effortlessly through the other. Deep whirlpools of a common time and world of reference, the same feeling of enlightenment, or as Heidegger would say, an imprint of essence. It's after 3 p.m. Dusk is falling. The trees on Vanadiskullen are dense and straggly shadows and the street lamps are already lit. There is still some snow on the hill and in Monica Zetterlund's shabby little park. Tomorrow I'm picking Sasha up in the afternoon. And we are meeting Vibeke after her afternoon rehearsal. Now I am writing the first line of *Rekviem*. I have no idea what year I will set it in, the end of the nineteenth century or a few years into the new century. It's a good point of departure to have not the slightest conception of what I am going to write, a point soon filled with everything I know I must *not* write, everything I have to write into emptiness, the white void. When you escape that effort the work, emptiness itself, is enviable. I am too tired to lift my eyes from the page. How could I sleep for such a long time and how could I be so tired when I woke up. What happened during that time. How far is Paris. To the end. One of our most distinguished comedians, Jarl Borssén, died yesterday aged only seventy-five, so born in 1937. He was funny in and of himself without effort or acting, his appearance was enough, the exhibition of his self. From Borås. I have written some notes for *Rekviem*. And I've started to look at the photographs in the big brown family album which I saved from the attic at Östermalmsgatan, a stream of people, now dead, unknown to me. I have also written half of page 100 of the prose book. Last night in bed I was thinking about Göran Greider's review of the Palme documentary which I haven't seen, where he criticises the portrayal of Palme as entirely separate from the workers' movement and its historic development. What I do know about the documentary is that it doesn't scrutinise Palme's actions vis-à-vis the IB affair[2] or his lies in defence of Geijer.[3] The documentary, therefore, spreads lies about truth instead of giving us truth about lies. That of course does not diminish Palme's symbolically important position in the history of Swedish politics, at least not now that he's distant enough in history that one doesn't have to denigrate him any more, but even so his real contributions were often mediocre and vague and have left few traces. It says something important about the slippage of the intellectual standards of our political history that Palme now appears as a great

[2] The IB scandal was the 1973 revelation that a secret security agency – the IB – kept tabs on communists and others regarded as a risk to the security of the nation.

[3] Lennart Geijer, the Minister of Justice, was known to frequent bordellos, and was for that reason identified by the police as a security risk.

politician. But his international efforts remain, at least in the name of several streets and squares in South America.

14 AUGUST 2015, STOCKHOLM

I'm very sad today. I know why, but I can't understand why I feel it so strongly. It's nothing – some clothes I ordered online and never received should have been paid for via the bank within forty-eight hours. I thought they would send a bill. How can a small thing like that get me down. But they were the most beautiful clothes I have seen, very hard to find, made from Japanese cotton, very rare, but it's all just material as Nelly likes to say. I know. It still darkens my day. I am going to repress it. I don't need them. I don't need the beauty they transmit. Went into town to find a dress for S, but couldn't find the shop Katja mentioned, where she buys clothes for her daughters. SMS from Linda. Wrote a fragment, started again with *Stilla Liv*. I'll have to start over again and again until it's done. It grows through regression, not progression. I must concentrate hard on keeping the sense of compulsion in a parallel story running alongside the main story, like memories of events to come. The compulsion to become a story is present in all material. It's the memories of what is to come which have to break through, that is the drama. It's difficult, demanding, anxiety-provoking. Why do the intense and existential moments always drop out of the context of a story when once it's over there's nothing else left anyway – those moments remain because they are bigger than the contexts they were created from. I am trying to escape from my disappointment. But the clothes were more than clothes. They usually are. I chose them because they are images which created something more in my imagination – reality as fantasy. How long will I have to think about it. It's childish. But the clothes, and I come back to this, are sort of poems. – I can't count the years I have left without calculating the years of absence I have lived. It's as simple as that. SMS from Martina Hoogland Ivanow. Wrote back and asked if we could meet for coffee at Kaffeverket, Snickarbacken, Saturday. I accidentally wrote 'Snickarbaken'. – Careful goodbye. Bought fish, spinach, potatoes and bread. – I want to show the new texts to Gunilla, whom I talked to this morning. They got back from Gotland yesterday. We agreed to set up a meeting with Eva soon. I also talked to Tarja and asked her to take care of the garden. She asked when we'd left and when I told her she worried about how dry it must be. She's going over to water it. Beckett's mother is burnt into his work. She is more or less present on every page. Sometimes she's also there in the sense of absence – her absence makes itself felt. Our mother is our God of absence.

10 DECEMBER 2020, STOCKHOLM

Grey days over and over again as though they were all one long day. Every evening after work I am drawn into battle with invisible companions about ethical matters arising from the text, concerns emerging out of the text I am writing. I have no defence against my inner accusers, except that I have to write. I notice whenever I get to the book reviews in the cultural pages how important it is to the task of the critic that they are moved; that they recognise something of themselves in the work and that the themes in the book are somehow current and alive for them. Yesterday the most important reason for Gunilla Brodrej to celebrate a novel about a marital break-up was that the setting of the novel spoke to memories from her own youth, and that was given as one of the most important reasons why she thought the book was so good. What do I care. I hope the book is good. Today I am going over to Nelly and Fredric's. I'll take my rubbish down and pick up my post on the way. The first thought I had when I sat down in my armchair was that I have to buy a TV for Linda. I miss her so much, I haven't seen her for such a long time. I don't know what we'll do about Christmas. Can we meet. S called yesterday and said, Since I have to ask before buying sweets, can I buy a doughnut.

I said yes. I have asked her to ring me every morning to tell me what's in her advent calendar. Sometimes she does. I am writing page 26 today. I got a question from Mikael yesterday about whether I read *Brighton Rock* when I was young. Yes, of course. He refers to Graham Greene's metaphor about pit ponies, and I know they come up in *Order*. I can see them now. In contrast to many readers, I very much like Louise Glück's disillusionment and her dialogue about the unceasing. In every ending she finds a new beginning. I love her quotidian sinkholes. I know that nothing is finished, and that often it doesn't even exist. That's what we are talking about. I don't really know who the person writing the slim volume of prose I am working on now is. The other night when I was brushing my teeth I suddenly looked wonderingly at my face for a long time – I didn't recognise it. Is that my face, I asked. The question was so deep and hard to answer that I suddenly felt insane. It's happened before, but only in a mood of melancholy and longing. I had an email from Françoise which I haven't yet answered. What am I reading. – I don't know. Added a line to the play about the mother and three daughters the other night. The most important time now is when I'm in bed in the dark talking to the characters in my texts. What else. I sent her a Gainsbourg song. I'm so glad the diary didn't cause more commotion. Just a bit of slag which hardly even stuck. But it might not be over yet. I feel gratitude to those who act to silence the book. I want to keep it to myself. I am aware of what I have created. Suzanne finds it difficult to stand her absence from the cultural conversation. Last night I was lying awake thinking again about what life at Bryor would look like. The move alone would destroy me but I could probably get over it. Most things are a matter of time. I don't know why I work, for what purpose. I don't know what waiting is and to what extent I contribute at all. I am worried, apart from every other reason to be worried, about how the vaccinations will be administered. I can't work until I have been to see Nelly. They are giving me some paper to take home. I remember when I bought the A4 paper I have now, which is almost finished. This existence has lasted for nine months, for all of us. Every morning,

I observe the small children arrive, a nice sight. They immediately begin to play, and the parents stop to talk to each other and then they leave. The ferries between the three quays feel more and more like Charon's ferry. They glide at a constant pace from quay to quay as though the invisible have boarded. That's how it is now. At times I glimpse their banners passing by. – It is what the character in the novel does with me that I am writing about.

18 DECEMBER 2020

I can't write the diary at the same time as working on the prose volume. I am up to page 51, working slowly, rewriting. I still don't have a sense of its value. I am not in a hurry. I mostly work on it in bed in the dark before falling asleep. The next day I often don't remember what I was thinking about. I have aged noticeably. It's a long way back and I have no hope. I'll go on for as long as I can. Had lunch, mozzarella, tomatoes and baguette, at Nelly and Fredric's, and collected a Farfetch package on the way. I ran out of milk yesterday but Fredric had three litres and I got some frozen salmon too. I haven't talked to S since last weekend. She rings Nelly regularly, so I get updates from her. She was at school today. The other day she cleaned the entire Hornsgatan flat, including the fridge. I have had some sporadic contact with Marianne. Mostly I am busy with Lisa Montgomery. I sent an email to the foreign minister Saturday and another one on Tuesday, and yesterday I got a bland answer which agreed that the death penalty is abhorrent and pointed to all the work the Swedish government does in support of its abolition. I wrote back urging the Foreign Office to focus on Lisa Montgomery's pending execution on January 12th next year, since it's imminent. Trump has already carried out ten of the thirteen executions he confirmed, the last of his brutal presidential decisions. Most of the prisoners, I believe, will die at Terre Haute, Indiana. I am very conscious of the anguish Lisa Montgomery must feel in the expectation of her transfer to Terre Haute to meet her death. Biden is sworn in January 20th and will probably suspend the death penalty, but that will be just a few days too late for her. I have no news about her lawyers recovering from Covid and whether they can now engage with her petition to commute the sentence to life in prison. I sometimes wonder if I want to meet her – travel to wherever she ends up if she survives. – I will at least write her a letter. I can do that now, tomorrow. I can write to tell her how deeply her fate resonates with me. – No winter this year and I don't even miss it. The weather is unchanging, mild, grey and still. But today it felt almost like spring as we walked over to Nelly and Fredric's. Nelly said we'll go to town tomorrow at about eleven to look at streets and houses. I want to go to Roslagsgatan, Sveavägen and past Vanadislunden, and what else . . . I started to wear a mask. Find out where you'll be vaccinated if you live in Hammarby Sjöstad. I would prefer to go to the health centre at Norrtullsgatan. I'll call my doctor tomorrow, she might know. No one is talking about how long the corona vaccine protects you, I suppose because they just don't know. It's not like the measles or polio vaccine. The water is crystal clear and the mirror image reflected in the water of the houses across the bay looks more real than the houses themselves. In the beginning it was very difficult and almost unethical to enter into Lisa Montgomery's life and existence. Now I go in and out of it as though she were only a literary character, but she is not. I am protective of her and sometimes I sense her presence. But perhaps I am deluding myself, creating a presence as a condition for writing. I am not clear why I sometimes use 'her' in the story and sometimes, without cause or explanation, let it become an 'I' narrating. The buildings look as though they were built and fixed in place by light. I am going to make the bed, have a shower, and then I'll lie down to read for a while. I haven't opened a book of philosophy for over a month.

20 DECEMBER 2020

My dialogue with Marianne has waned, maybe because we are both so tired of life. At times I really do feel a very strong sense of capitulation. How can a capitulation be strong. I am on page 56 of my small prose volume. Last night I lay in the dark and formulated a letter to her, to Lisa Montgomery. – Today I am thinking about how paedophilia has infiltrated our society, what the novel *Lolita* exposed. The men in Lisa Montgomery's life took every opportunity to uninhibitedly abuse a child. It's as if the paedophilia itself lies in wait before it breaks out, targeting unprotected children, the poor and the unhappy, as if the paedophiles are reaping a substance that has long grown in them, and the more it has previously been repressed the more brutal it becomes. I can't imagine what it's like to be in Fort Worth, Texas, waiting for the day of your execution. In my version Lisa is in a constant present, whatever is happening happens now, but the past is her existence. It's yet another grey day with just a hint more light than yesterday. It took me a long time to go to sleep after my unfinished letter to her. I don't know what I'll do for the rest of the day. I bought a jacket from Black Comme des Garçons yesterday. Peter rang earlier today, but I couldn't bring myself to answer. Will call him later. I am no longer alone in finding myself in a place beyond the world, I share that condition with my fellow human beings now. A long conversation with S yesterday, just as we passed her old school at Högbergsgatan, she recognised it, she said. I felt no nostalgia walking down Roslagsgatan, I saw the tailor Isa Menge who looked up sitting at his window. Every now and then I get a sense almost of a minor breakdown when I think about life there with S, the walk home from Bonk, from Fria Maria and now from school, bus 43, the pizzeria Meno Male, Sven and Sibirien's soup kitchen, the antique shop which turned into a Bag-all, but it's all because of S. Where are we. I miss reading Peter Handke's new book about walking through his garden in Vichy, the beginning of an extremely slow walk into the world, a walk consisting of shimmering small impressions. It's like experiencing Nathalie Sarraute again, however different they may be in their similarity. Can't I say anything more important. No, I don't think so. But still, despite the prolonged and paralysing immutability I feel an ever-stronger fear of the demands a world without the pandemic would bring for me. I am not sure how far I have adapted myself to the passive life or what is left of me to live it. Where will the vaccine be, how will we get the information. There's already a big group of parents and children in the playground below. I walk from the wardrobe to the kitchen, but I see nothing I have to fix or want to do. The shelf has arrived from Finland, but it can wait until next year. I don't know where I will keep all my shoes. I still haven't looked up Vibeke's address so that I can send her the diary. I hear nothing from Gunilla, and I haven't had the energy to answer Bobo's last SMS. Corona mustn't become a universal excuse, but it already is. I don't know out of what state I will get up and start to get organised. – A shipwreck loses its meaning if it goes on for too long. It's been almost ten months. – There is a pale light over the water and on the facades on the shoreline opposite

■

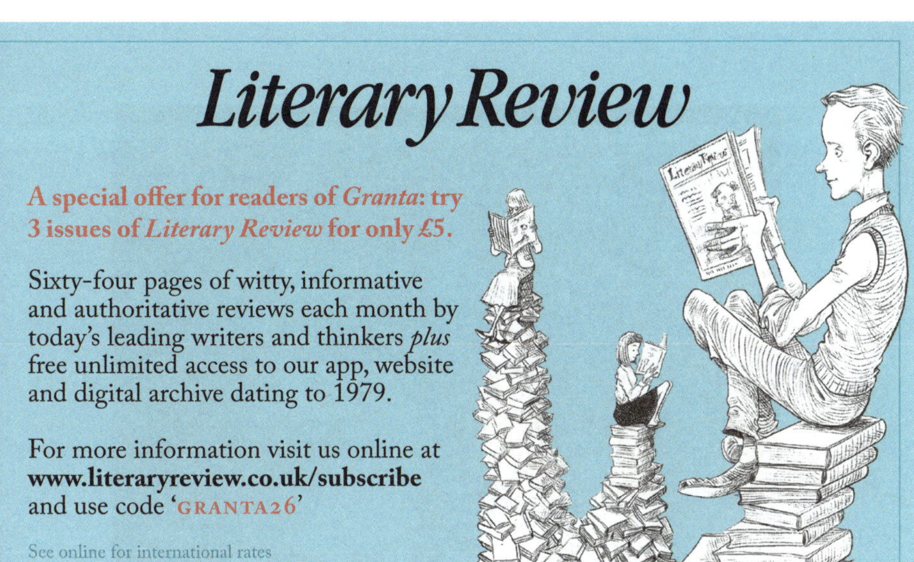
Literary Review
A special offer for readers of Granta: try 3 issues of Literary Review for only £5.
Sixty-four pages of witty, informative and authoritative reviews each month by today's leading writers and thinkers plus free unlimited access to our app, website and digital archive dating to 1979.
For more information visit us online at www.literaryreview.co.uk/subscribe and use code 'GRANTA26'
See online for international rates

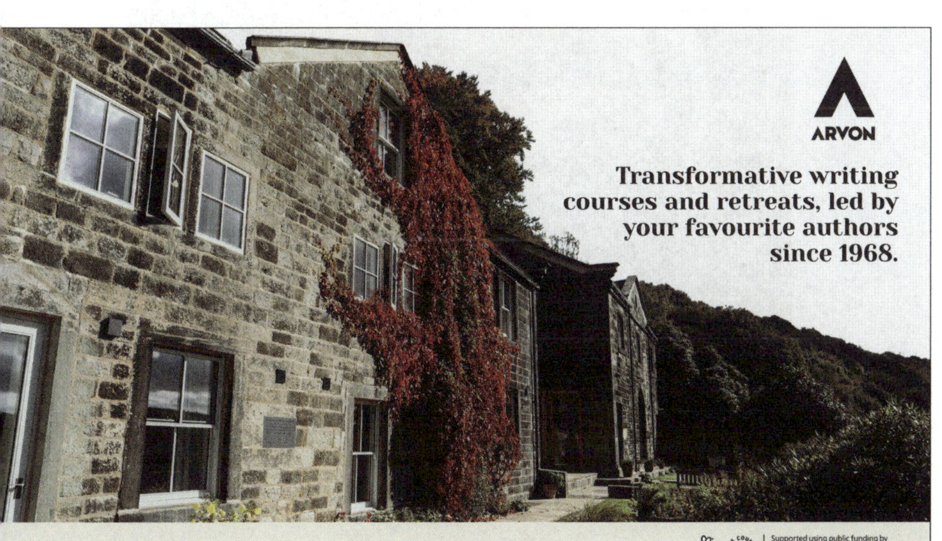
ARVON
Transformative writing courses and retreats, led by your favourite authors since 1968.
Explore courses at arvon.org
LOTTERY FUNDED
Supported using public funding by
ARTS COUNCIL ENGLAND

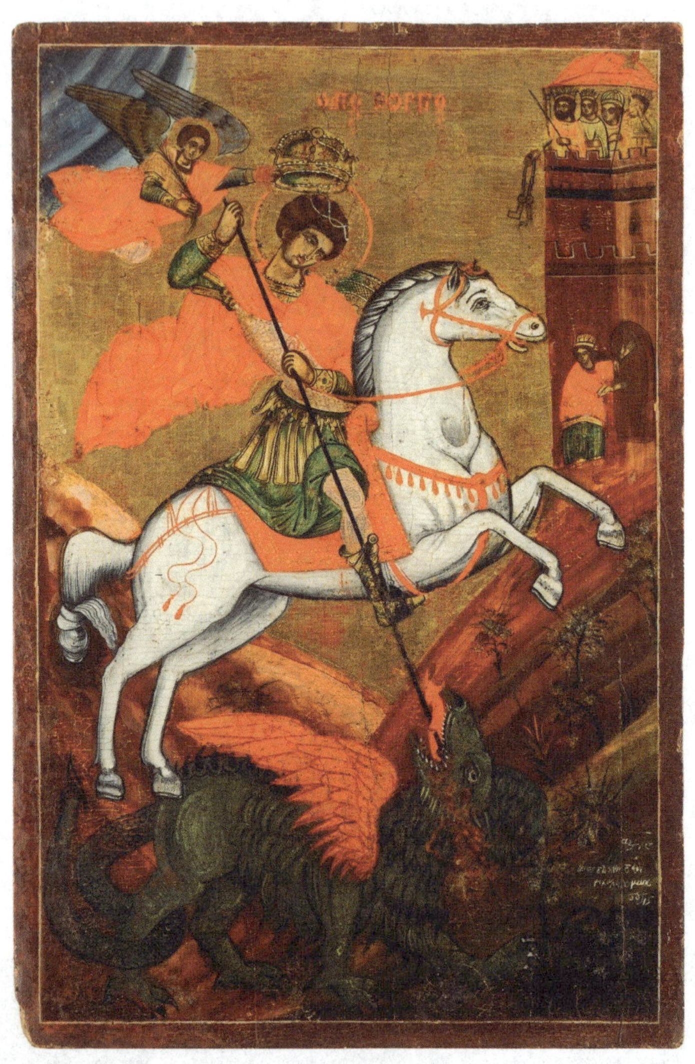

St. George Killing the Dragon, 1797

IOSEB

Pirkko Saisio

TRANSLATED FROM THE FINNISH BY ALEKSI KOPONEN

The rising sun stains the room red; the red glass of the vigil lamp that is burning before the icon turns St George equally red.

Father Christopher Charkviani stands in the doorway, looking at the boy. The boy is early. He stands motionless in front of the icon, staring at it.

He is small but muscular, with black hair, unlike Father Charkviani's own sons Ilya and Aslan, whom the priest sometimes looks at with incomprehension. The boys seem like the pale sprouts of a wintry potato.

The boy is on his way to school, is most likely flummoxed, perhaps scared. Father Charkviani steps into the room without making a sound.

The horse's tail is tied in a knot. Ioseb Besarionis dze Jughashvili has never seen a horse with a knotted tail – it has clearly been done on purpose.

It's unclear whether the rider is a man or a woman. The lips shine red, the way they turn after eating cherries, and the attire is strange.

The rider is holding a thin spear that pierces the throat of a fish – possibly a fish, or perhaps a skinned lamb, badly drawn at any rate.

A vigil lamp is burning in front of the icon. It stains the image ruddy, like at the hour of sunset.

'Well, then.'

Father Charkviani has stepped silently into the hall in a black ankle-length cassock, which looks like a skirt.

Ioseb keeps himself from looking at Father Christopher's skirt, he doesn't want one, not now or in the future, but it looks like they might well be pushing him to have a skirt.

Ioseb would like to ask him about the icon. It's the first time he's noticed it.

He's not yet been to this dimly lit hall that has a somewhat sour smell of decaying wood, even though he and his mother and father live in the house as Father Christopher's tenants.

He knows that his parents owe four months' rent to Father Christopher. It is uncomfortable and his father flushes bright red whenever his mother mentions it.

'Well, then.'

Father Christopher always speaks kindly and at such length that his listeners feel remorse for their drifting attention.

'Well, Ioseb, here you are,' Father Christopher says. 'Very well done for being on time. This is a great day for you, and for your family, for your father and mother, for all of us. You are about to take your first steps on the path of learning, with a mind full of humility and trust. I have put my faith in you, we all have. You have been chosen, as I am sure you understand, we've paved you a road to walk on, it's yours to step on. But do not veer astray, for you aren't alone on the road, not alone for a moment, God the Father will protect you, alongside your family, mother and father, the Gori School of Theology and all its teachers, your friends. And I'll try my best, Ioseb. Please don't hesitate to turn to me should you have any doubts or should you not understand what they teach you . . .'

Father speaks in quiet, even tones, once more at tedious length, punctuated by little coughs as if he was scared of speaking badly or in vain – and indeed he mostly repeats what Ioseb and others already know.

Father means well but Ioseb feels apprehensive. Why does Father keep one hand behind his back?

In the ten years of Ioseb's life, he has received nothing but hurtful or humiliating surprises from hands hidden behind backs: an empty sweet wrapper, sand thrown in his eyes, always the opposite of what was promised – once, even, a cream pastry that hid dried horse dung, which he'd had to keep spitting out long after it was gone from his mouth.

As the clock strikes its low peal, Father Christopher interrupts his speech and puts out his hand. He's holding a pretzel.

'A small bite to eat, Ioseb. Don't go yet, let me bless you first.'

Ioseb takes a bite of the pretzel and bends down. Father steps closer, standing right over Ioseb's lowered head, blesses him with a sign of the cross and recites a long prayer.

Ioseb gets pins and needles in his neck, his nose is uncomfortably close to Father Christopher's stomach, his black cassock has turned shiny from wear, it smells of resin and fried sulguni.

'Did it really happen?'

Father Charkviani stops his praying.

'What, then?'

'The man or woman who speared that fish or snake or whatever? Is it real or make-believe?'

The clock ticks and slices a minute-long sliver of time that drops silently into eternity.

'It's what's called a legend,' Father says. 'The legend of the Holy Great Martyr St George, the Victory-Bearer. It's not a fairy tale, nor, literally speaking, is it true, but at its utmost core the legend is truer than what appears true in everyday life.'

Once again, Father speaks in a tangled way and Ioseb gets frustrated.

'But did it really happen?'

'What is real and what is illusion,' says Father with an uncertain smile, as if Ioseb is making him nervous. 'What appears *real* is but a brief illusion in the eyes of an eternal God, and on the other hand –'

'Was there really a St George the Victory-Bearer?' Ioseb interrupts with impatience.

The clock lets out another tick and pushes Ioseb one minute further away from St George the Victory-Bearer – and one minute closer to the Gori School of Theology.

Father looks embarrassed. Ioseb doesn't understand why it is so difficult to answer a simple question.

'St George was a Roman soldier, a Christian among pagans, and that, taken literally, is true,' he finally says. 'The dragon, on the other hand, is a mythical creature. As for the city of Selem, we do not know whether it existed or whether it too is a myth. But they do say that Selem had a single well that would provide all the water for the townspeople. One day a dragon came flying into the city. Dragons can fly, as you well know – they are mythical creatures, as I might've mentioned – and it made its nest next to the well. The people of Selem were too scared to go to the well, for fear of the dragon who might breathe fire on them.

'Soon the city was overcome by need, people dried up and their tongues swelled with thirst. At last they went to the dragon and begged to draw water from the well. The dragon agreed, on the condition that every day the people of Selem brought it a lamb and a virgin –'

'What's a virgin?' Ioseb interrupts him without understanding why Father pauses to cough before answering.

'A virgin is a young woman.'

It seems to Ioseb that Father goes red.

'Innocent . . . and young . . . as I already said.'

'Beautiful, too?' Ioseb asks.

Father coughs a bit and stalls for time until the clock announces another lost minute. Father then gives his reply. 'Often, yes.'

'Did they give in to the dragon's demands?' Ioseb asks. 'The townspeople.'

'They had no choice. And every day they cast lots to see which young and innocent girl would be granted to the dragon. And, before long, it happened that Cleolinda, the king's daughter, was chosen. The king wept and moaned, and offered the dragon his gold and diamonds and castle, everything, if only mercy were shown to the princess, but the dragon would hear none of it. And at the very moment the dragon was holding the princess of Selem in his claws, God sent the Holy Great Martyr St George, the Victory-Bearer, on his white horse to Selem.

'When St George saw what was about to happen, he struck the dragon dead with his spear. And on the spot where the dragon's blood was spilled, a rose bush grew, which brings forth blood-red roses even to this day.'

The sun has risen and shines white, it is late. Father Christopher glances at the clock.

'You'll be late for school,' he says.

'Did they get married?' Ioseb asks.

'Who?'

'The princess and St George. Did they get married and live happily ever after?'

'Marriage does not exist in legends, Ioseb,' Father Christopher says. 'It does in fairy tales. And in real life, of course.'

'And they live happily ever after, right?' Ioseb says.

The clock strikes with a melancholy sound, a bird screeches outside.

'In fairy tales, at least. And in real life,' Father says. 'Most times. Sometimes.'

Once again it seems to Ioseb that Father's cheeks are turning red.

'On your way, now. If you're late, your teacher will strike your fingers with a ruler.'

Ioseb leaves reluctantly.

The corridor has little light, its floor wet and slippery. Father Christopher's maid, who with her eyebrows grown together looks frightening, is kneeling down in the doorway.

Ioseb walks to the door on his tiptoes. He knows women do not want boot prints on freshly washed floors. The tips of his boots leave behind small prints shaped like half-moons, enough for the maid to lash out at his feet with her wet mop.

The morning's still fresh, shadows dappling the ground at the front of the building, even though the boxwood branches are hanging down, clammy and forlorn, weary from the drawn-out autumn heat.

There are two things Ioseb doesn't understand.

How was it possible that the Holy Great Martyr St George, the Victory-Bearer, was already holy and bearing victory when he rode to Selem, before he had killed the dragon and saved the princess?

You had to be dead to be declared a martyr or a saint, not when you were still alive, and not just any dead person. Your death had to be as bloody and horrible as Christ's crucifixion.

A martyr could not die of a disease, a martyr had to die in battle for Christ and for Sakartvelo – or else tortured by Mohammedans or other heathens, for the glory of Christ.

And for Sakartvelo and the Kartvelians, of course.

The second question could not be put to Father Christopher, or the teachers in Gori School, or even his mother.

His mother was afraid of dangerous questions, afraid for her immortal soul.

Why did God send George to save the young, the virgin, only when she was a princess?

Did God consider princesses worthier than innocent young women with fathers who were cobblers or drunks or construction workers who'd lost all their pay at cards?

Would Christ's hot, sparkling tears not flow as he looked down from heaven and saw a dragon ripping apart a poor, innocent girl, who was screaming in horror?

Father Christopher looks out the window as Ioseb Besarionis dze Jughashvili crosses the yard to the gate.

It looks as though the pretzel is already gone. He must've had nothing by way of breakfast this morning.

Father Christopher feels ashamed. Ioseb has grown, and his blue trousers, already patched, only reach down to his calves.

Father Christopher gave him those trousers as a gift – they used to belong to Aslan. The trousers were serviceable enough, but anyone could see that Ioseb Jughashvili did not come from a family like the other students in the Gori School of Theology, sons of merchants, priests, clergymen and clerks.

Father Christopher makes a quick promise to God.

The next time the tailor visits the Charkvianis, he will have a suit made for Ioseb, similar to the ones Ilya and Aslan have.

If his wife says yes.

If his wife says yes.

Father blushes at this thought.

He sees Ekaterine Jughashvili drawing water from the well. She notices Ioseb and starts walking towards him, but then stops suddenly as if frightened by something. She turns and runs home, leaving a full water bucket by the well.

Ioseb looks frightened too. He runs to the boxwood for cover and presses himself against the bark.

Father Christopher opens the window. There's a muffled, raging cry at the gate.

'There . . . Keke . . . Kekeee . . . there there . . .'

The cobbler Besarion Jughashvili hobbles through the gate, swollen and beaten, and Father Christopher quickly closes his window.

Besarion's been drinking again. He is crying and fuming alone in the yard, entangling himself further and further in the web of sin, and the more he rants and rages, pitying himself, the tighter his suffering holds him captive.

Father Christopher resolves to speak with Besarion – once again – as soon as the man's had his cry and slept.

The almighty God created the crocodile, the snake, and quite possibly the dragon, which may indeed have existed at a time when humanity was still in a state of innocence, enjoying the wonderful fruit from the tree of life.

A blade of grass, a wife, a stork, a spider and a cobbler were all products of God's imagination and creation, and all had a place and purpose in the universe. Humanity had no right to judge the reason behind anything God placed upon the earth.

The task was to accept all creation as it was, listen to God with a keen ear and heart, and receive the tasks God set before them.

People were to love their neighbours as they loved themselves.

Besarion Jughashvili was Father Christopher's neighbour, and if it was easier to love the cobbler's son than the cobbler, that too held a purpose. God had sent Father Christopher this struggle.

The cobbler's head is submerged in a bucket of water. He seems to want to drown himself, as he has a few times thrown himself into the well. His conviction, however, fails him, and the man lifts his head, with a tirade of coughing and cursing.

Father Christopher retreats farther from the window, hiding behind a curtain, where he says a long prayer under his breath, and tries to forget what he knows.

He is afraid of the cobbler Jughashvili – afraid, like everyone.

And yet God has chosen Christopher Charkviani to serve as a shepherd to guard his flock, and as a warrior to fight for his neighbour.

Fear signifies distrust of God, and distrust of God is a sin.

As Father Charkviani steps back to the window, he sees Besarion turn to him with a grin like that of a wounded animal, and Father Charkviani finds himself stepping back behind the curtain.

Ioseb presses himself against the bark of the tree trunk.

His mother has pulled the door shut and he can hear noise from the inside. She drags furniture to bolt the door, to keep his father from entering.

Even the scary maid has shut the door. Ioseb can hear the metal clang as it locks.

The only thing he sees of Father Christopher at the window is his black cloak, the one that smells of sulguni, and his hand, tentatively rising and falling.

His father lifts his head from the bucket, splashing about, coughing, staring wildly around.

If his father notices him, no grown-up will come to help.

The tree trunk is slender. Ioseb holds his breath. He can hear his own heartbeat, tolling in his ears like the bells of Judgement Day, with a force that shakes his whole body. ■

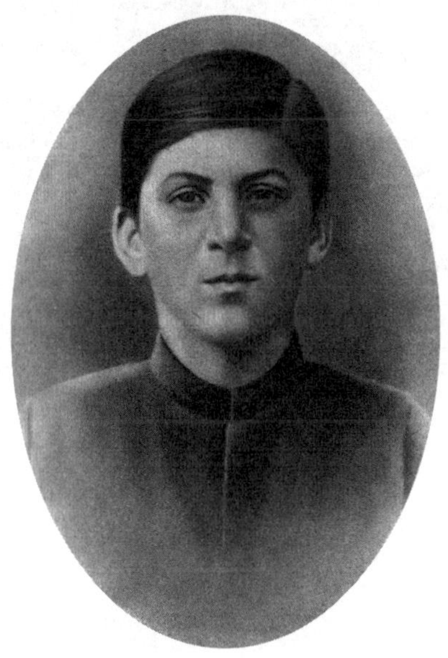

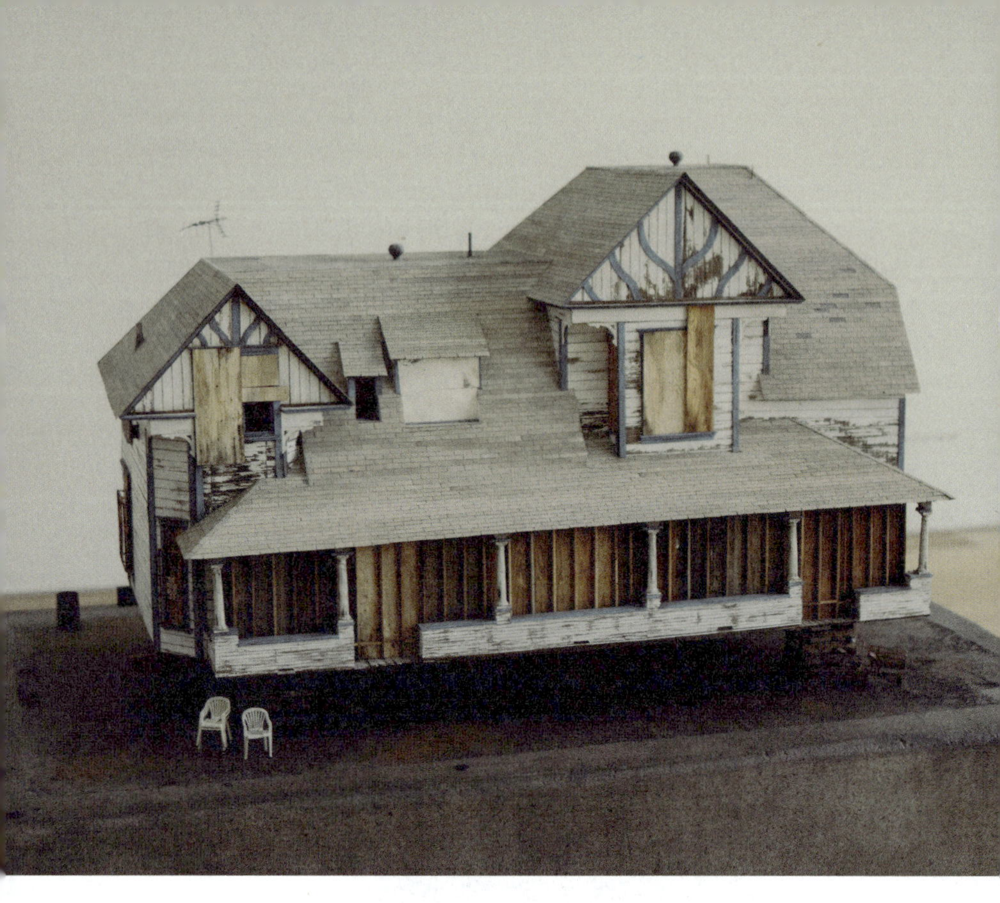

DEVASHISH GAUR
Artwork Sayre Gomez
Scale Replica of the Past, Present and Future (Peabody Werden House), 2023
Collection museum Voorlinden, Wassenaar

VAIM HOTEL

Jon Fosse

TRANSLATED FROM THE NORWEGIAN BY DAMION SEARLS

I was standing outside The Vaim General Store with this fishing set in my hand, and I thought why in the world had I bought myself a fishing rod, no, it had never once crossed my mind to buy fishing gear, because what was I supposed to do with it, it's true I had liked fishing when I was a boy, but, yes, that was quite a long time ago, still for all I knew it might be fun to stand there on The Quay and cast out the line and reel it in again, maybe, I thought and either way The Shopkeeper was a very good salesman, that was for sure, once you walk through the door of his shop there's no getting away from him, yes, I thought, and what now, well I'd been thinking I would go to the restaurant, to get dinner, yes because it had been several days since I'd had good hot food, so it would taste good, I thought, and besides I was probably pretty curious to see what it was like in that restaurant, but was I actually allowed to go in there carrying this fishing gear, because I didn't want to go back up to my room with it, because who knows, maybe I'd run into The Hotel Owner again, maybe with all Brita's nosiness she's gone up to my room again to see what I have in my suitcases, yes, she probably has, definitely, since I had nothing to hide she could look at every last thing in there if it made her happy, as far as I was concerned, but it was a bit ridiculous, that Brita woman wasn't entirely on the level, I thought and I noticed that

I had started walking down towards The Quay, not that I wanted to go fishing now, but sooner or later I'd have to try my hand at casting a line or two, I thought, but for now I just wanted go down to The Quay to look around before I went into the restaurant, Vaim Restaurant yes, I thought and I stopped and stood there and looked at the boat tied up there on The Quay, and it was a beautiful boat, big for the kind of boat it was, and the roof extended to almost cover the whole boat, and that was probably just as well, since it rained so much in this part of the country, and the boat was nicely lacquered, yes, the varnish was so shiny that it glittered, yes that boat was a sight to see, and the name it had, Eline, that was a beautiful name, I felt, but now it really was probably time to get some food in me, yes, I thought and then I cut across the parking lot towards the door with Vaim Restaurant painted on it and I opened the door and I could see it was bright and cozy in the restaurant, and a guy was sitting at a table in the far corner of the restaurant, about my age, he had a beer bottle and a glass on the table in front of him and he sat there staring into space, and he didn't notice that someone had come into the restaurant, he just sat there staring into space like before, there weren't that many tables in the restaurant, but they were nice old wooden tables, and there were wooden chairs like the one I had in my room around the tables, four wooden chairs for each table, and then on the left there was a counter with a cash register and the menu was written on a kind of blackboard on the wall behind the counter, and there were three dishes to choose from, meatballs, fishcakes, and stew, and below that it said that dessert was fruit cocktail with ice cream and that was it, and then there on the counter there was indeed a sheep bell, just like Brita had said and I went and leaned the fishing set against the wall behind the nearest table, the one closest to the door, and so the farthest away from the man sitting drinking a beer and staring straight ahead, and then I went over to the counter and picked up the sheep bell and shook it, and damn it made a loud sound, so I quickly put it back down on the counter, and the man sitting there with his glass of beer was still only staring straight ahead, yes yes, I thought and I guessed I had to just stand there at the counter and wait, I thought and all of this taken together really was a bit strange, I thought, The Vaim Hotel and The Vaim Restaurant and The Vaim General Store, yes, everything was kind of odd, and I wasn't so sure whether I liked it or not, no, there was almost something unreal about it all, I thought, and my car, I saw it when I left the store, didn't I, no, maybe not and I think I should go look out the door to see if it's there, and I go to the door and I open it, go outside, and yes, well, the car is right where I parked it, so as I can see everything's fine, I think and I go over to the car and I think that I should check to make sure the doors are locked and they are, every door, and so I should probably go back to the restaurant then, because somebody who can serve me probably has to come soon, I think and I go back into the restaurant and as soon as I'm through the door I see Brita standing there holding up the fishing set and she looks at me

Hello, she says

So you're checking out the restaurant, she says

Yes, good evening, I say

Yes well it's almost evening, she says

and I see that Brita is going back behind the counter with my fishing set in her hand, and I quickly look at the table where the other customer is sitting, and I see that there are now three beer bottles on his table, and I think why in the world is Brita taking my fishing set and she looks at me and she says that I probably want something to eat and she puts the fishing set down, leaning it against the wall behind the cash register, under the board with the menu

But you, I say

Yes, that, I say

Yes, she says

That fishing equipment, yes, I just bought that, I say

But the fishing set was there when you came in, she says

Yes, I say

Yes I just stepped out for a minute, I say

But the men's room's over there, Brita says

and she points towards the back of the restaurant

I didn't mean that, I say

and neither of us says anything, and it doesn't seem like Brita has any intention of giving me my fishing set back

But, that's my fishing set, I say

It's yours? Brita says

Yes, I say

But you, yes well, she says

and I can feel myself getting a little annoyed

I came in here, and put the fishing set down there, I say

and I point to the place where the fishing set was

You came in and then went back outside right away, Brita says

No, I stood here waiting for a long time, but no one came, I say

You can't have stood here that long, she says

Because I came almost as soon as I heard the bell, and then the other guest ordered some beer, she says

and I think that I really was standing there a long time, but that there's no point in contradicting Brita, I understand that much

So, you called, she says

Yes, I rang the bell, I say

What would you like, sir, she says

and I look at the menu

Maybe meatballs, I say

and Brita says that that's not a bad choice, she made the meatballs herself, following an old recipe, she got it from her mother and her mother got it from her mother, and who knows if her grandmother didn't get it from her own mother, she says

One order of meatballs then, she says

So you can just have a seat at one of the tables, wherever you want, she says

and I think that it really doesn't seem like she's going to give me my fishing set back, but I'll get it back, I just have to wait a bit

Where do you want to sit? Brita says

and I turn and point to the chair next to where the fishing set had been leaning against the wall and Brita says that that's fine

But wouldn't you like something to drink? she says

All right, maybe a glass of beer, I say

and I was actually just going to drink water, but since the other customer is sitting there drinking beer, yes, then I guess I can have a glass too, I think

One beer then, Brita says

But we only have bottles, she says

and I nod, and then I go and sit down at the nearest table, I put my shoulder bag down on the floor, and I see Brita open a bottle of beer and get a glass and then she comes to my table, tilts the glass, pours the beer into the glass, and puts the glass and the bottle down in front of me

Here you go, she says

I hope you like it, she says

Thanks, I say

It's a very good beer, she says

and Brita is already on her way back behind the counter, so she really doesn't plan to give me my fishing set back, I think, it wasn't that big a purchase either, but it's still infuriating, really, and after all if I have to I can always tell her that The Shopkeeper can confirm that I bought the fishing set from him, I think and I have a sip of the beer, and actually I've never really liked the taste of beer, but this beer is definitely not bad, I think, and I put the glass down and then I stare into space for a minute, what a mess with that fishing set, I think, but, shit, I think, who cares and I look at the man sitting in the back of the restaurant and I see that he's now put three empty beer bottles on the edge of the table and then there's a half-full bottle and another full bottle in front of him and he looks at me

You should've kept an eye on your fishing gear, he says

and I guess I never thought he'd say something to me, or even notice I was there, and so now I probably have to answer something

You think so, I say

Yes, he says

Once she takes it, yes, you'll never see it again, he says

Did you see me come in with the fishing set, I say

Yes, he says

But then you can just tell her it's mine, I say

That won't make a difference, he says

and I probably have to say something in response to that, but I don't know quite what to say

I've seen all this happen before, he says

That Brita's so sneaky, it's unbelievable, he says

And it was probably The Shopkeeper who sold you that fishing set, he says

Yes, you're right, I say

That fishing set has been sold many times over, he says

and now I don't understand what he means, I think, and I see him walk towards me with firm steps and then he goes behind the counter and then he takes the fishing set and goes back to his table and then I see him go to the restroom door that says GENTLEMEN and he goes inside, and he comes out again right away, without the fishing set

That's the safest place to leave it, he says

Because Brita doesn't go into the men's room, at least not when someone can see her doing it, he says

and he stops talking and I think that I'm understanding little or nothing of this, but I do at least understand that the fishing set has now been put in the men's room for some reason or another

That's how it goes, he says

and he looks at me

That's how it goes, he repeats

and he says that how it goes is that new guests at the hotel stop by The General Store and then The Shopkeeper gets them to buy that set of fishing gear, and the guest takes it with them to the hotel, usually to their room, and leaves it there, and then when the guest is out Brita sees her chance to unlock the room and go inside and take the fishing set, that's how it always goes, he says, and then when the guest checks out she brings it back to The Shopkeeper and then he sells it again to the next guest who comes to the hotel and stops by the shop, he says and I wonder how he can know all this, it's probably just drunken talk, but I don't say anything

It's true, by god, he says

But today, yes, well, today she saw her chance to take it when you stepped out, the set was just sitting there, he says

and he sort of points with his head at the wall behind me and he says that he's seen exactly the same thing happen before, the guest just had to attend to some urgent business and while he was away from the table Brita would come with the food or something and take the fishing set and then she'd usually take it out of the restaurant right away, not lean it against the wall behind the counter, he's never seen her do that before, but it was probably because she was about to bring him his beer that she did it like that, he said

Tricky, isn't she, he says

And how do I know that it's the same set, he says

Yes well, he says

Yes, well, when I saw this happen the first time, with the guest just going into the men's room, I stopped by The General Store the next day and tore a little notch in the packaging of the fishing gear, in the cardboard, and the next day the set was gone, and the day after that it was back again, he says

The Shopkeeper sells it, she gets hold of it somehow or another, she takes it back to The Shopkeeper, and then they probably split the profits in some way, he says

and I think he must be pretty drunk now, because this can't be true, now he's just making things up, I think

Yes, isn't that unbelievable, he says

It's so crazy that even though I've seen it with my own eyes I can hardly believe it myself, so to speak, he says

Mostly I think they're just doing it for fun, he says

By the way, everyone just calls me The Sailor, he says

and he pauses

But, he says

But there's not much money to be made from either the shop or the hotel, so they have to add a little extra wherever they can, he says

And it's not like it would be better if the shop, the restaurant, and the hotel all shut down, he says

So in a way it's probably fine, he says

and I see Brita come out from behind the counter and she's carrying a plate of meatballs and a knife and fork and a napkin and she hurries over to me and puts it all down in front of me

Here you go, she says

Hope you like it, she says

Thanks, I say

and then I hear the other customer, The Sailor I guess he's called, say that she could bring him a couple more bottles of beer, and she says that she certainly could and I see that I've ended up with a generous meal, four large meatballs, four potatoes with thick brown gravy, a big portion of mashed peas, and then a pretty large spoonful of the brightest red lingonberry jam on the side, and it looks good and then I hear Brita say that everything is homemade, not just the meatballs, but the lingonberry jam and the peas too, and of course the gravy, and she bought the potatoes from the farmer at the nearest farm, and she peeled them herself, she says and I see that she's already heading over to the other customer, to The Sailor, yes, with three bottles of beer before she rushes out again and I start eating and it all tastes excellent, to tell the truth I've never tasted better meatballs, I think, everything is good, the gravy, the mashed peas, the lingonberry jam, Brita can really cook at least, you've got to give her that, I think and I hear the other customer ask if I noticed that there was no price written next to the dinner dishes, and there's a reason for that, she charges a lot, and if the customer knew how much he was going to have to pay for the food and the beer he probably wouldn't buy it, he says, but it depends on who it is, she looks after her people, he himself has an agreement with her for a reasonable price on the beer, yes, it only costs him a little more here than it does at The Vaim General Store, he says, and that's why he can afford to have his beer here, he says and I think that it's true, she hadn't said how much a night at the hotel would cost, or how much the dinner would cost, or how much the beer would cost either, and I didn't see it written anywhere, so now Brita could probably charge me as much as she wanted, I thought, but the price probably can't be that outrageously crazy, I think, and after all she'd said she gave long-term guests a good deal, I think

On the other hand it's not that expensive if the guests are staying for a while, and if they come and have dinner here a lot, he says

You've got to give her that, he says

and I keep eating, because by now I was really hungry, and the food is genuinely delicious, I think and every now and then between bites I take a sip of beer and the beer tastes really good with the food, I think and then I hear The Sailor say that there's something familiar about me, we really must have met before, maybe I've been to Vaim before, because he definitely thinks he's seen me before and I say I doubt it, I've never been to Vaim, not as far as I can remember anyway and he says yes, yes, there's something familiar about me, but it may well be that he's thinking of someone who looks like me, someone he was on a boat with once or something, he says and just then I see Brita come into the restaurant and she looks for the fishing set and then she gives me a stern look and asks if I removed the fishing set, yes, she says removed, and I say that I haven't touched any fishing set, even though it was my set, I just bought it at The Vaim General Store, I say and Brita says yes yes and then she goes over to the guy sitting next to the wall and she asks him if he saw anyone take the fishing set

No, he says

The only thing I saw was that when the customer you just served came into the restaurant he had a fishing set with him, he says

and Brita shakes her head like this is the worst thing she's ever heard and I think that I can hardly remember ever having seen a greater lack of common decency, or whatever you'd call it, reasonable behavior, than all this, I think and then Brita comes walking towards me

Did you like the food, she says

Yes, very much, I say

Have you ever tasted better meatballs? she says

No, I was thinking that myself, I don't believe I have, I say

and I thought that this was probably the smartest thing to say to her, and when I think about it these really are some of the best meatballs I've ever had, it's true, but maybe that's partly because I was so hungry

These are some of the best meatballs I've ever had, I say

Maybe even the very best, she says

Yes, maybe, I say

and I think that now if The Sailor hadn't taken the fishing set and put it in the men's room, yes, then I'd of course have to tell her again that it's my fishing set and that I need to get it back, and maybe I can, or should, tell her that anyway

That was my fishing set, I say

Yes, Brita says

Yes, it's mine, so I'd like it back now, I say

Yours huh, she says

I bought it just now at The Vaim General Store, I say

You did, did you, she says

Yes I did, I say

and I see her standing there shaking her head

The Shopkeeper can confirm it, I say

The Shopkeeper, she says

and it's almost like she's shouting it into the air

Yes, I say

The Shopkeeper, the shopkeeper, she says

So, can you tell me where this fishing set is? she says

and I see her open the front door and go out and I hear The Sailor say sure, no reason why not, he says

No, I suppose not, I say

But the meatballs were good at least? he says

Very good, I say

Yes, she makes good meatballs, he says

And her fishcakes are good too, and the stew too, for that matter, yes, he says

and he falls silent and I calmly keep eating and I think my goodness it was good to get some food in me, and then I think what else could I think, that it was good to eat something is pretty much the only thing I could think and The Sailor says that the way Brita, yes, that's her name, he says, but she's probably told me that already, the way Brita manages to run both the hotel and the restaurant despite everything, and by herself too, yes, sometimes in the summer she'd get help from a girl in school, but usually, no, he doesn't understand it, he says, and she sure can cook, yes, he says, but since he doesn't have all the money in the world he basically has to choose between beer and food, and since he can easily manage to cook for himself the food he needs, well, he might as well spend his money on beer, he says and I take another sip and I'll never be a real beer drinker, I think, beer tastes okay, that's it, and the rush it gives you, no I've never really cared much for that either, I think, I just get kind of hot and fuzzy in the head, I think, and I don't like that feeling very much, so that's why I don't drink much, yes, little or nothing, but I don't need to tell The Sailor that since he clearly likes beer so much

Did you notice the boat tied up at The Quay, he says

Yes, I say

That's my boat, he says

and then he says that he's an old sailor, or not that old, actually, but when he retired it didn't take long before he bought himself the boat I saw tied up at The Quay, yes, he bought her for a lick, almost nothing, he says

and there's some pride in his voice

Yes, I got it cheap, he says

I've always wanted a boat like that, but I could never afford one, yes, you know, all this beer adds up, but would you believe it, a Strilelander from Sartor turned up here with a sjark, it was probably because of a woman, her name was Eline, yes, one night when we were sitting and drinking a little he offered to sell me his other boat for a reasonable price, yes, since he already had a sjark he would sell me the other boat for a reasonable price, is what he said, he really just wanted to get rid of it, so I got the boat practically for free, The Sailor said and then he says that the man who'd sold him the boat went back to Sartor in his sjark and he says that he's never been luckier, never gotten a better deal in his life, because the boat was built well and had been well cared for, she never had a single engine problem, it was apparently a boat builder up in the Hardanger Fjord that had built her, and he must have been an extremely talented boat builder, the only problem with the boat was that she was called Eline and it was apparently the boat's first owner who'd named her that, he'd apparently named the boat after his girlfriend or old lady or whoever it was, the way sailors get a tattoo of the name of the girl they're thinking about at the time, usually on the back of their hand, and then have to deal with it for the rest of their lives, because if they get a wife later, well, she usually has a different name, that's how it goes, he knew several guys in that situation, The Sailor said and everybody knew it was definitely bad luck to change a boat's name, so this boat was named Eline, he said

It's a magnificent boat, I say

Yes, I really feel attached to this boat, The Sailor says

I live on an island a little west of here, he says

And to get anywhere from that island I need a boat, he says

And I've had this boat now for many years, he says

Yes, when I was young, yes, the first thing I wanted to buy when I grew up, yes, was a boat, he says

And I noticed this boat a long time ago, he says

Her lacquer had such a nice shine to it, he says

And I always take good care about the spring cleaning and tune-up, ever since I got her, he says

So tar for the keel and lacquer for the sides have cost me a lot over the years, he says

Yes, a lot of money and a lot of work, he says

and neither of us says anything

Was that your car parked in front of the hotel, he says

Yes, I say

That looks like a nice car, he says

Yes, it works fine, I say

But I haven't had it that long, I bought it just yesterday, I say

and just then the front door opens and Brita comes in and walking behind her is The Shopkeeper, but now he's taken off his work smock, now he's wearing a regular coat and he has a hat on and I nod to The Shopkeeper and he nods back

So here you have the guy you supposedly bought that set of fishing gear from, now you can ask him about it, Brita says

and I say to The Shopkeeper that he probably remembers that I just now came by his shop and that I bought a fishing set, and he gives me a searching look

A fishing set, he says

Yes, I say

No, I don't remember that, says The Shopkeeper

and I look at him in surprise, is it me or him who's crazy, I think, because this, no, I don't understand this at all

Yes, you hear what the man says, Brita says

and The Shopkeeper looks at Brita

Was that everything? he says

Yes, thank you, thank you very much, she says

and The Shopkeeper bows to me and says goodnight and I say thanks same to you and then he looks at The Sailor and says goodnight to him too and The Sailor raises a hand and says goodnight to you too and then Brita opens the door for The Shopkeeper and he leaves and Brita looks at me

There, you heard what he said, she says ■

SCHOOL RUN

Stephen Gill

Introduction by Granta

Stephen Gill tends to take the same route when he does the school run, passing through the villages and flat farmland of Skåne, the southernmost county in Sweden. The drive lasts just over half an hour. He and his children discuss the day ahead, music, homework, black ice; the front passenger looks out for wild boar, deer and pheasants. Occasionally they spot a badger. In the winter months they leave in darkness and return in darkness.

Gill breaks up the solo journey home by making brief stops. He goes walking with his camera in hand. In that time he enters a state of mind that he calls 'extremely present and absent, equally, without needs, intent, a goal, or any kind of destination in mind.'

The photographs he has made on these walks – taken over a period of three years – capture the seasons of Skåne: its flora shrivelled and blanketed by snow, then verdant, in bloom. Extreme changes in scale estrange and transform natural phenomena: ice begins to resemble coral, cordyceps, blood platelets. Gill often photographs with out-of-date or instant film that he rests above the car's fan heater, resulting in a colour palette that leans away from how things appeared. In their informal focus and finish, deliberation is replaced by instinct and chance. 'I think it's healthy when life informs your practice,' Gill says, 'rather than practice informing your life.' ■

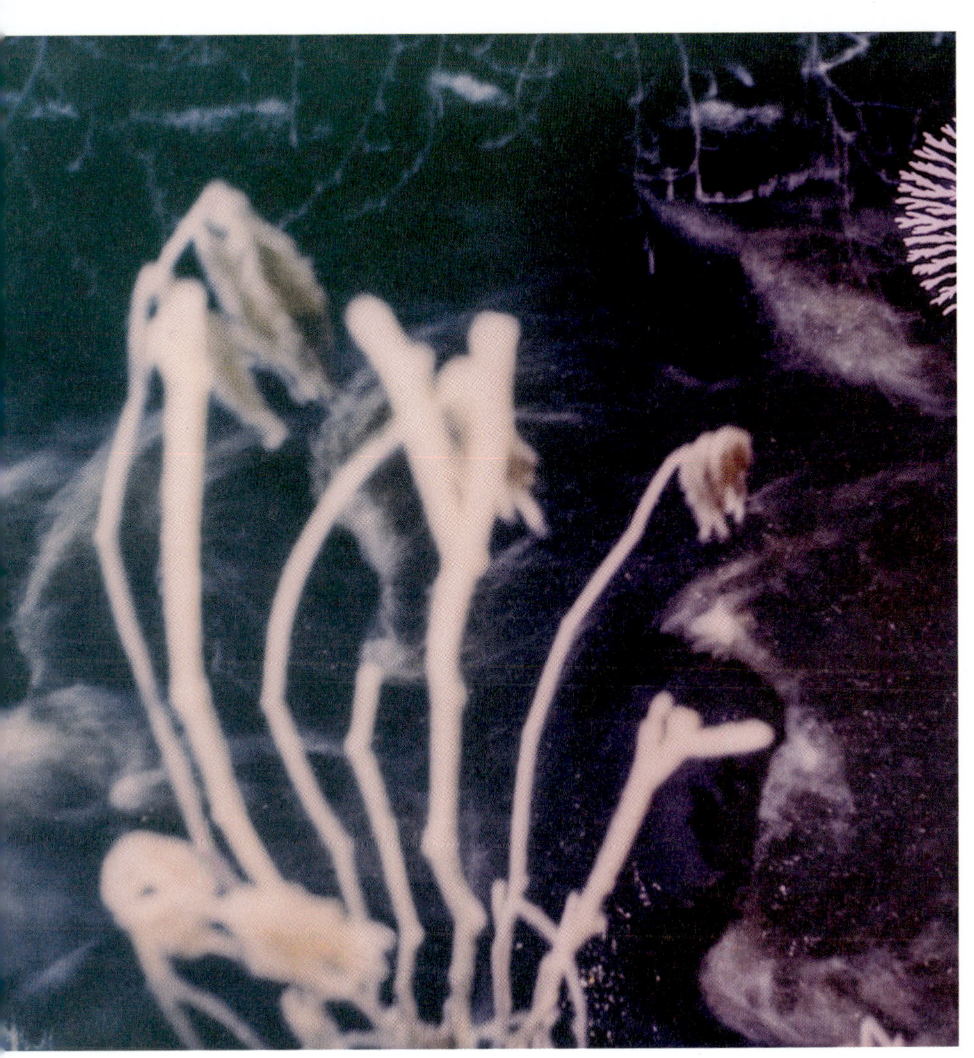

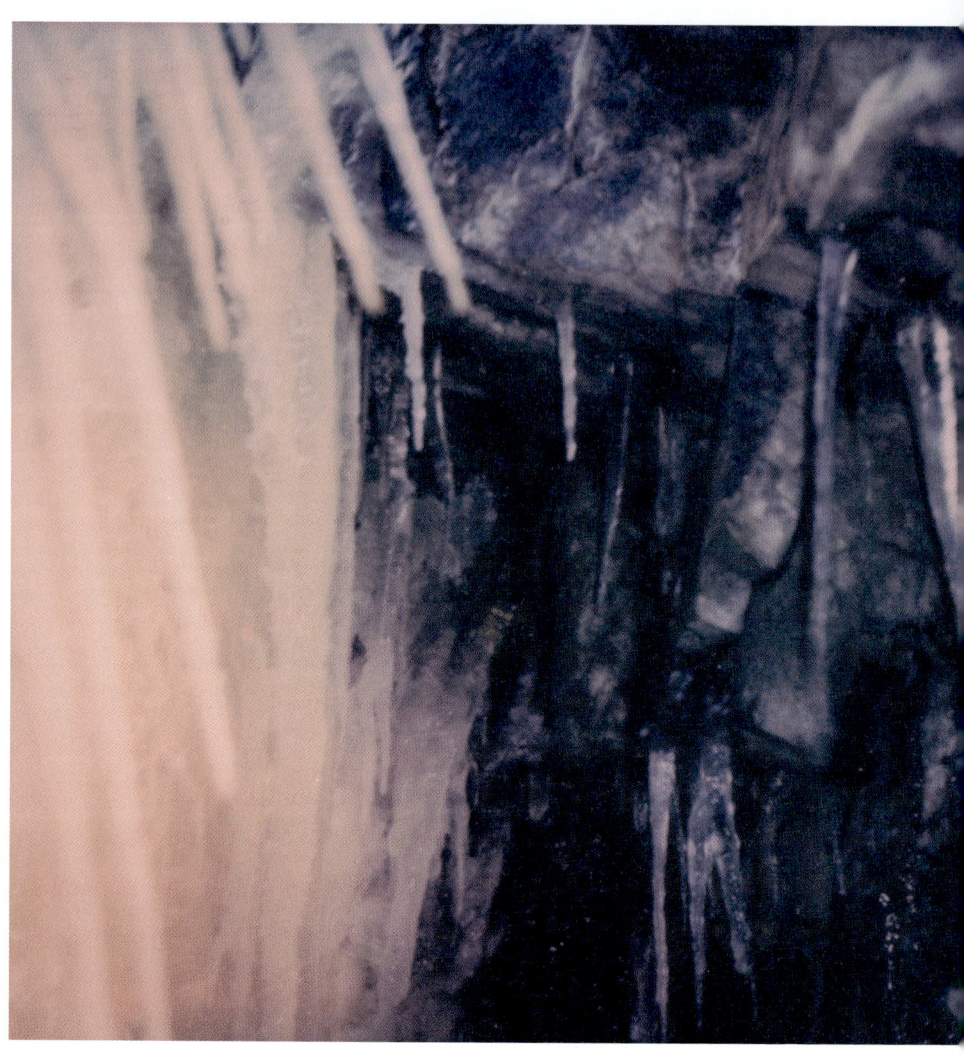

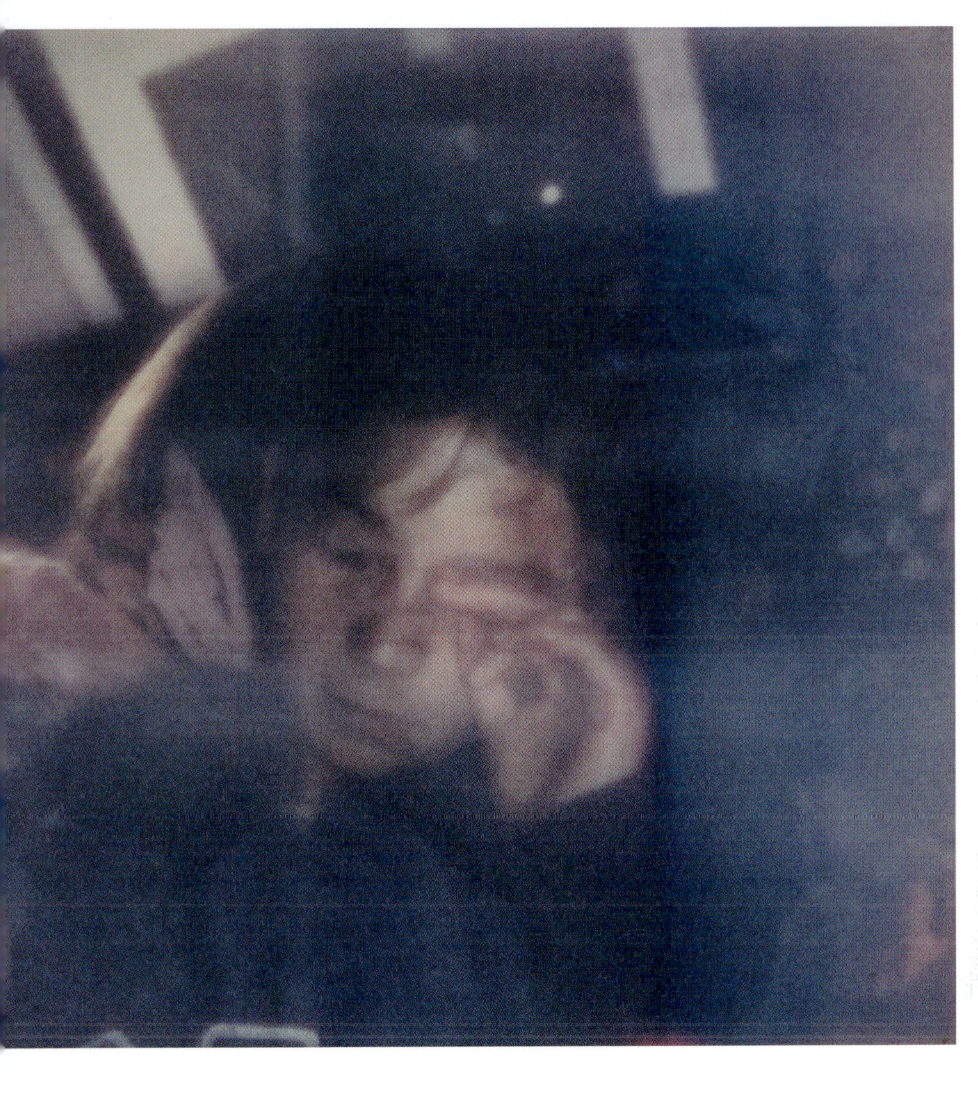

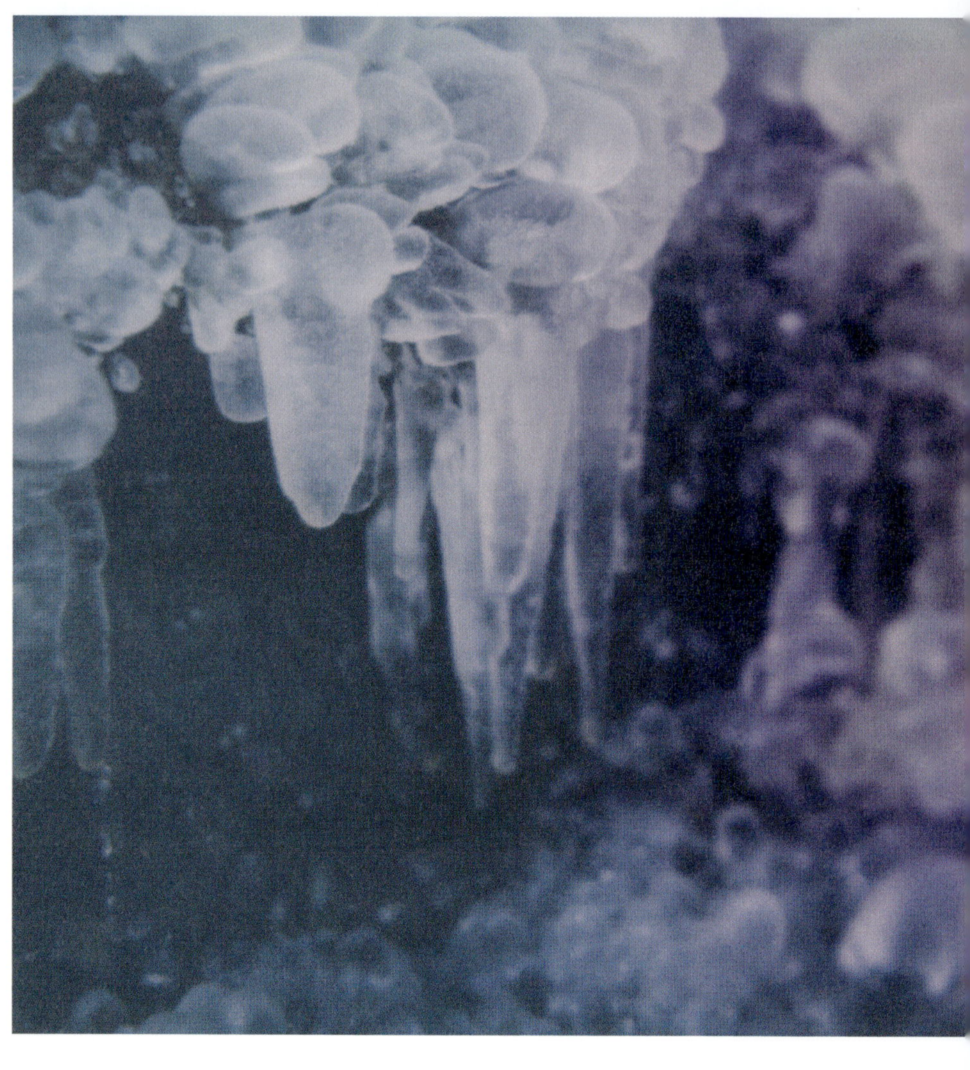

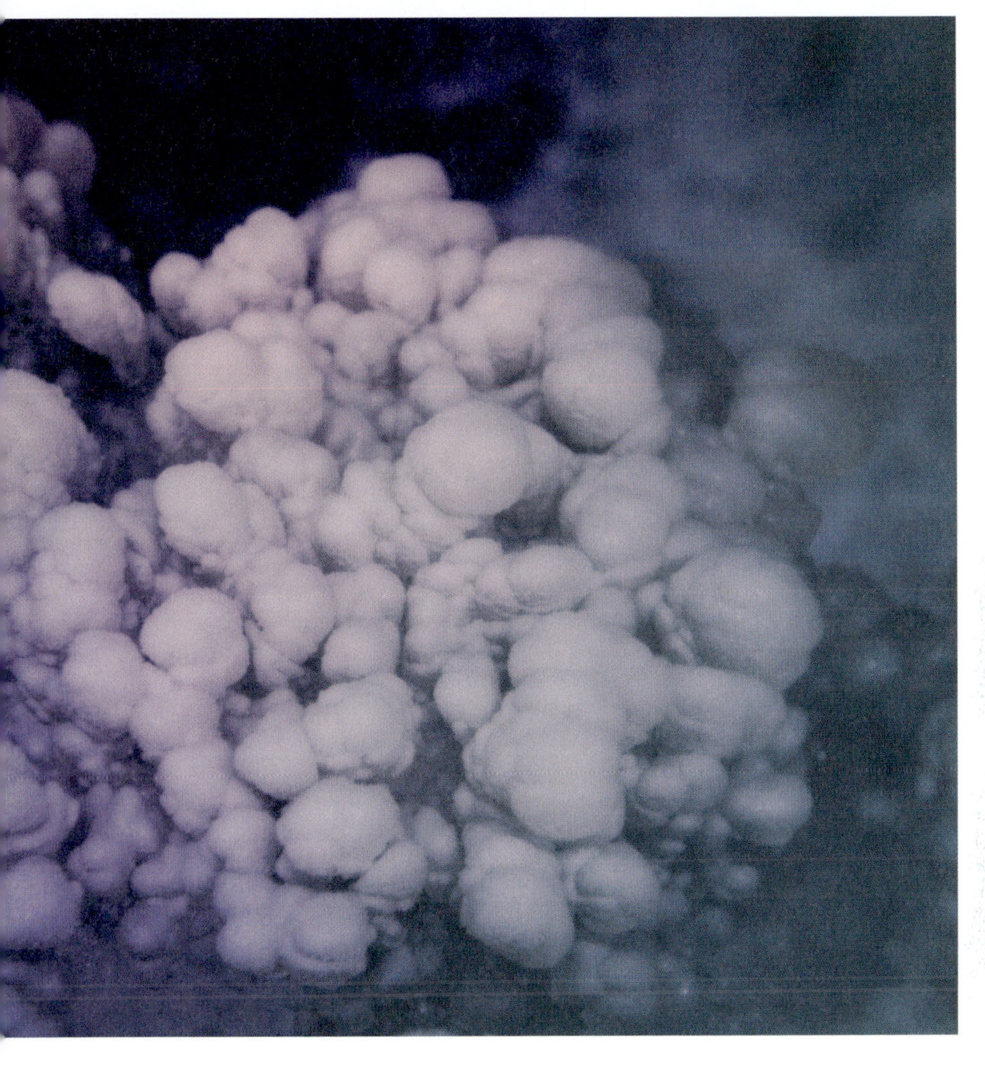

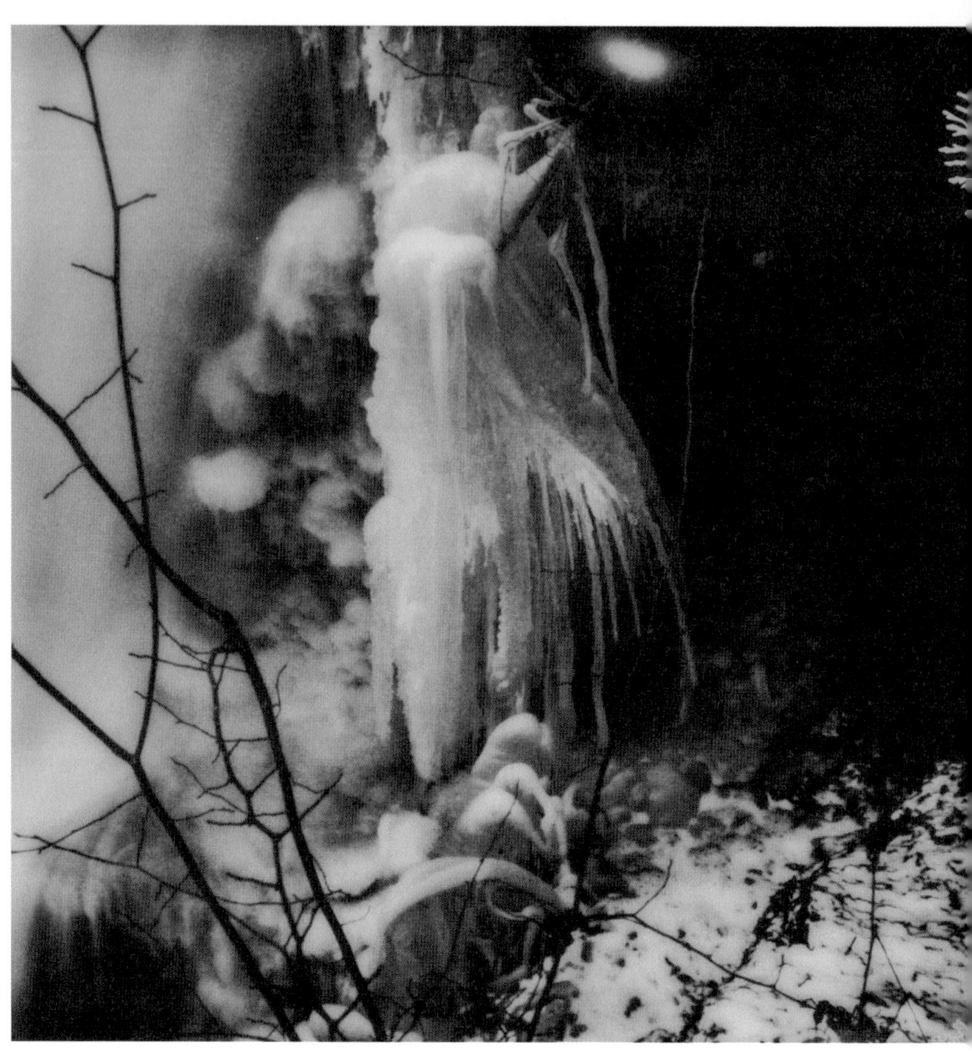

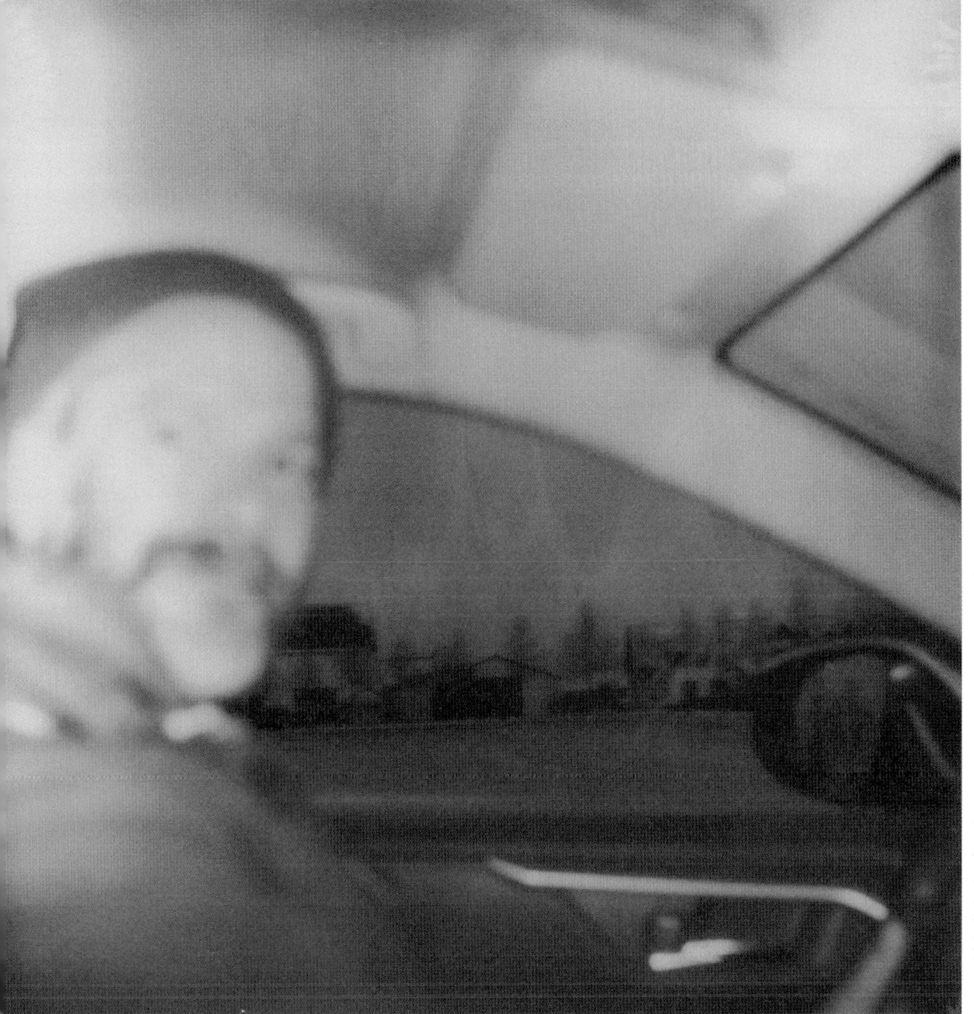

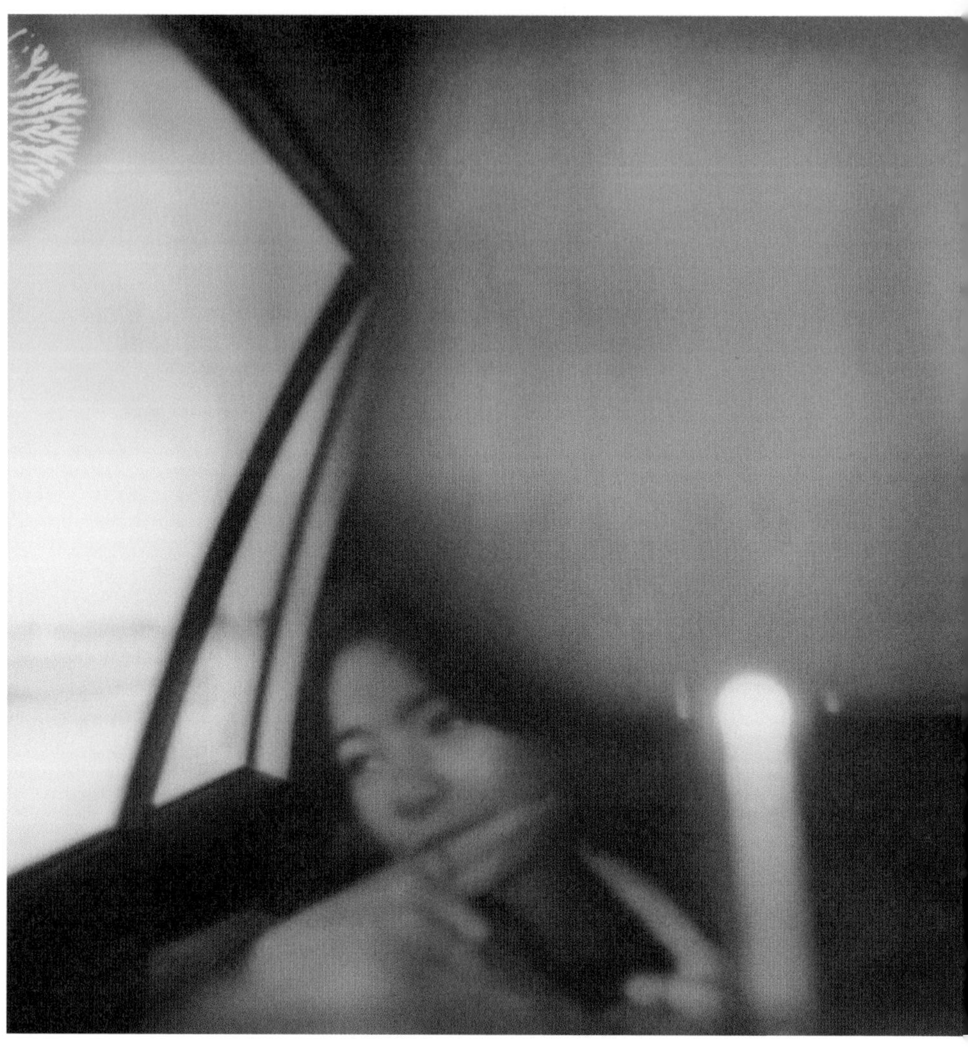

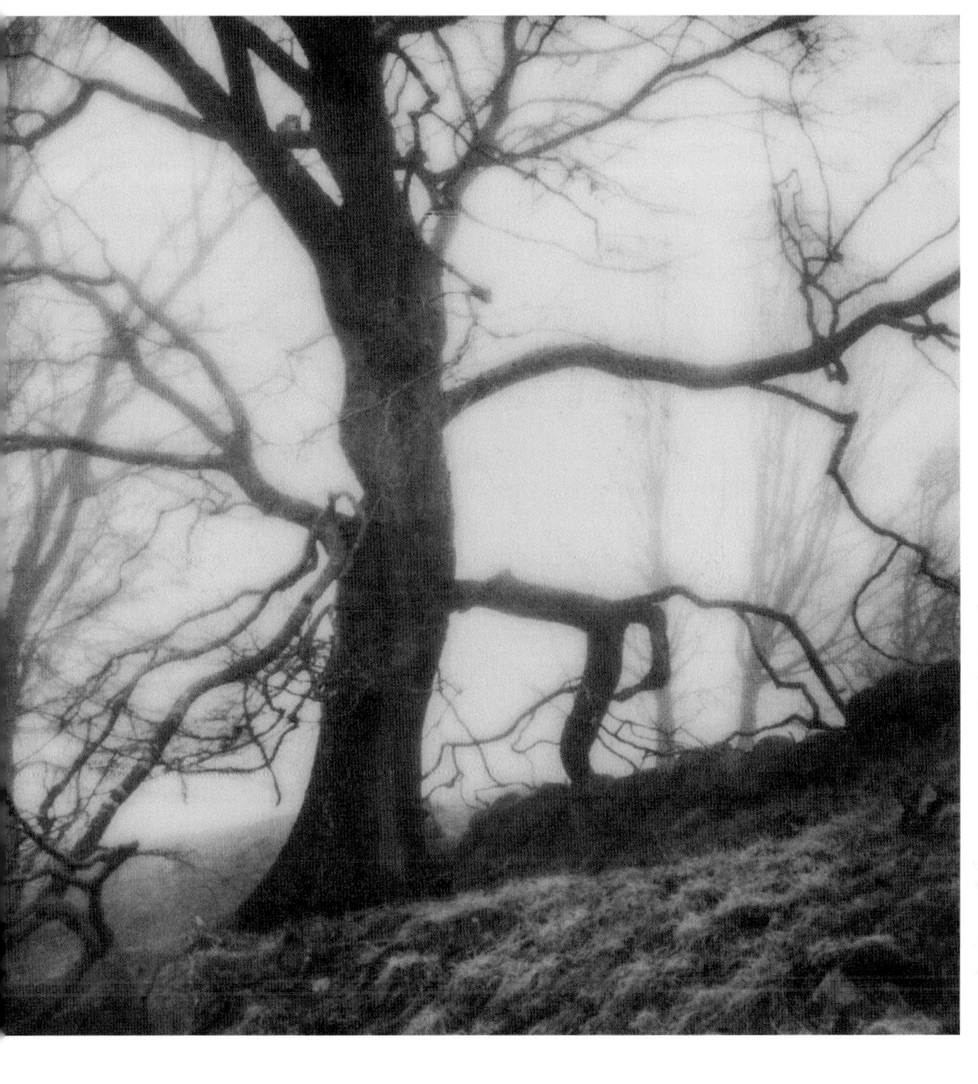

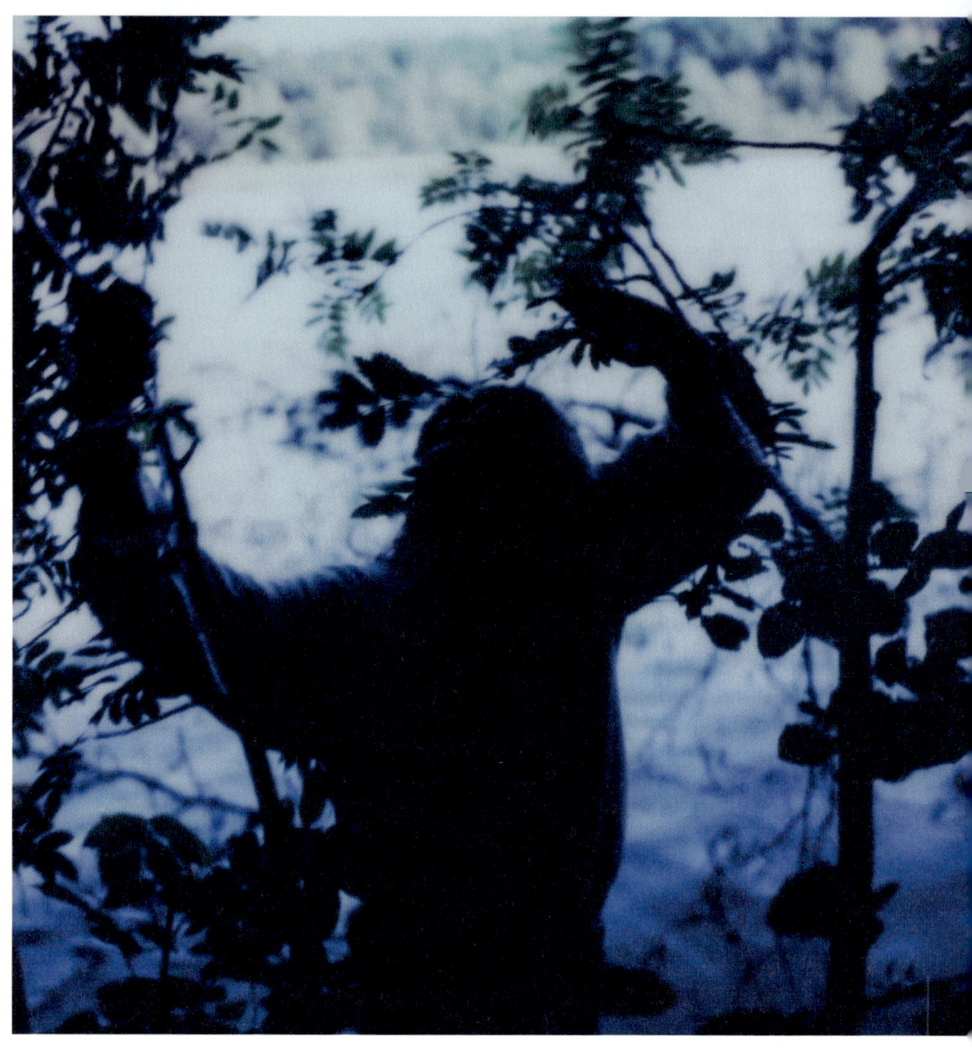

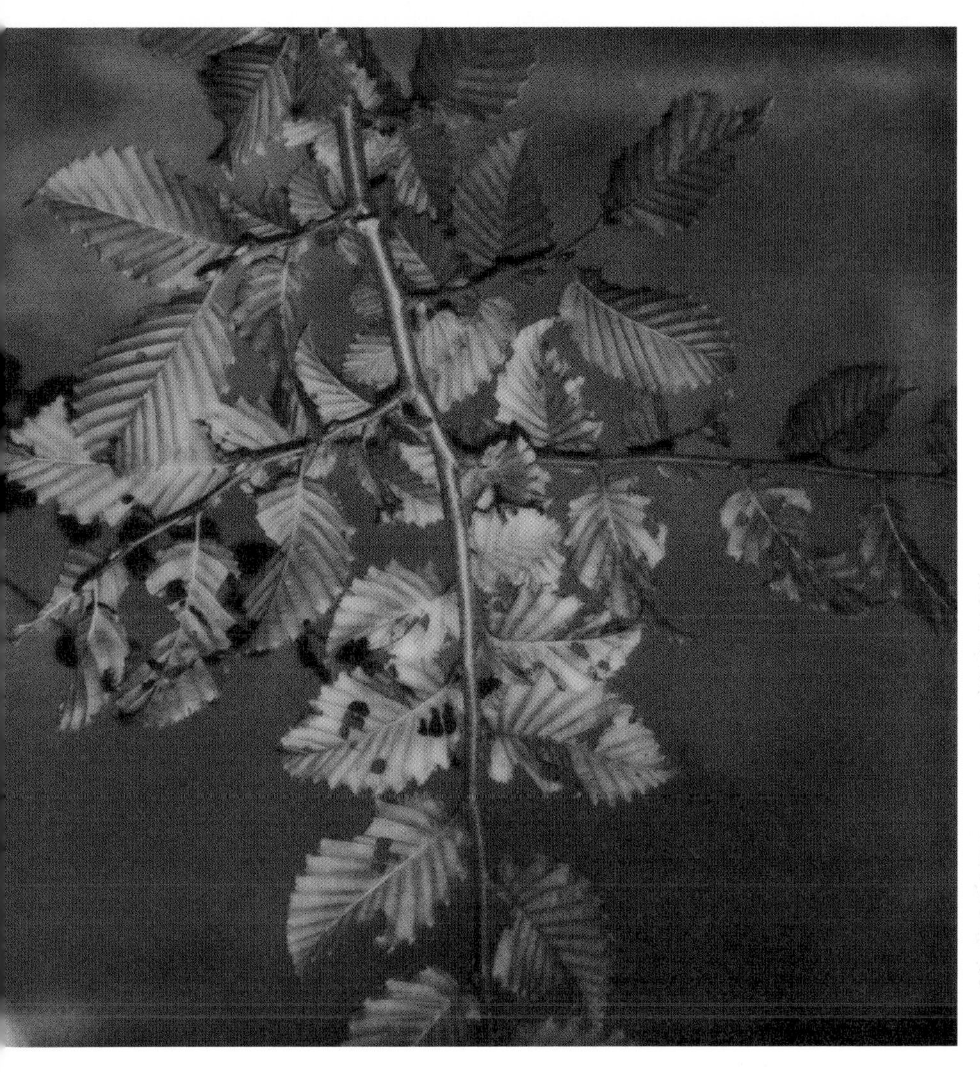

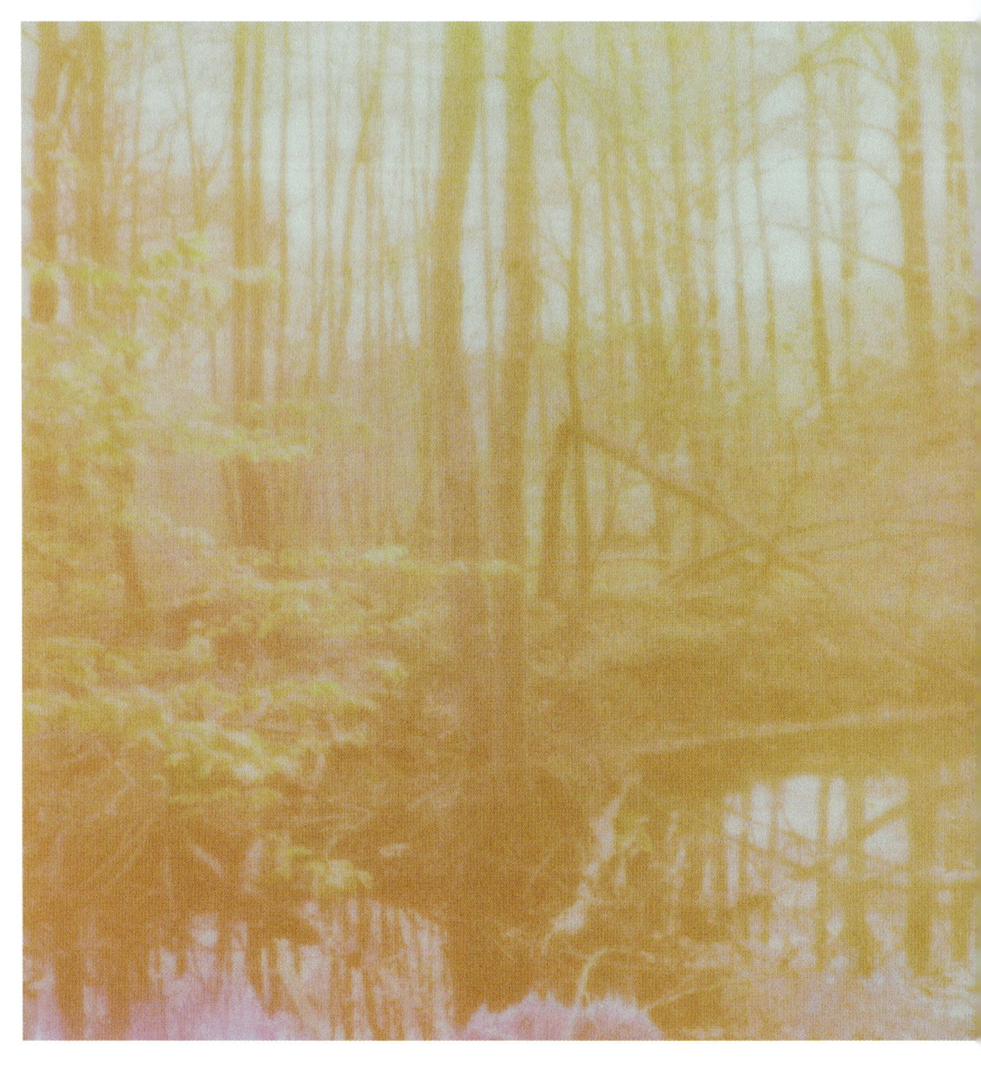

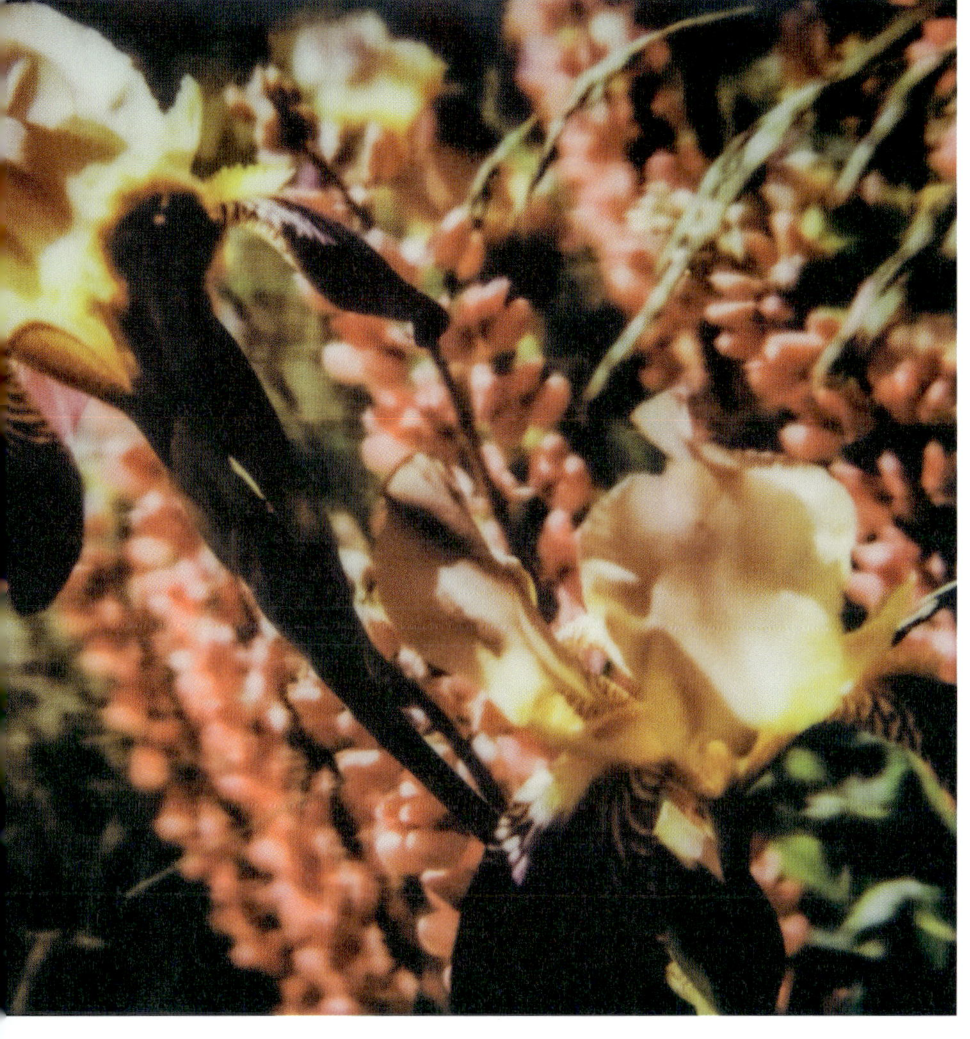

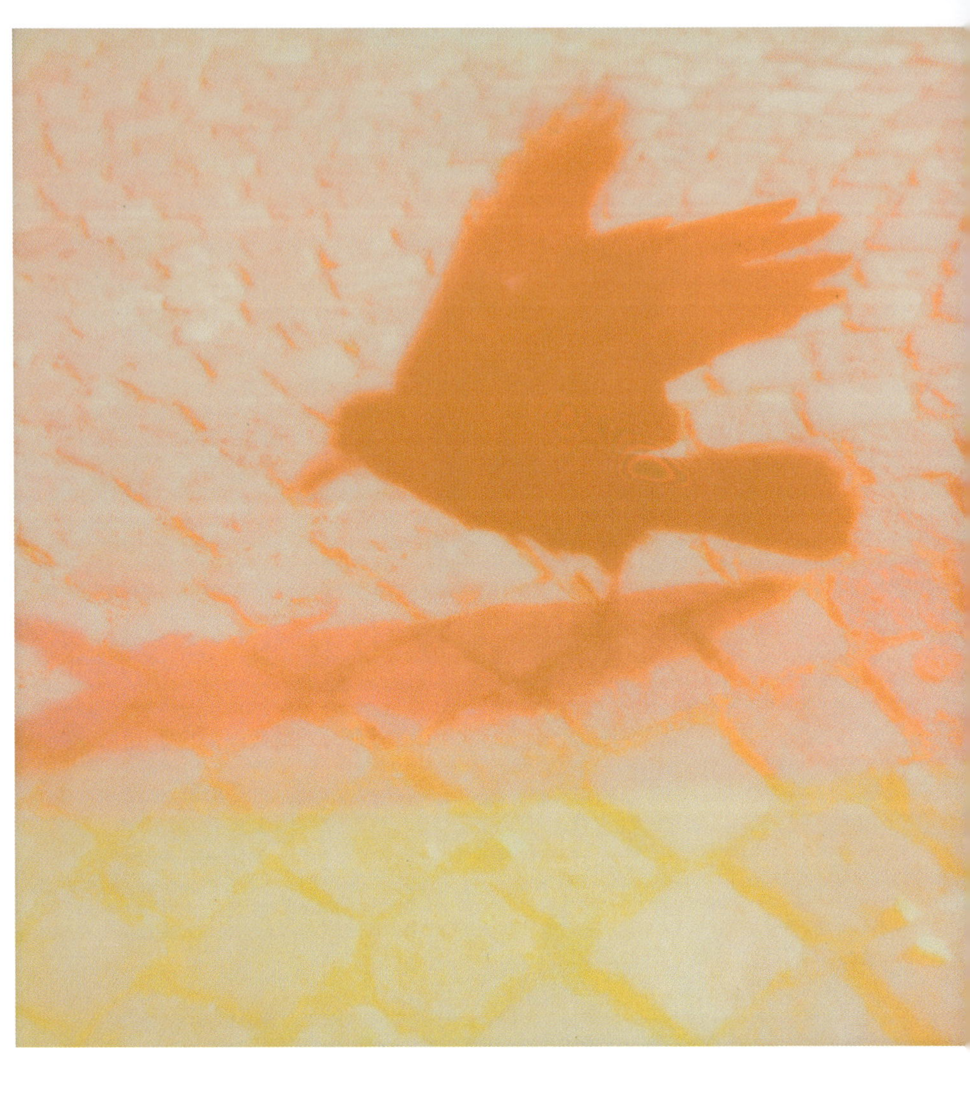

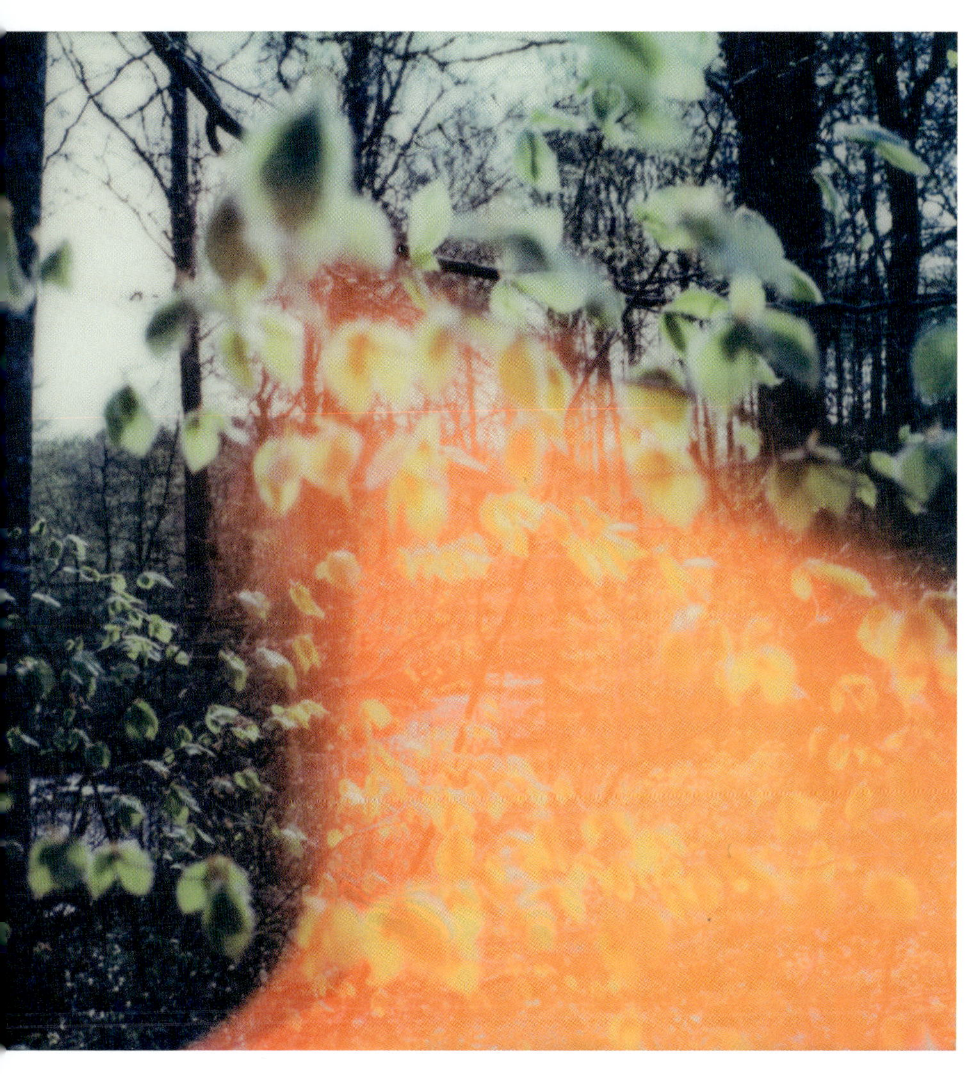

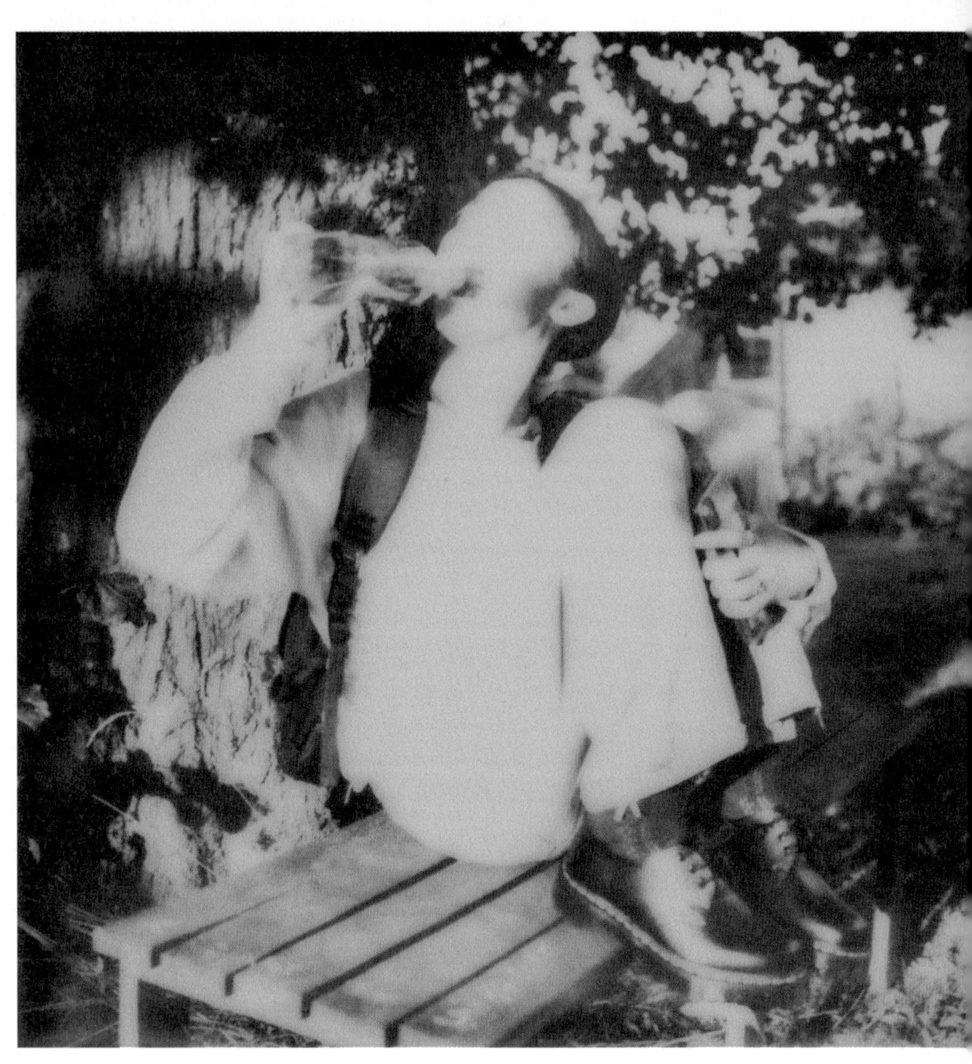

"*Senet* celebrates board games as an old-school pastime, but also pays homage to those who elevate them to an art form."
Monocle

"A gorgeously designed publication that is unashamedly analogue in a digital world."
Minerva Tabletop Games

"It's definitely a treat for the table and looks lovely next to tea and biscuits."
Staying In podcast

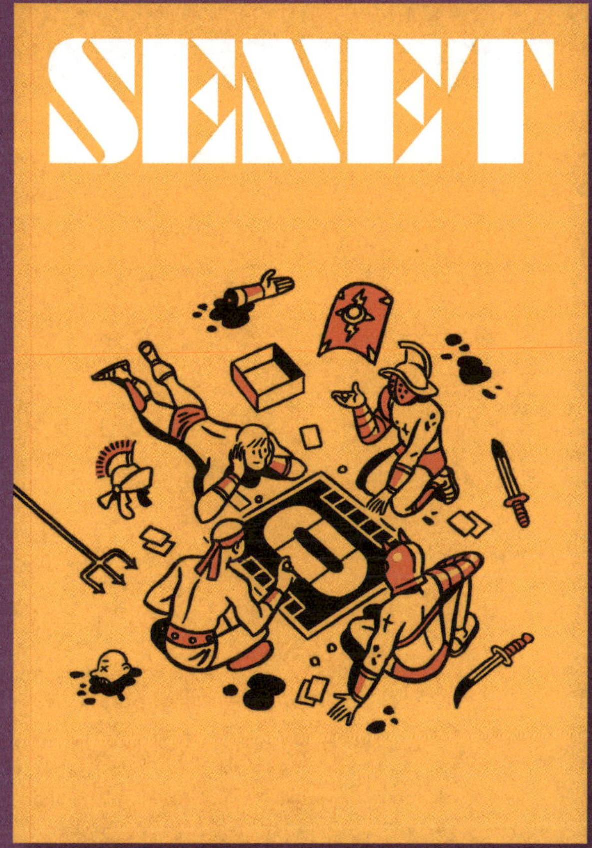

Board games are beautiful

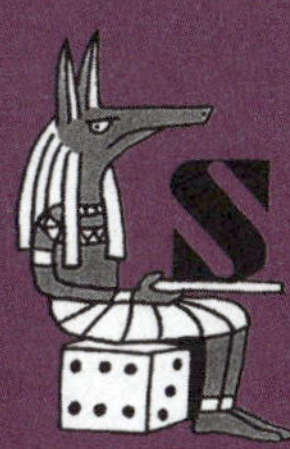

Senet is an award-winning independent print magazine about the craft, creativity and community of board games
Purchase the latest issue, back issues and subscriptions at senetmagazine.com

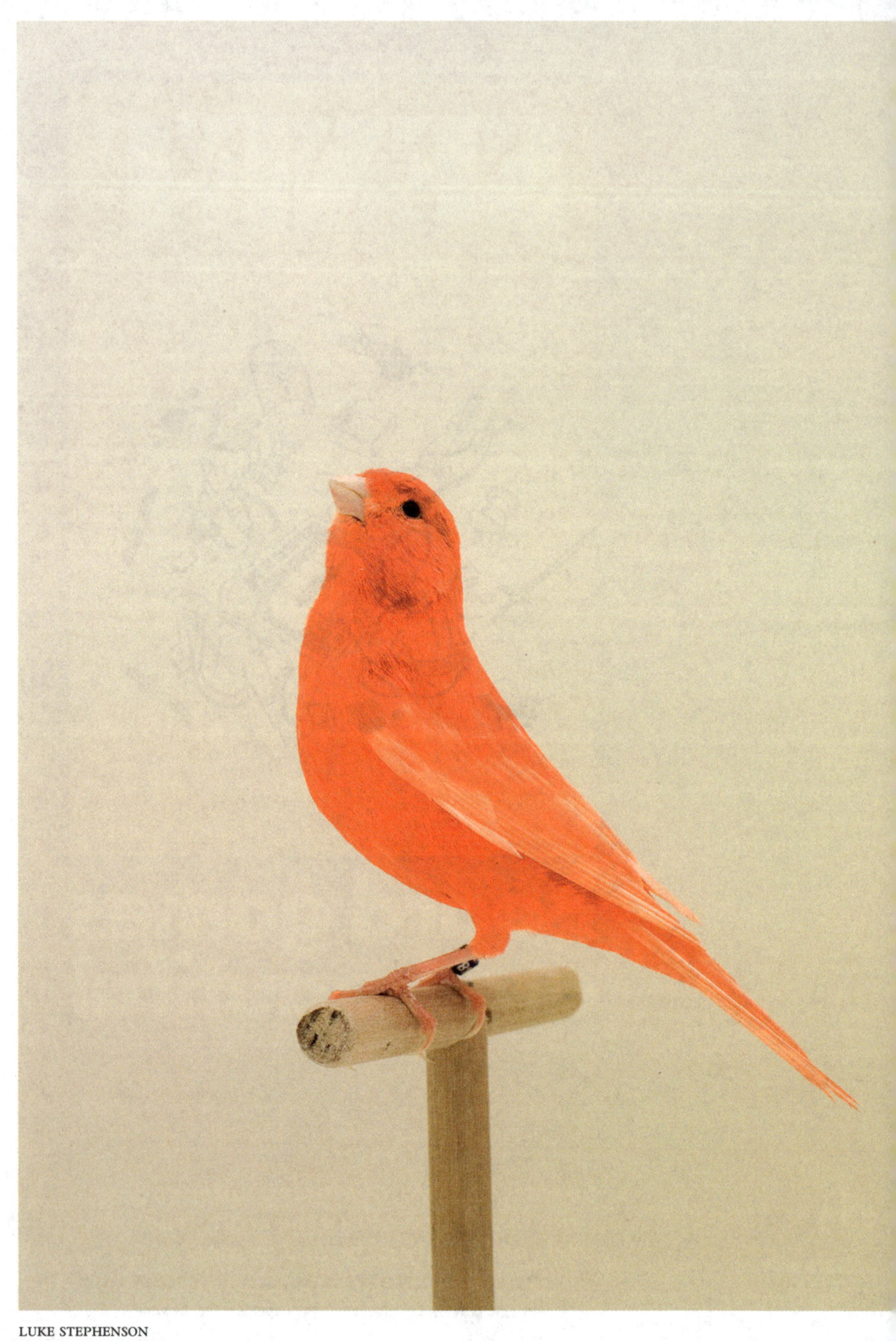

LUKE STEPHENSON
Red Canary #1, 2007

THE AVIARY

Solvej Balle

TRANSLATED FROM THE DANISH BY
SOPHIA HERSI SMITH AND JENNIFER RUSSELL

Will you play for us?

Maja took the lead. She crept closer and pointed at the guitar. I came up beside her.

Will you play for us?

Our mother had told us how to say this in English and we drew lots to decide who would speak. We had two slips spelling out our names: one said Martin, the other said Maja, and luckily it was Maja's name that got drawn.

We wanted to ask if she would play for us. That was what the words meant.

Joanna had arrived the previous evening, and she had a rucksack and a guitar with her. Now she was sitting on the grass, tuning her guitar.

'Will you play for us?' Maja had to ask the question several times, because she spoke so softly you almost couldn't hear her.

Joanna replied, and although we couldn't understand what she said, we could ask if she would play, and she did.

We had discovered Joanna that morning when we went out into the garden. She was lying in her sleeping bag on the grass. We went back in and told our mother but she already knew. She had picked up Joanna by the roadside on her way home from work the night before.

I asked what Joanna had been doing lying on the road since she needed picking up, but of course she hadn't been lying anywhere, she'd been standing with her thumb in the air to show she was waiting for a lift.

And then she ended up coming home with our mother and going to bed in the garden while we were asleep.

Our mother asked Joanna whether she'd like to stay another day, and she did, and then another night too. Out on the grass again. We wanted to sleep outside as well. Together with Joanna. And her guitar. Our mother spoke with Joanna in English and then she told us that yes, we could.

It grew dark, and the sky was almost pitch-black.

There was light in some of the windows in the house, and dots in the sky as if the stars too were holes covered with glass.

Gardens are a little scary at night. Mostly when the wind blows. But Joanna didn't care. She played her guitar and sang and taught us the words so we could sing along, but we didn't understand much.

We slept beside the big enclosure where the canaries were. It's called an aviary. The birds were silent, because birds don't sing at night. It was only Maja and me and Joanna who sang in the dark.

Maja had brought her new teddy-bear house into the garden. It sat beside her, and she had tucked two of the teddies into her sleeping bag. All was quiet, and the grass was a little damp when I walked across it in my bare feet. We were done singing, and I went inside to get my own teddy bear and also to wee and say goodnight and drink a glass of milk and see if anyone else had come to visit.

My mother was on the telephone, and I could hear that she was talking about Joanna.

'. . . yes, I suppose she'll stay for a few more days . . . I don't know . . . they're in the garden singing songs in English . . . here and there, from all over, she says . . . different places in Europe, that's all I know . . . she's mentioned a story she can't find but is looking for . . . yes, most likely . . . but she is really rather sweet . . . here's Martin, he's come in from the garden . . .'

I said goodnight and got my teddy bear and went to the loo and drank a glass of milk and said goodnight and fetched my pillow and went outside and shouted goodnight and walked across the grass.

Joanna had crawled deep into her sleeping bag. Maja was playing with her teddies and the teddy-bear house. Her teddies are tiny, no bigger than the foot of my bear. And mine has softer fur.

I hoped that Joanna wouldn't find the story she couldn't find, because then maybe she would stay. And also because if she were telling stories, she wouldn't be able to sing and play the guitar at the same time. And I wouldn't be able to understand the stories if they were in English.

We woke up early the next morning when the canaries in the cage began to sing.

We sat on the patio playing with Maja's teddy-bear house. It was made of wood and had four rooms across two storeys. Written across the front was THE TEDDY-BEAR HOUSE. We had almost finished decorating one of the rooms with wallpaper from a thick book when Joanna came over.

Maja wiped away the glue that had dripped along the wallpaper's edge and then wiped her hand on the flagstones while I put the furniture back into the room.

Joanna sat down beside us, picked up the scissors and a piece of pale green paper from the wallpaper book. Then she started cutting.

For a long time.

Joanna cut and cut the pale green paper, cutting sharp corners with the tip of the scissors and making skinny strips and small gaps. Tiny shreds of paper whirled about in the air and landed on the ground. Sometimes she stopped to inspect the paper, which was filling with angles and slits and curves.

Once she had cut away all the bits and left them scattered everywhere, the paper had become a birdcage. With thin bars and a rounded top and a patterned trim along the bottom.

She held out the birdcage. I took it and passed it to Maja, because she was about to tear it out of my hand and into pieces.

We looked at the cage and put it in the teddy-bear house.

'It needs some birds,' said Maja. 'We should ask Joanna to make us some.'

Joanna had gone back into the house and when she reappeared, she was carrying her rucksack.

I looked at her and asked if she was leaving, even though I knew that she couldn't understand what I was saying. But she nodded and pointed at the road.

I looked at the cage, which was sagging slightly against the wall in the newly wallpapered room. Then I asked Joanna if she had found her story.

I don't think she understood.

She took off her rucksack and sat down in front of the teddy-bear house. She found a pin and fastened the cage to the wet wallpaper.

'I'll just drop Joanna off by the motorway.'

It was our mother, stepping outside with the car keys in her hand.

Joanna stood and pulled on her rucksack. Our mother looked at the birdcage and said it was lovely. I mostly looked at Joanna. She looked happy, I think.

'All it needs is some birds,' said Maja.

'Why don't you make them out of paper?' said our mother. 'I'll be back in a tick.'

We waved as they drove off. Joanna was smiling.

We tried to cut birds out of the paper, but they didn't come out like birds at all. Just jagged scraps from a wallpaper book.

'Mother has a book about birds,' said Maja. 'We could cut those out.'

'You'd really cut up her books?'

'But we need birds for the cage. Do you think Joanna made us a birdcage just to hang on the wall as decoration?'

I looked at the cage. In fact, it didn't look like a paper cage at all.

And it would be wrong to fill it with wallpaper birds that didn't even look like proper birds. The cage had its own kind of rightness. Just not the metal kind.

The cage needed real birds, just as the house had real chairs and tables and teddy bears. Only flat. Otherwise they wouldn't fit inside. But we didn't dare cut the pictures out of our mother's book.

The only things we could think of that were both flat and real at the same time were our pressed flowers, which we kept in a big book. The flowers went completely flat when we pressed them between the pages with something heavy on top and left them to dry.

But you don't put flowers in a birdcage.

And the only birds we had were the canaries in the aviary.

We found a box to stand on to reach the hasp on the door to the aviary.

We knew that the birds would be hard to catch. They darted about, right beneath the netting up top where we couldn't reach. I think we were jumping around too much. In any case, the birds were frightened of us and fled to the corners.

'Maybe we should just make do with the flowers,' said Maja as we stood looking up at the birds that were impossible to reach. I nodded.

'I'll fetch the book,' said Maja. 'It's in the secret den.'

I stayed behind, watching the birds, wanting badly to touch them. Maybe if I stood perfectly still and waited. That would be the way to do it.

When Maja came back she laid the book on the ground, opened it and carefully removed the flowers, arranging them in thin stacks on the flagstones.

She looked over at the aviary, at me, and at the birds, which were beginning to settle back onto their perches one by one.

They sat like splotches of yellow and orange here and there, watching me with their black eyes. I watched back. That was all I did. I didn't move, and gradually they calmed.

Gently, I stretched out my hand towards one of the birds. It hopped away, but not far enough to be out of reach.

I held up a finger and touched it. You're supposed to hold your finger against its belly, then maybe it will hop onto it. I pressed my finger against its smooth feathers. The bird shifted a little and wrapped first one, then the other of its clawed feet around my finger. It held on, dipping forwards slightly as if about to lose its balance. Then it perched there, completely still.

Very slowly I took hold of its body with my other hand. It struggled a little but couldn't get away.

With the hand not holding any bird, I tried again, still keeping the other hand firmly wrapped around the first bird.

Then suddenly the second bird was in place. It was easier this time, but harder to get a proper grip since I only had one free hand. I lifted a finger and grasped its claws. I got a hold of just one foot, but held it tightly. Then I turned my hand over, retaining a tight grip. It flapped its wings and tried to escape, but I kept a firm grasp and managed to cup it in my palm, just as I had with the first one.

With a bird in each hand, I nudged open the door of the aviary and stepped out.

Maja had removed all the flowers from the book and just sat staring at me and the birds with their orange feathers in my hands.

I had caught two of the darkest birds.

Neither of us spoke.

Maja opened the book to the middle.

I held the birds down to the book's pages while she slowly closed it.

When the birds were in the right place, I pulled back my hands. We both huddled over the book with our hands held out in case the birds tried to get away.

At first it was soft, closing the book. Then a little difficult. So we both pressed down hard.

There was a strange sound. Then it went quiet beneath our hands.

Almost as if we had taken all the birds' sounds and their songs, put them in the book and pressed it shut, trapping them between the pages and flattening them like the letters and the pictures.

But the birds weren't completely flat, and they needed to be.

Like the cage.

We pressed even harder, and there were more sounds, different this time, as we squeezed the book closed, then a crunch that sounded hard and soft at once and there was sticky blood and bright orange feathers that looked like something on fire. The blood spread unlike anything I had ever seen, running flatly down the edges of the book and nearly reaching the ground.

It was completely silent inside the book.

And in the air. As if it too were flat when you breathed it in.

We breathed and said nothing.

'I think they'll need to dry for a long time,' Maja said at last.

I glanced over at the teddy-bear house and the cage, which suddenly seemed very small and possibly much too small for birds that were possibly much too big.

There came a gravelly sound and the hum of an engine, and we remembered our mother.

'We should probably hide the book,' said Maja.

I nodded, and she picked up the book and ran off to the foot of the garden.

I watched Maja dash across the flagstones, over the grass, and down to our den where no one else was allowed to go. The engine came to a halt.

There was a tapping right behind me. When I turned around, a yellow canary had landed on the roof of the teddy-bear house.

I looked towards the aviary and noticed the door. It was swinging back and forth, creaking. A quick splotch of yellow, the very last bird. It fluttered out and up into the air, and then the cage was empty.

I looked back at the teddy-bear house.

The bird hopped about on the roof.

At the sound of footsteps on the flagstones, it took off. ■

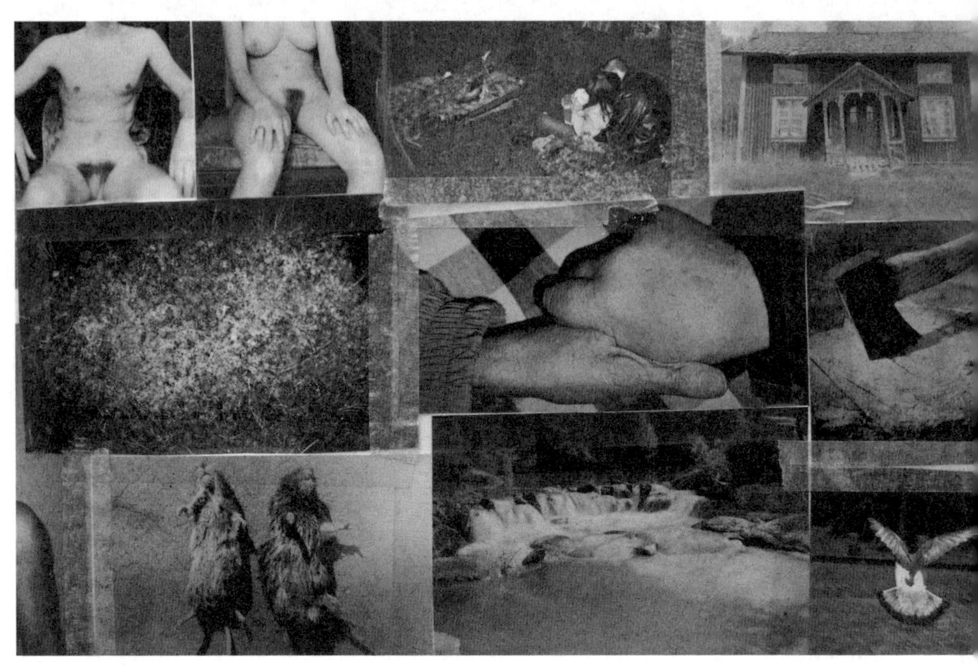

BACKWOODS FABLE

Sigbjørn Skåden

TRANSLATED FROM THE NORTH SÁMI
AND NORWEGIAN BY OLIVIA LASKY

The boarding house is cold. Huuva goes upstairs to his room where the heating is on and lies down on the bed. Sleep eludes him, his mind races. The image of the holy woman and the devil on the wall watch what he's getting up to. He goes to the bathroom and washes up when he's done, in the mirror his chest rises and falls with laboured breaths.

Is it the wind tightening its grip around the boarding-house walls, or is it his thoughts that are closing in? It's starting to get dark as Huuva heads towards the tavern a little while later. No lights are on in any of the houses along the way, not a person in sight. It isn't until he rounds Čoaffi that he spots a lone lamp above the tavern's stairs. The tavern is a low log building at the base of Čoaffi. No signs of life from outside. Huuva climbs the stairs and tries the door, giving it a solid tug to get it open. A wave of warmth floods over him as the inside infiltrates the outside, then come the sounds, the smells, and finally, the contours of the people milling about between the timber walls. The room is jam-packed. Huuva steps in and slams the door shut, but no one notices him. He weaves his way through the sea of people towards the counter, where the owner of the tavern, an unexpectedly tall man, is standing on the other side.

Yeah? he says.

I was hoping to get some food, says Huuva.

What? says the owner.

Can I buy some food here? Huuva shouts over the din, leaning forwards.

Meat stew, says the owner. Eleven crowns.

Huuva pays and waits while the tall man ladles stew from a pot and hands him a bowl.

Spoons and knives at the end of the counter, he says, peering down at Huuva. Bread, too! he shouts before turning to the next customer, a small old codger who wants to put another brew on his tab.

Huuva butters a slice of bread and brings his food over to the opposite side of the room, at the quieter end of a table. A large timber table with long benches on either side. A swathe of people are crammed at the other end, some eating, but most are just sitting there with bottles of beer. Huuva sets his food down and sits. No one looks in his direction, everyone is absorbed in their own banter.

He eats. The stew trickles down his gullet, warms his belly. There aren't any windows in the tavern. The logs encircle them in there, the door Huuva just entered the only opening to the outside world. Someone at the other end of the table shrieks so hysterically that the bench almost tips over just as Huuva bites into the first piece of meat – liver. It's been stewing for a long time, gotten tender, he hardly even needs to chew.

Huuva ate with relish the inner organs of beasts and fowls. He liked thick giblet soup, nutty gizzards, a stuffed roast heart, liverslices fried with crustcrumbs, fried hencods' roes. Most of all he liked grilled mutton kidneys which gave to his palate a fine tang of faintly scented urine. And now, as he swallows the liver – lamb liver most likely – the small old codger plops down across from him with his brew.

You from Food Standards? he asks, cocking his head at Huuva with a mischievous grin.

Huuva looks up from his meat stew that's a liver stew. He has to swallow a few pieces of liver and potato before he can answer.

Nope, criminal police. The name's Huuva, he replies automatically.

The codger widens his eyes and looks around before that mischievous grin of his returns.

So is that why you're here? Because you think the stew is *criminally* good?

Huuva smiles.

Or is there something else that brings you to our neck of the woods? the old codger continues. What'd you say your name was?

Huuva, Huuva repeats.

Where're you from with that kind of name? They got criminal police in Kiruna?

No, I'm from here, or, my father's from here, Huuva explains, straightening up and bracing for a reaction.

From here in Láŋtdievvá?

Yes.

Aha, now it's all starting to make sense, the codger nods.

Oh? Huuva says cautiously.

You're Ragnar Pedersen's boy, the codger says.

That's right, Huuva responds, surprised.

I'd heard tell that Ragnar's dáža-kid took a Sámi name, he says. And now I know it's true.

Huuva doesn't reply. Just then, a tall shadow slides in between them.

He bothering you? the tavern owner calls from the rafters, looking down at them.

I'm going, I'm going, the old codger says, and disappears before Huuva can even open his mouth.

He wasn't any bother, says Huuva, but the codger doesn't hear and the owner doesn't seem to care.

Want a top-up? the owner asks. Four crowns.

Huuva finishes what's left in his bowl and gets some more. Once that's been consumed, the owner comes with coffee, strong and black. As he sips the coffee, Huuva starts taking a proper look around the tavern. There are fewer people at his table now; a group has started gathering on the opposite side of the room, where something seems to be brewing. Huuva drinks slowly. The faces in the room are unfamiliar, but the features are recognisable. As if cast in the same mould. But one familiar face sticks out in the crowd: Josva Johnsen is sitting alone at a table, looking over at the swarm of people. The only lamp in the tavern is hanging above him, he is sitting right where the light spills into the corners.

Huuva goes to the counter and buys two beers, then zeroes in on Josva.

Hello, Josva, I thought I might treat you to a beer, Huuva says, handing him a bottle.

Well, I'll be damned, are you here, too? Josva asks, taking the bottle and indicating Huuva should sit down with a friendly nod.

You're here alone? Huuva asks.

Looks like it, Josva replies.

Something happens in the throng. It parts. A broad-chested fellow strides nonchalantly through the opening, clambers up onto the table, and positions himself beneath the lamp. Huuva gives Josva a perplexed look, but Josva is no longer paying attention to him, he's fixated on the fellow who is now standing confidently on the table between them with his face turned up towards the light. The fellow starts stomping his feet, first carefully, then harder and harder until the whole table is shaking beneath him. He stops abruptly, every sense in the room is now trained on him. Someone shouts to the owner that he needs to bring over the pot with the meat stew, he argues there's still some good food at the bottom and instead brings yesterday's pot of fish soup that he saved, that'll have to damn well do, he barks, heaving the pot onto the table at the fellow's feet. The fellow on the table howls as though the pot landed on his toes then bends down and embraces it, rocking it as though it were a child, or is he just swaying? He starts to croon.

Huuva looks around, confused, as the people around him start to join in. The fellow croons for a long time as he rocks the pot of fish soup, a choir of voices murmuring beneath him like birds gathered for the autumn migration. Then slowly, slowly, the choir gets quieter and quieter until the room is completely silent. The fellow lifts the pot to his lips and starts to drink. It runs down his chin and throat, fish heads and intestines smacking the table around his feet. When he finally lowers the pot, he falls to his knees right in front of Huuva. The fellow howls. A howl so terrible it's like the insides of his body are being squeezed out of his flesh. Huuva jolts and tries to get to his feet, but someone behind him holds him down. Meanwhile the fellow undresses as he whimpers plaintively. Maybe it's a joik.

Once he's undressed, the fellow lies down buck naked flat against the table, and two teenage girls sit beside him. One of them has brought some bread and butter from the counter and begins tenderly massaging the fellow's skin with butter and breadcrumbs. The other girl takes hold of the pot and does the same with what's left of the fish soup. The fellow lies motionless as the girls continue rubbing his body until it's completely greased up. When they're done, the girl with the pot moves up towards the fellow's crotch, dutifully massaging his cock and balls with what's left. She looks up, her eyes rolled back in her head. The girl begins to preach:

The river flows between the trees, the bow-stave birches stoop over the churning water, waiting only for the snow that is yet to fall, the girl begins. In the ravine, there is a girl who has a mother who isn't her mother, she lies in contentment beneath the bow staves, but *it* sees her, the girl continues, indicating with a gesture that she means the fellow whose genitals she is massaging. The winds rush, autumn settles, a black bird flies above, a raven circles between the crags, it makes a ring over she who lies so contentedly down below, a black ring that grows smaller and smaller.

The other girl has moved to the fellow's feet and started rubbing them gently with butter and breadcrumbs. She, too, starts to preach beneath the voice of the first girl, like waves, their voices rising and falling disproportionately.

Blow, winds, says the girl by the feet, eyes rolled back in her head as well. Blow through our earth, turn our heads inside out, ravage, root and rip so that everything grows clear, the leaves in the ravine will fall one by one, fall so the branches are clean, so the ground is covered, o, o, dear Láŋtdievvá, our withered Láŋtdievvá, o, o, the ring is a black devil coming closer, gliding slowly in between the stooped trees where a girl who has a mother who isn't her mother lies in contentment.

The first girl's voice rises. She's started rubbing faster, pouring soup over the fellow's crotch and massaging his member with the other. Only now does Huuva notice that the girl has six fingers on one hand, and the six fingers caress the fellow's cock and balls.

Beware the river's roar, the girl chants. Beware the rapids' maw, you who are trapped in the ring, you already bear the mark, ah uh, it rushes and roars, ah uh, it blows and it pulls, the black ring ensnares.

Air suddenly erupts out of the fellow on the table and he wails. An acrid tobacco-like smell spreads throughout the room. Not your average Petterøes 3; this is something else. Not a caustic odour; this is deeper, more sophisticated. A worldly scent. Or more biting? Or is it one and the same? Tiedemanns red? Maybe. Distinguishable, at the very least. Difficult to inhale, like a mind-dulling porridge.

Aaaaaoooo, continues the girl rubbing the fellow's member with her six-fingered hand. Aaaaaoooo, the ravine vanishes, I see a crossroads where two roads spread in opposite directions, there is a stone I sit upon at this crossroads, three roads now, westwards, eastwards, and back from whence I came, I sit on this stone for a long time listening to the rushing winds, watching the dancing leaves, and then a child appears before me. Take me westwards, the child says, but my feet won't carry me. Take me eastwards, the child says, but my feet won't carry me. The child pleads. It pleads pleadingly, and each time it makes a sound, the child grows smaller, little by little it grows smaller. I sit on the stone until the child is gone. When at last I rise, my legs carry me back from whence I came. I see the hill where wild strawberries grow and I walk past it, I see the plain someone baptised pubic hair plain because the grass there grows thinly like pubic hair, I see the scree where you can find treasures and the hill where the children stomp the snow to make ski jumps in the winter and then I see Čoaffi before me on the road and I keep walking, and when I've climbed over Čoaffi I see on my right side the dark timber that encircles this place, I slowly walk down towards the door, the withered grass flutters on both sides, and now I'm standing outside, let me in.

The gathering turns collectively towards the door and then commandingly towards the owner. The owner meets their gazes with defiance but eventually shrugs and takes a few ambivalent steps towards the door. He jostles it open with a theatrical shove. There is nothing outside. The owner slams the door shut and returns to his spot at the counter. The gathering turns its attention back to what's happening on the table, where the two girls have started talking over one another with raised voices.

The scents fill me, the girls chant. The visions that come. The sounds that pound into the skull. Is that Josva sitting there? Josva. Rise, Josva.

Josva springs to his feet. The girls' eyes, however rolled back in their heads they may be, are looking straight at him.

Josvaaaaa, the girls say as they rub and knead. I see your path. So clearly. It's getting dark where you are. It's time to get moving. There is a clearing on the other side of the river. You walk, Josva. You walk through the river. Now you are on C6. You've chosen your path. Your path, blackling, was set from the beginning. You don't choose the path, the path chooses you. C5, Josva. Don't look back. The clearing is at C4. Go. Go there, blackling. And before you, the castle rises. You can fend for yourself, Josva. You've managed well. You have two choices left now, Josva. Stay or move. You move. C3. To the base of the castle. The castle lets nothing past. Since childhood you have seen that white-headed sentinel looming over our village, it lures but lets nothing past, and bishops circle round like predatory animals. You have no weapons. No help in sight. You are a blackling out in the world, you are out of place. You have no choice, you say? You yourself took the first step, Josva. You yourself chose what looked like a better place when the gloaming descended upon where you had once been. And now you are here. You can go no further. You cannot retreat. And the predators draw ever closer.

Josva leans against the table and weeps. The two girls are still looking at him, eyes rolled back. Can such eyes see with mercy?

It isn't you, Josva. Predators will be predators, they do only what they were made to do. Look up at the castle. The castle remains even though you have been erased. Is that a comfort? You've made it far, Josva. You've managed in this world for a long time. I now grant you peace.

The fellow on the table moves suddenly. First the left foot. Then the right. Then his hands. People around him have started to stand up. Someone at the end of the table is supporting Josva, who looks like he's about to pass out. When the fellow on the table finally gets up and raises his arms towards the light, naked and shining with butter and soup, everyone in the tavern is on their feet. The crowd howls as though flush with victory, practically lifting the roof. The fellow on the table takes in the people's tribute for a long time before the howling quiets little by little and people instead start to chatter among themselves, the aftermath of the event still etched in their faces.

Huuva has also got to his feet, but doesn't speak to anyone. As the episode was drawing to a close, he kept a close eye on the six-fingered girl, who has turned towards the door unnoticed. She carefully opens the door and steps out into the night. As she closes it behind her, Huuva quickly winds through the throng towards the door. Two old geezers follow him with their eyes. Huuva doesn't notice them. The geezers stand with their heads close together, whispering as they watch Huuva, who can't hear their conversation beneath the din of voices.

The seers' words were coloured by him being here, says one geezer, nodding in Huuva's direction. That's for sure.

How d'you think? asks the other.

I know a thing or two about him.

The policeman?

Yep.

What d'you mean?

I know him from back in the day, when he used to come round here in the summer with his old man. He has special powers, I've seen it myself.

Noaidi-powers? Like he sees things other people don't? Is that why he joined the police, because he can tell the future and see right through people?

No, no, what are you talking about? the first geezer says, exasperated. I'm talking about chess! He's a chess genius! Lemme tell you, I've never seen anyone who can even hold a candle to him, who can show that kind of insane control and virtuosity with a chessboard.

Really? says the other. Tell me!

So, here's the thing, the old geezer begins. You might remember I worked down south for a few years logging for Borregaard, you could make good money in a job like that.

'Course I remember, says the other.

Alrighty, says the first. And then there was this one time at the Mo Market, you know, it's world-famous now, they show it on TV and everything.

'Course I know about that, says the other. They show it on TV and everything.

Sure, but they were already having it way back then.

Really?

They sure did, and it wasn't too far from Sarpsborg where I was living, they have the Mo Market in a place called Mysen. And all kinds of celebrities were flocking there, and then we heard that Sonny Liston himself was gonna be there, would you believe it.

You know, when you say it now, I think you might've told me this before, says the other.

Maybe about Liston, says the first. So, we were a couple of guys from Borregaard who hopped in the car, off the cuff, to go to Mysen. There was no way we were gonna miss Liston, chances like that don't come twice. This was when Liston was still world champion. He was unbeatable, they said.

Sure, before Clay came around.

Yeah, yeah, but that's a whole 'nother story, says the first. Anyway, we gunned it over from Sarpsborg and there were so many cars it was near impossible to find any parking, but anyway. We managed to get in after a lot of back and forth, and you gotta believe it was chock-full of people. We practically had to fight for a spot, but in the end we got to see Liston. And I'll say this: I've never seen anything like it, before or since. Big black fella the size of a troll, it sounded like goddamn dynamite was going off when he went at the bag!

Yeah, says the other. That part I've heard before. And then?

And then after Liston was done, we took a round of the marketplace. And I was mucking around there for a while when I came across this little tent where there was some kind of chess show. And inside the tent there was a little table where a young boy was sitting in front of a chessboard and people were taking turns challenging him. Believe me when I tell you that kid made easy work of anyone who dared sit across from him. I'm talking just a couple of moves. And I was watching this when it hit me, didn't I know this boy from somewhere? And then I realised that it was Ragnar Pedersen's boy, I'd seen him around here in Láŋtdievvá every summer, back when Ragnar was still alive.

And you've never brought this up before? asks the other.

I honestly didn't remember it 'til I saw him here just now, says the first. Seeing Liston kinda overshadowed everything else that happened that day. But now when I saw him again and heard the seers' words it all came back to me, that I'd seen him as the star of that chess show at the Mo Market all those years ago.

And he was a little odd?

You got that right, says the first. The boy sat there still as a statue. The only thing he moved was the hand that held the pieces, otherwise it was like he was made of stone, he didn't bat an eye, just stared straight ahead like a sleepwalker. And the other thing was that it was like he knew what his opponent was gonna do before they did it, the boy'd already reached over the board to make his countermove before his opponent had even put their piece down, it was crazy. And he just sat like that. The opponents came and went and he just kept on sitting. I don't know how long he was sitting that way, but I watched him for a pretty long time and he was still sitting there when I left.

You didn't go over and talk to him?

He didn't really seem like he was present in this world, says the first. I didn't really know the boy either, so I just let him sit. But it was really something, seeing him in action.

Sure wish I'd been there, says the other.

Ain't that the truth, says the first. ■

'Backwoods Fable' is an excerpt from the novel *Láŋtdievvá* (North Sámi) / *Planterhaug* (Norwegian) by Sigbjørn Skåden. The novel was written and published simultaneously in North Sámi and Norwegian in 2025.

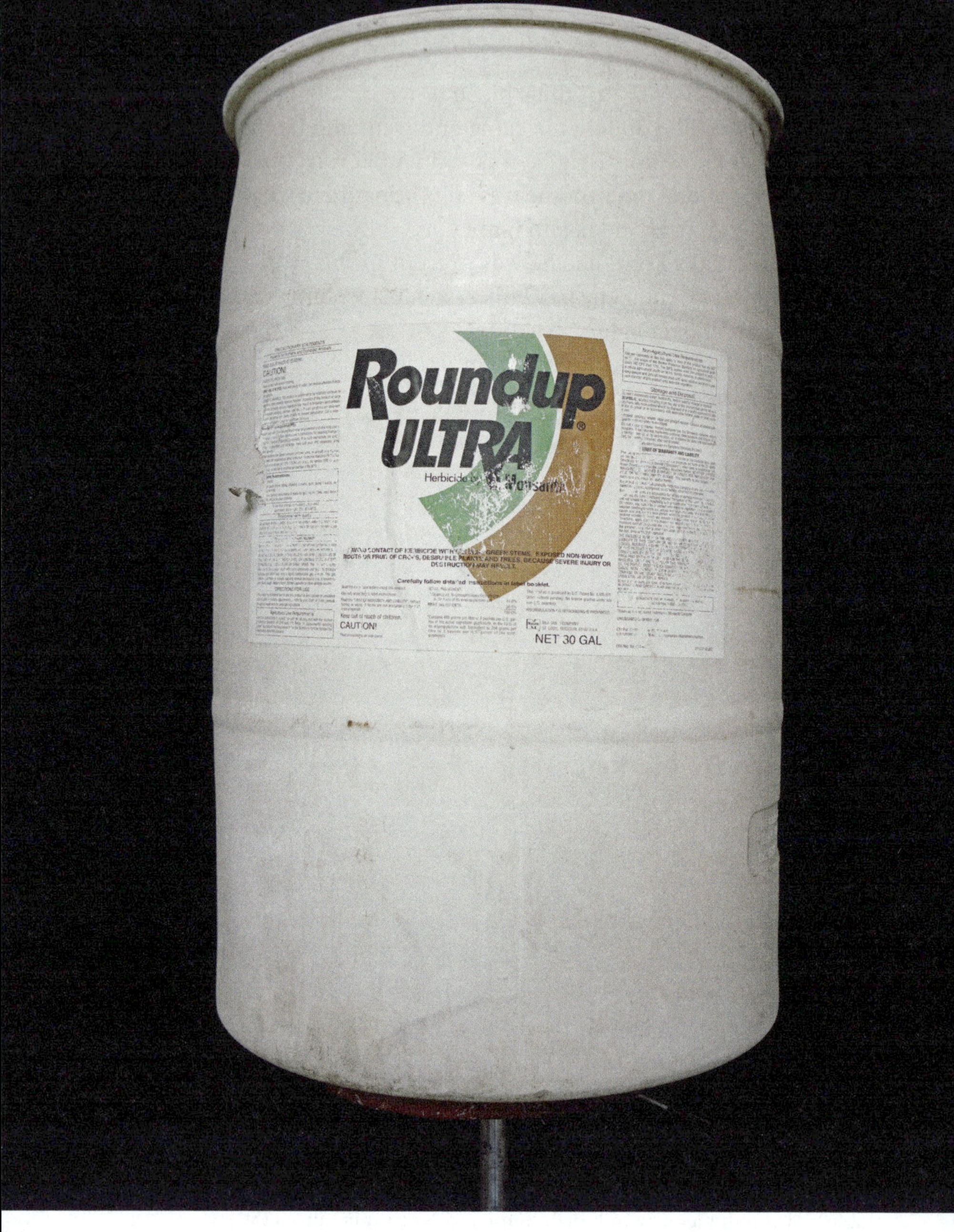

MATHIEU ASSELIN
from *Monsanto: A Photographic Investigation*

BLOW UP THE FACTORY

Malte Tellerup

TRANSLATED FROM THE DANISH BY DENISE ROSE HANSEN

No hope, no soil

When May comes around and the tousled, lightward sprouts of Nanna, Martin, and Rasmus's husbandry come surging from the ground; when five years of tilling, composting, and nurturing the depleted soil – a real desert of soil – have turned it into a healthy basis for the life of vegetables and countless other creatures; when the fruit of their hard work sprawls at their feet, that's when a farmer named Mikkelsen turns up.

He is the kind of middle-aged man who thinks nothing of pairing a blue shirt with a cowboy hat when he goes out to strike a deal, a pair of blindingly white trainers the finishing touch. Mikkelsen. He's a man who knows what works and how to make money. All his life he has reared pigs on the Hedevej 10 estate, just as his father did. Above all, he understands that owning land is always worthwhile. So Mikkelsen owns land, and he buys more. Evil tongues call him Hogfather Mikkelsen – though well-meaning tongues call him that too. It's not straightforward to get the measure of Mikkelsen. But no matter what you think of him, Mikkelsen owns pigs, he owns land, and he is married to a woman named Vibeke. He sees real promise in Power-to-X, so much so that he has gone into partnership with the municipality and leading local businesses. Power-to-X may well become the west coast's most ambitious renewable-energy venture.

But of course Mikkelsen doesn't mention any of this when he knocks on the door, wearing his cowboy hat, blue shirt and white trainers. He commends the young people for their perseverance, admitting that when they rocked up from Aarhus, some folks – including himself – didn't believe that they could raise such an impressive kitchen garden. At this, Nanna – the person who answered the door and invited Mikkelsen in for coffee, which they take standing in the kitchen, because Mikkelsen regretfully doesn't have time to sit – has to interject and correct him: 'regenerative farm'. And he does correct himself, 'Yes, a vegetable farm like that – who'd have thought you could get so much from the soil out here? It isn't exactly the fairest in the kingdom.' Mikkelsen tastes his coffee and his words, visibly enjoying the old turn of phrase that sprang to mind just as he finished his sentence. As he sips the coffee and relishes his own locution, one of the young men – Mikkelsen has already forgotten their names – talks about courgettes and winter squash and all that sort of thing. But when the young man mentions synergy Mikkelsen perks up, because he likes that word, 'synergy'.

And he interrupts the young man, 'Yes certainly. What I wanted to put to you – what I'm actually going round and putting to all your neighbours – is something you should have a good think about, because one needs to consider these things carefully. But the fact of the matter is that we're going to have a real renewable-energy adventure out here, and that means I'm going from door to door, as I said, offering everyone who's committed themselves to this beautiful speck on the map a good price for their land –'

'You're what?' Martin cuts in.

Mikkelsen continues speaking, as though flicking a fly off his nose.

'– so that's the thing, and of course you ought to think carefully before saying yes, but I can guarantee that the price will be good. It will be close to double the valuation price, so you can be very pleased about that.'

'But we aren't going to sell you anything,' says Martin.

'No, no, of course you should stay and sell your vegetables and do one final season – this won't be until autumn. But that's the way things are going, because, well, I might as well say it like it is, and you seem like the sort who like to hear the truth about things, so yes, you see, once we start in on building it'll be uninhabitable out here – absolutely unliveable. Everyone will get three years' notice before we start construction. If you haven't sold by then . . . well. But that's not what you should concern yourself with, you should concern yourself with the money and what you want to do with it,' says Mikkelsen, setting his cup down on the counter.

He reaches for the hem of his shirtsleeves, tugging at them a little like he always does once he's delivered his message. Then he walks out of the kitchen and climbs into his four-wheel drive, leaving the message to settle.

'The bastards are in on it too!' shouts Rasmus, in front of a computer at the local library in Ulfborg.

'What's up?' Nanna says, coming over to him.

'Cheminova – they're involved, it says so right here. I found an article in the local paper that says how pleased the director is about the positive contribution the plant is making to the area, and that supporting the local community is one of the factory's trademarks. What a hypocrite.'

'That's a load if ever I heard one,' says Martin.

'A load? No, it's the last straw,' says Rasmus. 'A factory that dumps poison into the groundwater, the sea, and the fjord, a factory that makes pesticides so toxic they can't be sold in Denmark or most of Europe, is claiming to support the local community? It's just too much.' Rasmus bolts up, seething, and stomps out of the library for a smoke.

Nanna and Martin keep reading. All of Cheminova's chemicals are patented, and therefore secret, but the vast majority aren't sold in Denmark because of the environmental standards. As they read, something begins to take shape between them: an unspoken conviction, maybe even a kind of certainty.

The factory complex itself is enormous; it fills the entire Rønland area. From north to south runs the production line P0–P3, designed for the processing of parathion, a key chemical in highly potent pesticides that can no longer be legally manufactured in Denmark. For this reason, Cheminova moved production of the poison to India in 1997, where it is used in cotton farming, causing enormous harm to people and the environment. They simultaneously expanded their reach to the Brazilian plantation sector, with equally devastating consequences. It's the same story with dimethoate and other organophosphates, except that these are still being produced in Denmark. Where does the poison go after it's exported? Some dubious sources speculate that they were mixed into Saddam Hussein's chemical weapons. An intriguing idea, though it feels like conspiracy. For them, for Nanna, Martin, and Rasmus, it's enough to know that the factory produces poisons that people like Mikkelsen are becoming rich from, while depleting the local soil.

There are treatment plants and dilution tanks – open vats that show up as striking greenish hues on the satellite images – and it's impossible to figure out what they actually contain. Two wastewater pipes run out from them under the factory and into the North Sea at Jetty 42, where the outlets end five hundred metres off the coast. Jetty 42 is a well-known site for pollution; here decades of toxins lie buried in the sand, a persistent threat.

To the east of the factory site are the sulphur depots, where old parathion remnants are stored in both liquid and solid form. They are buried right there in the ground, sealed in a grid of concrete sarcophagi. Further to the west is the dispatch warehouse, filled with barrels of packaged chemicals destined for the market. Beside the warehouse are several freight trains, stacked with containers ready to be loaded and shipped off. It is largely due to the factory that a railway line was built out here in the first place. To the south lies the laboratory division and the power plant. This part is important.

Nanna prints out a satellite map. Then she finds a series of old maps of the factory site. Rasmus comes back in and watches her screen with a knowing nod. He grabs more printer paper. Martin finds a sabotage manual online and starts watching YouTube tutorials. Together they carefully write the instructions out by hand. Then they walk to the car and drive back home. At the farm they mark out the key points on the satellite map and then hang it up in the barn. What should they strike first? And how can they create a chain reaction of explosions?

Then there's nothing for it but to go and compare the map to reality.

On the country lane south of the factory they manage to shake surveillance, despite the road being so straight and long. But they have no intention of driving back to the farm now – it's time to act. They continue on through the countryside.

Their first stop is the station town of Vemb. Martin, who has been managing the farm's accounts, withdraws their entire bank balance. Nanna inserts her own card into the machine, but the machine swallows it. They look at each other, smile, and Martin shakes his head as though to say, 'No need for it now anyway.' They feel united. Tempered by struggle, their anger seems to have hardened into the shape of a three-headed iron hoe, ready to rip out weeds.

Martin hands Rasmus four hundred kroner, who goes into the Co-op for matches and nail varnish remover. Nanna and Martin flop onto a bench, sunglasses on, and smoke. Martin counts out what's left. Not enough: they need more money. A man comes staggering past from the pub. He stops when he sees them. Stares for a moment. Then lurches on, saying, 'What's up, girls?' without looking at them.

Nanna gets up and walks into the town kiosk, her hand closed around the folding knife in her pocket. The only customers are a Swedish family – dad, mum, son – who have just been served burger meals. The father is drinking beer. The waitress has poufy hair and wears oversized glasses and a grey T-shirt, white shorts and clogs. She smiles at Nanna as she comes in. Nanna smiles back. A mosquito is zapped on the insect lamp above the refrigerator.

'I'd like to order a coffee and a hot dog,' she says to the waitress. 'For here.' Then she walks over to the family.

'Hiya,' she says, squatting down between the dad and the child. 'I really hope you're enjoying your holiday here in Denmark.' She smiles at each one of them. 'I'd recommend you all stay calm when I go up to the till in a moment for the money.'

The dad freezes mid-bite over his burger, jaw dropping open above and below the bun. 'I hope you have a safe trip back to Sweden.'

Nanna gets up and walks to the counter. Calmly she pulls the folding knife from her pocket and swings over the counter just as the waitress comes out of the back room with a pile of frozen hot-dog buns.

She smiles at the waitress and points the blade in her direction. She rings up the coffee and hot dog on the register. 'I'd like to pay right away. That'd be forty-five kroner, and I gave you a hundred, so you owe me fifty-five in change.' The register pops open with a clatter. She takes all the banknotes, then stuffs her pockets with ten- and twenty-kroner coins while looking over at the waitress, who is still standing there unmoving, arms filled with hot-dog buns.

Nanna comes out of the kiosk and strolls over to the car without a change in expression, and then Martin drives them recklessly through the countryside. The car rattles and creaks but holds its speed. They tear across the central Jutland heathland, past wild land and cultivated land. The gorse rises along the hillside, bursting into magnificent yellow. Rasmus puts on music. The road is deserted. They see a man kneeling in the middle of a large brown field. He's on a plastic sheet, a black bucket on either side of him. He doesn't look up. He's digging a hole in the centre of the field, his car is parked on the roadside, hazard lights flashing. Martin keeps his foot on the accelerator. Nanna rolls down the window and lets herself be blasted by the wind.

They turn off at the congress centre in Herning, where they're folded into the sea of cars funnelling towards the Agromek livestock fair. The Home Guard has been called in to direct traffic. Uniformed under their high-vis vests, berets perched on their heads, they wave their arms. People and cars stretch as far as the eye can see, as though all of Jutland has been crowded together here. When they've parked the car, they join a queue of men in leather shoes and padded jackets to have their tickets scanned, then split up. Nanna and Rasmus drift among shiny new agricultural machines that stand mighty and dead, like the polished skeletons of dinosaurs. Martin walks on alone, looking for the stand of the Danish Agricultural Grocery Company. He finds it, and is met by a young salesman barely twenty years old, wearing a T-shirt that is slightly too tight, a lanyard around his neck, and a product folder resting on his forearm.

'Hello, hello,' says Martin. 'I'm looking for a good deal on a fertiliser mix.'

'We've got that. Do you have a preferred brand?' the salesman asks, leafing through his folder.

'Well, that one there,' Martin replies, leaning forward and pointing to one of the pages. 'Though I don't see the one we usually get . . . the blend with 35 per cent nitrogen?'

'Uh, yes, let me have a look,' says the salesman, flipping a bit further. 'Hmm. It doesn't look like we have anything above 28 per cent. Let me check . . .'

'That's the one we usually get.'

'Yes, yes, I'll just need to check with one of my colleagues.' He hops over and pulls an older man in their direction, a man who is very much radiating 'agricultural consultant' for today's Agromek: short-sleeved chequered shirt, work trousers, and safety shoes.

'So you're looking for . . . ?' he asks, one eyebrow raised.

'My dad sent me along to get some of the strong, low-cost stuff we usually buy from you. But your colleague here can't find it.'

'No, we don't sell it just like that.'

'Oh, I wouldn't know. I've got our company registration and the account number we have with you.'

'Right, let me see then,' says the man, walking over to a computer stand. Martin shows him the numbers, and the man types them in.

'And of course that drought we had last summer . . .' Martin says, projecting his voice into the exhibition hall, '. . . it really wore down our already thin margins, that's safe to say, so we really need something with a bit of kick to it.'

'Uhum, hum,' the salesman replies. 'Dry it was . . .' He looks at the screen. 'Mikkelsen's, up at Hedevej?'

'That's the one.'

'Alright then. How much do you need?'

'Mm, three Big Bags.'

'The large ones or the small?'

'Large. And do we get any sort of discount?'

'Yes, yes, I'll shave off a bit.'

'Oh, thanks for that. Will you send me an invoice, or is cash better?'

'That's up to you.'

'I've got the money with me now, so you might as well take it,' says Martin, fishing an envelope out of his pocket marked FERTILISER.

The man takes the envelope and smiles.

'Alright then,' he says. 'I hope you manage to turn things around from last year.'

'Thank you, thank you. We'll see. It's just a matter of pressing on, then maybe prices will go up. Thanks for the deal.'

'Yes, indeed. Goodbye and thank you.'

They shake hands.

Martin turns to leave, then says, 'Oh, right – one more thing. It's to be delivered to number 18, not number 10. We've expanded.'

'Very well.'

'Good then. Thanks.'

Martin finds Nanna and Rasmus again. They're standing by pens filled with the perversely perfect cows that are about to be paraded into a ring to receive prizes. Men in shirts gleaming with chlorine, sharp monochrome ties, and white paper hats are starting to lead their finest animals out for inspection. The group exchange sardonic glances and hurry out. In the car park, Martin steals a flower planter shaped like a swan and climbs into the back seat with it.

They drive on. In Brande they head into the town centre to find a hardware shop. The town is a wasteland, dominated by a billionaire enterprise called Bestseller, whose warehouses and office buildings huddle among the trees. The place looks like some kind of Scientology compound in its eccentric style, with soft natural stone colours paired with glossy glass facades – a striking contrast to the usual stripped-back steel-and-glass boxes of industry. Here Bestseller plans to build a tower for itself – a 320-metre skyscraper that will rise like a monumental phallus out of the flat landscape, proclaiming to the world the great ideas and ingenuity that can spring from central Jutland's commercial mentality. Brande exists for Bestseller. Another obvious target. In the hardware shop they buy aluminium powder, hydrogen peroxide, sulphuric acid, wire, and tape. Again Martin gives Mikkelsen's company registration number at the till, though this time he lets them charge the account. No one bats an eyelid. Now Mikkelsen's chipped in a bit as well. They fill the boot of the car.

They drive towards Give. The Siemens wind-turbine test facility looms square and cynical. It stares back at them, all glass and steel. Various turbine components lie ready to be assembled. They may be producing green power, but the manufacturing of the turbines is indefensibly toxic. What happens to a retired wind turbine? Its blades are buried in landfills, the fibreglass left to decay beneath heaps of soil. Chimneys jut into the sky. With that, they've already passed the town; Give is but a gap between Siemens and Givskud Zoo. On the far side of town a large concrete and cement works sits in a permanent cloud of dust. It's all of this, all of it, endlessly producing growth while degrading the world, destroying anything that isn't profit. It's all of this that has to die. ■

AFTER THE EVENT

Mamma Andersson

Introduction by Granta

Mamma Andersson paints from pre-existing images. Her compositions are derived from combinations of archival photography, film stills, clippings from old magazines, period design, crime scenes, sketches of theatre sets, as well as the landscapes of northern Sweden, where she was raised. After Andersson narrows these down to a handful of sources, she applies brushstrokes of oil and acrylic: 'I paint slowly, gently, thin, beautiful, ugly, thick, hard.'

This method lends her work an eerie dissonance, like witnessing an actor wandering onto the wrong stage. The surrealism from these juxtapositions is paired with gestures towards nineteenth-century romanticism, both through her sublime, psychologically layered treatment of the natural world and her bold use of colour.

In the work featured here, paintings live within paintings, and the natural world appears like a ruin. Largely devoid of people, if bodies do inhabit the frame, they are withdrawn and provisional. Absence is made conspicuous, as if the images in front of us have been half-remembered, details elided. We have entered *after* the event. The paintings provoke a sense of menace and melancholy, particularly in 'Wood Cut', where a lone trunk stands with its branches severed, rough daubs of red and brown, a mutilated hand grasping upwards. But Andersson also finds tranquillity and something approaching respite in the Swedish landscape: a thin tree is symmetrically flanked by forest; the sea is glimpsed from the aperture of a cave's mouth. ■

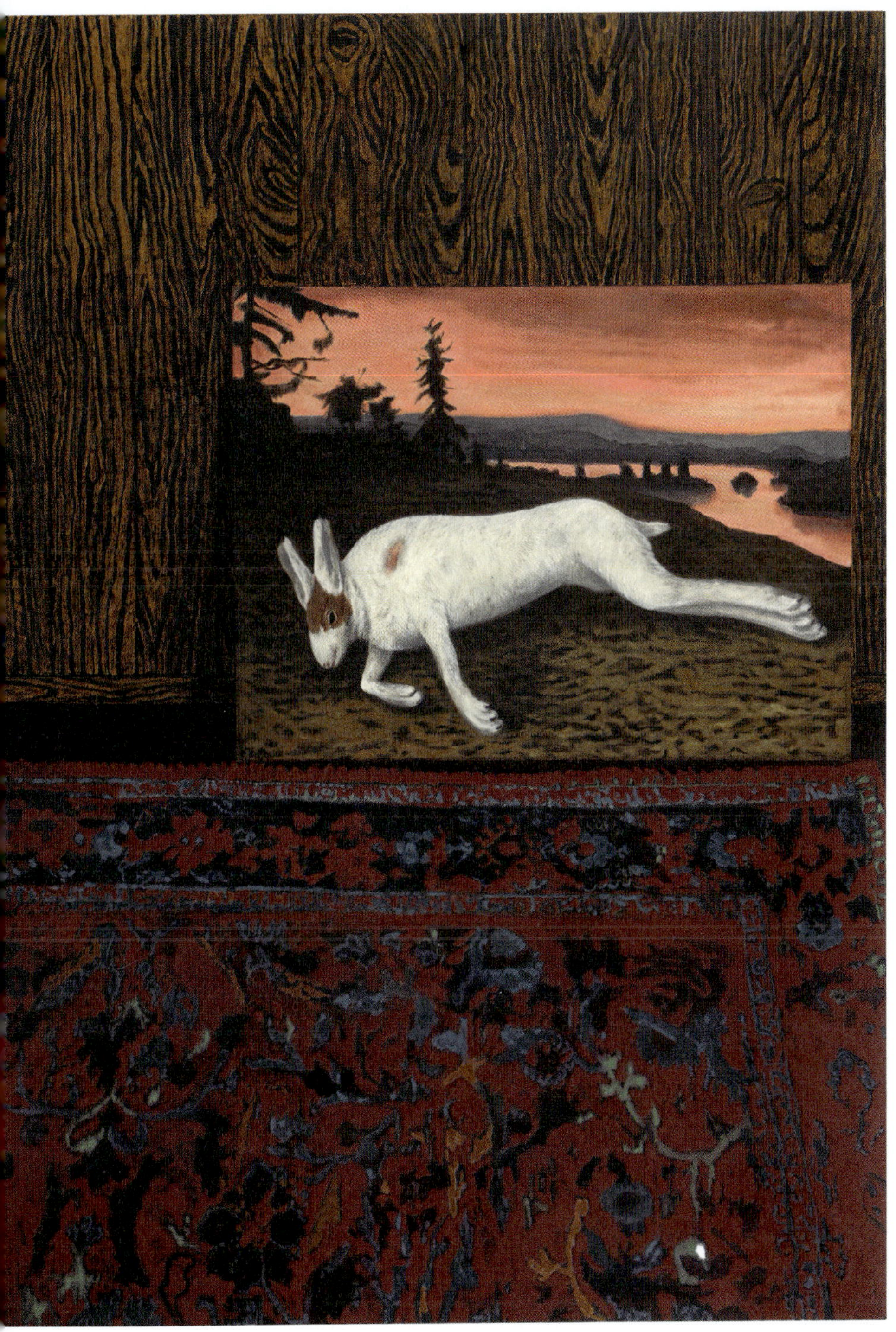

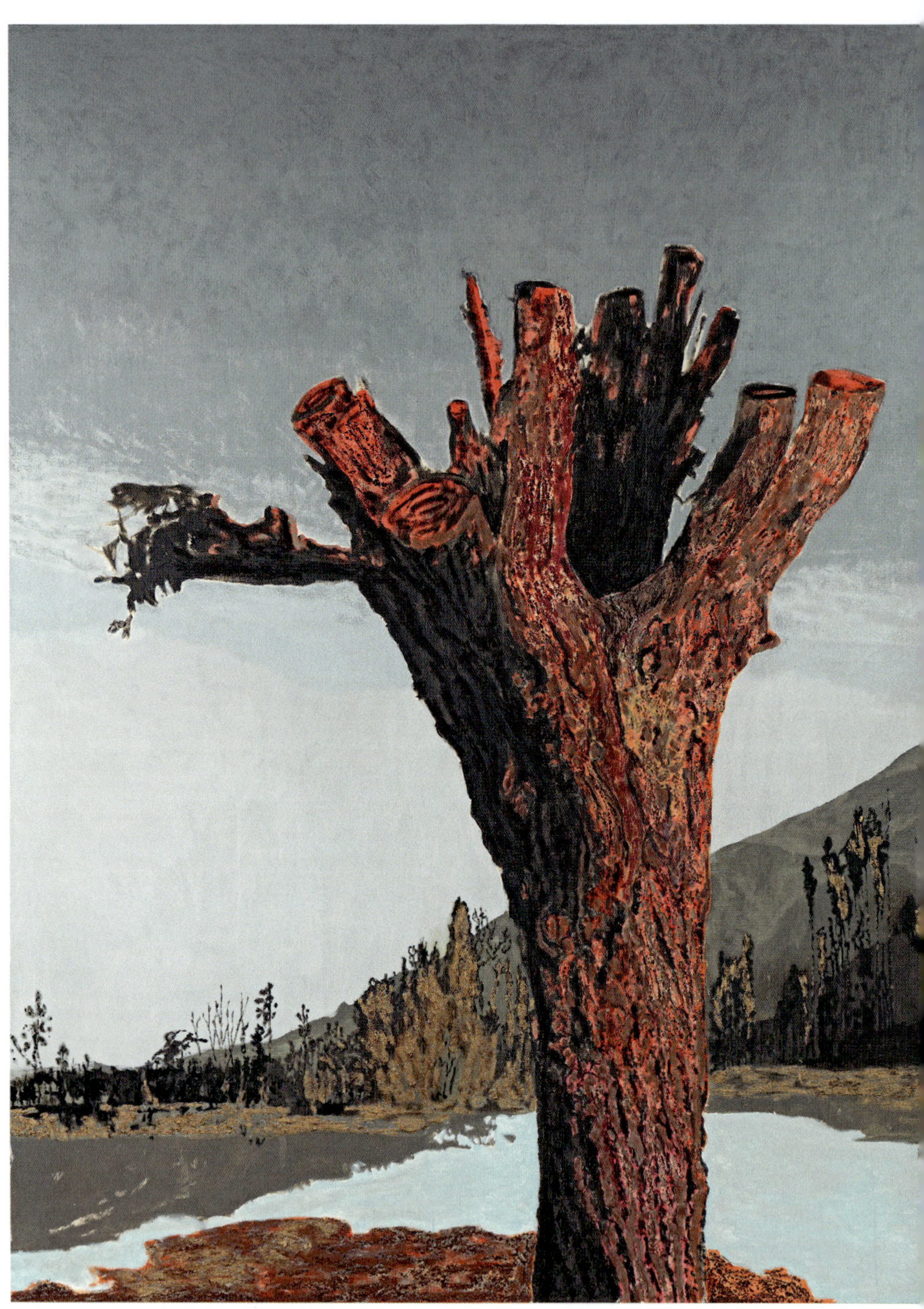

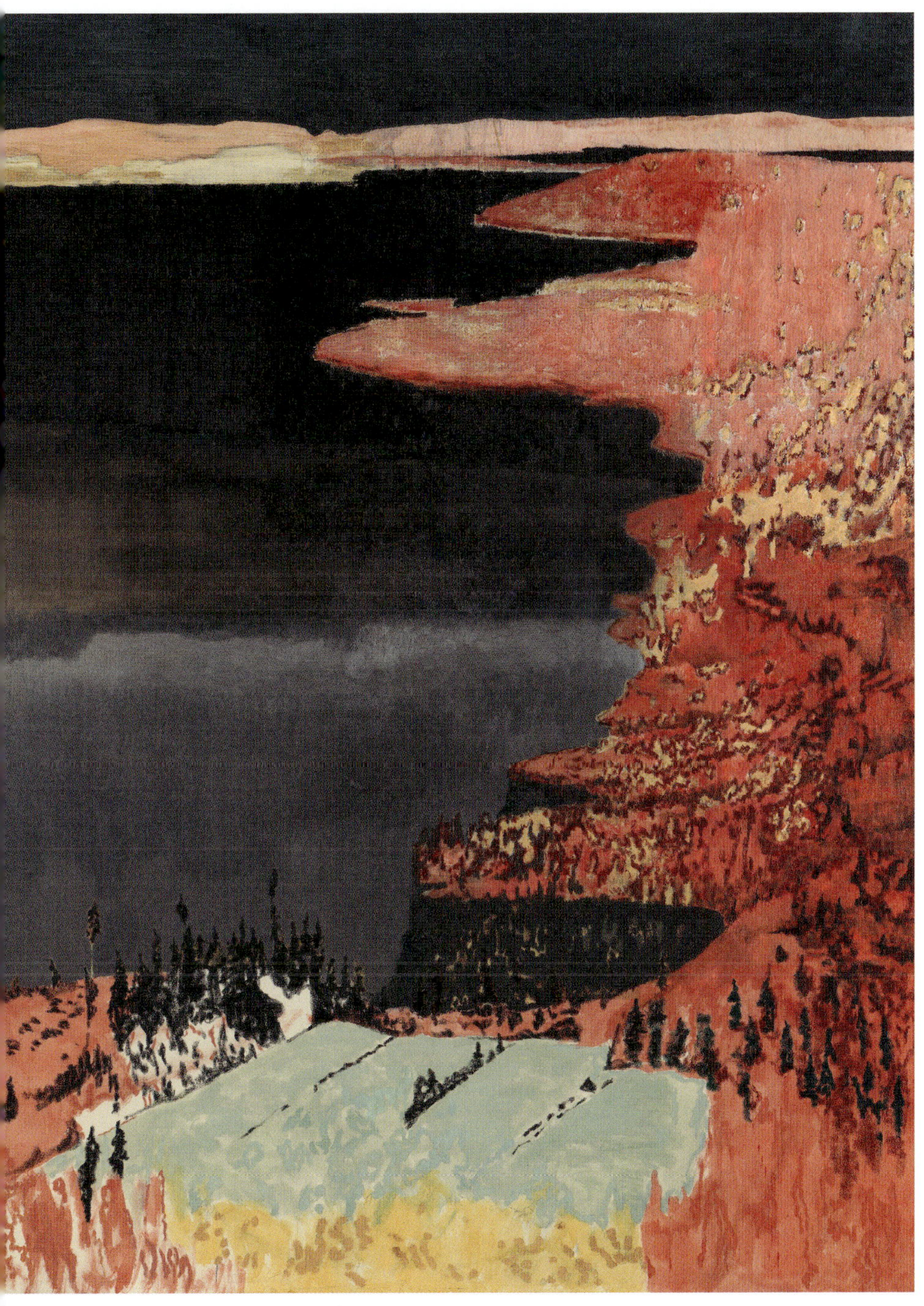

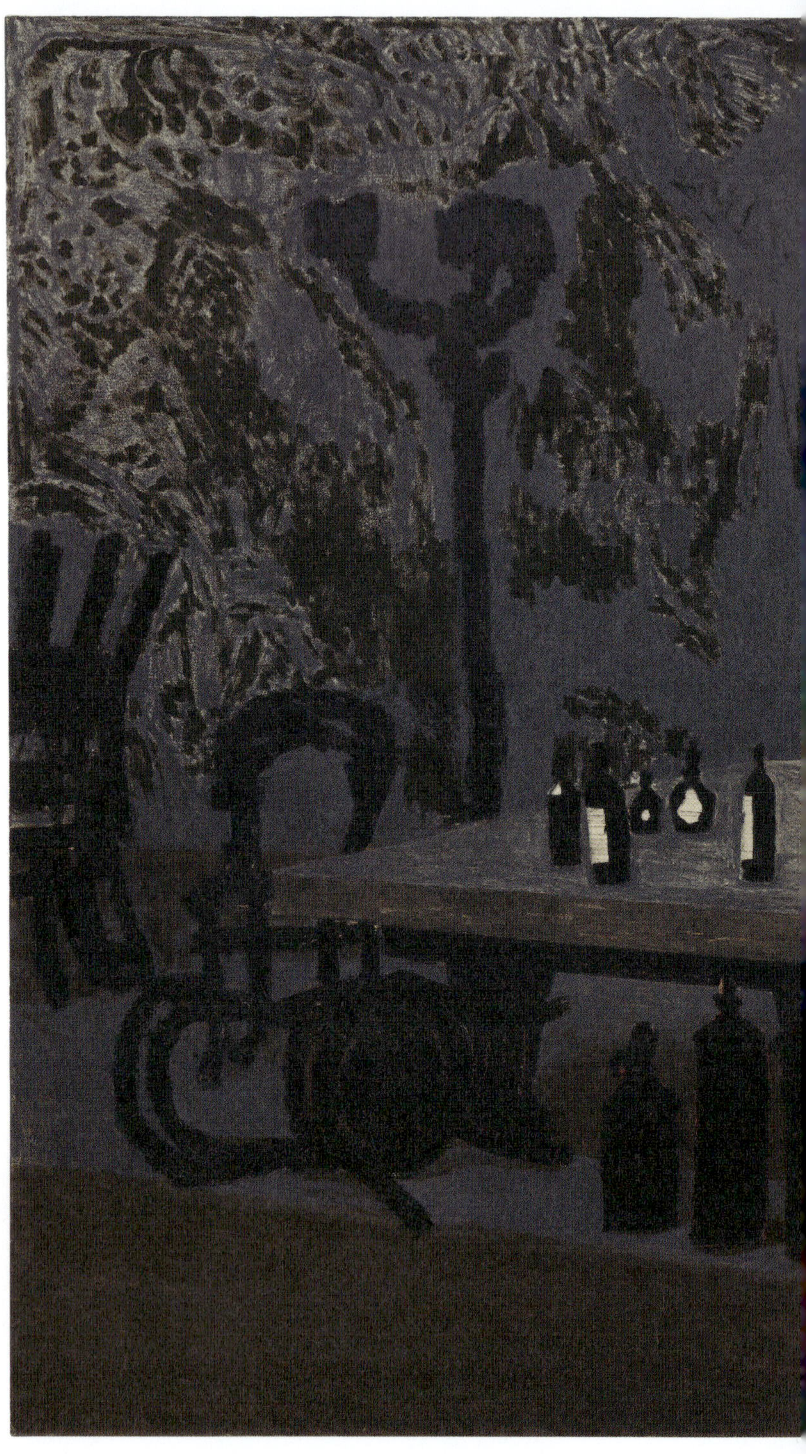

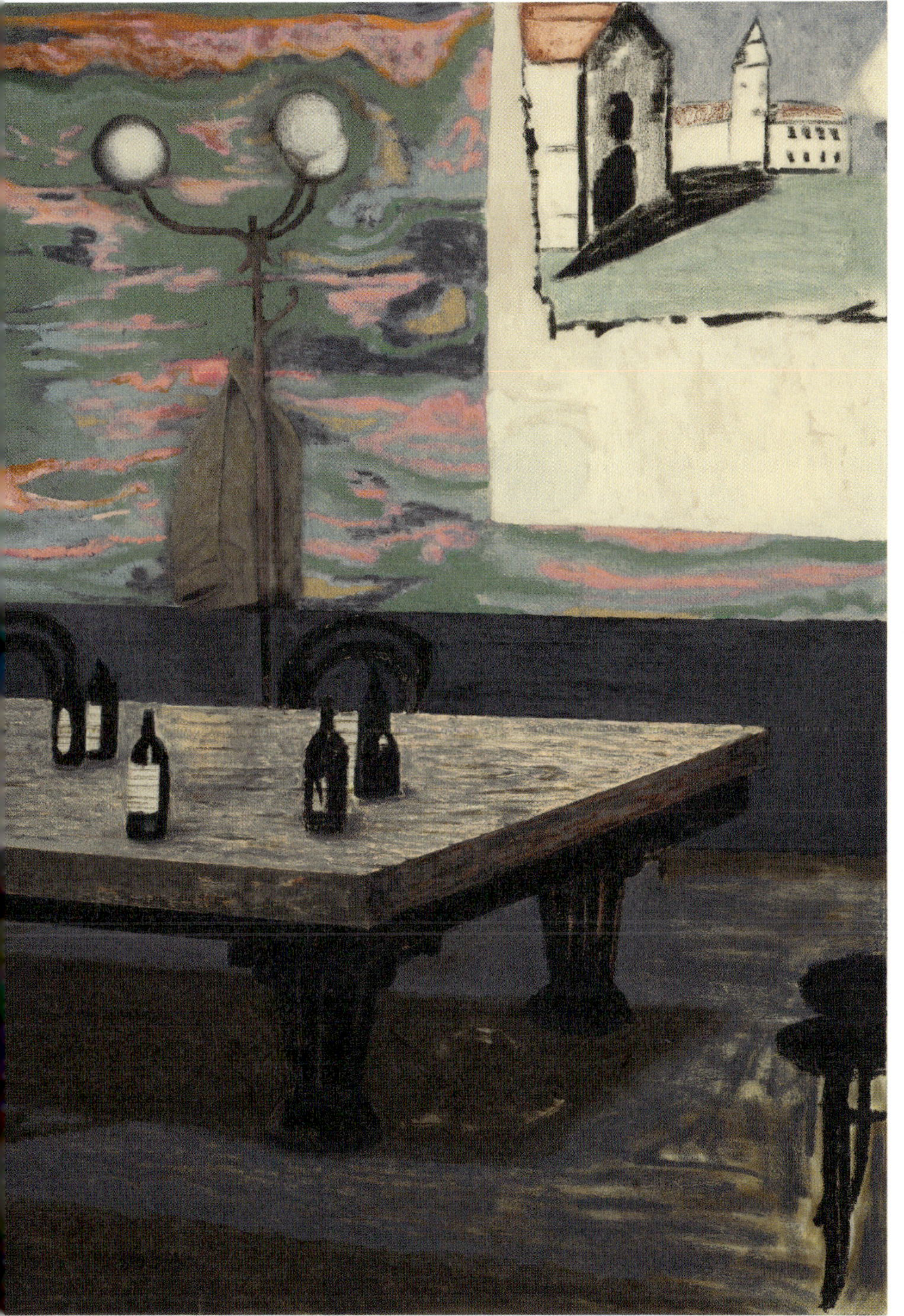

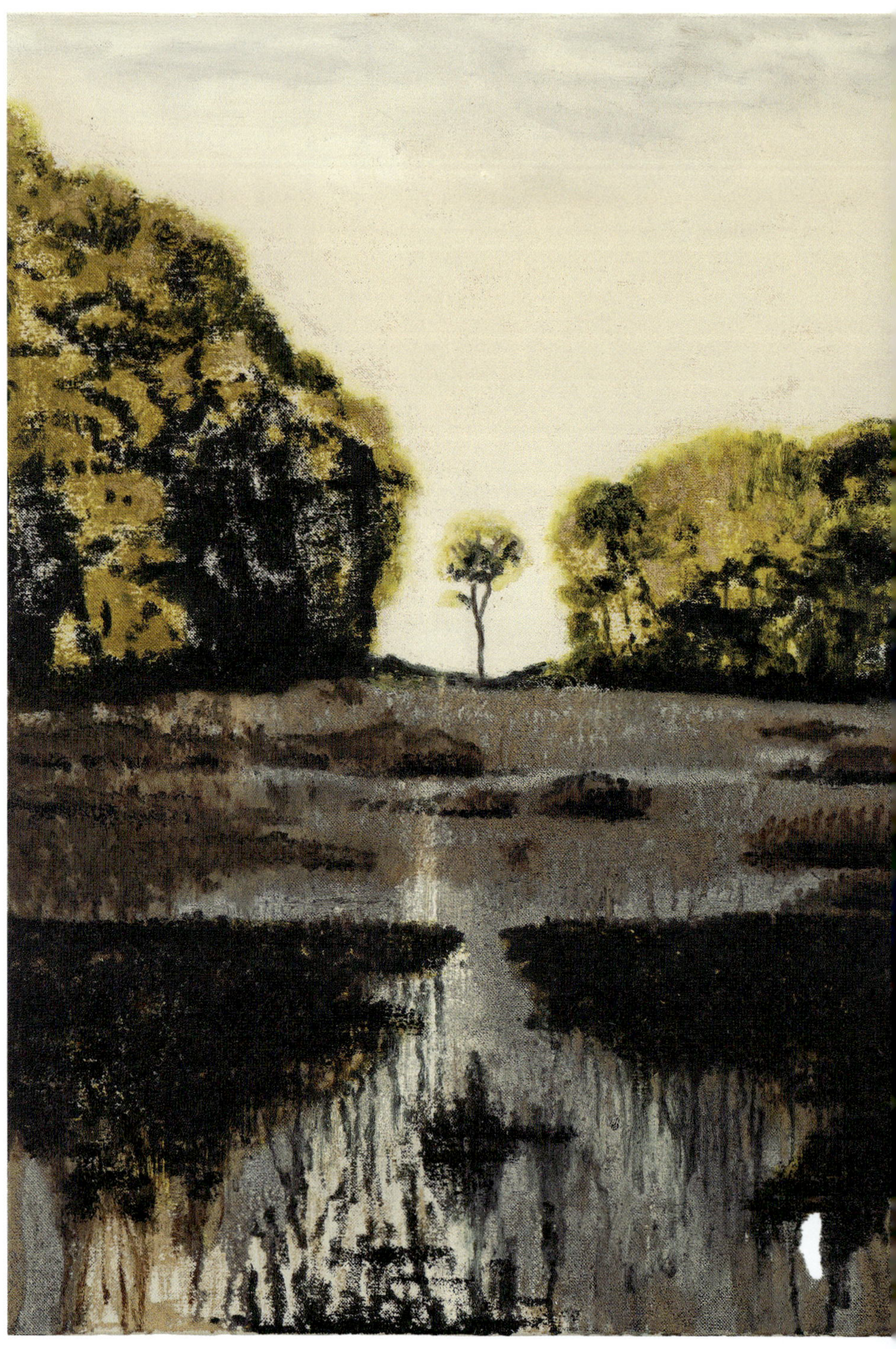

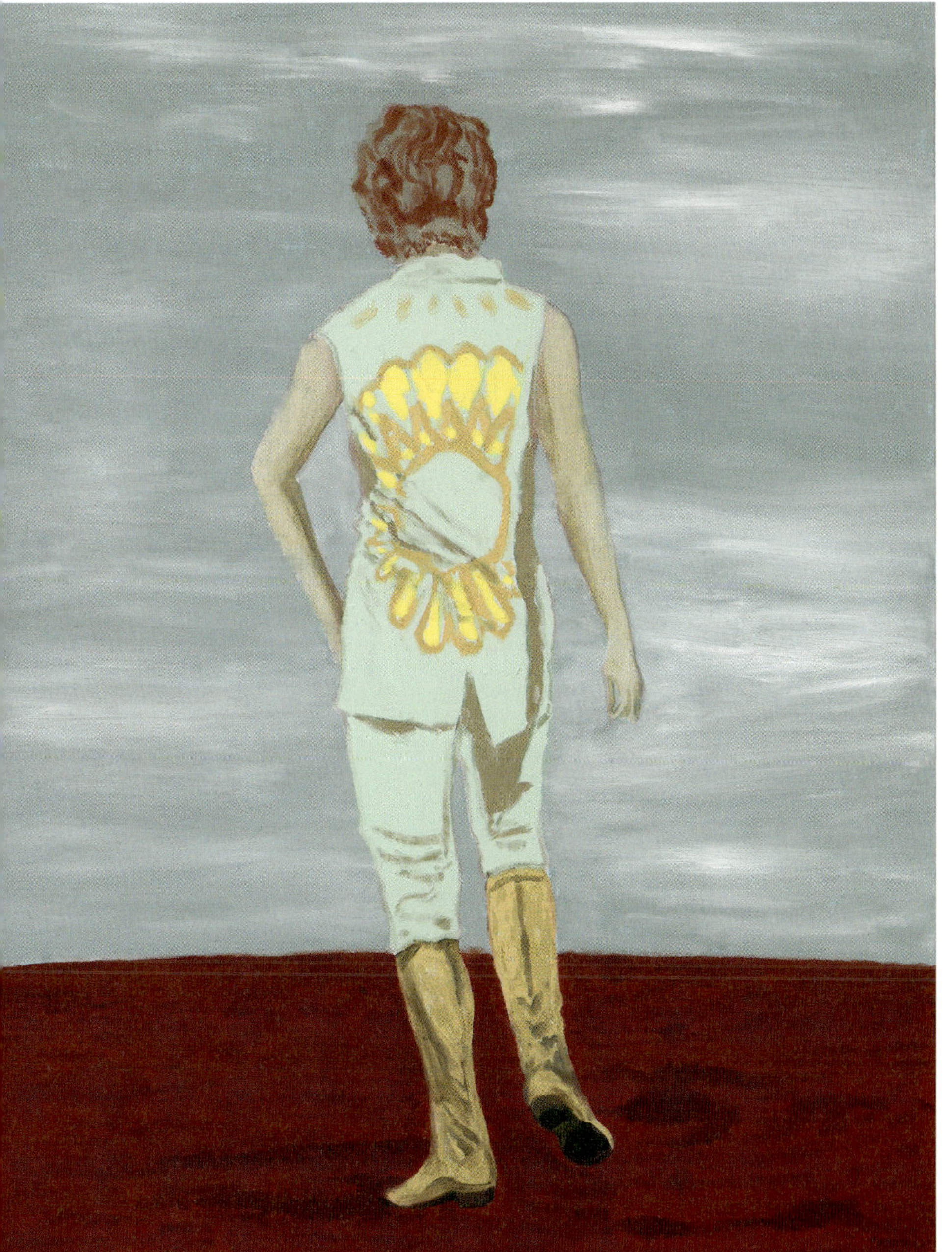

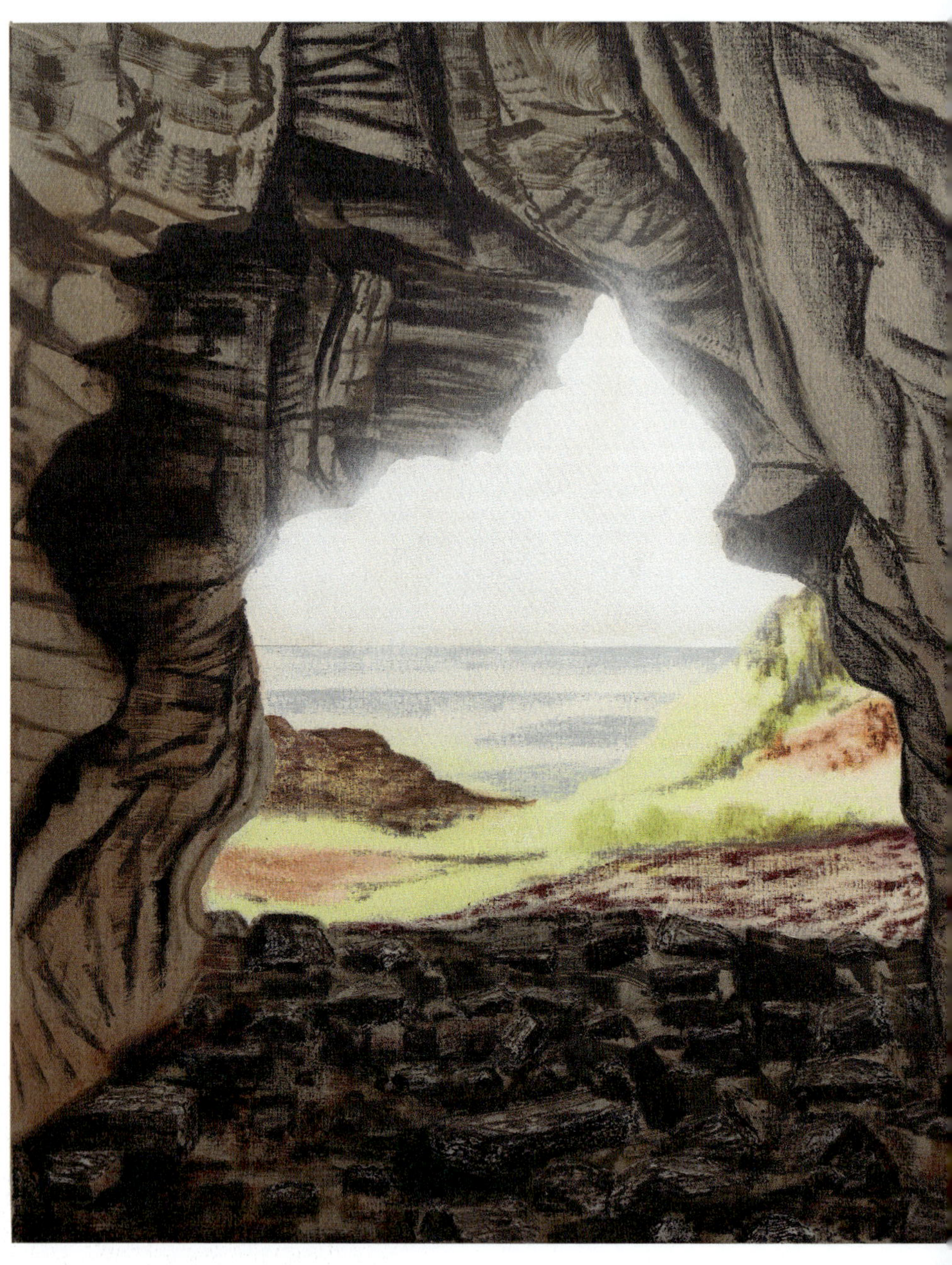

All artwork by Mamma Andersson, courtesy of the artist and David Zwirner

1. *Lièvre Mort d'Ehrenstrahl*, 2023
Oil on canvas
© 2026 Mamma Andersson/DACS, London/Bildupphovsrätt, Sweden
Photo by Per-Erik Adamsson

2. *Wood Cut*, 2019
Oil and acrylic on canvas
© 2026 Mamma Andersson/DACS, London/Bildupphovsrätt, Sweden
Photo by Per-Erik Adamsson

3. *Dagen efter / The Day After*, 2020
Oil on canvas
© 2026 Mamma Andersson/DACS, London/Bildupphovsrätt, Sweden
Courtesy the artist, David Zwirner and Galeri Magnus Karlsson
Photo by Poul Buchard / Broendum & Co

4. *Last Waltz*, 2020
Oil and acrylic on canvas
© 2026 Mamma Andersson/DACS, London/Bildupphovsrätt, Sweden
Courtesy Kerry McFate

5. *Vespera*, 2023
Oil on canvas
© 2026 Mamma Andersson/DACS, London/Bildupphovsrätt, Sweden
Photo by Clare Dorn

6. *The Lost Paradise I*, 2020
Oil and acrylic on linen
© 2026 Mamma Andersson/DACS, London/Bildupphovsrätt, Sweden
Photo by Per-Erik Adamsson

7. *New Morning*, 2025
Oil on linen
© 2026 Mamma Andersson/DACS, London/Bildupphovsrätt, Sweden
Photo by Per-Erik Adamsson

Espen Stueland

Dummy Genealogy

Sierra Susie was the first
She was developed by the US Air Force in 1970
for use in testing to calculate how a body ejected from a fighter
plane
reacts to the abnormal acceleration
One of the researchers noticed that the pilots' accident rate was
higher
in their cars to and from the airport than in the air
and conjectured that the tests at the airbase
could be applied to the auto industry

A biomechanist painted a smile on Sierra Susie
then she was wished godspeed
Shards of her head poked through the windscreen, the rest ricocheted
back
into the seat while glass splinters whirled towards the concrete wall
in front of the car in slow motion Next to go was a dead pig
The fibres in pork and human flesh are sufficiently similar
that tests performed on pigs are valid also for humans
notwithstanding their distinct anatomies
The pork ribs were crushed against the steering wheel
The orthopaedist explained: It takes quite a bit of force
to break a bone wrapped in tendons and flesh. Try it yourself (with
a pig)
In either case the neck is the weak point
and snaps right off without a head restraint

After these pathbreaking trials the dummy industry flourished
Dummies were no longer the exclusive domain of the military
    industry
photos of them increasingly appeared in the tabloid press
and in time they made their appearance in music videos
as symbols of the frailty of the human body
with film icons' tragic death by car fresh in memory
Later airbags were invented
which wrapped around the faces of babies, suffocating them
A forensic medical expert in Heidelberg
– referred to by *Die Zeit* only as Professor Horror – determined that
pigs could be substituted
very successfully by dead children in further trials
Public opinion was whipped up in an instant
and the trials were aborted

Susie has a jacket pocket weighed down by tiny bits of glass
from a smashed windscreen in the street, scooped up in her hand
after a few turns around the block she stops
pulls out the lining of her jacket pocket and tosses the bits of glass
    into the air
They rain down over her   The meaning of life
is to be abandoned
What could upend that

Translated from the Norwegian by Ingvild Burkey

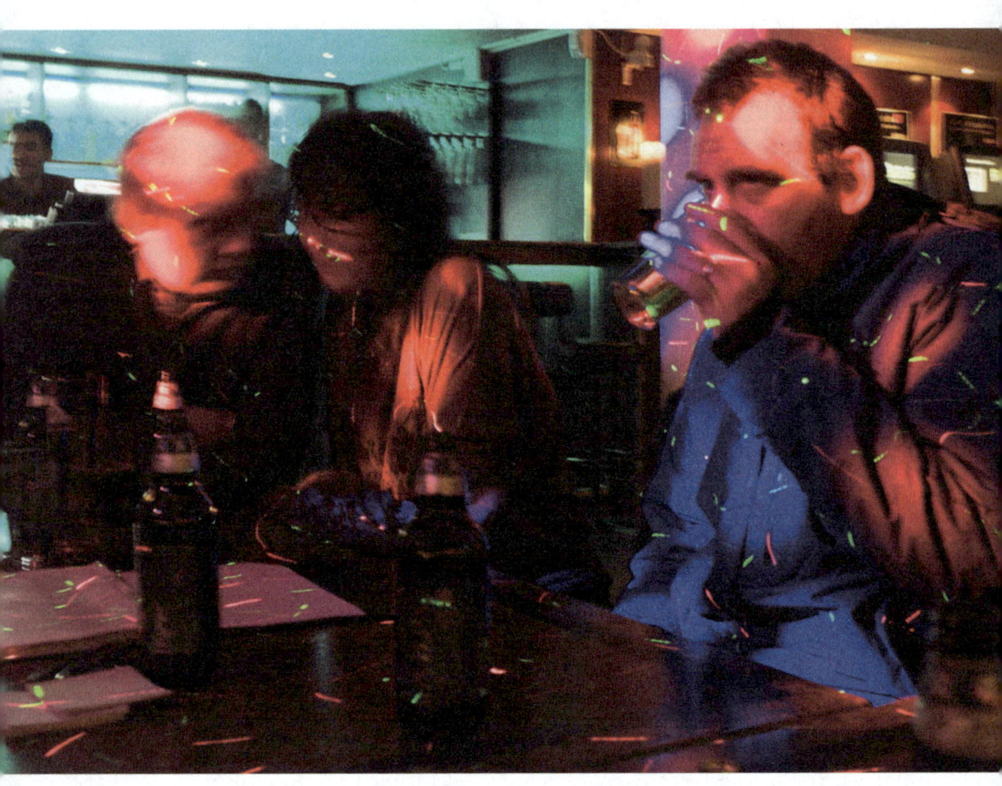

THE GOOD PERSON OF SANDVIKA

Vigdis Hjorth

TRANSLATED FROM THE NORWEGIAN
BY CHARLOTTE BARSLUND

Some years ago I was a frequent visitor to a brown pub in Sandvika, it lasted a couple of years. To start with I went there because it was near the station. When I arrived on the train from Oslo and had a long wait for my bus, it was tempting to go inside, especially in the autumn and winter, when it was blustery or there was rain or snow in the air. Eventually, I started going there in the spring and summer as well, it became a habit, the pub felt like home. Today I know it went deeper than that. An intense love affair had ended and my children had flown the nest, my house was empty and cold, and besides, it was November, the hard month.

I was very productive at the pub, working to the hum of other people's voices. More and more I ended up not catching the bus home I had aimed for, but a later one, quite often the last one which left just after eleven at night. I didn't talk to anyone at the pub, but in time I started greeting a few of those who came there as often as I did, we became nodding acquaintances, as it were. They left me alone, we left each other alone, most sat on their own staring pensively into the glass in front of them. Some were obviously couples, they didn't say very much either, but they would arrive and leave together, at times they would fetch some of the newspapers lying on the counter and flick through them for a while. In a corner at the back an old TV was mounted on the wall, on Sundays guests would sometimes sit down in front of it to watch the football or the ice hockey. We provided each other with a kind of companionship would be my guess, as it would have been cheaper for all of us to have stayed at home. I don't suppose most of the people there had very much money, they certainly didn't look as if they did, going by their clothes and shoes, their hair, the fraying wallets they would open to pay for something, the way they counted out banknotes, coins. A very different clientele would turn up at the weekends, people having a drink while they waited for the train to Oslo to go to the theatre or to a party; later on, patrons would emerge from the cinema or the local arts centre and pop in for a drink to discuss the experience while they waited for their train or bus. And yet another clientele, different from that of the dark, hard months, would come in the spring and summer because the pub would then offer an outdoor service, tables and chairs were set out on the decking by the entrance which got the sun from early morning to late evening. And during these bright, crowded summer months, they, we, the regulars, would look forward to autumn.

Whenever I was writing that winter, whenever I took a break and looked up from my laptop, I would study a slightly plump, possibly naive woman in the corner of the pub, who was most definitely on benefits. One afternoon she came over to ask if she could say hello to my dog, I nodded, she greeted the dog and from then on she would come over to say hello to it whenever we were there together, her name was Ada.

I learned that she bought a lottery ticket, almost furtively, every Saturday. One Saturday she won, almost furtively, except I noticed. I realised she had won, she realised I was aware of it, and she confided in me. I was lost for words. Should I – or should I not – give into the temptation, this irresistible temptation to warn her against acting on her altruistic impulse and give away her winnings to the deserving as well as the undeserving poor in the pub?

I watched Ada even more intensely than before, but I was also more scared of being found out, she had to be wary of me now as I was the only one who knew what I knew. She didn't drink more than usual, but not less either, would be my guess, she drank in the same slow tempo as before, but why had she played the lottery every Saturday if winning didn't change anything? Did she not have any plans for this what if?

Perhaps her winnings represented insurance against all kinds of what ifs that had always worried her. What if the dishwasher breaks down, what if my shoes fall apart, what if the rent goes up, what if bus tickets become more expensive, what if everything does, what if she got ill, what if she lost a tooth. So she must be less worried now than she was before or so it seemed to me and that was good for her and somehow also for me. I wondered if she would keep playing the lottery and she did. The first Saturday after that Saturday she played it again and in the exact same way, it would appear, but then again I had no idea what was going on inside her mind. If she felt more hopeful now because she had realised that winning was indeed possible, not just in theory, or less hopeful because she was already rich or because statistically it was rare for people to win twice in a row. Or she continued because the routine was reassuringly familiar like routines are, like my walks with the dog to the pub. Soon, however, I sort of forgot about it, time passed and I told myself that the money must have reached her bank account and was safe there. There was no rush, on the contrary, her best option was to keep the money in the bank. I had evidently believed that people played the lottery to get something specific, a car, a boat, that it was purely the hope of finally being able to afford a car or a boat that made grown men and women take part in such silly things and pay to do so, even risking a TV appearance and having to talk to one of those irritating lottery-show hosts with their fake excitement and go along with their false bonhomie as if they cared. Once in Accra, Ghana, I had seen queues several hundred metres long of clearly impoverished people outside the tiny state-run lottery sales points and thought that it was a cheap way for the authorities to give people hope so that rather than organise themselves, take on the exhausting and risky task of bringing about political reform, they put their faith in a winning ticket. Did that explain why they didn't join forces – because they were too busy sitting on their own, their eyes switching between their lottery tickets and the state-run TV channel?

Ada had not wanted anything specific, it would appear, just a break from the constant uncertainty which all the what ifs induced, but I couldn't know that, I was just speculating about that as well because for all I knew she might have bought a boat and a car, but I knew she hadn't done so. I couldn't know, true, but I was sure. I am guessing her relationship with money had the same unhurried quality that characterised all of her, her walk, her speech, her drinking, a calm which my dog liked and which I lacked.

I continued watching her until the last Saturday in September when I knew the benefit payments had been paid out. The trees were blazing red and orange and rosehip blushed in the verges of Brattheiveien, the benefit payments were here and the pub was packed, the outdoor tables were still there and the sun was high in the sky so people who arrived early could find a spot where the sun's rays could reach them and would keep reaching them for some time. I was one of the lucky or clever ones who got there early to secure such a spot where I knew from experience the sun would warm me the longest, it was close to the neighbouring building which would soon be demolished, the whole neighbourhood would be demolished to make way for something which, as of today, 10 July 2025, has yet to be finished. Apartment blocks, it seems, going by the pictures on the fences surrounding the enormous construction site. But back then, on the last Saturday in September, there was a kind of square in front of the pub's decking. My dog settled down in the shade under the table and I was looking forward to a cold, foaming beer after my long walk in the late-summer heat, I went inside and there she was at her usual table, she never ventured outside under the open sky, we nodded and smiled, I got my beer and went back outside. I was drinking and working when Hiccup-Per stumbled in, I hadn't seen him for a while. He didn't see me, but staggered through the door and Janus, the barman, looked worried, I could see, I was sitting so that I could see inside when I leaned forwards. Janus weighed up the pros and cons and landed on the pros, fortunately, I was pleased about that, as was Ada, I could see, we identified strongly with the very thirsty ones. Hiccup-Per was wretched, beyond wretched, it was plain for all to see judging by his gait and his face, his sagging doggy eyes, but once he had had a drink, he would tell all and I would go inside before that. He was standing holding a glass in his trembling right hand looking about, eyes swimming, but all the tables were taken so he sat down by Ada's table, right opposite her. I suppose he thought he knew her in his own way, like we knew each other, we who came here, in our very own way.

If he started telling his story now, I wouldn't be able to hear him, but there were no seats nearby and in any case I would hear about it later so I carried on with my reading, I don't know what it was now, but whatever I was reading calmed me down.

An hour later the sun began to set and people disappeared from the decking, some running to catch their train. Through the window I could see that my usual table was now free, I untied my dog and went inside, my dog dragged me towards Ada who had a treat for it in her pocket as always. Aren't you lucky, I said, what a lucky dog, I said, isn't Ada nice, I said, and Hiccup-Per nodded and took a deep breath, looked at me with eyes as red as the filthy, stained silk neckerchief around his neck, Ada is an angel, he hiccupped and he said it again, an angel in my hour of need, imagine, he said and he looked on the verge of tears, but then Ada shook her head, no, no, I was missing something.

I tied the dog to the table, took out my laptop and carried on working. She left, I saw, without looking at me, no nodding or smiling and that puzzled me, Hiccup-Per started to look around, then he got up and walked on unsteady legs in my direction, he sat down opposite me and whispered in a loud voice that he wasn't able to buy cognac from Janus, could I get him a dram? He had had one for his right leg, but he needed one for his left to avoid imbalance. I went up to the bar and asked Janus for a Larsen cognac, he knew who it was really for, but it was better this way as it meant he wasn't technically breaking the law. When his left leg had had its cognac, Hiccup-Per told me an exceedingly rambling and incoherent story about how the angel Ada had saved him, it went roughly like this: since his wife throwing him out and divorcing him and him losing his job, he had lived in a damp basement room belonging to a friend, but it was tough for his friend and his family with two children to have another person sharing their bathroom and their fridge, and today they had told him he had to move out. And he realised he had to, but where would he go? He already had debts he couldn't pay, so renting a place was out of the question and for that reason he had decided to drink away the last of his money to summon up the courage to throw himself in the River Sandvikselva at its deepest point, he knew where that was. He had bought beer from the supermarket and drunk it in the basement of a multi-storey car park, but by the time he had finished his beer, the supermarket had closed and so he had come here instead and yes, he had to admit that he was now somewhat the worse for wear, he was swaying dangerously on the chair. He had come here and bumped into Ada and told her all his troubles and mourned his fate and then she had offered to help him, she said she had some money he could have. He had refused to believe her, where would she get money from, but she had assured him that she had more than enough so he was not to worry and please don't think about throwing yourself in the river, they would talk more tomorrow. Again he started crying and sobbing that she was an angel, a chubby cherub with a trombone, he hadn't thought they existed, but now he knew that angels were real. I could feel myself grow pale, how the blood ran from my head to my feet so they refused to move. I untied the dog from the table with arms that were still working and hobbled off without saying a word and anyway he wouldn't remember this tomorrow, that was the great thing about going to the pub, the next morning few people would be able to remember what had happened the day before.

Ada had not been drunk, she did not get drunk, I had never seen her intoxicated or overexcited, she was quiet in her frugal ways so it wasn't the drink talking, she must be serious, but this madness was intolerable. Every Saturday she had sat in front of that television, finally she had won and now she would risk it all to help a casual acquaintance, a hopeless drunk. Something in me wanted to call her, it was a matter of urgency, the money was in her account and newspapers and television channels were full of appeals to her irrepressible benevolence, but I didn't have her number and I couldn't find it listed online and I couldn't take a taxi up there late on a Saturday night because that would be intrusive. I imagined myself ringing her doorbell, her asking who it was and me saying it was me and her knowing what I was going to say when she didn't want to hear it, that was what I had sensed, she didn't want my advice and why was I even getting involved, why did I care?

Sunday morning I got in my car and went up to Brattheiveien. As I approached the supermarket, I slowed down and drove the last stretch at twenty kilometres per hour while the dog got up in its cage in the back. The horses stood silent under the sky, their eyes and muzzles down as if they had never experienced the anxiety that plagued me, but perhaps that was because they were tame? But I, too, was tame! I was just another docile creature, wasn't I, because what exactly would I say if she turned up? Don't be so good? ■

Audun Mortensen

sunset

i’m too childish
to write a poem titled
self-portrait at forty
too childish
to pay attention to age
to contemplate ageing
to rage against
the attention economy
to contemplate the beauty
of the sunset
to be afraid of dying

news

i'm too childish
to not read
the local newspaper
to not take a close look
at the photos
of the grown-ups
who enjoyed themselves
out on the town
i'm too childish
to enjoy myself
out on the town
i'm too childish
to not envy the grown-ups
who enjoyed themselves
i'm too childish
to not write a poem
about my local newspaper
and its photos
of local grown-ups
enjoying themselves
out on the town

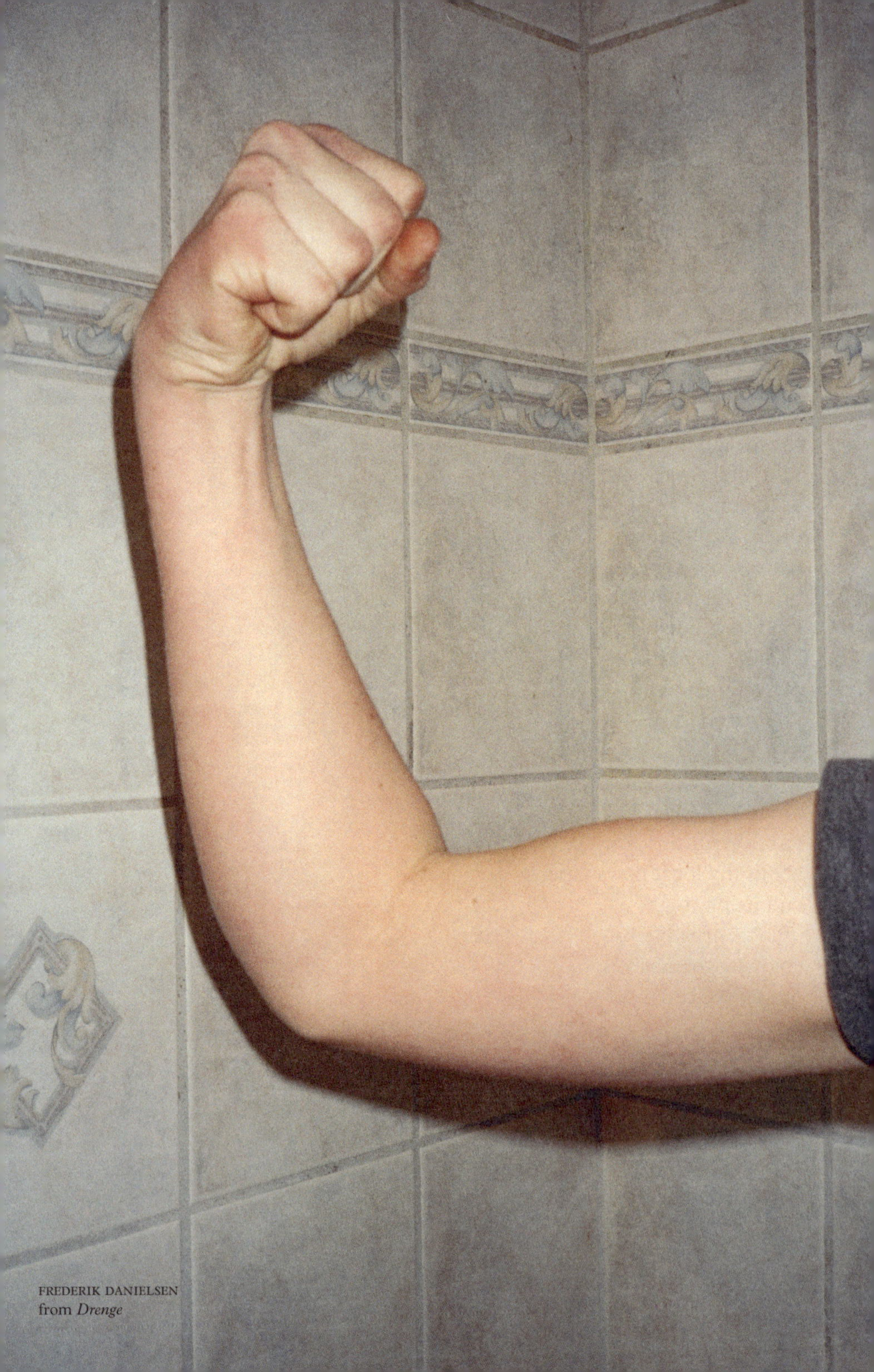

FREDERIK DANIELSEN
from *Drenge*

FURTHERMORE, I CONSIDER THAT CARTHAGE MUST BE DESTROYED

Kyrre Andreassen

TRANSLATED FROM THE NORWEGIAN BY LUCY MOFFATT

I had to give up working as an electrician after slipping a few discs. When years of tightening screws in awkward positions leaves you wearing a corset to work – an actual *corset*, like it's the Middle Ages – you can only take it for so long. I was out of a job for more than a year. That's unlikely to put you in the best of moods. But then I got a job, as a teacher of all things – way outside my comfort zone in other words. I told the people in charge, I said I was no professor, but they were in no position to be picky, they desperately needed people to teach adult foreigners Norwegian. The chap at social security and the school managers said my experience was valuable, more valuable than all the education in the world, they reckoned.

Was I motivated? Well, it kept me going at any rate, it kept me going for a while. But of course if you spend one day drilling a group of foreigners on labour law and the next putting out feelers for off-book workers to those same foreigners, well, it doesn't look so good. But I wasn't really putting out feelers. I can see it might have seemed that way to outsiders, but I wasn't putting out feelers. Fact is, I felt sorry for Magomed, and when he heard my request, when I asked if he'd be willing to put up a pergola for us, for Marianne and me – well, good Lord, he just lit up. It wasn't about exploitation, it was about stimulation. Magomed was a furniture maker from Chechnya and I'd seen some of his work – ornamentation and craftsmanship that went back almost to the days of the Byzantine Empire – and here all he was graciously permitted to do was work a couple of evenings a week at a lumber company's warehouse. Of course he lit up. It was about giving people a chance to grow and Magomed, a man who never said a word in class, became almost chatty. Not problem, he said. Not problem, teacher. And maybe he went round and blabbed, maybe that's how it came out – he blabbed in the corridors because he was excited. In any case, someone got wind of it and that person snitched higher up in the system. And then how it rained down, my God – my God, how the abuse rained down from senior management, and those so-called colleagues of mine, priggish sheep that they were. They all thought Krister Larsen had behaved quite disgracefully.

Me, who wasn't even interested in the pergola. Couldn't give a damn. It was Marianne, she thought it'd look elegant to have a pergola in the garden. The idea barged its way out after a trip to Rome, a long weekend at Easter, when we happened to eat at a restaurant down there called La Pergola. That's where she got the idea. I'd barely managed to lug our suitcases into the house before she was in full swing outside, inspecting the lawn. She stood there, waving her arms about and giving directions. The snow hadn't even melted yet.

Can you picture it? said Marianne. But just because you've sat on a pavement in Rome with all kinds of hanging plants dangling about your ears, gorging yourself on fine food and wine with the whole of antiquity shoved up in your face, that doesn't mean you're necessarily going to get the same feeling of opulence from throwing up a few planks between your house and your garage. I said it was naive. A bit naive, I toned myself down, and then I said it was also a question of finances. I mentioned credit, how much we'd splashed out on the flight, and the hotel, and presents for Andreas – all kinds of things on the card. And who was it who'd bought all those shoes and clothes? The leather jacket for example. There she stood on the snowdrift in a shiny new leather jacket, dark green – cost over three thousand – so dark it was almost black, and it stopped at a strategic point, right above you know where, and she'd poured herself into some jeans and high heels. There were still a few unresolved tensions left over from the holiday – four child-free days – tensions of the best possible kind, granted.

When you've been married more than fifteen years, it'd be a miracle if there wasn't a bit of wear and tear, and once a bit of wear and tear sets in, well, that's when you start longing for new perspectives. That's why we took the trip to Rome, to look for new perspectives. We were as happy as clams in Rome. Symbiotic, as they say. Even the Pope would've been impressed if he could've seen our acrobatics down there. We'd been living in a bubble in Rome, and when Marianne went trotting around in the snow spouting her fantasy about building a pergola, she was still in that bubble. And I didn't mean to be negative. When I dropped those hints about credit it wasn't negativity, it was reality, and Marianne understood that. She trotted across the lawn, stood in front of me and put her hands on my cheeks. She bit my lip. It was those tensions. Bloody killjoy, she said, and pressed her hands together, as if she was trying to squeeze the air out of a beach ball, but it wasn't a beach ball, it was my head, my cheeks, but it didn't hurt.

What's that thing people say? Romance blossoms in the Eternal City. Talk about starry-eyed – the way we wandered around those cobbled streets going on about the marvellous atmosphere, because there was the Colosseum and there was the Pantheon and marble sculptures all over the place. The Sistine and Michelangelo and God and the finger. Arm in arm along the cobblestones. I reckon the pair of us lost it a bit. I talked about things like the whisper of history, and wasn't it wonderful to be on holiday, to be in new surroundings, because it gave you new perspectives – but perspectives, who gets new perspectives from four days in Rome? There's any number of ways to fool yourself. And as for all that marvellous atmosphere – well, we could've left the atmosphere altogether, flown to the moon even, but we'd still have had to come back down to Earth sooner or later and park our spaceship.

The bubble soon bursts. There's this thing called reality, and trivialities, all those trivialities. We got called into a meeting at Andreas's school. His form teacher was the one that called, only days after our minibreak in Rome. A meeting to agree on the rules for the road that lay ahead. Those were the words the form teacher used on the phone, although it turned out to be not so much agreeing as dictating because when we arrived, Marianne and Andreas and I, when we innocently traipsed into the classroom, we found that the form teacher had forged an alliance with the head of department, and the headmaster, and even a pregnant school nurse, all of them with ring binders, and then there was little doubt about who was going to set the rules for the road that lay ahead.

Andreas had, regrettably, slapped one of his classmates. A boy called Chrisander, of all things. As the form teacher spoke about the incident, the others sat there – the headmaster and his underlings – they sat and listened with solemn faces. You'd have thought this Chrisander was lying in a coma in intensive care, but he wasn't, although he *had* had a nosebleed, which was apparently just as bad.

I'd always found the form teacher a likeable bloke. He's a jolly ginger chubster who usually carries the banner for the marching band on Constitution Day, the one who keeps time and blows the whistle. A likeable bloke, at any rate. When he was done with his little story, the head of department took over and talked about zero tolerance of violence. An energetic type, the head of department, he talked a lot and quickly. A blond moustache, a wispy blond beard that only grew on his chin so it looked like somebody had grated cheese on it. His right hand constantly crept up his face to check if his hair was in place, stroking and smoothing the moustache, stroking and smoothing the beard, and he talked and talked, he talked about Andreas as if Andreas wasn't there: he has to understand that this kind of behaviour is not acceptable. But then as he spoke he stared at Andreas – all four of them did, with their solemn faces.

Andreas sat there biting his nails, a habit of his. They call it making music, don't they? It looks like he's playing some instrument when he bites them; he vanishes out of this world. Lord knows I did my best to make eye contact with him but it was awkward because he was sitting on the other side of Marianne; we were all sitting in a row, tic-tac-toe in front of the tribunal. Marianne just looked at the four of them, chewing the inside of her cheek and scratching behind her ear because anything to do with school makes her anxious. Just the smell, she says, the empty milk cartons. Besides, the way they'd mobilised and were staring at Andreas was enough to make anyone anxious, drumming their fingers on their ring binders – and what kind of information was there in the binders anyway? Were they synchronised by the colour of the dividers? It didn't feel like we had much to bring to the table. They sat there with the upper hand, and as for Andreas, who would be his advocate?

I tried a spot of diplomacy. I said I thought it was great that they were taking things in hand, but I'm a teacher myself, I said, and it isn't exactly unusual for eleven-year-old boys to have conflicts. But there are conflicts and there are conflicts, I was told. It was the head of department who said that, because the headmaster, the top dog, the headmaster just sat there looking as if he might up and retire any second. Must have been pushing seventy, in a brown wool blazer with even browner leather patches on the elbows. Liver spots on his forehead. Clearly only hauled in to demonstrate the gravity of the affair.

And the school nurse, she was making notes on a sheet of paper she'd laid on top of her ring binder. It was pretty mysterious, really. What kind of dissertation could she be working on? She was keeping an eye on Andreas. He sat there, twisting his head to get a better grip on the cuticles he was chewing. Marianne didn't notice a thing. The school nurse kept writing. A pregnant lady, ready to pop. She looked like a dairymaid – the way dairymaids looked in the olden days when they rode on pigs and churned the butter for their supper, fol-de-diddle-day, with rosy cheeks and all. I thought I'd seen her somewhere before, but this wasn't the time to ponder where that might have been. The head of department was demanding our attention. Perhaps he thought it made him look imposing to thrust out his chin and fiddle with his wispy beard. When it escalates, he said, we cannot let it escalate. Then he said more about the nosebleed and the school's anti-bullying campaign, and mentioned 'zero tolerance' a dozen times.

The form teacher stepped in. He was the eyewitness and he'd never seen anything like it, he said. Violence was the only word for it. He said it was frightening and sad, and he was about to say more, but then he stopped suddenly mid-sentence and went quiet, shutting his eyes. Mid-sentence? Sheer play-acting. Fact is, he was sitting with his eyes closed to show that he was searching all the atrocities he could see in his mind's eye, looking for the right words. None of the others said a thing. And the seconds ticked by, and evening came and morning came – the sixth day, and the form teacher opened his eyes and said he had been shocked. By the brutality, he said. I don't wish to trivialise matters, but if what the form teacher claimed was true, if it *was* the case that Andreas had sat on top of Chrisander and slapped him about the chops, then of course that wasn't great, but it would amaze me if what he said was the truth and nothing but the truth, and really I thought the form teacher was laying it on a bit thick. What was his base of comparison? This ginger wimp didn't exactly exude life experience. It probably wouldn't take a lot to shock him. If it actually had been such a shocking experience, why hadn't he mentioned anything about it when he rang about the meeting? All he'd mentioned on the call was rules of the road because there'd been an incident. But how do you define an incident? I mean, he'd even said it was a *minor* incident. At any rate, he hadn't said anything about violence and brutality. He'd conducted the telephone conversation in a comradely, jovial tone, a tone that had now evaporated as he laid it on with a trowel and embellished and turned the whole thing into a tragedy.

It probably had something to do with the internal balance of power. The balance of power at the school. The headmaster might as well have retired already since nobody took any notice of him. The head of department was the *primus motor*, the driving force. And, as for the form teacher, talk about a toady. Every time the form teacher said anything, he'd peer over at the head of department, grovelling for confirmation that what he'd said was correct and intelligent and right on target – imagine being in such a subservient position. Andreas, said the form teacher, you remember those nice talks we had, don't you? But it didn't look like Andreas heard what the form teacher said. He just sat there chewing his nails. Lost to the world, doing those weird facial tics he gets when he's carrying on like that. Seeing them pained me to the very depths of my soul. The form teacher said, I was very disappointed. He said, Mum and Dad are probably disappointed too. Marianne nodded. She was disappointed of course. And he looked at me then, Andreas did. I registered it out of the corner of my eye, but instead of turning to him and meeting his gaze, sending him a smile maybe, instead of that I looked at the form teacher. Must have been hypnotism. God help me if I didn't nod at the form teacher, that merry drum major. I nodded, and he nodded back, so vigorously that the red hair danced on top of his head. I sided with the form teacher against my own son. Nodded and nodded. As if some great trophy awaited me for my efforts. It was hypnotism, pure and simple. I wasn't in the least bit disappointed about anything. But what with the form teacher and the department head, the way they whipped up the atmosphere and hypnotised each other, and hypnotised the rest of us there – how easy is it to speak out in a situation like that? They hypnotised us with their solemnity. I didn't reflect on it so much there and then, but that's what happened. If you didn't fully grasp the solemnity, you weren't a human being. That was the way it felt. You weren't a human being. But in my defence, as I sat there nodding like a sensible smart-arse, I did feel uneasy. ■

Ingela Strandberg

from *Ingenstans mitt segel* (2022)

1.

We invented you, say the barns

We are the seers of memory

You are matter
beckoned and lost
in fields of wild oats

Come in
and we'll make you believe
that there is still an evening some place
where cows slumber
and butterfly-orchids bloom to death

Stop a moment
in the troubled sleep of cows

Kiss their terror

Kiss the foam from their mouths

Remember it

Carry their wet foreheads
out through the fog
and forever

You are of them

Bend down

Sink down to the flowers

To the thin white lips

Kiss them

Get drunk
on the temptation of sticky lips

You are in the house of the dreamers

2.

The small station houses
clung to the railway bank

Wild strawberries and blue flowers grew between them

My father repaired the houses
I don't know why I wanted to go with him
Perhaps because then I saw who we were

 We lugged the briefcase of sandwiches
 and milk Sat on the toolbox to eat
 Came into being Streaming milk-like
 white and bloody from the cosmic udder

It was always summer

 Oh, warm softness

I spent hours in the waiting rooms
studying my birthmark
it looked like the constellation Little Fox

    But we should never have discovered the words
    But we should have trundled on like cattle
    But we should have slept by the precipices
    But we should have remained deaf

    to every greeting   To every minor key echo
    on the rails

Cosmos was an udder

We approached it like thirsty flies   Meandering

Tempted by white veins
and starry shining heads

3.

You could never have become anyone else, say the barns

You think you choose

But we own you

From liver to coat

4.

At Christmas parties I wandered out
alone to ice-cold bare verandas
and felt with my fingers the fabric
of the women's coats

Coarse wool smelling of barns sex
and scent

I tried on some of the coats but then
the women's souls stepped out of the linings
and tried to choke me

Through icy panes of glass
I admired instead
the stance of the planets

Certain of that
which cares for the dead
and the weak

from *När jag var snö* (2024)

5.

With the dead cat on the back seat
we drive through the deceitful light
of the land

The cherry trees are in their bridal dress

The maples are shameless with sugar

The cat, eyes wide open,
watches the death-meadow
clover

Nature has lifted her skirt

She's nothing but a whore

Offering passion and suffering

In an endless number of coffins hidden in other
coffins she collects us seduces us
with stars and power until we bend
to our knees in her unfathomable catacombs

We dig the grave together

The unspoken between us

deepens with the hole in the dirt

The cat cools in the grass

6.

I carried a child inside me

No larger than a Barbie doll
but already I loved it

I sat with my back
to the lighthouse
all the way out by the sea

Every time the light called out
it made its way into my body

As warmth
As hunger

We would be happy

I said to the child
that we would play

We would always just play

Always be free

Only let them call us back
late in the evenings

To food and the dark

Never have I been as happy
as when I was crossing the herring-run
road of light in the waters by Subbe lighthouse
led by the simmering
sea

Under me death above me the stars

Translated from the Swedish by Sigrid Rausing

ROSENGÅRD & MÖLLEVÅNGEN

Ikram Abdulkadir

Introduction by Granta

When Ikram Abdulkadir first began experimenting with a camera, she found herself mimicking other people's work – the overly tidy architecture and landscape photos that flood Instagram. Dissatisfied, she stopped shooting. During a trip a few years later to Nairobi – where she was born in 1995 – Abdulkadir began to record everything around her, especially relatives, some of whom up until that point had existed only in second-hand stories and photo albums. Since then, the self-taught artist has become an established portrait photographer, alongside documenting friends and family in the Rosengård neighbourhood of Malmö, where she grew up, and Möllevången, where she now lives. Located on the south-western tip of Sweden and directly connected to Copenhagen by the Øresund Bridge, it is one of Scandinavia's most culturally diverse municipalities. 'It's a beautiful working-class city,' Abdulkadir told *Granta*, 'with a blend of people from so many places.'

Abdulkadir carries a point-and-shoot everywhere she goes. Casually, she captures Malmö on the move: mothers gather in the park for the end of Ramadan; children play in the snow; we join crowds at protests, gigs, in hazy clubs; traverse the city on foot and busy buses. There is a candour and ease to these quotidian scenes – the viewer is often met with the backs of subjects – balanced with careful framing. 'It's a way of seeing the small things,' Abdulkadir says of her art, 'instead of rushing to your destination.' ■

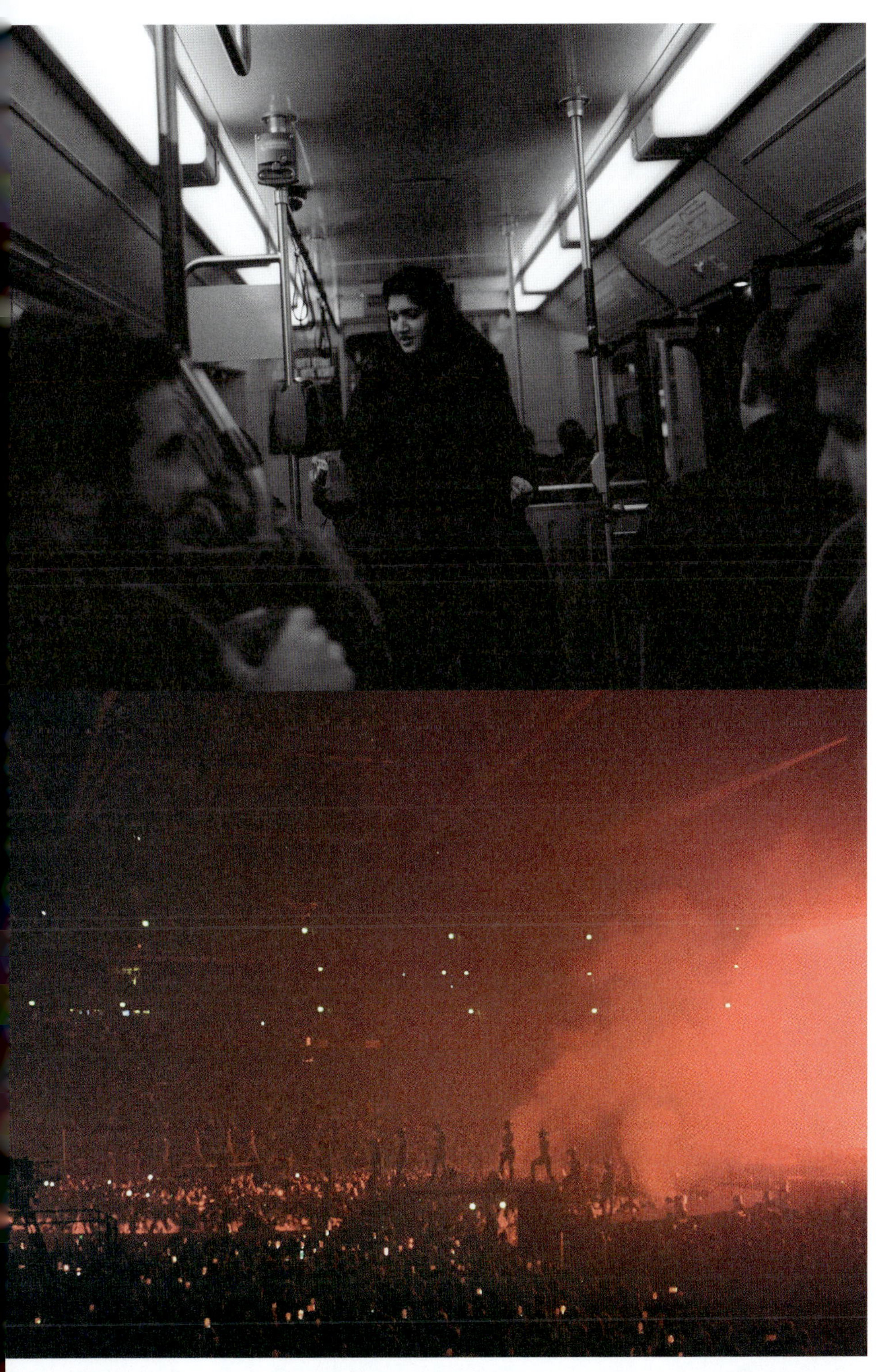

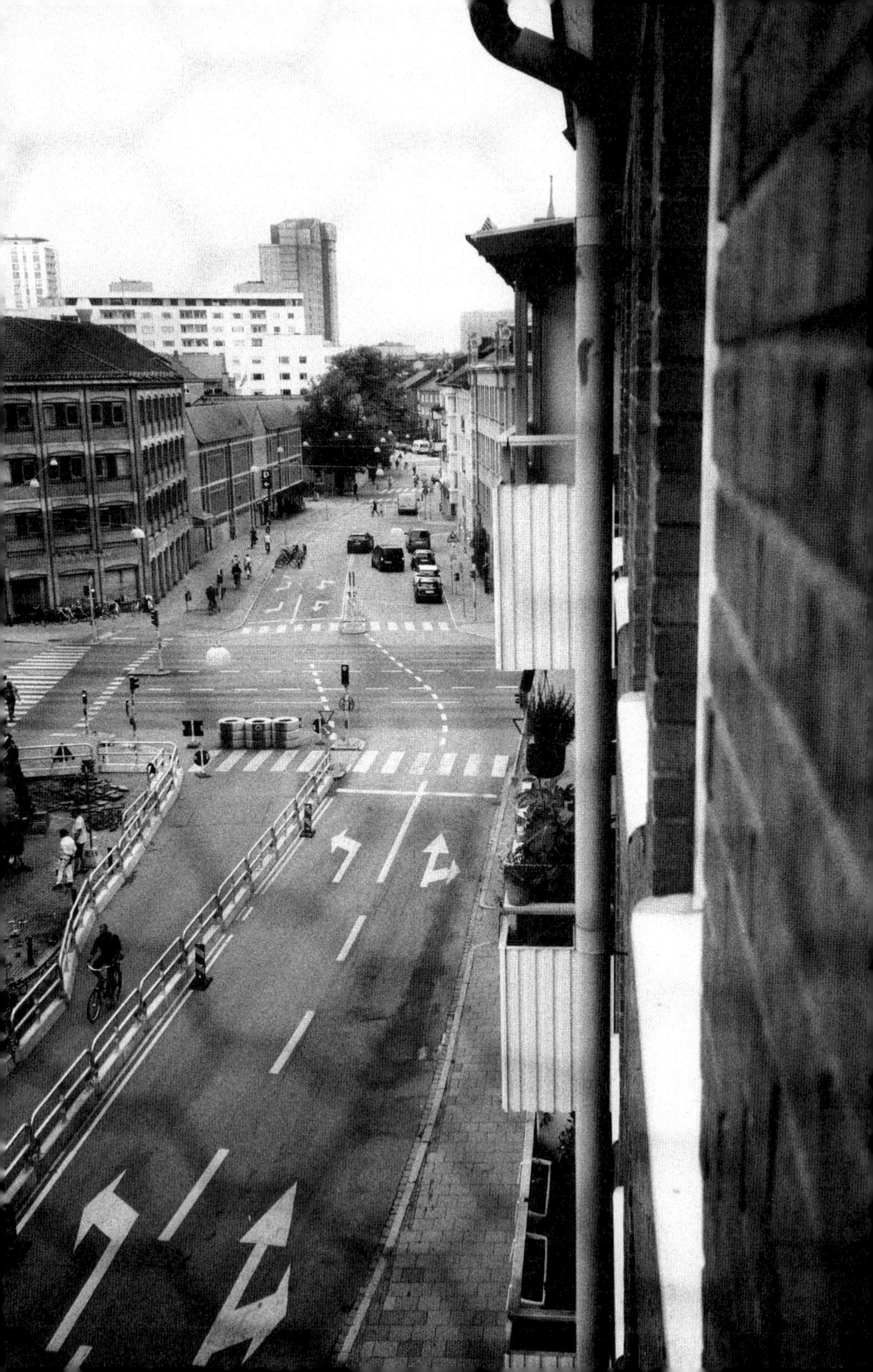

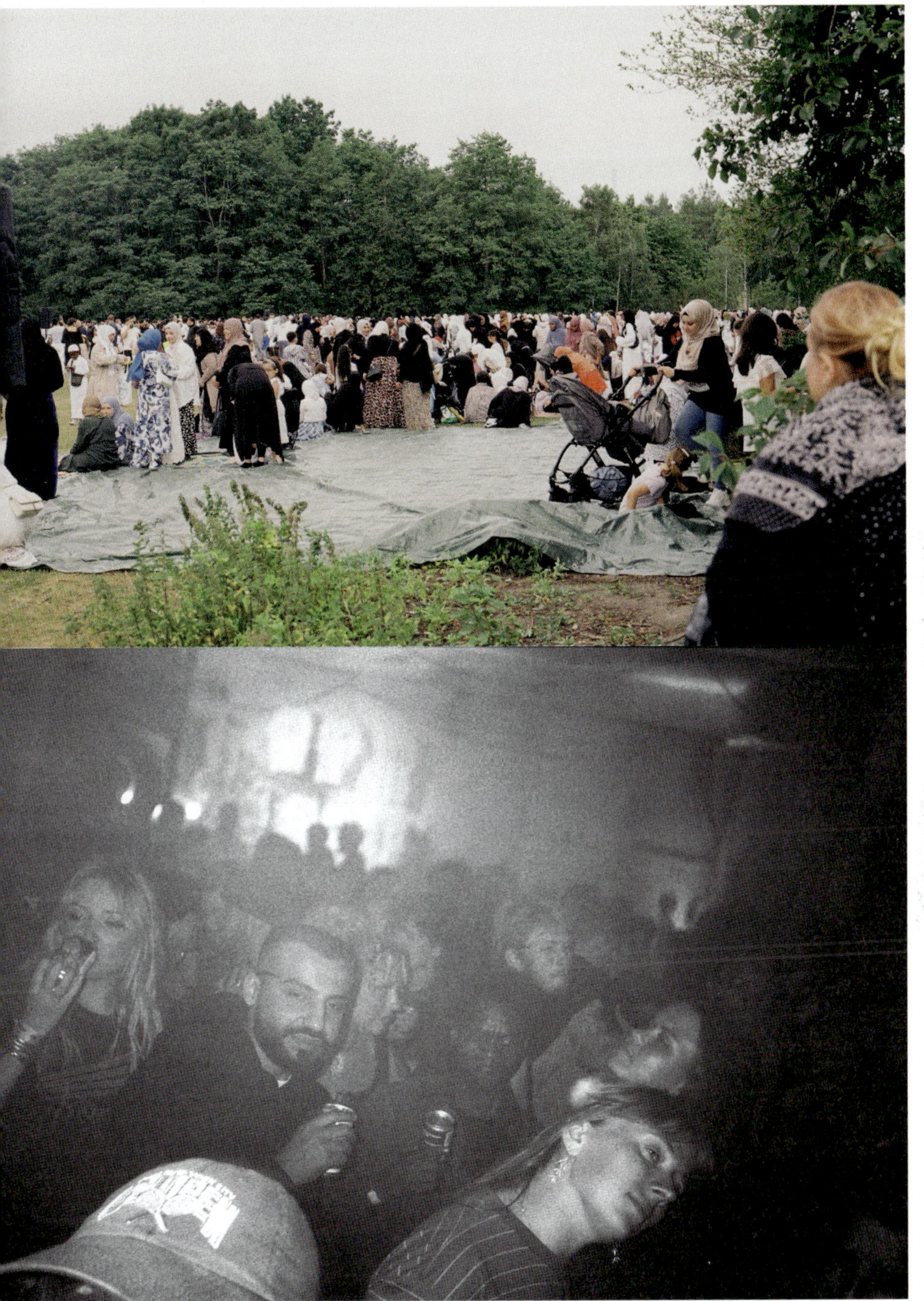

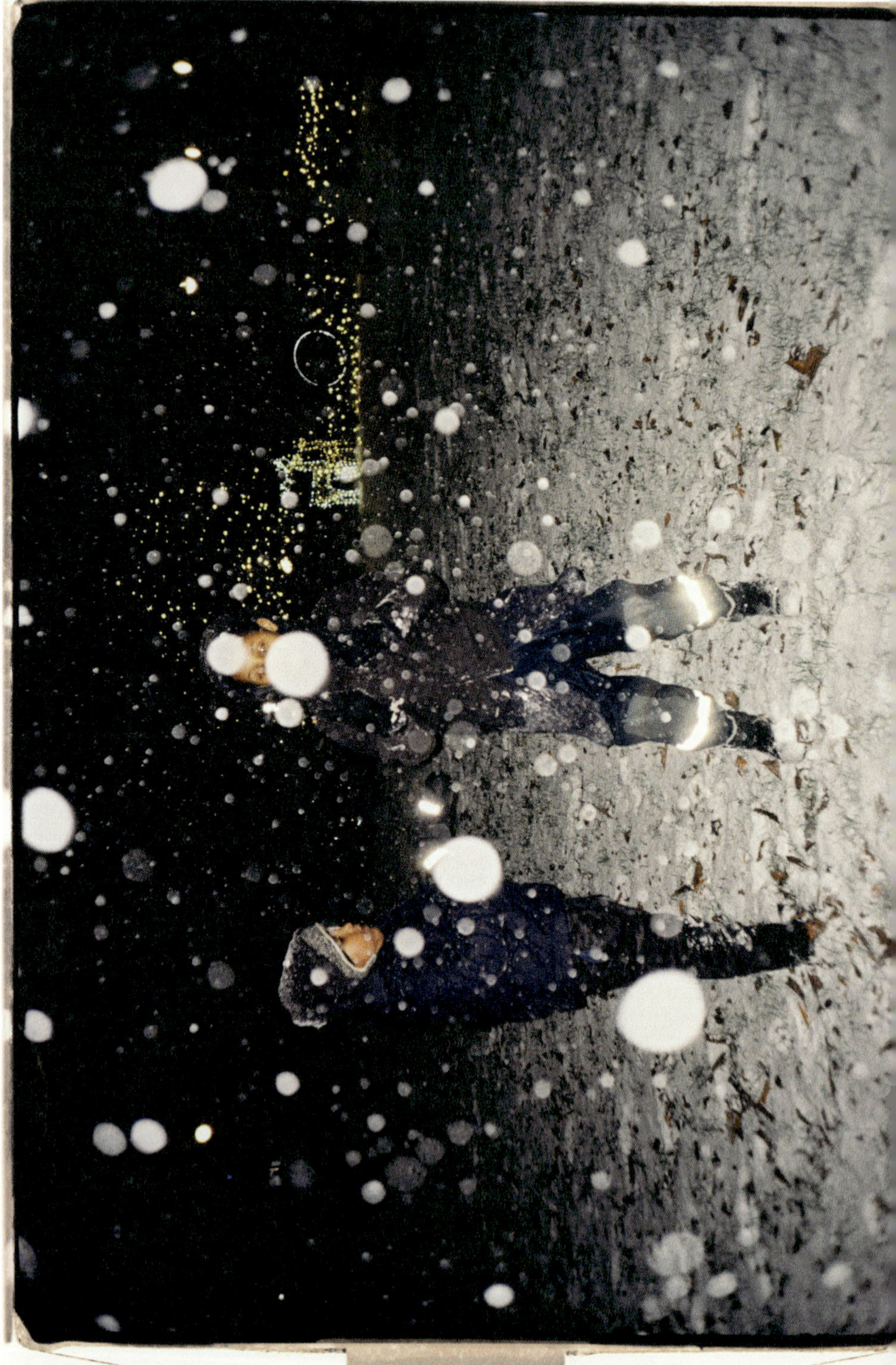

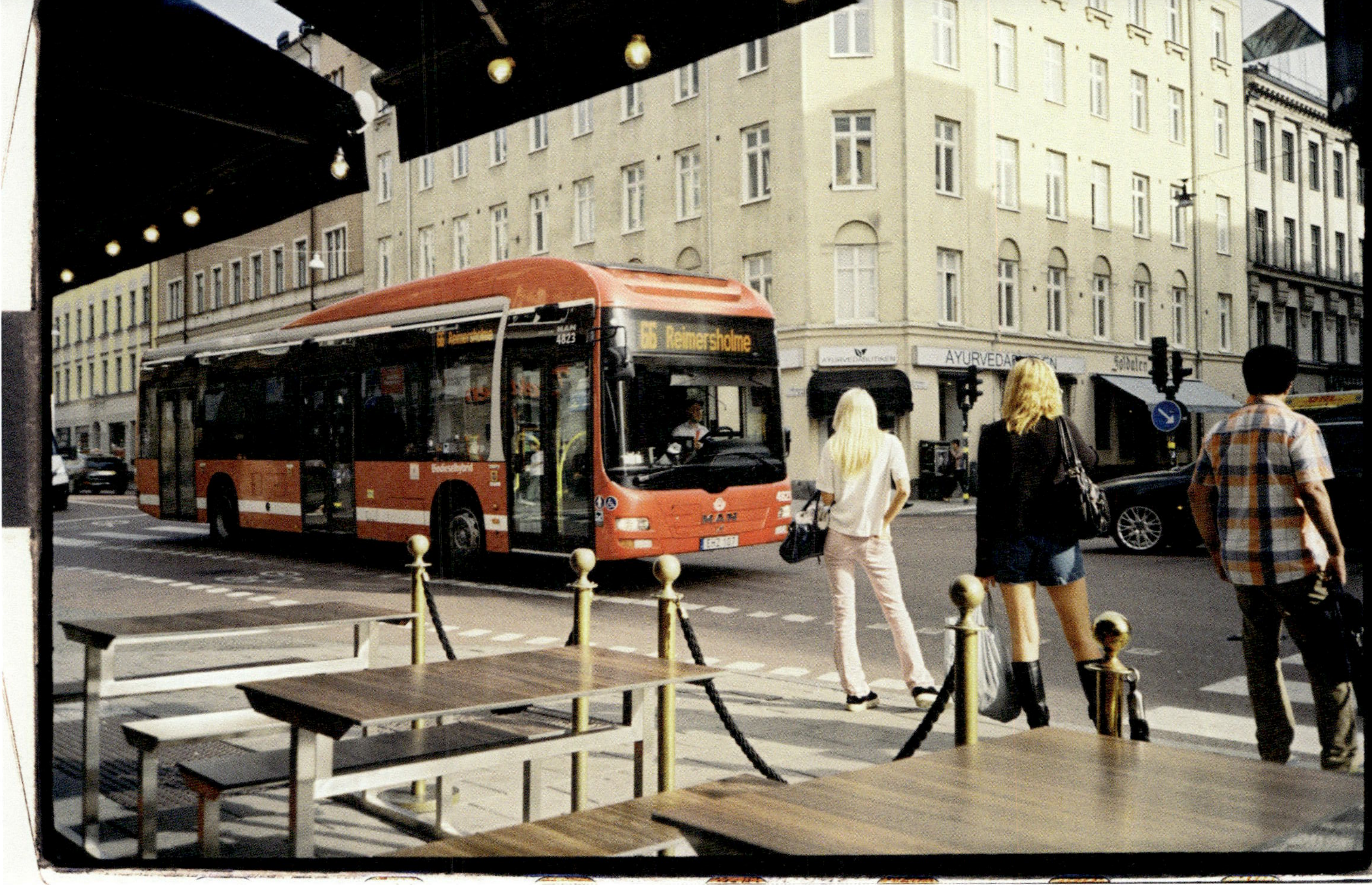
66 Reimersholme
MAN
4823
AYURVEDABUTIKEN
DHL

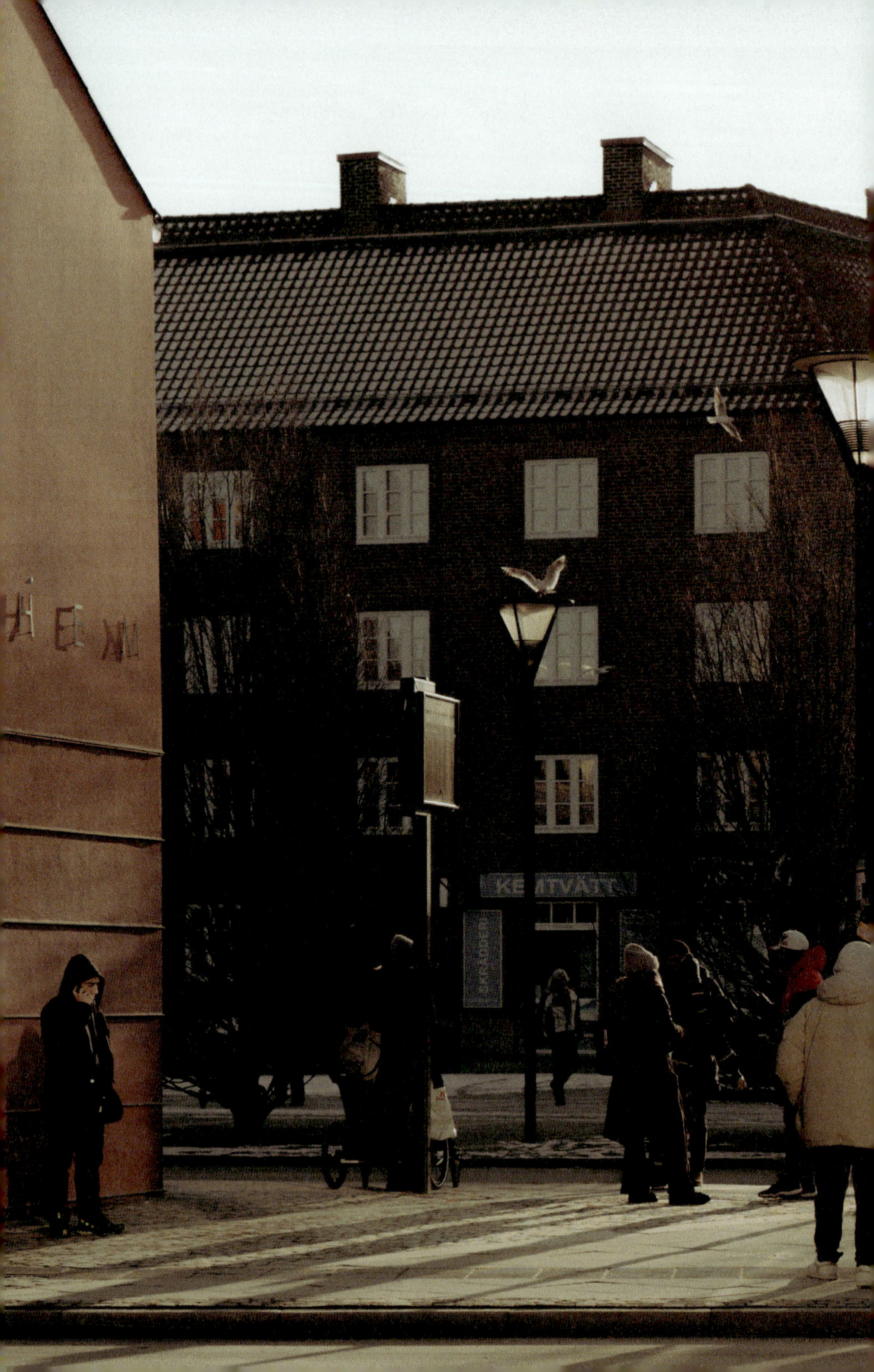

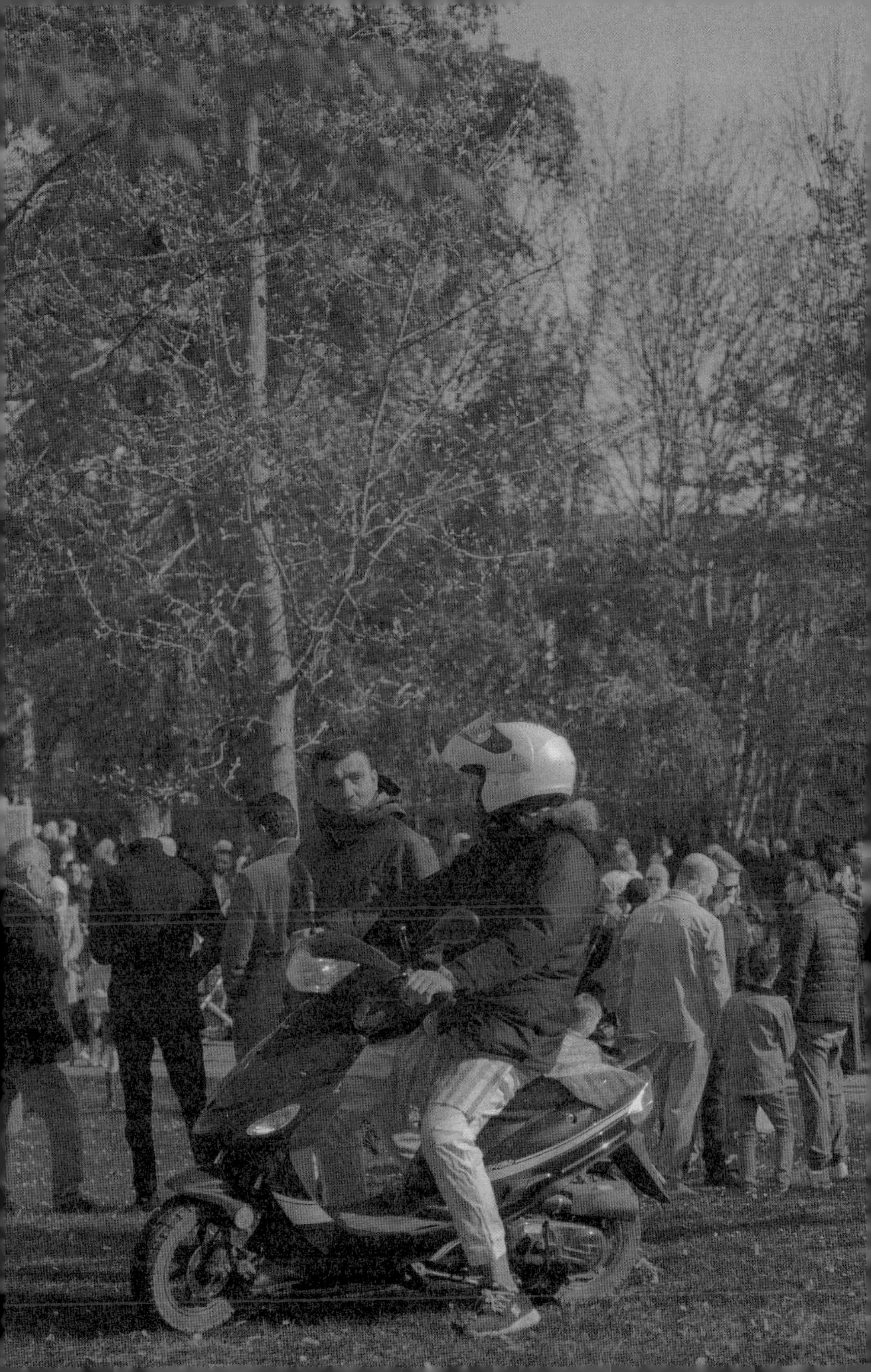

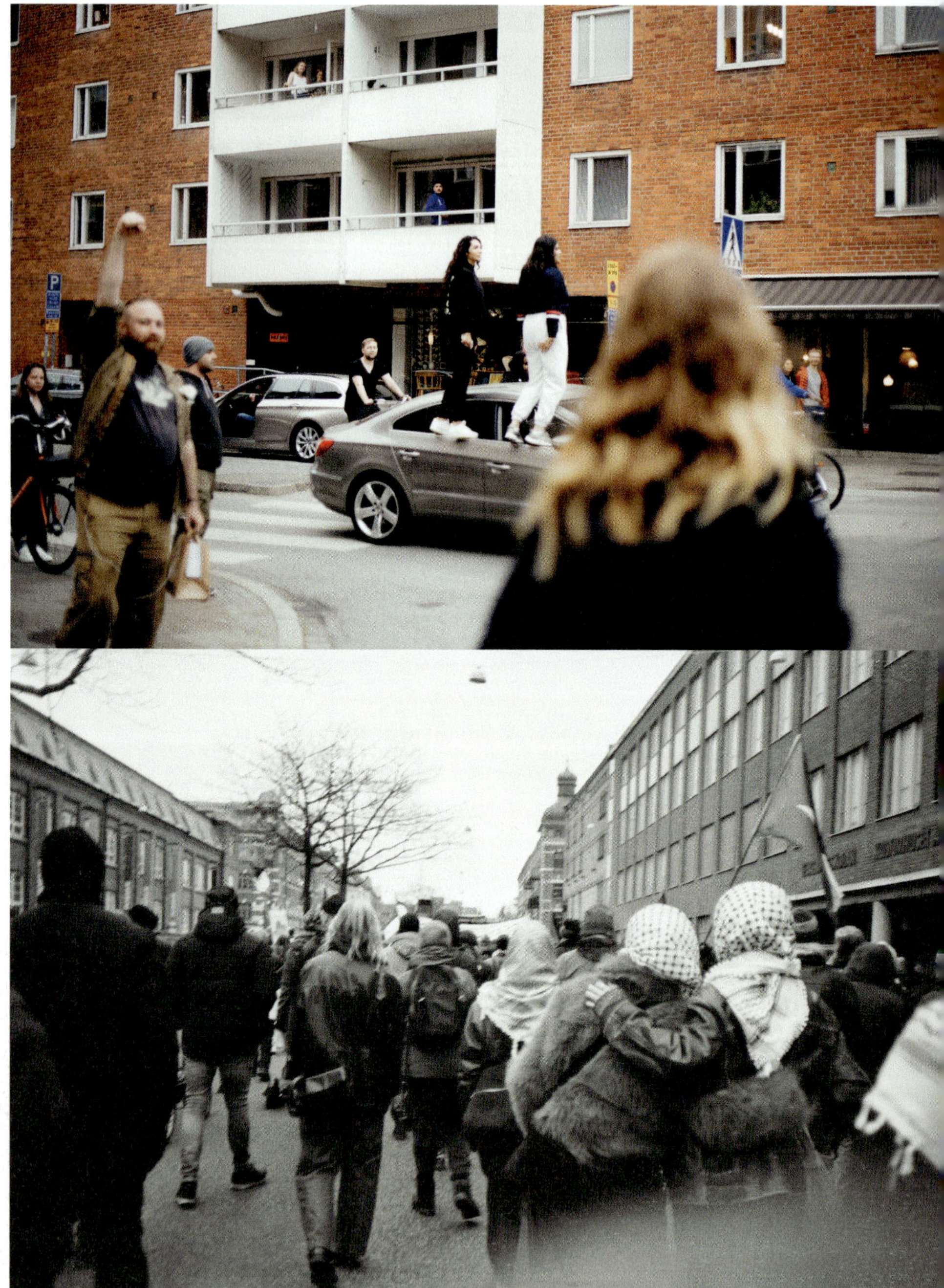

Søren Ulrik Thomsen

from *The Worst and the Best*

The best are the Lutheran Psalms'
dizzying towers of strictness and light

to cross Flanders on a rattling night train
while reading a tattered old thriller called
Never Too Late to Die, is the best

though the best thing I read this summer
was the milky foam writing of the waves as they broke,
all light, bright alliteration
          and the cold sizzle along Sigerslev Cliffs
of silence hissing in the black wind

the best thing I can see from my east window
is a military helicopter dropping straight down
onto the lawn in front of the University Hospital,
carrying, maybe, somebody's new lung

the river's flickering reflection under a bridge &
the sound of hard rain on an asphalt alley
is the best

and the best is that I'm now so old
I don't even have to pretend I'm somebody else
to forget who I am:

          That to me is the best.

The worst is playing the role of your poor self
just to avoid losing face

coming across an atrocious old poem
that I myself god help me have written is the worst

the worst is when the roots of one's teeth
have just started to show at the gums

trains that stop in dark tunnels
& 'life coaches' are the worst
and sitting at cultural conferences until your bones
are bored down to dust

the worst is finally realizing
that you long ago lost respect
for a man you'd give anything to admire

that everything can still happen is the worst

the worst is all those ghosts
roaming my apartment;
the lurching footsteps of everyone I ever failed
and the faint, sweet whiff of their breath
cursing my name:

That to me is the worst.

The best is when the dark, like an inky blue powder, dissolves
into the summer night's liquid sky,
    so the glowing light of the huge, silent houses
grows more concentrated and saturated, minute by minute

that the greatest revelations strike each time
with the same discrete clarity as the sound
of a drop hitting the bottom of a stainless steel sink
is the best

the best is turning off all the lights
and listening to the voices in a radio play
as the receiver's strange little lights
    pulse in the dark

words like blood sugar, snarl, and zephyr are the best
and best is that autumn smell of half-rotten leaves

the lower end of Nordre Frihavnsgade
    where the wind whips up from the harbor
and the elevated S-train roars past
is the best

the best is to give up at last
    and suddenly feel everything beginning again:

    That to me is the best.

Translated from the Danish by Patrick Phillips

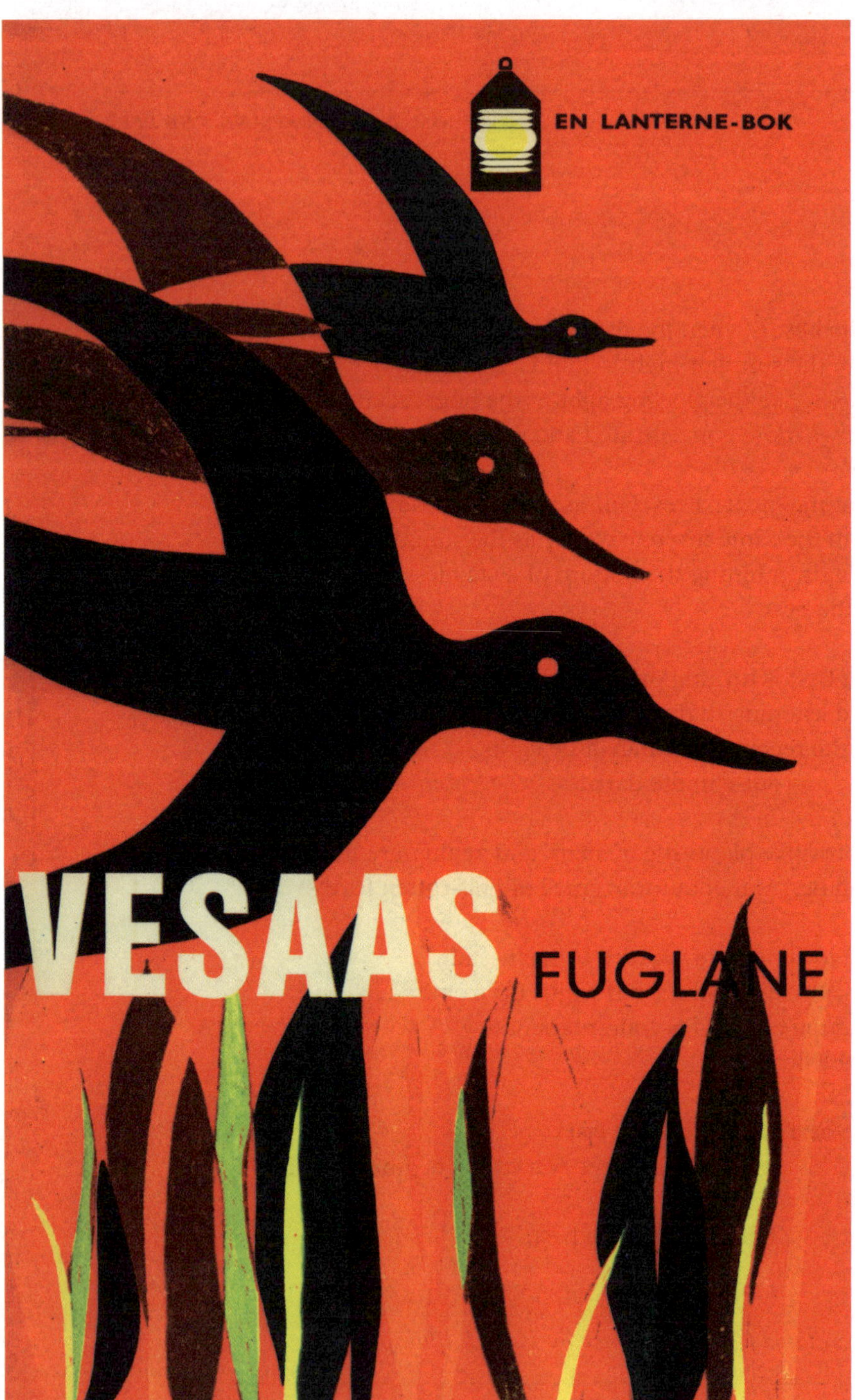

INGHILD STRAND
Gyldendal Norsk Forlag, 1962

A STRANGE BIRD'S CRY

Karl Ove Knausgård

The Norwegian author Tarjei Vesaas was born in 1897, the same year as William Faulkner, and two years before Jorge Luis Borges, Vladimir Nabokov and Ernest Hemingway. Vesaas is not usually mentioned in the same breath as the others in this generation, obviously because his books are hardly read outside Scandinavia and, I suppose, because it is easy to think that his books are hardly read outside Scandinavia for a reason, and that reason can only be that they are not as good. But they are.

Fuglane (*The Birds*), Vesaas's masterpiece from 1957, is in my opinion one of the best novels ever written in Norwegian, if not *the* best. Vesaas himself was a taciturn and modest man who probably would not have minded that his books remained largely a Norwegian secret, indeed, he would probably have been more than satisfied, and perhaps even surprised, that his books were still being read here, more than fifty years after his death. Most books remain in the world in which they were written, representing that world and not much else, and they are left behind when that world changes. Not so with *The Birds*. I read it for the first time as a teenager and have read it three times since. Seventy years after Vesaas sat down and wrote it, it still feels important. The same applies to his other late masterpiece, *Is-slottet* (*The Ice Palace*). Both of these novels have protagonists who are completely outside the mainstream and utterly powerless: the protagonist in *The Birds* is called Mattis, a dysfunctional man in his late thirties, a child at heart, helpless in the world, cared for by his sister, with whom he lives. The main character in *The Ice Palace* is called Siss, an eleven-year-old girl who, as she is discovering her own burgeoning sexuality, is confronted with death. The lust for life and the paralysis of it in an icy, snow-filled landscape – that is *The Ice Palace*.

For a long time these were the only two books by Vesaas that I had read. And that is a bit weird, because he was a fiercely productive writer, his oeuvre spanning some fifty years. He made his debut in 1923 with the novel *Menneskebonn* (*Children of Man*), and published forty books in all, ending with the posthumous collection of poems *Liv ved straumen* (*Life by the Stream*), which came out in 1970. I never picked up any of them. The reason being I had the notion that Vesaas wrote two definitive masterpieces, and that the rest of his work was competent but uneven and not very exciting – that all his other books in some way led to those two.

Why did I think that?

A prejudice is an assumption borrowed from others, an opinion that lacks grounding in experience. I must have come across this judgement of Vesaas's work in more places than one, not necessarily in so many words, but perhaps casually intimated, a disparaging sentence here, a perfunctory remark there, which, without my consciously assessing them, nonetheless slipped into my mind to clandestinely build a case there against Vesaas's early work – for in the mind a prejudice is never a prejudice but a truth.

At any rate, I just couldn't get interested in any of his other work.

Even when I was asked last year to give the annual Vesaas lecture in his home town, Vinje, it didn't occur to me that I could delve deeper into his writing – I thought I would talk about *The Birds* and *The Ice Palace*; the other thirty-eight books I kind of 'knew' anyway.

But then, a couple of months before the lecture was to be held,

I happened to be in the book town of Fjærland, browsing the shelf-metres of titles old and new, Norwegian and foreign, which included a good selection of Vesaas's books, when it struck me that I could perhaps buy some of his older novels and at least have a look at them, if only for appearances' sake, yes, out of courtesy almost. After all, I was going to give a lecture on his writing in his home town.

So a big stack of these novels ended up in my study, a stack I had to go past every day to get to my desk, but which I then forgot about as soon as I switched on the computer. Until one evening in early autumn. I needed something to read and was standing in the doorway looking in at the man-high towers of books on the floor. My eyes fell upon Vesaas. Maybe. Yes, why not? A quick skim wouldn't hurt, surely?

The first book on the pile was the novel *Bleikeplassen* (*The Bleaching Yard*), and I picked it up and took it with me over to the bed where I stretched out to read.

I was devastated. How could such a stunningly good novel, such a consummate, vital, absorbing work have so completely passed me by?

My senses sharpened as I read, the book seized my full attention, and all the time I kept thinking: this is important, this is important, I must remember this.

In the haze of my prejudicial notions about Vesaas, *The Bleaching Yard* was about someone who dried sheets for people on a 1920s farm, and wasn't there a sullen youngster too who didn't want to take the place on after his father? Don't ask me where I got this from. Because now I'm going to write something about what to my mind makes *The Bleaching Yard* such a brilliant novel.

The story takes place over a single day and night, and in a single place. This narrow frame creates the sense of being in a kind of room from which nothing can escape. The narrative is present tense, what goes on is in the here and now, in front of our eyes. These elements, the novel's form, impart almost single-handedly an urgent, intense feel to the events. And this is crucial, since what the novel tries to encircle, as I see it, is the relationship between emotions and actions, between inner life and outer world, though not seen in isolation, not in the way they play out in the individual; on the contrary, the novel's concern is the collective, the interplay between people, which is to say human relations. The way something inside a person can manifest outwardly and how its ripples spread and affect everyone. Vesaas wrote *The Bleaching Yard* during the Nazi occupation and buried his manuscript in the forest, where it remained until the war was over and the book could be published in 1946. It would not seem unreasonable, therefore, to think that in this novel Vesaas was seeking to explore the relationship between emotion and action, between hatred and violence, not on the grand scale, but in terms of its minutest components, its germ, such as we all recognise those things in ourselves. How do emotions arise, and what forces lie within them? The novel makes no mention of the war, nor is it in any way necessary to one's reading of it: *The Bleaching Yard* constitutes its own reality, complete in itself, like any other significant novel.

The events are set in a laundry in a small town. The laundry is run by Johan Tander and his wife Elise. They have three people working for them: an older woman by the name of Marte, and two young women, Vera and Anna. The laundry is in the basement of a large house owned by an old man, Olsen, who also owns large areas of forest land. Besides the Tander couple, three young men, forest workers, live in the house too: Jan Vang, Amund and Stein.

The lives of these various people are intertwined. But much of the tissue that connects them is hidden, existing only within the individuals themselves, without any external form. Johan Tander, for instance, while married to Elise, has a soft spot for Vera. It's no more than that. He perks up when he sees her, he enjoys talking to her. Nothing happens, he doesn't do anything, he simply feels good whenever she's around. When the novel begins, Jan Vang, one of the men who works in the forest, is in a relationship with Vera. Anna had a relationship with him earlier, and she's jealous. Johan Tander is jealous too. Not that he thinks he has a chance with her, something in him just wants her to stay pure. Elise, his wife, sees this. She realises the kind of feelings Johan has for Vera, and how it makes him feel towards Jan Vang. This is the situation as the novel opens. Nothing bad has happened, nothing bad has been done. Elise sees how tortured her husband is, it fills her with despair and she decides to do something to make him snap out of it, something radical that will make him realise how good he has it. She goes over the street and with big letters on the front of the house opposite writes: NO ONE HAS EVER CARED FOR JOHAN TANDER. This utterance becomes the catalyst for everything that happens next. Again, it's only a small thing, a few words scrawled on a wall with chalk – is that anything to get worked up about? But for Johan Tander the words are humiliating and demeaning, and if you take that sentence in it's hardly surprising. Because what it says is that Johan Tander is no use to anyone. And if you're no use to anyone, what are you then but no one?

The novel itself contains no such overarching thoughts or drawn-out lines of reasoning. It's completely down to earth, follows its characters closely, and they sense only their own thoughts and feelings, not those of the others, and for that reason none of them has any kind of overview of what is happening or why. The dialogue is everyday, though laden with meaning, and Vesaas seems to follow the exchanges as they are absorbed, describing their effects on the characters' inner lives. This was perhaps his greatest gift as a writer, to articulate what is wordless between people as it is shaped *inside* people. The picture that emerges is that dependence on others is total, but also hidden and therefore often unrecognised. Johan Tander too is dependent on others, and when conversely it is made plain to him that no one is dependent on him, and that accordingly he is no one, he turns his feelings outwards in the form of hatred, for hatred leaves its mark, it is he who has made it, and in that, he becomes someone to the others.

Alongside this story, in which hatred spirals and ends in death, albeit unintentionally, runs another story, that of Krister, an old man who shuffles about in the area and who on this particular day wakes up with 'rubble' in his heart. He knows he's going to die and gets it into his head that he must have a clean shirt on when it happens. He thinks: 'I need to see a sign that I've been among people, that I haven't lived for nothing. And that is the sign: I must have that shirt right away.'

Novels that employ a heavy symbol are often problematic in that they can easily steer our understanding with too firm a hand, it being crucial to a novel's quality that the reader remain free, but when it's done well, the gains can be enormous. Think of the white whale in Melville's *Moby-Dick* or the castle in Kafka's *The Castle*. *The Bleaching Yard* is not at that level – only a handful of novels in the history of literature are – but there's something deeply satisfying about the symbol in this novel, since it's so fully integrated into the realistic flow of events: the action surrounds a laundry, where people bring their dirty clothes, they're washed and then hung to dry, spotless and white – and at the same time it functions as a distilled image of what takes place in the story.

The Bleaching Yard is a novel about people and the relationships between them, nature has no part in what is told, with the exception of a short passage in which the narrative follows the three young men out into the forest. And there this sentence stands shining, all on its own:

'The tree is a thousand things that go unreckoned, denied a voice.'

That sentence could be a motto for Tarjei Vesaas's collected works – and it points forwards to *The Birds*. But we are not quite there yet, because after I'd put *The Bleaching Yard* down I took the next book from the top of my Vesaas stack. It was *Tårnet* (*The Tower*). And *The Tower* too was written during the occupation, and its manuscript buried in the ground together with that of *The Bleaching Yard*.

I was expecting a Kafka-like novel dense with symbolism, and was pretty certain it couldn't possibly match the same high level as *The Bleaching Yard*. My prejudice about Vesaas's early novels had turned out to be wrong, granted, but it still had to have come from somewhere, been prompted by someone's reasoning, it couldn't have just arisen out of thin air.

Again I was wrong. Shamefully wrong, in fact.

In spite of all its qualities, *The Bleaching Yard* didn't quite clutch at my heart. *The Tower* did. It reduced me to tears at one point, and my emotions rose and fell throughout, and when suddenly a deep sigh escaped me, my wife asked me what the matter was. I suppose she thought something had happened in real life, so I told her about what happened in Vesaas's *The Tower*. She wanted to read it herself, but she's English and the book has never been published in English. (One major upside to being Norwegian is that we can read Vesaas in his own language . . .)

But yes, *Tårnet*.

It takes place on a farm called Sund where two families live. One house is occupied by the Sund family themselves, who run the farm – Olav and Sigrid and their three adolescent children – in the other live Randolv and Jorunn and their two children; the main character Nils, who is fifteen, and Vesla, who is twelve. Randolv runs a garage. All around are rolling fields and forest, there is a strait with a bridge crossing over it, and there is a road that passes by with a lot of traffic. We're talking everyday Norwegian life in the 1930s.

At the beginning of the novel Jorunn is expecting a child. This has driven a wedge between Nils and Vesla and their parents. The child is born, and Vesaas, who never recoiled from depicting even the most unfamiliar lives from within, describes the infant's world:

> The newborn is now, and only now! He is not something that was.
>
> He lies up on the veranda that Randolv's father built in order to see the strait. And the last-born lies there and sees the strait and clouds all day.
>
> The bassinet has been put down there and all he has to do is see.
>
> He faces out, and his hazy eyes strain into the vastness that has become his, but they make no headway. The glitter from the strait comes to him as something unfamiliar which he reaches out to grasp. It is all he

> knows of gleaming straits and such.
>
> Land, land! He has been put down here so as to take it in and be filled by it – and his hazy eyes strain and seek to comprehend. In vain. But nonetheless it shall lie spread out in front of him in its lush abundance. It will enter him long before he knows it.
>
> Free, wide straits will engender something in him. Clouds, sun and straits – and kind, rounded faces. Together and in turn.
>
> It is for him. He has arrived.
>
> He is lifted up, and the one who lifts him is good, and turned towards him. She faces him towards the water and the fields and the bridge, and the dark hills beyond. He will become attached to this place such that the place will be his, regardless of where he later may roam. For here I have carried and given birth to you.
>
> High up on the veranda. The strait glitters.
>
> Words are said to him. Sounds he thinks are a thing that may be grasped by a hand when they bubble in his ears. He reaches out for it. All he has learned is that everything is his.

Pure serenity. The two other children are won over, Randolv even takes several weeks off work to spend time with the little one. And then events take an abrupt turn, a tragedy occurs, and the rest of the novel is about a family coming undone. The mother withdraws completely into herself, shuts herself off from everyone, while the father becomes obsessed with his work, and this unhealthy state of affairs, which gathers in strength on both sides, also consumes the two children, who are loyal and try to cope as best they can, yet are likewise dragged down into the same cruel, cold and bewildering place. All the while hoping it will change for the better. As is his habit, Vesaas describes his characters from within, and his portrayal of the mother, for instance as she wanders restlessly about the fields having lost her grip on what is real and what is not, is not only shockingly well turned, but yields the paradox of the novel's perspective becoming more elevated the deeper it reaches within. She has let go, and we understand why, for she is destroyed by grief. The novel tells us: this can happen. It's no one's fault. It's a catastrophe, a catastrophe within the collective. It is a tearing of the bonds that hold people together. And the novel encompasses this in two movements: one that turns away, and one that turns towards. The mother turns away from Nils and does not see him. Nils, pulled ever deeper into this slow collapse, leaves the house one day, he goes over to the neighbouring farm – the people there have seen what is happening and have been helpless to intervene – and there the young Astrid looks after him. She turns towards him and sees him. And it saves him.

This goodness in people, always present in Vesaas's novels, isn't it a tad sentimental? Something drawn from half-forgotten pockets of Romantic literature rather than from life?

One might think so. But take away goodness from Vesaas's books and we take away their essence – we take away the kernel, and only the husk remains. Vesaas was the poet of goodness. That's how I look at him. And it's why his books steer towards what is painful, difficult, unmanageable, dark – death is central to *The Bleaching Yard*, to *The Tower*, to *The Birds*, and to *The Ice Palace*. Why? Simply because it exists. Why does it exist, and how does its presence work on us? These are the questions his books raise. And if there is hope, where is that hope? Hope, goodness and evil are, in Vesaas's novels, concepts that are in no way firm, the universal does not exist, what he shows us is something occurring among people, something in motion, something living, and which belongs to the moment and the situation. Astrid is neither good nor evil, but what she does is good, more than she herself understands.

With these thoughts printed out and packed in my luggage, I took the plane to Oslo and drove from there down into the country, to Vinje in Telemark, the sparsely populated mountain village where Vesaas was born and where he lived his entire life. In the hall where the lecture was to be held, Vesaas's two children, Olav and Guri, aged eighty-nine and eighty-six respectively, were present. Both are well-known names in Norway, Olav as a journalist and author, Guri as an editor and translator. They invited me to their childhood home the next day, the Midtbø farm, which Vesaas bought in 1930 and which was not only the place where he had written almost all his books, but also a place of pilgrimage: in the 1960s, many young writers travelled here from Oslo to meet Vesaas. The new generation of writers in Norway at the end of the 1960s, led by Dag Solstad and Jan Erik Vold, represented something radically new and were relatively uninterested in the generations before them, with two notable exceptions: Tarjei Vesaas and Olav H. Hauge.

The next morning, I stood there myself. A small, ochre-yellow, well-maintained farmhouse on a slope, surrounded by dark, unpainted farm buildings, with a view down to a lake, wooded hills and, in the distance, high mountains. The zinc boxes containing the manuscripts of *Bleikeplassen* and *Tårnet* were buried in the woods behind the house, Olav told me, under a tree marked by Vesaas. I knew he had had a cabin nearby, where he sometimes sat and wrote, and when I asked where it was Olav pointed further along the lake. It was impossible to see that lake and the surrounding landscape without thinking of the landscape and lake in *The Birds*.

We went inside. The living room was small and painted in bright colours: light green ceiling, dark green wooden walls, red wooden doors and chairs. Tarjei had painted everything himself, Olav said, and it had remained unchanged since the 1930s. An old, antique farm bed stood in the corner, contrasting with the modernist paintings, one of which I immediately recognised as being by Kai Fjell. Olav told me that Tarjei had received it from the artist after he had spent a summer there. The home-made, green-painted bookshelves contained mostly Scandinavian poetry collections from the 1920s through to the 1960s. Olav came over while I was looking at the titles and told me that they had held secret poetry readings here during the war, friends and neighbours gathering in the living room in the evening while Tarjei read Nordahl Grieg, the poet who was shot down over Germany in 1943. The bedroom upstairs was painted yellow with orange window frames and an orange bed, and contained Vesaas's study, small as a closet, with books from floor to ceiling. Guri talked about how soothing the sound of the clattering typewriter had been when they were growing up – their bedroom was on the other side of the wall – when they heard it, everything was fine.

Vesaas himself grew up on a farm a few kilometres away. It was called Vesås and had been in the family for ten generations. Tarjei was the eldest of three brothers and was supposed to take over the farm, but he gave up his share because he wanted to write. The costs must have been considerable, as must have the inner conflict. You are born into a family that has run the same farm since the 1600s, and as the eldest son it is not only expected that you will take over from your father, it is a given. How strong must the urge to write be to overcome that? Writing is, after all, something weak, incorporeal, a few thin pencil strokes on a small sheet of paper; it can't really be called work, because you sit almost completely still while it's happening, and most of this so-called 'work' consists of staring at the blank sheet of paper, and, if you've come to a complete standstill, perhaps taking a stroll outside. And what is written, the context formed by the words, is just as weak and incorporeal, some vague impulses you have inside you that almost never lead to any kind of action. They have to be put down on paper, and when they are, the 'work' is done. How can the urge to do this, so infinitely trivial, overcome the demand and the obvious expectation to run the farm, whose work is hard and physical and measurable, and which must be done, because that is where the food comes from, that is where the clothes come from, and in doing that work you may be incorporated into a line of men, of fathers and sons, going back as far as anyone can remember, a few hundred years, until they disappear somewhere in the depths of history?

But that was exactly what Vesaas did. He stepped out of the line, out of the family, out of the context and into, well, where? A hut where he could sit alone and fiddle with his pencil? Probably.

But what does it mean to have the urge to write?

What does it mean to write?

Let's say that one morning in late September you stop on the hillside and look over at the mountains on the other side of the water. It has snowed during the night. The fog has begun to lift, the water is black, the air greyish. The colours along the lower part of the mountainside, dark green, red, orange, yellow, shine brightly and intensely against the thin, white veil, and farther up, where no trees grow, it is as if the mountain, suddenly defined by the fresh snow, has moved closer. It is a magnificent sight, and it fills you with awe. You don't know why, but it has to do with the feeling of being. Of being alive. Perhaps your father comes by and stops, perhaps your mother. They see the same thing you do. But the feelings it fills you with cannot be shared. You can say that it is nice, perhaps even beautiful, even though that is not a word that is used much where you live, but that is all. You cannot know what your mother or father thinks about it, what they feel, whether it is anything like what you feel, or something completely different. You are alone with this, of course. And so it is with almost everything else too. When you eat dinner a couple of hours later, it is about so much more than just eating. Your mother radiates something, your father radiates something, both who they are and what they are feeling right now, even though nothing is said. You notice their wills, and what happens when they meet, because it's not as if their wills, personalities and feelings live in isolation, one by one. No, they meet all the time, gently and nicely or harshly and brutally, and everything in between, so that new moods arise continuously, and you take part in these moods, they colour you, your thoughts and feelings, sometimes in violent bursts. They come not only from people, but also from animals, such as the cries of fear from a pig when it realises it is about to be slaughtered, or the joyful somersaults of swallows as they swoop through the quiet summer sky, and every place has its own mood, something unique that you encounter when you are there. But what is it? And where does it take place? In you, of course, but that is only where it manifests itself, not where it originates; it happens outside of you. But it is invisible and indefinable – it is not like a mountain, which emerges and becomes clear when snow falls on it. It is as if two realities exist side by side. One physical, concrete, tangible. It is the one in which work takes place, cooking and eating, it is the one in which bodies move. Handles made for hands, rakes made for the grassy slope, spades made for the earth. Fences to keep the animals in, barns to store the hay, cowsheds for the cows in winter. Beds for the people, tables and chairs. Greasy chops on the plates. Faces dimly lit by the light from the window, faces in the sunshine outside on the porch, faces in the darkness on their way in. Happy eyes, angry eyes, tired eyes. Lips pressed together, lips opening. Voices whispering, voices mumbling, voices talking, voices shouting. Someone crying somewhere. Laughter spreading and dying away. A black bucket of water glinting in the sunlight on the tram. Out of all this, out of all the faces and bodies and what they move between, another reality rises up. It is invisible, almost ghostly, sometimes vague to the point of imperceptibility, sometimes so powerful that it makes the inside tremble, adults cry. But of these two realities, only one really counts, only one has language and can be talked about. What do you do then if the other one is the one that matters, that fills you, and that is the one you actually live in? When you are alone with all these feelings – it is not that the others don't have them, just that you have them one by one, and perhaps assess them differently, perhaps feel them to varying degrees, so that for others they are completely manageable, the feelings can somehow be incorporated into practical life and actually make it more robust, but that is not as it is for you, for you it stands in the way of practical life – when you are alone with all this, because it not only stands in the way, but also cannot be shared, it is as if you are isolated, and what then tears and wears you down is loneliness and its companion, meaninglessness.

But what does the urge to write have to do with all this?

The urge to write does not arise from nothing; it arises from the urge to read. And what is reading?

Yes, what is literature?

Literature is the place where the other reality, the one that takes place between people, animals, things and places, and which cannot be seen but is invisible, literature is the place where all this takes shape. It is the place where it comes to light. It is also the place where the inner self of one person, no matter how closed off on the outside, can emerge. Literature is simply the other, and the otherness.

To write is to give form to that which has no form – what else could it be? – and in that way make it present. There are as many ways of doing this as there are writers. Vesaas himself highlighted two who had meant a great deal to him as a young man. They were Knut Hamsun and Selma Lagerlöf. It is not difficult to see from his writing why they were important to him. Hamsun's novels are characterised by heightened presence, which is what still makes his books so readable, while Lagerlöf's novels are characterised by a great concern for people on the margins of society. Presence is basically a question of literary technique – i.e. aesthetics – care and a heartfelt concern for ethics, but as we know, there is no such thing as a neutral literary technique or aesthetic; it always involves morality, whether the author is aware of it or not.

Presence and care: is this perhaps as good a description of what goes on in *The Birds* as any other?

Formulated in this way, 'presence and care', the concepts are abstract and rather empty, meaning that you, the reader, can fill them with whatever you want. Neither presence nor care exist in themselves, but only in relation to something else – what you come close to, what you care about. In *The Birds*, it is a mind. To get so close, Vesaas must have sat virtually motionless and listened, allowing the inner self space to unfold. This absolutely necessary passivity must have occurred simultaneously with the writing, which implies the opposite; it is an active action and it takes up space. Language itself has a form, it is a tool, something other than what it describes, and if the words are too heavy, too crude, too harsh, they can close themselves off from the reality they want to open up and make present. Then we see language, plot, characterisation, style, convention, literature. In order to get close to something else, literature must go against the nature of words, from being something that takes up space to becoming something that makes space, by fine-tuning them, making them light, lasting, so that what they describe can seep in between them and be found there, that is, in the spaces between the words, in much the same way as it is found in the spaces between people. In *The Birds*, Vesaas is close to language, language is close to Mattis, Mattis is close to existence – he is not someone who does, he cannot, he just is. And his being is filled to the brim with the being around him – his sister's, but also that of the birds, the trees, the sky, the water. Instead of close, one could also say open – Vesaas is open to language, language is open to Mattis, Mattis is open to existence. It flows through him, that is, through language, and via language through us. And the same applies to the reader as to Vesaas: in the same way that he worked to make room for something in language, the reader must make room for language within themselves. That is why it is so difficult to say anything about *The Birds*, because it is precisely about what cannot be said, only sensed, and a statement, almost any statement, destroys the sensation through its sheer weight.

None of the four times I read *The Birds* did I think about this. I just read, and I came close. But how? I wonder now as I write about it. What did Vesaas do with language that allowed Mattis's reality to seep into mine? It must necessarily have happened imperceptibly, because if I had noticed it, that is, become aware of the means the author used, a distance would have arisen and I would no longer have been close to the text, close to Mattis, close to his experience of reality.

Allow me to take a look at the very first sentence of the novel.

> Mattis looked to see if the sky was clear and cloudless tonight, and the sky was.

The sentence is simple and uncomplicated – a man named Mattis looks to see if the evening sky is cloudless. But the sentence is also slightly unusual. The expected or normal way to write it would perhaps be to use 'it' instead of repeating 'the sky'. Like this: 'Mattis looked to see if the sky was clear and cloudless this evening, and it was.'

What does the repetition do?

By its mere presence, it suggests that we are close to something that is not quite normal, something that in a still undefined way breaks with expectations, but more importantly, it affects the tone: by repeating 'sky', it introduces something childlike, but also something solemn, with the faint echo of the repetitions in biblical language. This creates a mood that surrounds Mattis from the very beginning, without a word being said about it, and which the reader can relate to: Mattis is surrounded by something childlike and something solemn, and he looks up at the sky.

That was the first sentence. In the next three, we are taken further into Mattis's world:

> Then he said to his sister Hege, to cheer her up:
> 'You're like lightning, you' he said to her.
> He shuddered a little at the words he had uttered,
> but in a safe way, since the sky was nice.

In addition to the information provided – Mattis has a sister named Hege and she needs cheering up, so she must be weighed down by something – there is a new repetition. This time it is more prosaic, without any obvious resonance from anything else and without containing any new information, thus seemingly unnecessary: why write 'he said to his sister Hege' and then add 'he said to her' after the line? It is not rational, the same information is given twice, and what is repeated is not important either, there is no major event being emphasised in this way. The language is otherwise sparse, there is no waste of words here. So why the repetition of 'he said'? For an author who has learned a lot from Vesaas, namely Jon Fosse, repetitions are central; they do not relate so much to the individual characters or the plot, but are part of the style in which they are written, a slow avalanche of words, which thus takes on the leading role. In Fosse's novels, all characters, all descriptions, all thoughts are part of this avalanche, a bit like how the various instruments, regardless of their distinctive characteristics, submit to the logic of the symphony they are playing in. In Fosse's work, the language thickens, becomes visible as language, and it is through this, the slow avalanche of words, that the moods and emotions arise, not through the characters, who are barely distinguishable from one another. In Vesaas, on the other hand, the language is close to the characters and works quietly, with shifts so subtle they are almost invisible:

> Then he said to his sister Hege, to cheer her up:
> 'You're like lightning, you' he said to her.

An eager child may repeat words unnecessarily, and there is an element of that here, but in what is repeated there may also lie security, a bit like wrapping the rope around the rack with the skis on the car roof one extra time, even though you know that, strictly speaking, it is not necessary. In other words, Vesaas, close to Mattis, secures his space with repetition. In the next sentence, a connection between words/language and security/insecurity is made explicit: 'He shuddered a little at the word he had uttered, but in a safe way, since the sky was nice.'

This opening, these first four sentences, draw the reader straight into the universe of the novel, but not by telling them about it ('His name was Mattis and he was called Tusten. He lived with his sister, Hege, who took care of him after their parents died. Mattis was not like others, did not think like others, thought more like a child, but there was also something solemn about his thoughts, filled with awe for nature as he was. One evening, the two sat on the porch outside the house, and he looked up at the sky') or by showing it through scenes ('The sun was setting in the west. The air was warm and still, the sky was completely clear, blue with a touch of red where the sun's rays made it flare up. Mattis, a thin man of thirty-seven with an open, almost childlike face, sat on the porch next to his sister, Hege, who was four years older, and looked up at the sky. There was silence between them. Mattis turned to Hege. His eyes were sparkling. She seemed older than her years, weighed down by something. Then Mattis took a deep breath and said: "You're like lightning."') In Vesaas's work, it is within the language that the essential things happen, through tones, sounds, rhythms – not in the words themselves, but what the words convey, what rises from them and the spaces between them:

> Mattis looked to see if the sky was clear and cloudless tonight, and the sky was.
>
> Then he said to his sister Hege, to cheer her up:
>
> 'You're like lightning, you' he said to her.
>
> He shuddered a little at the words he had uttered but in a safe way, since the sky was nice.

The third repetition of 'the sky' both closes the scene and opens it up, of course towards the sky through which the birds fly and which arches over the siblings sitting there, but also towards a web of calm and unrest, safety and danger, openness and closedness that Mattis finds himself within.

When I read this opening, I still do not know who Mattis is, I still have no idea about his personality, but it is nevertheless as if I am getting close to him, that I feel him, have him. A bit like when you meet someone for the first time, their unique presence, that which escapes your thoughts, is nevertheless noticeable. The fact that the text manages to convey this has to do with the tone, and that should be impossible, because it is just a few words that Vesaas has put together, but the way he has done it, the sensitivity he has shown, means that something Mattis-like flows towards me and into me when I read these four sentences. It is as if Vesaas's language does not construct Mattis, but listens its way to him. Through this, Mattis's own relationship with language takes on weight, becoming like a heavy stone in a net, since it represents the exact opposite – for Mattis, words and actions are so closely connected that saying 'lightning' is dangerous because it can invoke lightning. In other words, the relationship between language and reality is magical. For Mattis, words are as real as reality, or are directly connected to it.

In these first four sentences, we are not only introduced to the main character and his world, we are also introduced to what is perhaps the most important but also the most elusive theme in *The Birds*, which is – at least as I experience the novel – what meaning is. And thus, as a necessary consequence, what language is. The key scene in this regard is when Mattis, sitting at the steps outside in the dusk, sees a woodcock passing over the rooftop, and realises it is a roding, the bird's mating route:

> But then there was a tiny sound! A strange noise all of a sudden. And at the same time he got a glimpse of some quick, flailing wingbeats in the air above him. Then some faint calls again, in a helpless bird language.
>
> It went straight across the house.
>
> But it went straight through Mattis as well. Muted and agitated inside, he sat wide awake and confused.
>
> Was it something unnatural?
>
> No, anything but, and yet . . .

Mattis has no doubt that this is a significant event, and that it has great meaning. Something has been revealed. He does not know what, he does not know why, only that it has happened. Something has been revealed.

If one were to lift the event up and place it in a language other than Mattis's, one could perhaps say that it possesses many of the characteristics of the sacred. According to Rudolf Otto, the experience of the sacred is characterised by a thrilling sense of a presence, nameless and divine, which he called 'the wholly other'. According to Émile Durkheim, the sacred was something for which a society at any given time created a separate category, outside of everyday life. To Mattis, the flight of the woodcock is sacred in both senses of the word; something vast, yet obscure, has drawn near, and he creates a separate category for it. The roding is a revelation: it changes the house, which becomes like a different house, and it changes Mattis ('He was clearly different inside'). And it will change Hege when she finds out about it – as he goes in to wake her up and tell her about the revelation, he thinks *Now Hege would be different too.*

Crucial to the novel is that this momentous event for Mattis takes place outside the realm of grand words, outside concepts of the sacred and revelation, but entirely within Mattis's consciousness, filled as it is with sensations and premonitions, as if on the threshold of language, and based on his understanding, where the magnitude and significance of the event are self-evident. He knows. And knowing something is important to Mattis; it is what sets him apart from everyone else, that they know and he does not. *Now I know something*, he thinks as he sits on the tram after seeing the bird for the third time, just before it strikes him that it will also change Hege. Bursting with the urge to tell her what he knows, with a feeling that he is now perhaps even more important than she is, he goes inside. In a scene as luminous as the previous one, he tries to explain what has happened. Hege, angry and grumpy at being woken up, but also patient with her unreasonable brother, listens to what he has to say and understands, saying kindly:

> The roding? Oh yes. Go back to sleep, Mattis.

Mattis doesn't give up, keeps banging on about the roding, until Hege snaps, shouts at him and finally starts crying in despair. Mattis doesn't understand why; he interprets it as her not believing him when he said the roding had come. He goes outside again:

> That's it for tonight. Because now the bird has found his girlfriend.
>
> When he looked up, there were streaks of light where the woodcock had flown. Right above his house.

Here, two completely different meanings meet – the solemn, almost religious feeling that the sudden presence of the woodcock fills Mattis with, when the traces of the roding glow like a halo in the air, and then the biological or zoological function that the roding has, in that it is part of a mating ritual, something the male does to attract females. That same night, Mattis dreams about girls, in a context where he himself does everything right, he is strong and powerful, perfectly normal and someone the girls look up to and want, a dream he associates with the mating call – something new has begun. All of Mattis's longing is directed towards the social, the only thing he really wants is to be like everyone else, and there is a painful irony in the fact that he believes the roding is his ticket, his pass, the thing that will make him like everyone else, both through his identification with the bird – it flies over his house and attracts females, so soon he will also attract females – and through the fact that by having seen this, he has also become someone who knows. For the opposite happens, of course: the revelation and everything it represents increases his distance to others, drives him further and further out, until on the last page he lies in the dark water and desperately calls his own name, which on the desolate water 'sounded like a strange bird's cry'.

The Birds can easily be read as a psychological portrait of an immature mind, a kind of restoration of human dignity for all who are like Mattis, or as an investigation of the mechanisms of exclusion and the conditions of loneliness. But it also seems essential to me that this mind is so open, and that what it is open to and filled with comes to light in a fierce ambivalence: humanity on the one hand, nature on the other. Action on the one hand, inaction on the other. Mattis, the scene of these contradictions, in the middle. He cannot communicate the significance that the flight of the woodcock has for him. He tries, mentioning it to everyone he meets. The reference is the same, a roding, but the meaning is too different for communication to be possible. The roding is a sign in a language that Mattis believes is universal, but which only makes sense to him.

When he can't communicate the meaning of the bird's behaviour to anyone, he goes the other way and starts communicating with the bird itself. He finds traces of the bird in a ditch, it looks like writing, and he writes something to it in the same language with a stick. He is so attuned to his surroundings that he is afraid to take up space, thinking that just being there could scare the bird and cause something to break. Something important. What could that be? The bond he has with the bird, perhaps, which is so fragile that it would take very little to break. The very sense of belonging. When a lumberjack enters his life towards the end of the book, as his sister Hege's boyfriend, and takes him into the forest, everything is different. There is no sensitivity, no responsiveness, no finely tuned language. The lumberjack wants to make him into a man, and the forest is about work, about cutting down trees, chopping them up and clearing them away. It fills the space completely. Everything is rough and efficient, nothing goes in, everything goes out, and in Mattis, thoughts grow, tangle themselves up and make action impossible. When he finally acts, it is not according to social logic, which has to do with work and rationality, but according to the other logic, which until then has had to do with signs, which he has interpreted based on the belief that what happens in nature predicts what happens to humans. He places his life in the hands of fate, something passive in itself, but which Mattis now fills with action: he rows out onto the water, kicks a hole in the boat, lets it sink, grabs the oars and floats on them. Fate will decide what happens next, whether he goes under and drowns or manages to save himself and live on. The ambivalence in the action, the ambivalence in Mattis, the ambivalence in the novel finds its final expression when, in deep despair, he shouts his own name out there in the darkness on the water. The name has been given to him by the others, it comes from their language, so he calls himself in a strange way from outside, and the cry is distorted over the deserted water and becomes the cry of a bird. Mattis cannot hear it, only the novel can, and the reader of it. ■

Sunna Dís Másdóttir

Bow

Don't cross your legs
my grandmother says
you'll get cellulite

but I was a girl scout
I knit my own knots
weave my own net

I whittle in winter
over crime dramas
one arrow for each
woman murdered

Sit up tall
I tell my sister
open your legs

steady your pubis against them
taut
like a bowstring

Translated from the Icelandic by Esja Alyssa Matich

Jam

This is nothing new of course

women
have always gathered
in houses by the sea
at harvest time

we work ourselves warm
a bead of sweat between my breasts
milk pearling on one nipple

the sugar we buy in turns
shuttle it in wheeled suitcases
we bought in street markets
and airports
pink belts buckled around their middles
so we'd recognize them

tattered Louis Vuitton logos
remind us of our trip to Turkey
a year or so ago
when we first tasted pistachio paste

the pot was a communal
investment
containing as many liters
as run through our veins

the jam simmers
maybe someone cries
sugar syrup sweating in a pan
thickening in our veins

we set out crackers
a jar of olives
maybe after we'll get in the hot pot

skim the sugar
crusted atop the jam
we never throw it away
but carry it outside in a red bowl

let it seep slowly into the soil
that is coming into being
just like us

Translated from the Icelandic by Larissa Kyzer

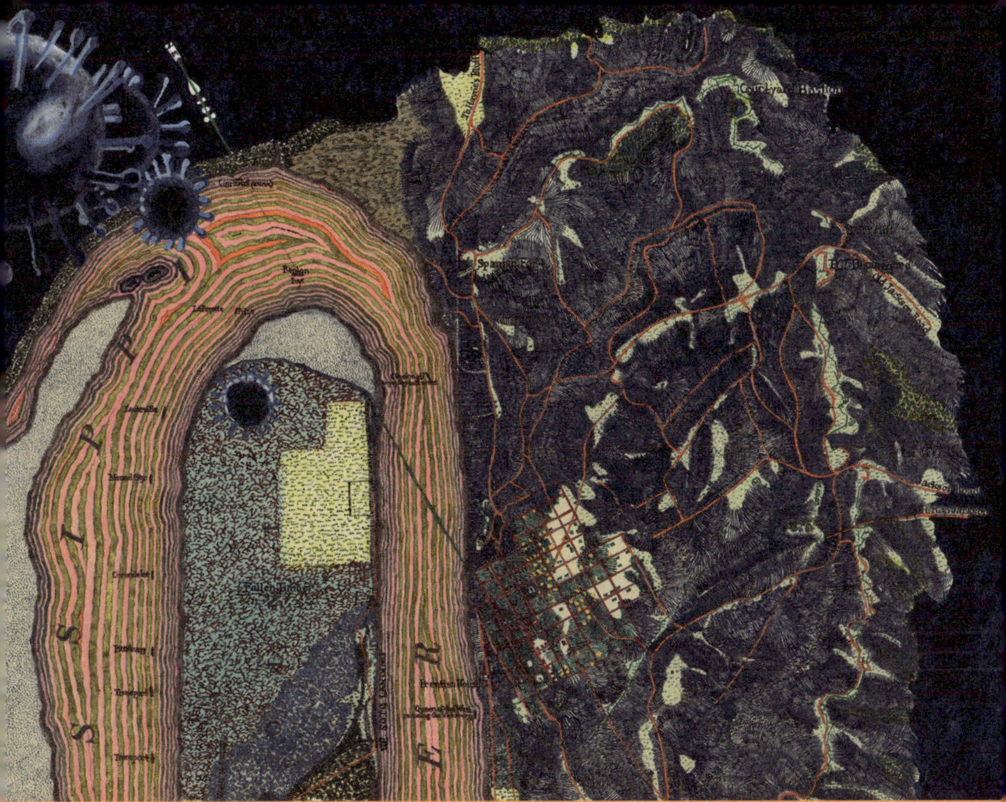

JOURNAL ISSUE 13

A free, peer-reviewed journal on contemporary art

LIVE NOW

ISSUE 14 COMING SOON

contemporary.burlington.org.uk/journal

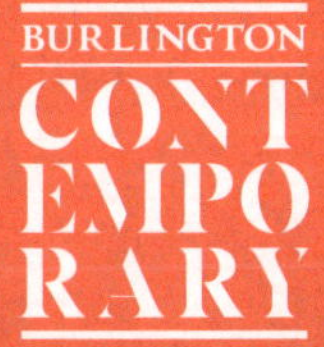

Uncivil Wars: Battle of Vicksburg, by Joyce Kozloff. 2020. Acrylic on canvas, 152 by 102 cm. (Private collection; courtesy the artist and DC Moore Gallery, New York; photograph Steven Bates).

PORCELAIN SOULS

Inuuteq Storch

Introduction by Granta

In the mid 1980s, Inuuteq Storch's parents were separated by 1,800 miles of water and ice. His mother was studying in Aarhus, Denmark, while his father had returned home from Copenhagen to Sisimiut, Greenland. They were apart for a number of years and regularly sent letters to one another.

Storch's 'Porcelain Souls' pairs this physical correspondence with found photography also taken by the pair, stretching from the late 1960s to the early 1980s. Pictured here are moments in the lives of the Kalaallit – the largest group of Inuit people in Greenland – at the close of the last century, as the territory underwent rapid modernisation. Denmark ended Greenland's status as a colony in 1953, and Home Rule was achieved in 1979.

In Storch's project, desaturated portraits of friends, family and co-workers are often coyly posed, eyes fixed into the middle distance, cigarette in hand. These sit alongside shots of fishing boats that are frozen in place; in one sweeping panorama, dog sleds lie scattered over a vast white tundra. Storch's work acts as a quiet rebuke to the archival and administrative photography that has been wielded to record, map and lay claim to Greenland. 'It's about telling our own history through our perspective,' he told *Granta*. ■

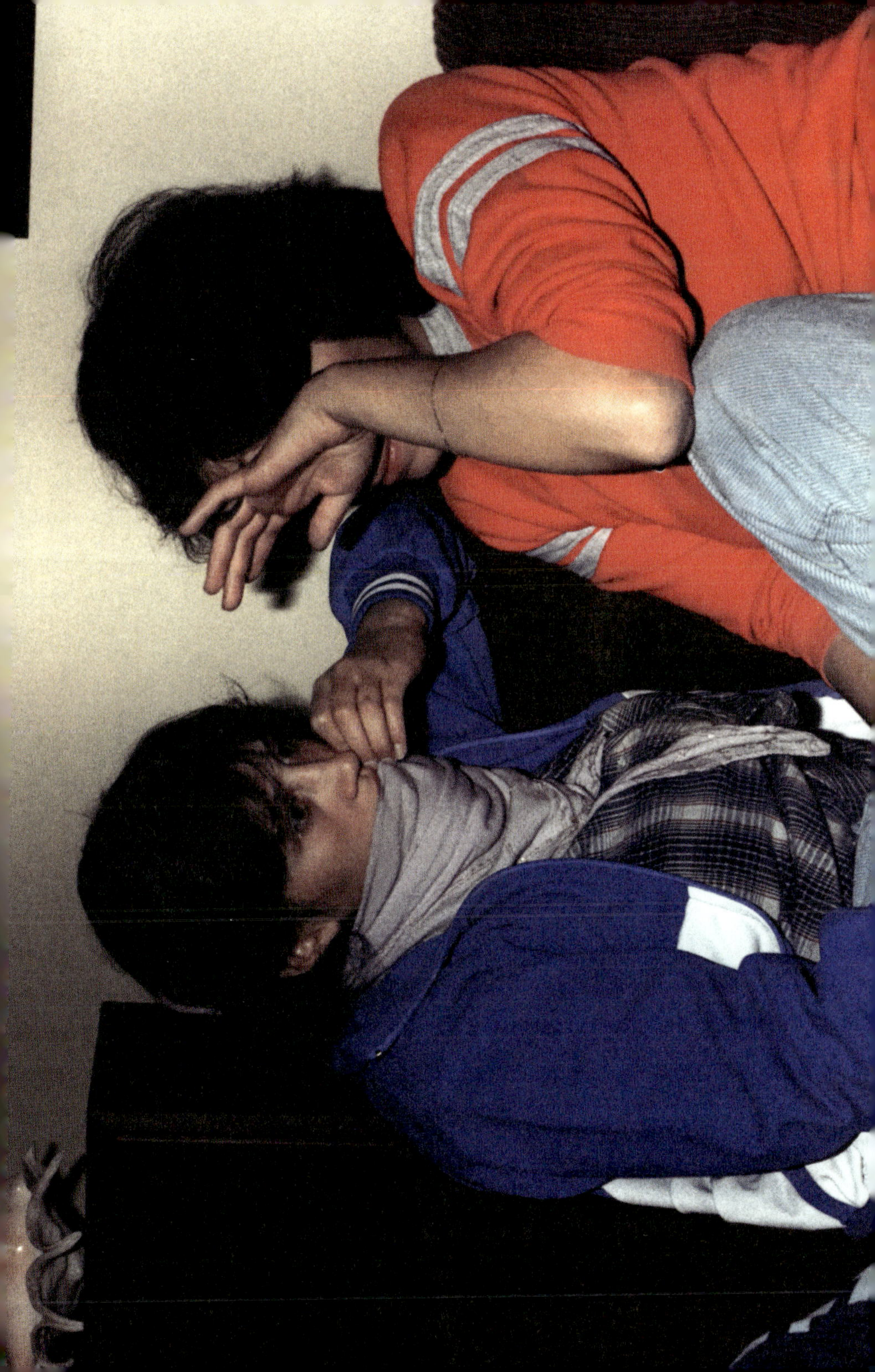

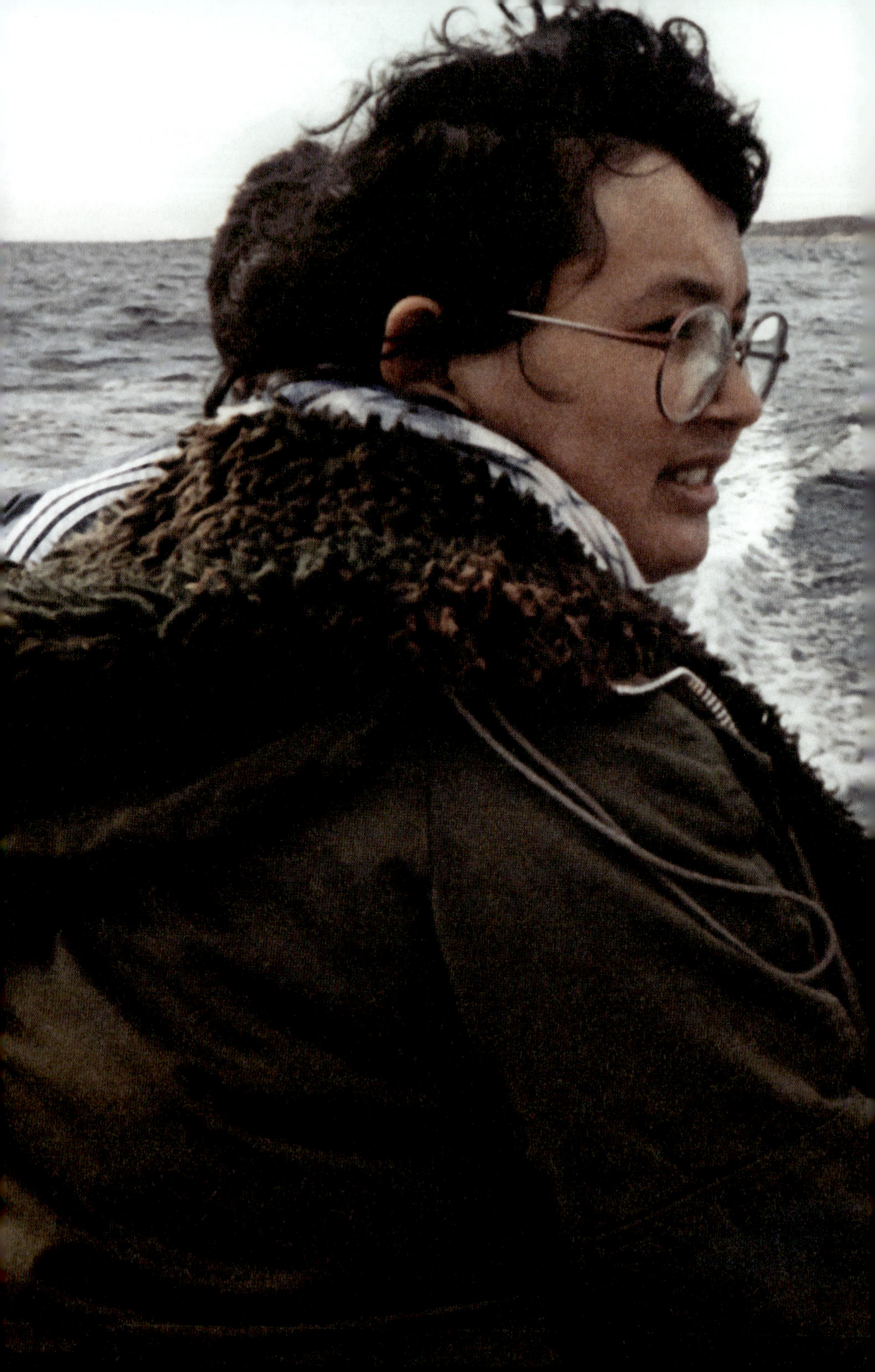

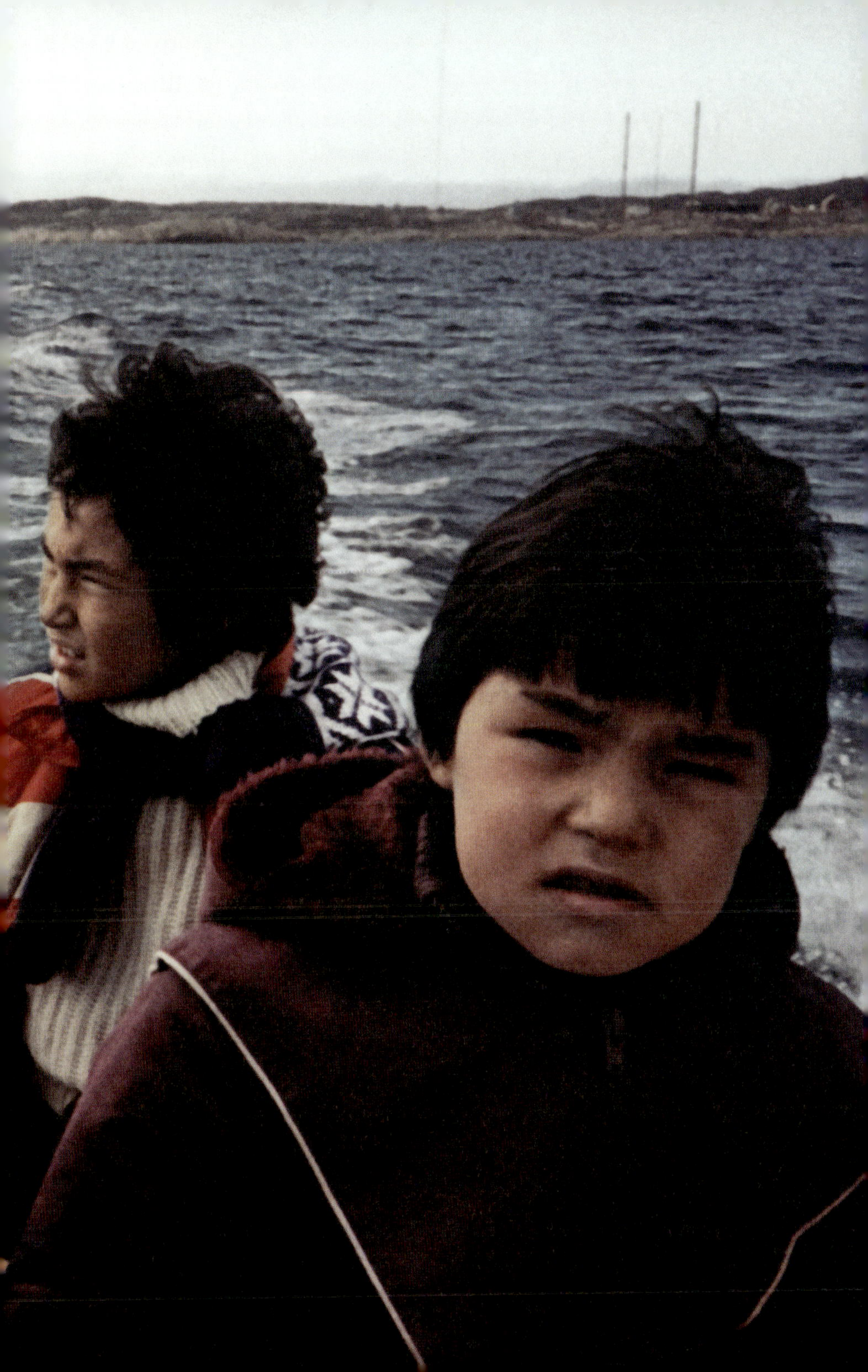

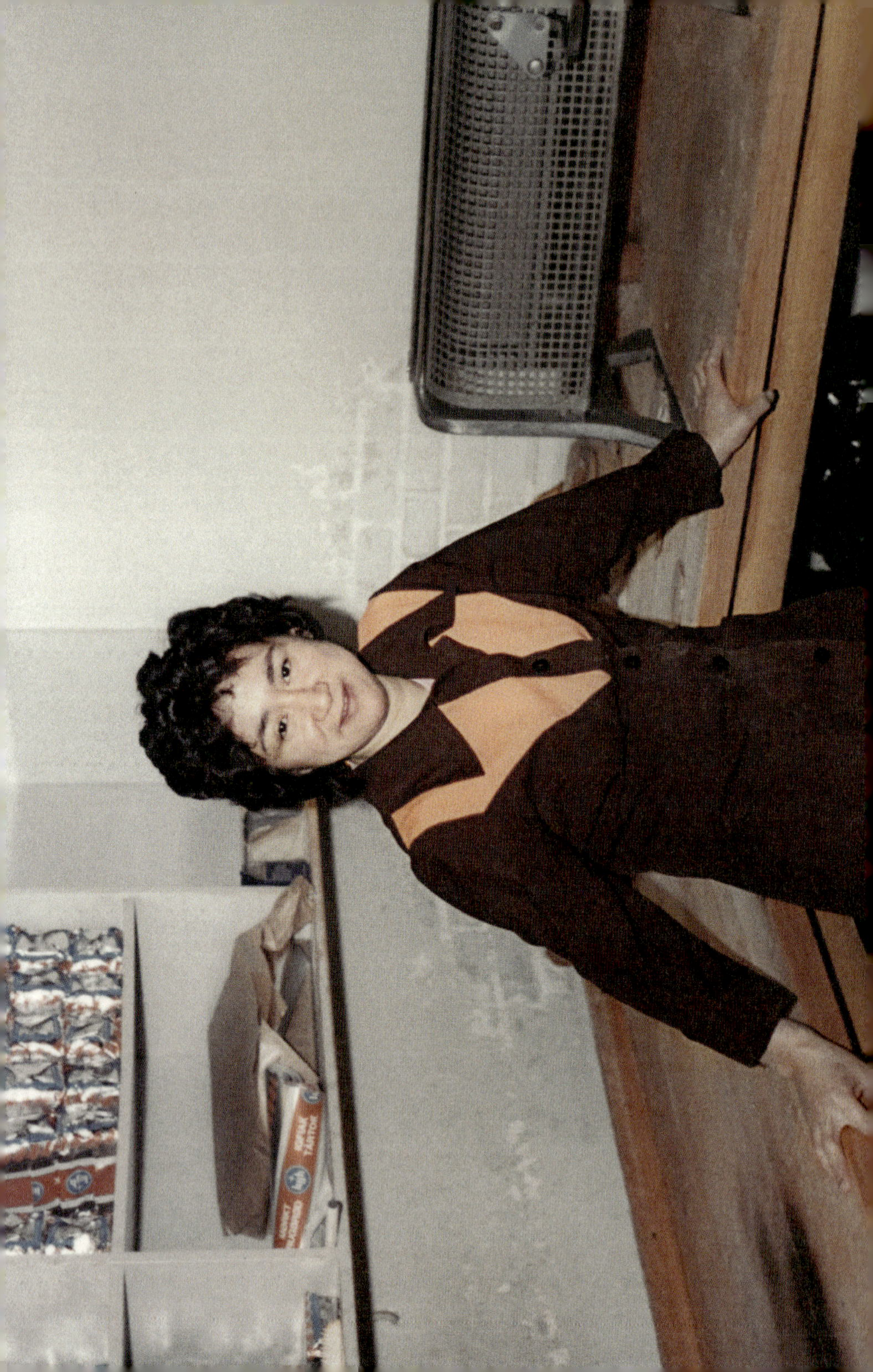

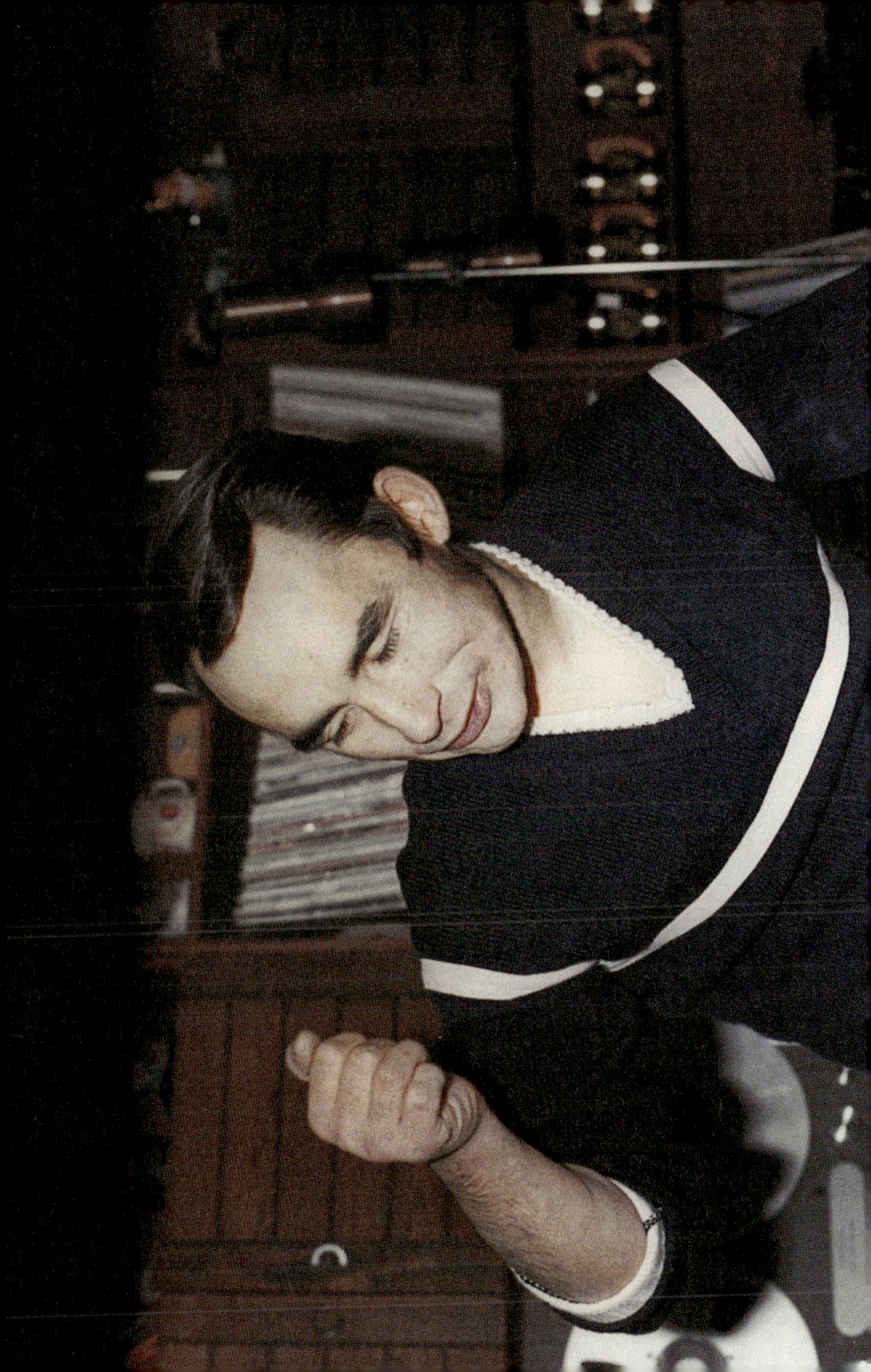

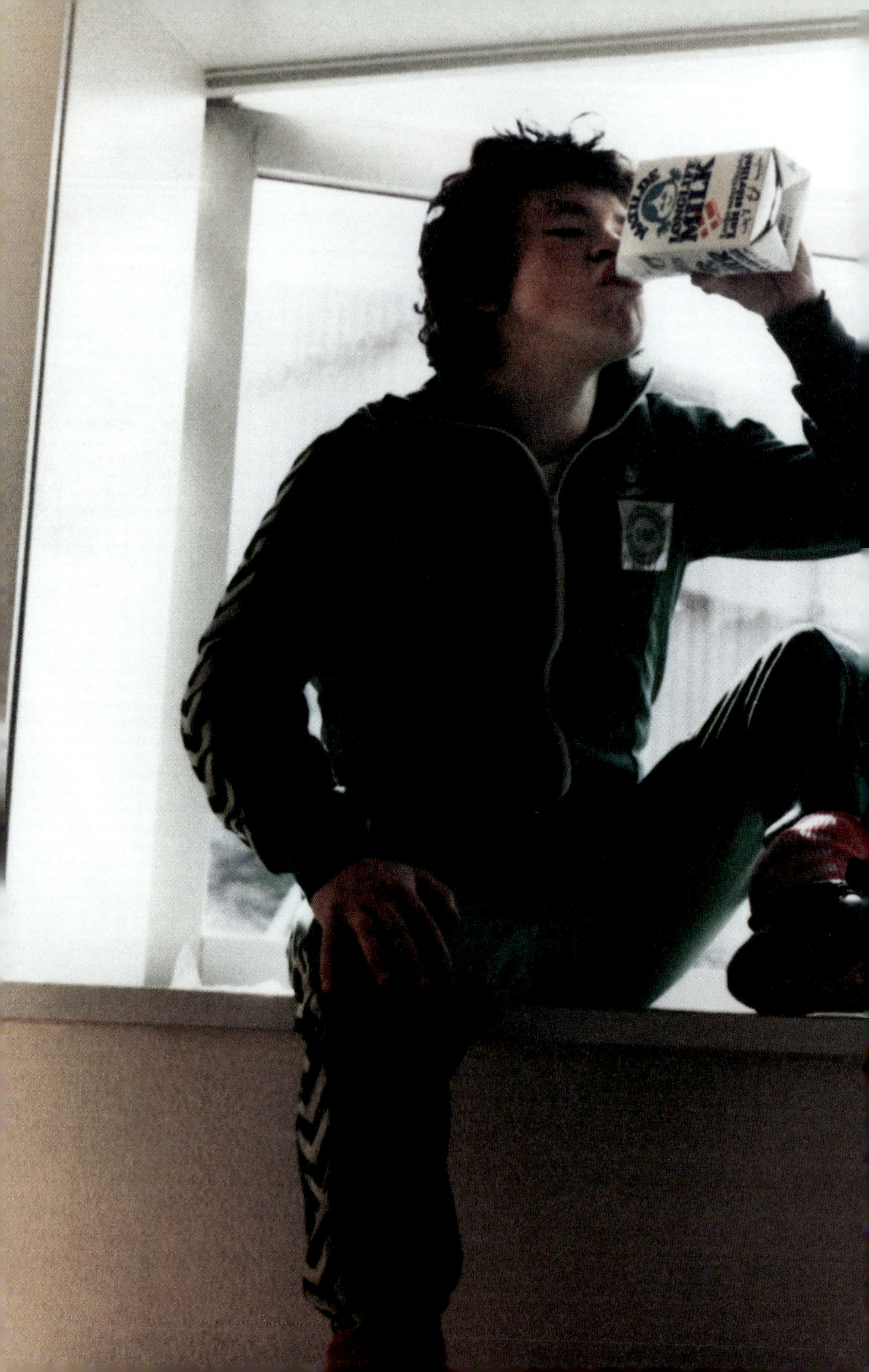

Sep 85 Århus

Asasara Jan-u Emmaqa.

Qanoq ik'. Manga ajunngil- Ikkaluarpunga. (Kisian- sami ~~ma~~ taamani iser- nangajalerlunga allappunngiiviippara naluna- llummummut maani attaa. maassagitit allatak- lersuisi. ...samanngorpat neriinissamik assut sangu- ...qittara

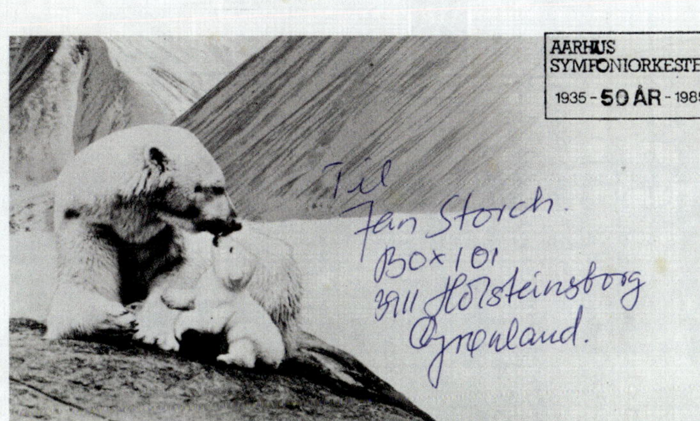

...
(nukkama) kammani ... ilumut imminut
ingasaralunga onnik ajoranik
immikkoortinneq ilAaqqa.
nerani nuersagassaq
Aviaja nalliqeqaara. C...
qulliqer. Tassani taam...
mineq isummami eqqar...
Tassaniuna nalunaru...
ngammik qimaqqallumi...
ngaataa Anda aamma...
vittu sigorusullugu. M...
ger takunikuulluqu...
nikitigalun tassa a...
lereer pala. Sooruaami m...
qarsaatigigaani.
atuarfimmi ulapilaaqaa...
mut. Ilummumi atuarfi...

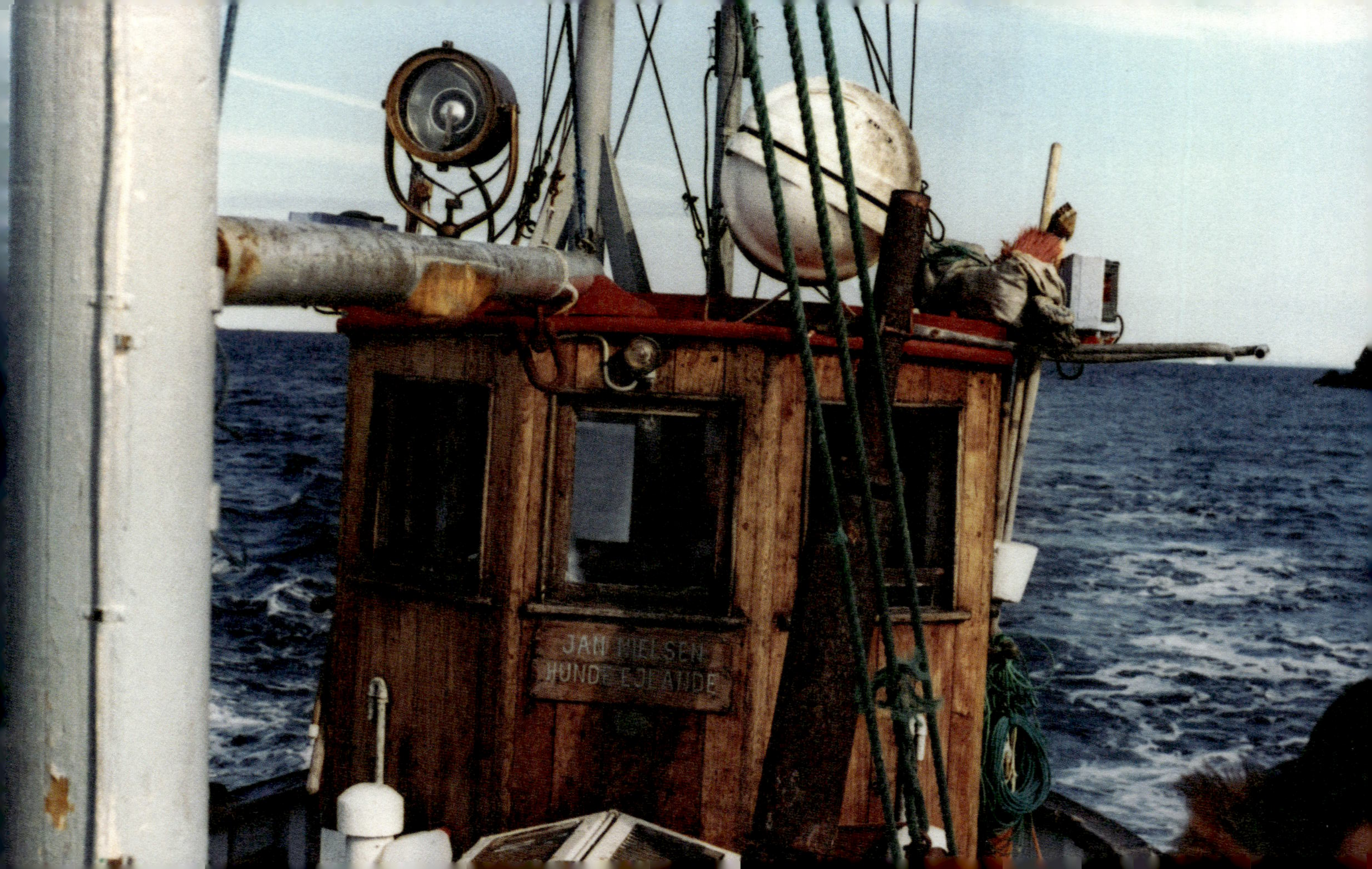
JAN NIELSEN

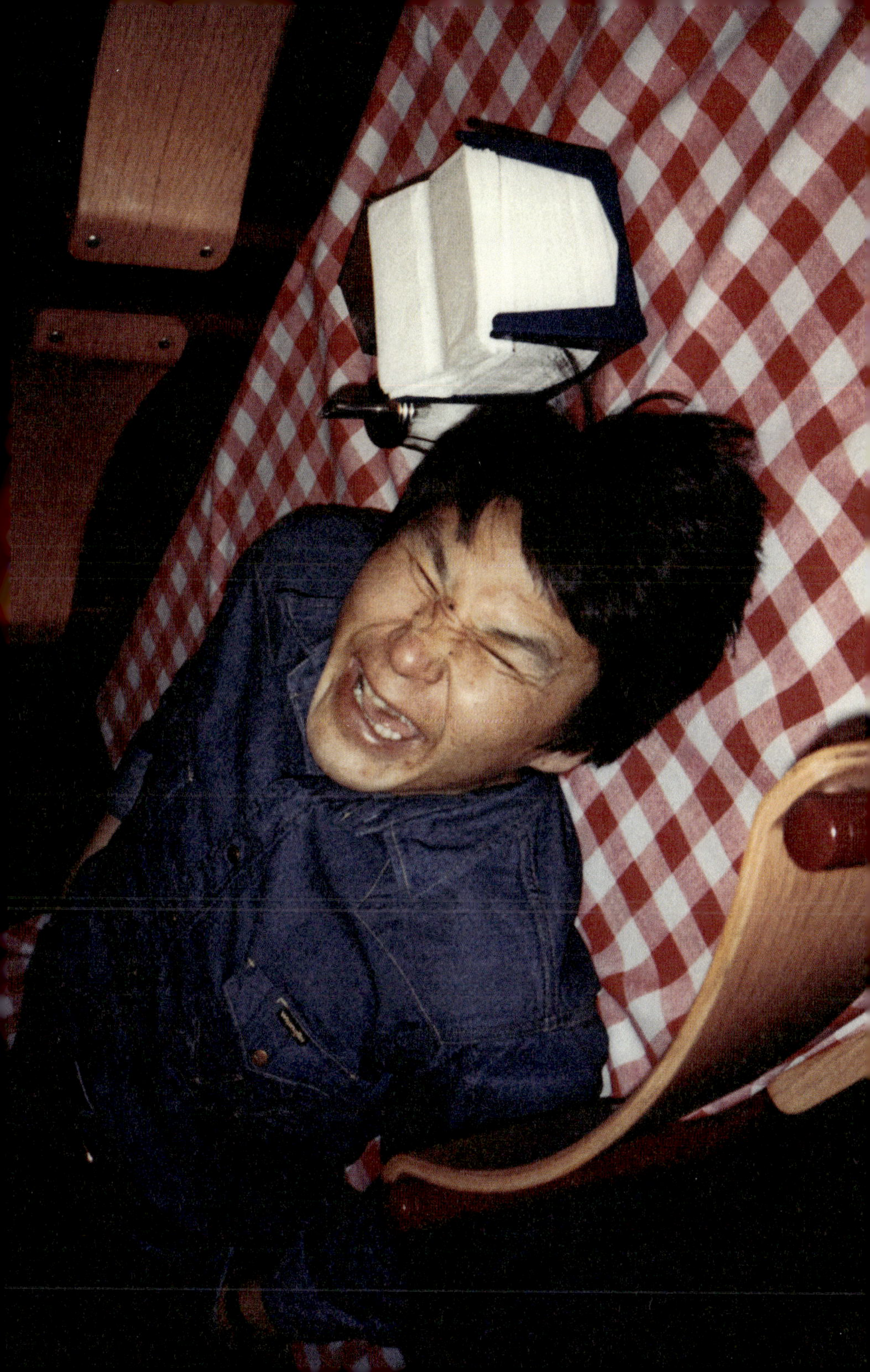

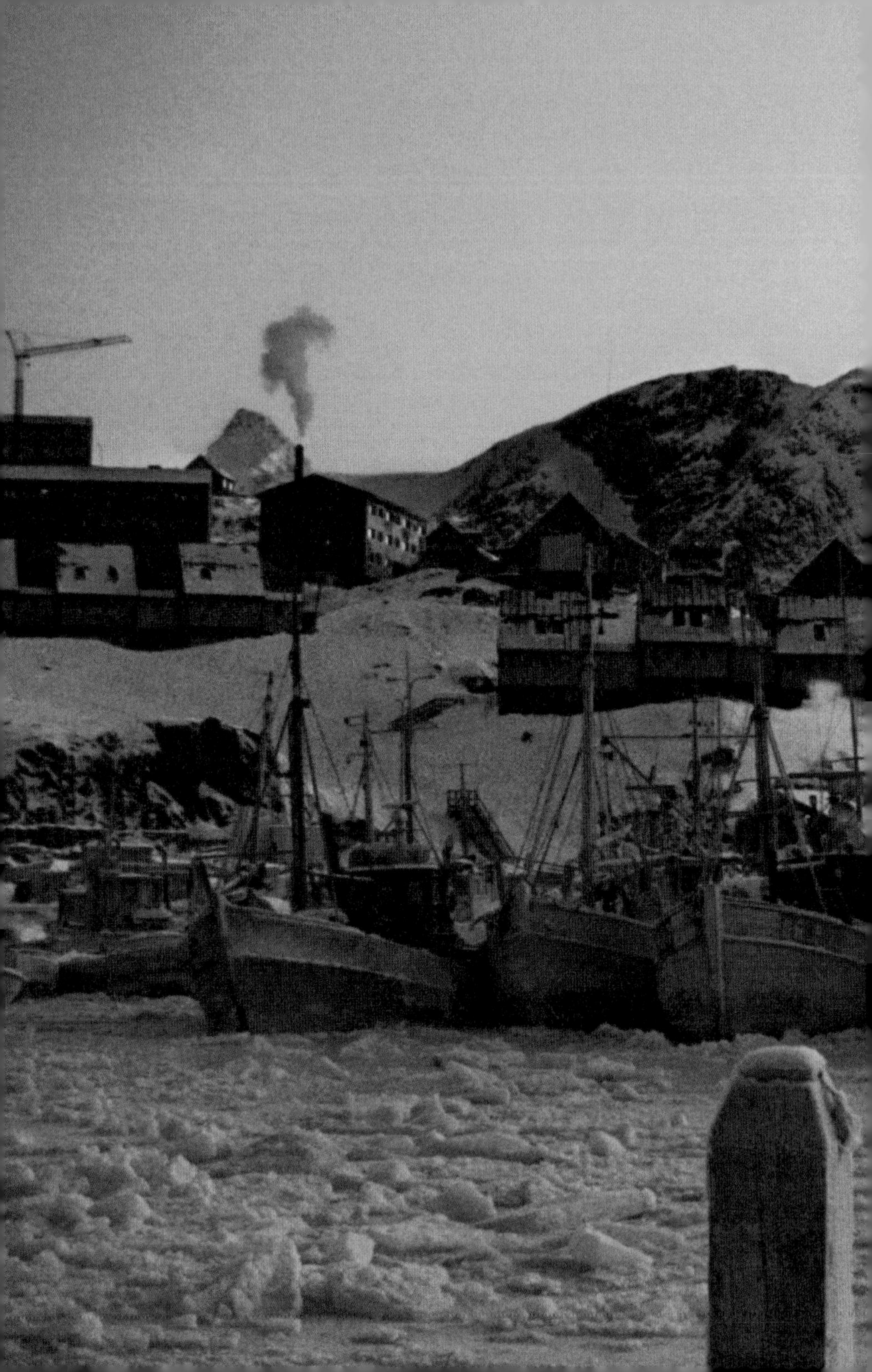

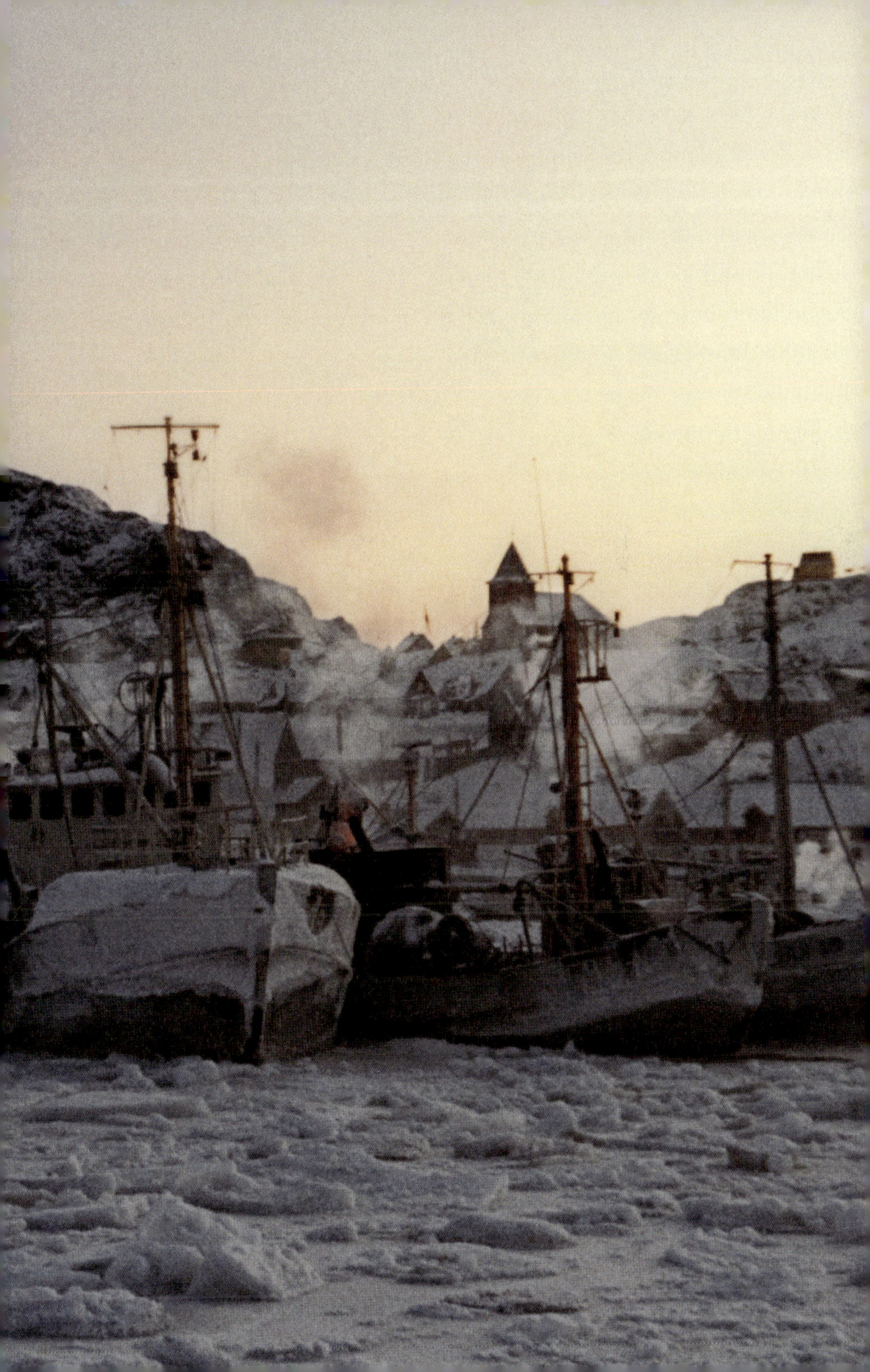

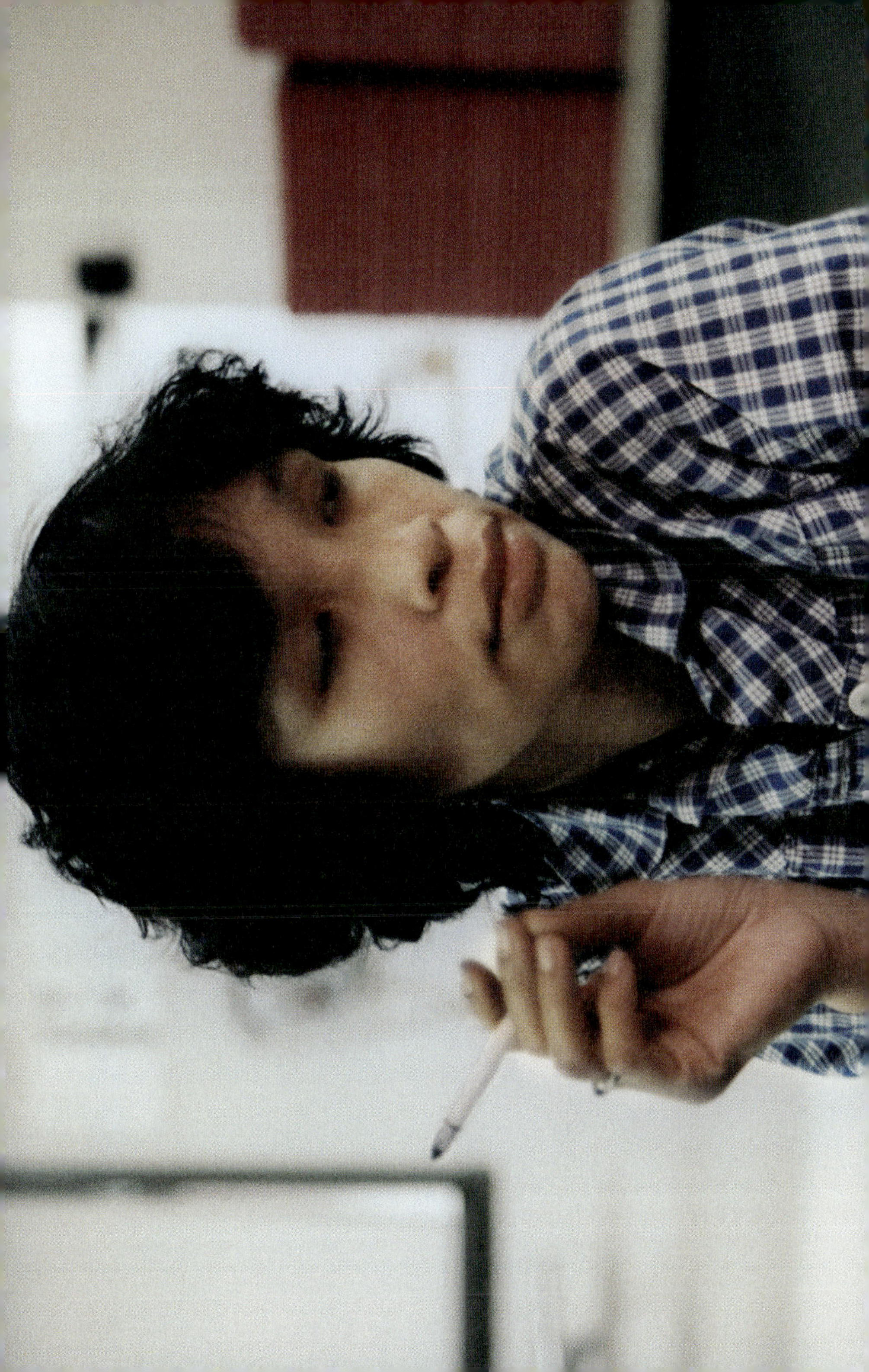

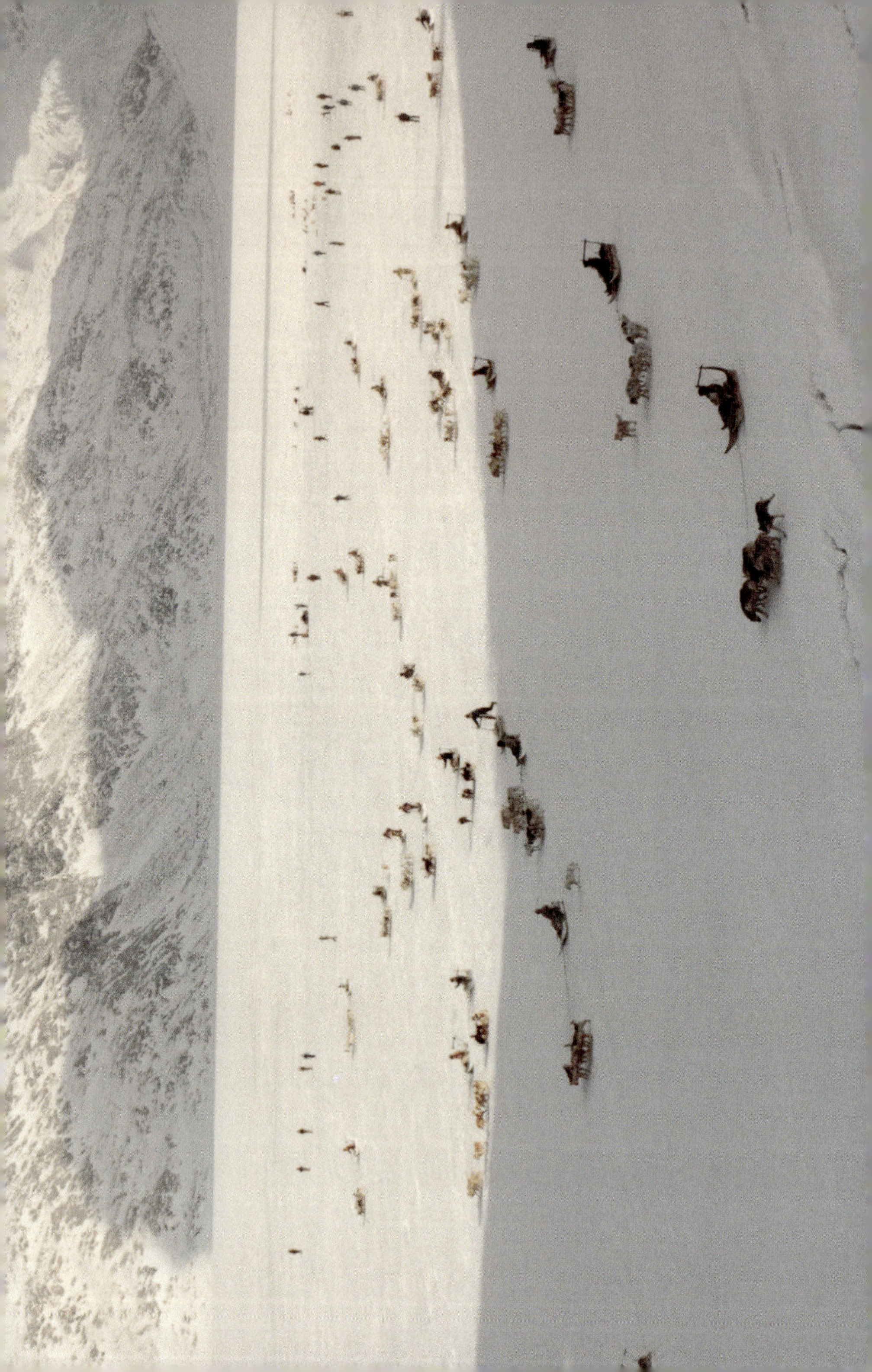

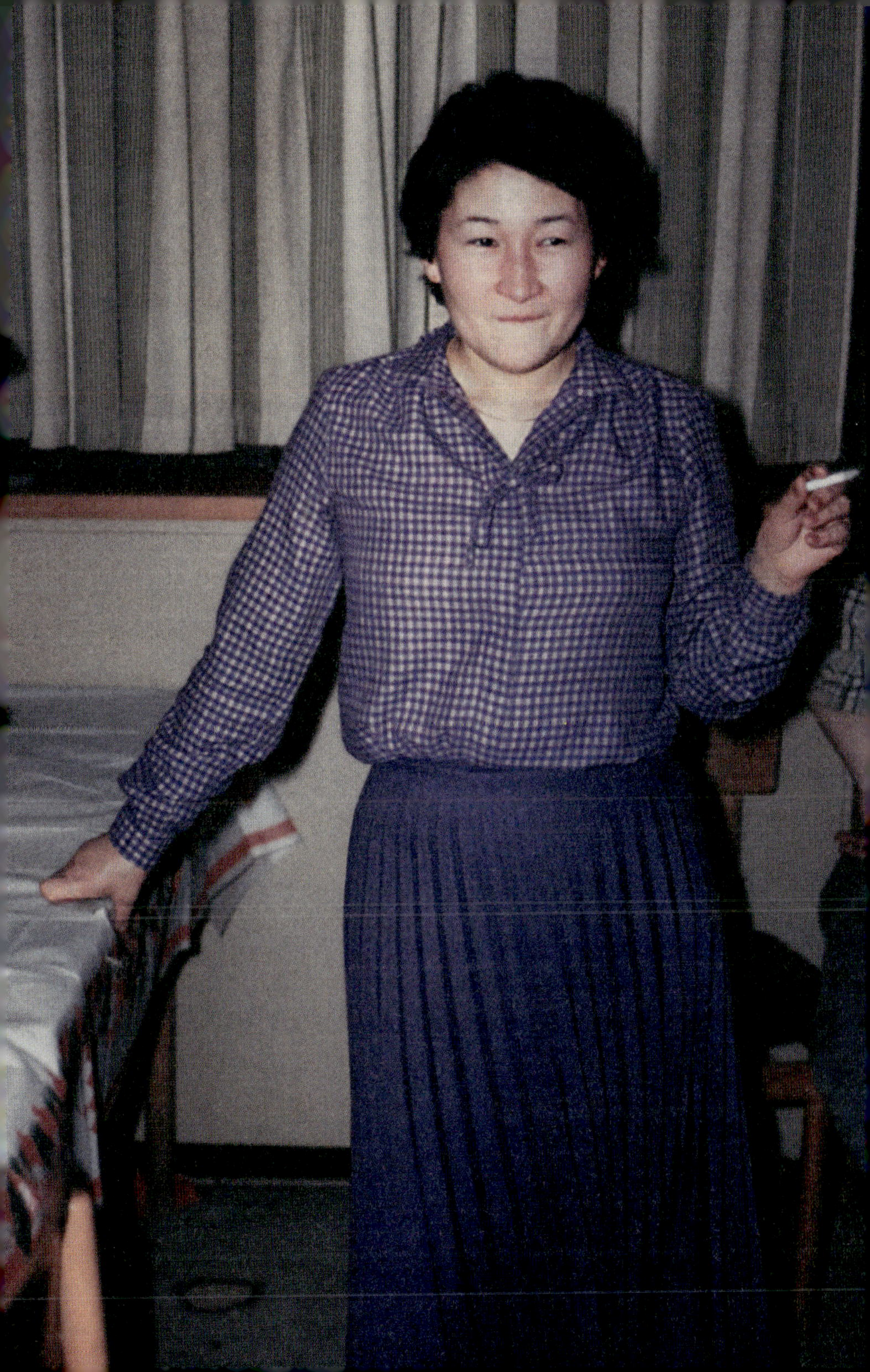

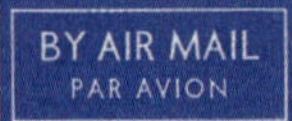

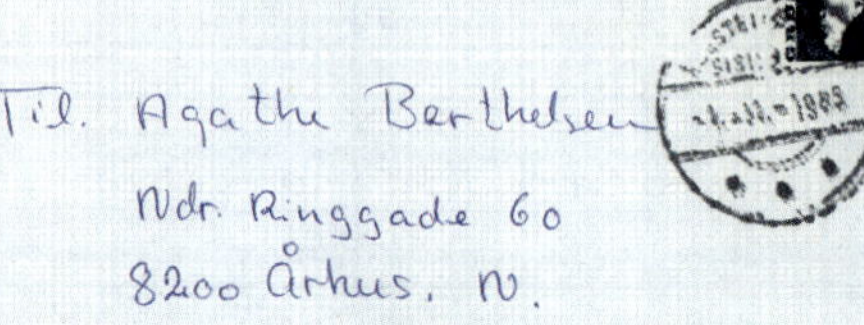

Sisimiut 31-10-85

asasara Aqqa.
kanoq ippit uvanga ajunngilanga asuliuna
naatunnguanik allalaaginnarniarlunga.
Sisimiut ulluni makkunani ajornaqaaq sialler-
nermut kiisa tassa aqusineq kuutuinnanngorput
kiisa sialussiuserluta anisalerpugut, aputituannguaq
kiisa nuguleropoq.
Aqqa neriuppunga Finlandi-mut aqalalluarsimassasutit
nuannertunik alutornartunillu misigissaqarsimassa-
sutit aatsaalli ilangalutit takusassasi[illegible]ugatingalutit
nuannisaqaluvarpoq ippassaq allatitarinikuusara.
aasaq Marmorilimmiillunga. Duun-jakke tikikkami
assut kusanarpoq oqurunarlunilu. merke-qarpoq.
Fjell-ræven. Ekspidistion
Arfininngorpat 02-11. hallimi S 68 festissaqut assut
nuannerunarpoq maaniissaqaluvaravit nuannernerus-
sangaluarpoq aama sapaatiupat hallimi sulifiqar.
fiit arsaqattaarlutit aallartissapput qanorlia illarnar-
torqartigissava nuannerunaqaq.
Asasannguara allamik oqaasissaarutilerpunga
neriuppunga aqalalluarsimassasutit nuannisaar-
lutillu

Asannittumik inuulluarit asasit Jan.

P.S. tassa takunissatinnut qaamatip aapa affanan-
ngulerpoq ilaa ajunaminerarssuaq ilaa erininaq.
pissanganarlunilu. asanannguvaqaatit
takujumaarpugut. baj boj

London Review
OF BOOKS

Repays your attention

12 issues for £12

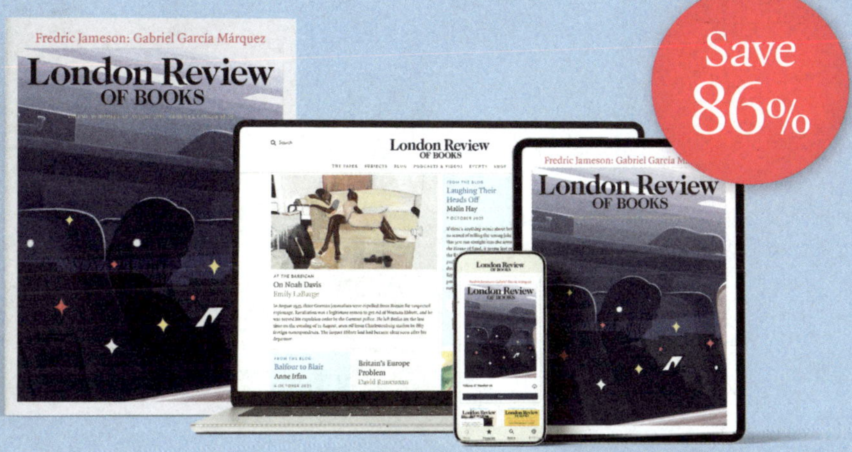

At the *London Review of Books*,
we'll never tell you what to think,
but we'll always make you think.

Subscribe to the *LRB* and enjoy:

- The magazine delivered to your door twice a month.
- Access to the entire *LRB* online archive of more than 18,000 pieces.
- The latest issue FREE on your mobile device through the *LRB* app.
- The ability to cancel at any time.

Subscribe now at: **lrb.me/granta26**

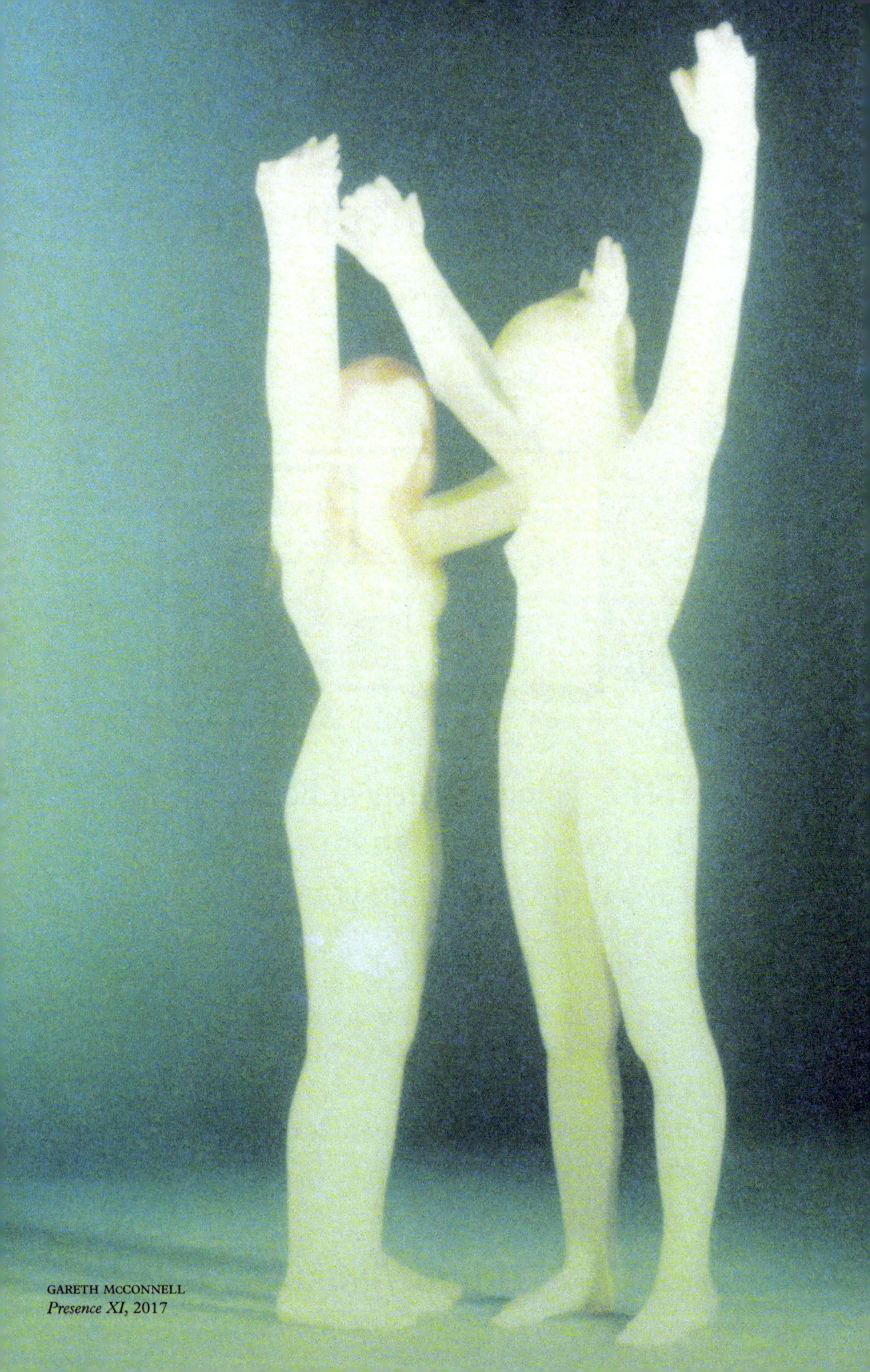

GARETH McCONNELL
Presence XI, 2017

THE FOREST KINDERGARTNERS

Jonas Eika

TRANSLATED FROM THE DANISH BY SHERILYN HELLBERG

Burger – Adda said – we just call it little burger; yeah – Dani said – we haven't found the right name yet, detecting a flash of concern in Sanne's silvery eyes, maybe even discomfort at the *it* which Dani and Paula had also taught Adda to use when she spoke about her little sibling, and Dani was tempted to say that *it* was as good a word as any for this very wonderful and lively but still not-yet-fully-human being that was sleepily smacking its lips on their chest, just as it had been for Adda when she was a baby, even though back then *it* had been just as difficult to hold onto, already in the maternity ward, just seconds after Adda was born, when the midwife, from the foot of the bed, had leaned into Dani and Paula's field of vision and asked*: should I hold it up so you can see what it is?* and Dani could still recall their confusion, of being completely unable to respond, but also their immediate sense that the misplacement of the question didn't lie in the *it*, which was entirely fitting for the body that lay blue, bloody and, as far as Dani could see, still completely limp on Paula's chest, but in the *what* that needed to be answered, filled out, dislodged immediately, and in the moment, still panicked by how close death had seemed for both Paula and the child just minutes earlier, Dani managed to say: *no – no – I just want to know that it's alive!* and it was, and for a long time after, that remained a kind of refrain for Dani, a point of control, a fact to defend against the trite tree of life that the orderly, on the way down to the postnatal ward, asked them to adorn with either a bow or a bow tie, and then later against their father, who from day one insisted on calling Adda 'little lady', against the new government policy that was proposed at some point in the first few groggy months, about 'a child's right to have a mother and a father', against the visiting nurse who came more often than she was supposed to, and who seemed to be, from the corner of her eye, scanning the apartment, Paula and Dani alike for signs of unfitness, as she wrapped a muslin around Adda to weigh her or tested her motor skills by applying pressure to the soles of her feet, and against the demand of a gender that tried to contain the obvious and overwhelming *aliveness* of the child, of its grunting, greedy breath, its gaping stare and its constantly wriggling limbs trying to learn their limits and their strength, a vitality that also emerged in Dani, in the strangely attentive sleep they sank into at night, where they could hear every sound in the apartment and feel their whole body, their buzzing limbs and mouth that autonomously kept mimicking Adda's small smacking motions, the whirr of the organs that took turns being busy through the night, the heart valves that opened and closed, a warm, blue-red feeling of the blood that streamed from one chamber to another and out into the arteries, and when, on rare occasions, the blood sought downwards and gathered in their lap, it felt more like an opening, as if their ass and crotch merged together into one soft and receptive tissue, aliveness against gender, Dani thought again, as they looked at Sanne's worn feet in her black Tevas, even though that was also too simple, reductive, wasn't it, to say that the two existed in opposition to each other, the gendered body and the living body, because, in fact, that initial, half-symbiotic period with Paula and Adda had also triggered a feminization in Dani, or at least a hope of feminization, feeling their mouth become more pursed, their jaw more delicate, their chest softer from the days spent imitating Adda's slightest movements, which sometimes, in the all-too-alert sleep that made the night yawn like a chasm in the pillow between Adda's wake-ups, especially when Dani's breasts were still blooming from having given her milk with the Supplemental Nursing System whenever Paula was out for the night, made Dani wonder if they even needed to medically transition, if perhaps Adda was already giving them all the hormones they needed, but then, when it was finally time for Dani to take their parental leave, their hormone levels started to stabilize and their vitality faded into a dullness in their skin, something pale and blurry in their senses, a vast, gray-white sense of being disconnected from their own body and thus also from Adda's, of maybe not even knowing her yet, not really loving her, yes, and maybe they had never really loved, grieved, felt tenderness or compassion but had only adopted those feelings, learned to mimic them to a tee that made it difficult to tell the difference, and there they had resided, in the gray-white place, for several months when, one day, they found themself in Fælledparken with Adda, early October but still mild, still study groups and mothers' groups scattered across the grass, finches and warblers in the trees, chirping among the lazy gunshots from the new military training site in Nordhavn, and Adda had just fallen asleep in the stroller as they passed the little cruising spot along the bike path, the hidden passage of shadowy paths and hollows beneath the leafy trees, and just the act of recalling it now, here, with Sanne who was being so patient with Adda today, it already felt like a confession, it provoked an instantaneous urge to apologize and explain, because *Adda had just fallen asleep*, which meant that it would be approximately forty-two minutes before she'd wake up again, that was her sleep cycle, *trust me,* you could set your watch by it, while Sanne reminded Adda about the little aquarium that they built out in the forest, didn't she want to check on it today, and Dani had parked the stroller under an ash tree, slipped in the monitor and stood there for a moment, listening to her breathing, *I always listen to her breathing*, the three little nasal gasps, with three small sighs at the end, before leaving the stroller and entering, through the rumpled opening in the foliage, into the first dark enclosure beneath the branches, while the other monitor dangled like a drowsy amulet from their neck and their eyes adjusted to the darkness, the tree trunks, the used napkins and smell of wet earth against the skin that rises and listens: there, in the shrubbery ahead, someone was walking towards them, in shadows and spots of buzzing light, in gray-blue jeans and a windbreaker, with one hand resting at the top of his hip, tender and self-assured, fingers pointing at his groin, and Dani had kneeled and held his gaze, an open and patient gaze, and *was it really so bad*, Dani could have been sitting at a cafe, sipping their coffee like the other parents, who might have forgotten to turn on their monitors and might not have even heard their child crying in the stroller outside, and *that wouldn't be so bad*, really? – Adda asked, her skepticism sliding into curiosity as Sanne told her that the dragonflies might finally have hatched – and if it wasn't so inextricably bound to their dysphoria, if it wasn't so damn gender-affirming to be fucked in the face like that, thoroughly and anonymously, maybe – Sanne said – we have to go and see, and Dani remembered the flickering light in their eyes and the good, deep pain-pleasure from the asshole, spreading through the lower abdomen, suddenly there had been an insistent vibration against Dani's chest, mechanical, from the monitor flashing the round, bawling face, and then they heard it too, from the monitor and further away, through the foliage and the moans behind them, the cries, Adda's cries, but fortunately she managed to hold them back today, to give Dani a hug and voluntarily board the bus, though only because she was carried by Sanne's firm care, her practiced, mildly deflective way of ushering the kids into the day, and Dani thanked her and turned to walk back home, still springy in their legs, with a hand under the baby in the carrier, past the other parents and down Ryesgade with their gaze fixed on the linden trees at the other end of the street, with a knotty discomfort in their bare shoulders, their legs and hips which were accentuated by the platform sandals and the high-waisted denim shorts that barely reached the crop top, why the fuck had they worn a crop top, why had they dressed so slutty today? ■

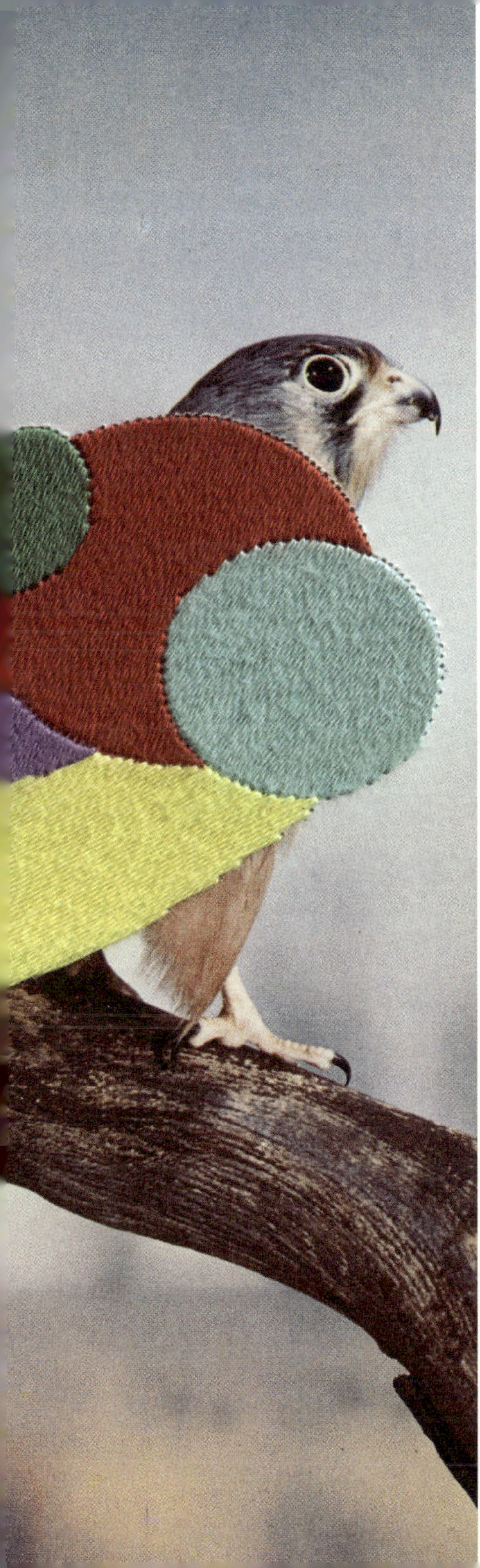

GRANTA
WRITERS'
WORKSHOPS

NATURE WRITING
SHORT FICTION
THE NOVEL
NARRATIVE NON-FICTION
MEMOIR

'This is one of the most rigorous courses I've ever attended. A lifetime's knowledge of literature and writing, a compilation of enriching materials, videos, readings and references that will last a writer a long while.'
– MEIKO KO, COURSE GRADUATE

'Granta's course gave me the confidence and tools to produce, pitch, and publish long-form journalism for the first time. It's a fantastic opportunity for anyone eager to hone skills and guide ambition.'
– COCO PICKARD, COURSE GRADUATE

Image © Julie Cockburn

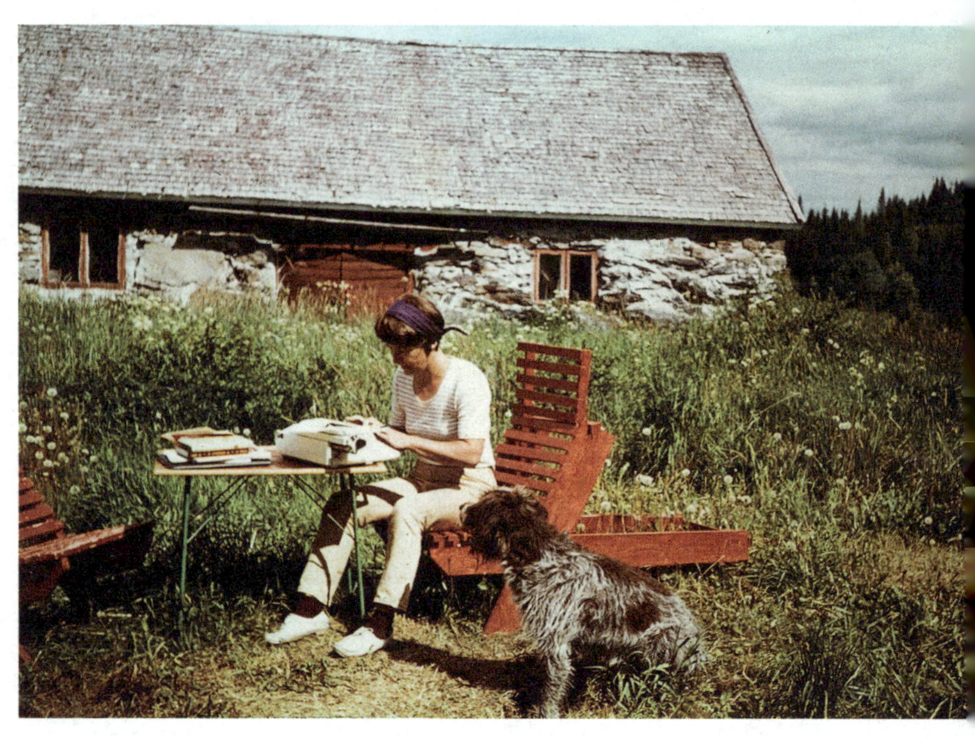

Eeva Kilpi at her cabin in Piskola
Courtesy of the author

JUNE

Eeva Kilpi

TRANSLATED FROM THE FINNISH BY MIA SPANGENBERG

AT THE CABIN, A COLD, GREY THURSDAY.

The first hint of a normal state of mind since Saturday. After evening tea, close to ten, my anger and disappointment ease for a moment.

Just as my anger and anxiety recede, I feel the need to fart. People fart the evil out of themselves.

My difficulty is with close relationships. I can't handle them. What is it that's ruined me?

I've been in a strange state of mind all winter, in truth, since last summer. Only now, in this moment of clarity, do I see it. Am I losing my mind? What is this melancholy, this absence of joy? I'm overcome with the urge to isolate myself. I've cut all ties for the summer. The freedom I've longed for is slowly taking hold. It's a draining transformation.

Cold air streams between the north and north-west. The oil heater ticks. It's night. I imagine a dog breathing in the next bed.

FRIDAY. ABOUT 16.30.

The sun is like a party you unexpectedly stumble into, and, to your surprise, enjoy, despite the depression.

It seems to be getting warmer, contrary to the forecast. It's been beautiful. I've been lounging on the rock in the yard and reading; then I went looking for false morel mushrooms on a whim, without a basket of course, that's the magic. I found eighteen: it could be my best harvest here. I gathered them into my red scarf. A bonus: a bouquet of birch branches to place in the butter churn. I wonder why the junipers have died. The ones in the field are all dead. And the ones bordering the woods are turning brown.

9AM. PENTECOST. SATURDAY.

Today I've said all of two sentences. The first in the late morning: 'Why play that song of all things?' after an announcement on the radio that the next piece would be 'The Last Flowers of Autumn'. I said the second one a moment ago. It went: 'A salami sandwich!' I've just made one for myself, and now I'm going to eat it while I read.

The air is cold as a refrigerator. I get to have my beer cold. What a luxury.

I feel no joy, not even the desire to live – yet my optimism shows faint signs of returning.

I can't be bothered to feel apprehensive about potential visitors these days. I don't bother to put the key in the door before midday – if someone assumes I'm not at home, then so be it. I've decided I'm not even going to try to smile if someone visits. I'll replace my welcoming smile with a look of surprise. It requires less effort and wouldn't offend. How worked up I've made myself anticipating guests in summers past! Always with the thought 'in case someone shows up' at the back of my mind.

I've had the strong urge to isolate myself even before this, most recently last winter, when I was at my parents' cabin in the countryside until the bitter cold drove me away. That phase ended with a trip abroad, giving talks, being in the public eye, and after that I was happy to come home and appreciated the children being close by. A pleasant period that led to this severe spring neurosis, to this pain and depression as the leaves were budding. It's only eased now that I'm here. I mean that literally: it has simply stopped. I feel no joy or euphoria. Only a loose and sour stillness, the consistency of viili yoghurt. A joyless curdling. And a renewed need to be alone. I'm tired of interviews and literary events, the endless questions and appearances. Wish I could hide in a bush. Disappear from the world entirely. Stop smiling. Escape being recognised. To be a plant, unnoticed but intensely alive. With my roots in the soil and my crown in the sun. I want to get my brain working again. Rid myself of my pain and find peace. Return to a normal state of mind. Without any demands. To the life force that is nature. And God willing: to write again. Productively.

If only I didn't need to go to the library, give a friendly hello and present as a writer enjoying their summer. But I must. I've almost finished reading the three books I borrowed, and I'm craving more. That's the only sign of life in me right now.

I dread being around people. Only love could save me from this feeling. But I have no love in me right now.

I don't even feel the desire to call my children, to make contact in any way. Not with them nor with anyone else. Perhaps a little with my parents.

I'm turning into a plant. I think I'll go unnoticed in the woods from now on.

SUNDAY, BEAUTIFUL AND COLD.

I slept a little restlessly. I dreamed about Ilkka and military exercises.

For the first time since last Saturday I find myself able to think of him more favourably. I let myself wonder what it would feel like to invite them here, what it would feel like if they came? Would Ilkka upset me again? Or would it be better if I didn't get involved for a month while he studies for his resit exam alongside his work on the farm? Or would he feel rejected, without a home or family?

The last thought horrifies me, and rouses my maternal sense of self-sacrifice and forgiveness.

I turn it over in my mind.

I spent the morning sleeping and reading. Only drank one cup of coffee, then a cup of tea; I made my bed and combed my hair – my accomplishments for the day. But what is it that's bothering me? That just now I noticed how the skin on my face sags when I looked in the mirror? I can no longer deny it: I have the wrinkled face of an old woman. It's only in the right lighting, when I'm carefully made up – 'dressed' as Mother would say – that I still look like someone.

Children are powerful events in a person's life, natural disasters like weather, the seasons – landslides, floods, or earthquakes. Beyond anyone's will. Something that happened to me without anyone asking my opinion.

Depression latched onto me like a fish hook. If you try to pull it out, it tightens its grip, embeds itself deeper.

AFTERNOON. 3.40.

I listened to the first part of *Salka Valka*. Unlocked the shed. Looked inside. Wasp nests scattered across the floor. I made a birch broom and set it in the water bucket. Now I'm sitting on the rock out front. It's warmer outside than I expected. The rock is completely warm. Not much of a breeze either. Clouds. Sky. Sun. Small flies. The sounds of birds.

I'm suddenly drained of all strength. And tired. I don't have the energy for anything. I just feel bad. It's like a disease. Perhaps it is.

I'll say it now – in case I kill myself – this doesn't have anything to do with the boys, nor because of anything or anyone else. There is no reason for me to be this depressed, this often. If by accident I were to kill myself, it would be because I'm overcome again and again by a depression that I'm powerless to withstand, and which is difficult to endure – as pain is – and leaves me paralysed. It is so severe that I have a few times thought that someone might kill themselves without knowing they were doing so. Just to stop having to endure it. They try to kill the depression and end up killing themselves. It's never occurred to me before that this could happen.

That is why I want to be clear: it doesn't have anything to do with the boys.

I know of no reason for my depression that I can name or understand. Unless there's something in my brain, or I'm suffering from some extreme hormonal imbalance.

Once again I find myself wondering: would the presence of a dog help me at a time like this?

If there's anything I truly long for, it is dogs and swallows.

People need physical pleasure. Without it we become anxious and depressed. Children experience pleasure through their bodies, through intimacy and touch. From cradle to grave, we crave it as we do nourishment.

Skin comes alive to the touch and withers without it. That's why we need cosmetics, massage, and physical therapy.

For the book: love, money, and food – if you have them, they mean little and are taken for granted; when you don't, they assume vast significance.

MONDAY.

The moon appears to be waxing again – yesterday at noon it was only a white sliver in the southern sky. I dread the approaching nights when the moon will be full. It always affects my sleep.

A lonely, suffering person is the epitome of self-centredness and self-scrutiny! A dog would dispel much of that. And a dog is, without question – it's raining, good, everything needs the rain, even me – a dog, without question, drives away self-centredness and loneliness; my contentment here in previous years was in large part thanks to the dog. It didn't just depend on my dog, though, it wasn't solely due to him. There was also the joy of discovering this new place, and the challenges associated with experimenting and adapting. The problems come after such a period, that is – now. But this phase too will grow old. And, unfortunately, so will I.

The young spruces have light green tips. Even the large trees are still growing.

This getting used to things could make me colder and more 'realistic'. Subtleties fade into a painlessness, and into pain again soon as well. This is what middle age does to a person: it coarsens, makes you cold – easily. And what of old age? Will I have the energy to feel anything then? Or will I harden myself in self-defence, to spare my soul further suffering with all its subtleties?

I'm in good spirits – and after such a long time. I knock on wood in my mind. For a whole hour I've felt good. Euphoria? It would be great if it lasted.

The situation in the Middle East is extremely serious. Syrians and Lebanese are fighting in the streets of Beirut. Syria launched a major offensive last night. Egypt has severed diplomatic relations with Syria.

I think about Robin a lot, but I don't miss him. Though one time yesterday – amid the depression – I thought I might still have time to take back my refusal to let him come with a telegram. But then I remembered how much tending he requires. I thought of him the entire time I was in the woods: it felt like he was beside me looking at Mustalampi pond and hunting for false morels with me.

I found one more morel on the path leading to the pond. As I carried it, it suddenly began to feel like a penis in my hand – firm and sensitive, smooth and slightly wrinkled, a little moist like skin, fragile and swollen. It had an exceptionally smooth cap for a false morel.

The radio has decided to offer an abundance of comedy today. Just now her royal highness of solitude was enlivened with an episode of *Radiolääkäri* called 'A Gynaecological Summer Memo'. What dangers lie in wait for the social at this time of year: lice, gonorrhoea, and the ultimate catastrophe: a child! Urinary tract infections and trichomonas. You must be on guard at every moment if you happen to have dealings with the opposite sex. What horrors I'm spared! I'm not even among those that so-called 'doctor' called 'casual pleasure-seekers', as opposed to married couples and people in stable relationships. The latter aren't threatened with gonorrhoea as punishment, nor presumably by lice, those pesky vermin that 'lead a jolly life down in your pubic hair'. The pill must be taken right on time. Even being off by a few hours can result in a 'catastrophe'.

I wonder how anyone will dare to fall in love after listening to that nonsense. Its greatest merit was that those who didn't listen to it were spared a great deal. May the good Lord shield us from such a life!

My meal: false-morel stew picked by the artist herself + a tomato (large one) and rye bread (dark) with a Finlandia beer. Then a cup of lemon tea and a vanilla bagel to top it off.

(Could it be that my intermittent waves of arousal are due to the vanilla biscuits?) Now once again I have the strength to endure beauty. And just as I'm finishing my meal, the sun comes in through the window for dessert. The rain has stopped, and my bird is singing. The spruces are light green. The pines are tipped with candles.

Sex, money, food, potency are all alike. They don't mean much when you have them. But if you don't, they override everything.

Writing requires an atmosphere of complete immersion. Within that lies the faith needed to create a new world, one that lives and breathes on its own terms. It's like a lily pad you float on while writing. It's like falling in love, like the mind becoming erotically charged and coloured by a dominant tone. It's faith, an obsession. It's the trickling source of a spring that must not be touched, only drawn from.

This atmosphere can be cultivated by reading, thinking, walking, by dedicating yourself to it, carrying your typewriter and paper to the table, as I did today. It's like foreplay.

I hate this typewriter of mine, supposedly a good make. I've now taken it from its case and set it on the table. It may well be the main culprit behind my neck and shoulder pain – they're so stiff. It's ruined my neck vertebrae. And yet it enjoys a fine reputation. Granted, it may be quite durable: I'll break before it does.

22.00.

A generous half-moon glows in the south-west in a light sky. The eternal wonders of a summer night.

Frost threatens again. I feel a powerless rage even though I don't grow anything. It stunts growth, freezes the lilac buds, torments the birds.

I still remember from my early days as a writer how some task or subject would excite me, how I'd drive myself to the point of mental exhaustion so that I could squeeze something extraordinary even from ordinary work. I had the feeling – and still have – that if something can't be done in an original way, it's not worth doing at all.

The conventional truly is not worth the effort.

But enthusiasm like that no longer comes so easily. I'm more self-critical now. And the only recognition I've received has come from women's magazines. Never from the critics in Helsinki. Sometimes I wonder what my 'career' would have become had I been praised more generously: would it have strengthened my confidence? We writers long for encouragement, endlessly so. As it is, I've been left with my continued attempts to write, despite the lack of recognition and how random it is. For some reason I haven't received much recognition – it's been paltry. And I hate such meanness. Perhaps people think I'm conceited, though I'm merely self-centred. Demanding in my work, but otherwise modest.

Anna died. Four days ago. In the evening.

Yki sent me a telegram the next day, but I didn't go to the letter box until today, on my way into town. I couldn't reach Yki by telephone. Nor my mother. I sent a card to Ilkka, a greeting. Suddenly it felt natural and clear.

Anna's death depresses me and brings me to tears, although it's unquestionably for the best. What a victory for death, to finally get that emaciated person! It makes me think I'd rather not give death the satisfaction of deciding when to end a person's suffering, how long to torture them. What must Anna's sister and brothers feel, soon to be facing death themselves, when I feel like this? I've never before understood the horror of death. Now I do. There is nothing noble about death. It is nothing but horrifying. Against life and humanity.

Life appears to be nothing more than a hopeless endeavour, doomed to fail right from the start, a disorder, an anomaly.

I wonder whether I will ever feel the will to live again. It's superficial, but I would love to have a share. How can anyone bear to live confronted by the void?

Everything loses its meaning and purpose. It's superficiality that creates meaning.

I'm not afraid of death; I'm horrified, repulsed by it. I understand the caricatures that have been made of death, by Simberg and others, the dancing spectres from the Middle Ages. It is this feeling that led to those symbols. I didn't understand them before; I didn't feel this way. Perhaps everyone feels this way once. But how can you live, how can you desire to live, how can you let death decide? How can you live at the mercy of death?

The only salvation left for us is naivete.

MORNING. THE SUN IS SHINING. 11.20.

My dog's grave is growing lily of the valley, cow parsley, speedwell, and raspberry. I moved some moss to the gravestone, by the polypody ferns. It's a good place for him to rest, by a beautiful hillock, beneath the rocks, mosses, and lichen that I've gathered myself.

In a melancholy mood, I went for a walk in the woods, with a basket in case I found some false morels. Of course I found none, having come prepared; the mushrooms were in hiding. One thought kept running through my mind: you must become friends with life's sorrows . . .

It seems to be getting warmer as the forecasters predicted, but there's a strong wind. The frost bites deep, and the air has been so cold that the dandelions are only now beginning to bloom more abundantly and take over the fields. The wind rattles the cabin. Every now and then I think I hear voices, people talking. The tall, dead grasses rustle in the wind as if someone were approaching.

I've thought about it, and I've decided not to go to Anna's funeral, though I promised her I would when she asked me. I'll fulfil my promise from here, I'll be with her in spirit. I know she would understand. There will be strangers at the funeral, but no Anna. I would be further away from her there than I am here. I'll ask Yki to send a bouquet.

21.22.

I cleaned the sauna, heated it and bathed. It felt good. As though even my dizziness eased somewhat in the löyly, the steam rising from the stones. It's a beautiful, cool evening. The wind has died down. My soul was bathed and feels at peace.

A moon two days short of full looks at me from the southern sky, and it makes me happy to think that I managed to begin writing during the waxing moon.

People in this region always say that work, sowing, planting, building – everything you want to grow and prosper – must be started during the waxing moon. Then it will succeed. In any case I've begun: I wrote the first chapter, and I read it and accepted it. It forces me to keep going.

WEDNESDAY. 20.40.

I drove the letter for Ilkka to the letter box (which has been moved from the school to the old store and is emptied at six in the morning). It's such an awkward letter. While typing it – so that he might actually bother to read it through, fearing he wouldn't and wishing that he would – I realised how truly helpless I am as a mother. I was never able to relate naturally to the boys, except when they were little things who appealed to my senses and acted in accordance with their own. The truth is I should never have had children I could ruin. I don't know how to be a mother. I never have. And both the boys and I have suffered because of it.

And yet I must say: even though I've been a bad mother, I don't deserve to be rejected or treated badly in return. None of my three children keep in touch with me, not one thinks that I might like a hello or a visit; no one lets me know of their comings and goings, often not even when they're gone for long periods of time. Not one sends me his address, let alone cares how I'm doing. I need wood. I'm going to get sick from all this sawing. My shoulders and arms ache. And it's been so cold that I've been forced to heat the cabin. I shouldn't be carrying things. I have an oil heater, but I have to carry in the oil for it. At least Yki informed me of Anna's death in a proper and respectful manner.

Perhaps it's when your children are grown up, after caring for them for so long, for decades, that you begin to wish that they in turn would take on the responsibility of staying in touch, that they would take the initiative, since they're the ones who are more mobile, and scattered far and wide.

I'm trying to think about the men I know and what they're like. Are they all men who don't stay in touch with their parents? Is it really true that only daughters maintain contact and sons don't, as my sisters and I have discussed, assuring one another that we'll be left all alone in our old age because we only have sons? It's too much for a lonely mother like me. You raise three boys and then you end up alone and forgotten, forgotten three times over. It's not fair.

What makes boys so cold emotionally?

The most difficult relationship between men and women must be between sons and their mothers. Another woman always gets in the way. And if one doesn't, it's even worse. Sons become distant because of the 'other woman' – and usually needlessly so. Nature is ruthless. It's hard for parents to be abandoned in their old age.

I've been divorced for ten years now, and I'm still alone. And that, after all, was the intention. The divorce for me was a choice between living alone and being married. My dog is dead. My children are almost gone. As then – during that summer, ten years ago – I've been lying awake at night in anguish. I can only conclude that this pain is an integral part of my life, no matter what my circumstances may be. Strangely enough I'm always alone, abandoned in one way or another. Perhaps it's inevitable.

FRIDAY.

A clear day. I woke up in pain and prayed. I'm very worried about Ilkka and long for intimacy. I began the second chapter.

I just saw my shadow on the wall of the outhouse. Despite everything it looked human. It had a few curls in its hair. I looked at it kindly.

SATURDAY. BEAUTIFUL, COLD.

The day Anna will be buried and the day Robin could have come.

My neighbours were here yesterday evening. We had a good time. And this morning I'm in no pain at all. I instinctively prayed for Ilkka as soon as I woke up.

I'm drinking coffee and eating the good barley flatbread the neighbours brought, and reading Laxness. They also brought me roast veal, from the calf I saw hanging from their awning when I drove past.

Laxness reminded me of an old thought of mine, one I've had about Mother: the way someone experiences things determines whether they find richness in everyday life or not. Mother does. For her, everything is exciting, fascinating or pitiful, sad or solemn. I've inherited this rewarding but burdensome trait from her. Laxness – no matter what he's writing about – transforms everything into something mythical and magical. This mindset could be taught to children. Mothers could do it. It's an emotional thing and is learned in emotional contexts.

'A person can't be blessed with a man every summer!' I came up with this answer for Mr Ventonen, one of my summer neighbours. I was in the sauna washing my nightgown and imagining him coming over to chat; I heard voices coming from the Ventonens' cabin, and their boat was on the shore.

MONDAY.

A heavy meal requires a heavy dessert. I ate the rest of the roast veal with two potatoes and some sliced cucumber. Plus the beer brought by Heikki and Tuulikki. And to top it all off: two chocolate cookies and one cream cracker spread with marmalade. I'm about to burst.

And: I finished the second chapter. Note: I'm tired after writing. I've been sitting for too long. My body is tingling. I think I'll go heat the sauna. Tomorrow I'll probably have to go into town. I'm out of bread. The coffee and tea are running low. Etc. What bliss: no pain today. An unexpected, unforeseen gift for someone like me. I read Laxness while I ate. Laxness has made me understand again, after a long time, how you should write. In Laxness nothing has destroyed his fundamental trust in the correspondence between experience and expression, which is essential for a work to feel natural.

The sky has cleared for the night. Moisture condenses on the blades of grass. It means a sharp drop in temperature, perhaps frost.

It's half past ten in the evening. I've had my sauna and a dip in the pond. The water was as cold as in a well: it was a quick dip. I sawed and chopped firewood. No one blesses me with any. I've also done a little laundry almost every day. Yesterday my nightgown, today a scarf. Mist creeps out from under the rocks, trails along the tips of the grass and out onto the paths. I feel sorry for nature.

Many nights I've slept in my clothes, in trousers and a woollen jumper, sometimes because of the cold, sometimes from sheer exhaustion. Mother would regard it as a mark of severe decline. I'm doing it tonight, too. My hair's damp. It's cold. I don't want to disrupt my body's thermal economy any further by changing into a nightgown. I console myself with the thought that this is how people sleep in cabins in Lapland, too, and no one thinks anything of it.

I've calmed down. My sense of reality has held. I'm here on the ground and not about to evaporate into space or to dissolve into the mist; I'm not merging with plants or decomposing into the soil. And I've been writing. I finished the second chapter, five and a half pages.

THURSDAY, AND STRONG WINDS AGAIN, AS YESTERDAY.

The neighbours were here last night. I've realised that despite my anxiety, I enjoy these sorts of evenings. We drank many cups of tea – the usual kind and rose hip – because it was extremely cold, and I burned beautiful twigs in the stove the whole time. It grew warm because the doors were shut. The night sky was light and clear, but the wind brutally strong.

I slept well and until 11! Almost around the clock.

I ate a meagre lunch, and without an appetite. Andalusian soup seasoned with local chives. Half a beer. Sourdough bread. A piece of cheese. And plum brandy, Murska Sobota Slivovitz straight from the bottle – which only made me cry. The Saalem Church choir sang 'The Crystal Stream' in the background, and my eyes obeyed. The cloud hanging over the cabin released its rain.

I'm beginning to see and as it were, to understand. I've 'returned' from somewhere. Laing speaks of 'the journey'. I've just returned from a journey into suffering which for some reason I was compelled to undertake. All along I felt I couldn't avoid it, I could only go through with it; that it has a purpose, and that I must understand something; that it burned a path through something, from one state into another, and though it hurt, my only choice was to follow. Now I may have made it through. I feel battered, but the pain has stopped. I don't know what it was for yet.

FRIDAY, COLD, CLOUDY, RAW. 12.53.

The sun is shining weakly. The cabin creaks, stretching its stiff limbs. The forecast all across Finland: rain and clouds. No interest in mentioning the temperature in numbers. They only said it would 'remain steady or drop a little'.

MONDAY.

There is no meal more beautiful and delicious than the one I have just set down for myself for the first time in a good long while: green nettle soup in a yellow bowl on an orange-checked tablecloth, and beside it a long chunk of sourdough bread with cheese, a bottle of Finlandia beer, and Osip Mandelstam's *The Noise of Time*. Along with the sun, and some smoke from the damp stove.

Every evening I seem to hear distant voices approaching, awakening a curious anticipation, as if a cheerful crowd were coming down the road chattering and bringing with them a surprise that would transform this dreary life. It certainly is dreary, I mean joyless, even though I feel fine now except for the pain in my shoulder. My only thrills are literary ones. At least I have those.

I wrote two and a half pages today, and there won't be more. No clouds. The sky is clear. 15–18 degrees is the forecast for tomorrow. That will have to do. If only it wouldn't rain.

TUESDAY. 15.34.

I ate deliberately, cautiously, and as may soon become apparent, with skill, because I'll probably avoid the depression that's been threatening me so insistently. I'm tired; the feeling of having 'low blood sugar' is both physical and mental. If, for instance, I'd drunk a beer on an empty stomach, no possible power could have prevented me from collapsing into tears. But I remained calm, moved carefully, and talked to myself slowly, in a soothing voice, as I pulled the carts filled with the groceries into the yard. I pretended to be walking along the edge of a jagged precipice, knowing that only patience would bring me back to safe ground again. I ate some peeled cucumber first. It was refreshing. I remembered the cucumber sellers on the streets of Istanbul and the trip I took there with Ilkka six years ago. I thought too that those kinds of trips might well be behind me by now. It was good that I got to travel with the boys when they still wanted to travel with me. Fortunately I had remembered myself at the store: I had bought warm pork ribs. I was thankful to myself as I ate them with fresh sourdough bread. The meat wasn't too salty like last time, but just right, mild and juicy. I only drank the other half of the open bottle of beer and now a cup of tea: I had put some water in the Thermos, and it was hot. I think I will survive, though my conversation with Ilkka threatened to crush me. He 'ended the call' as he had threatened he would, and I let him. I kept my voice friendly throughout, but I would have liked to talk about his finances in more detail. He's run out of money again, but refused to discuss it further. I wrote him a card. He hadn't read my letter until he got home just now. He didn't mention it. He has his English exam tomorrow. That's the main thing that helped me to be friendly, but I also felt that I can't go on always praying for my children. I can't help it if he wants to be angry with me. I walked the streets repeating this sentence like a mantra in my mind.

I also talked to Yki. It was a civil conversation and gave me some comfort. Yki is leaving for Crete the same week I must go home for a quick visit.

Now I'm going to sink into bed.

I long for the life lie. Ibsen is right. How can anyone bear to live without it. How much more welcome the lie of a formal, superficial, friendly conversation would be than this harsh truthfulness!

I don't know how to be a mother. And perhaps the boys don't know how to be children either.

I can't go on living in this state of depression. Not for years. Not like this.

I think much that is valuable can be written from experience – if you survive and still have some strength left to do it.

I must endure this pain, see what's on the other side.

Every now and then I get light-headed and feel my mind fading. 'Blacking out' as Father would say.

I keep getting up to look down the road though I'm not expecting anyone. And I hear voices, conversations, as if people were speaking to one another.

22.31.

The sky has cleared, it's grown quiet, and I feel a little better.

I had no energy to write. Another day wasted. ■

GRANTA TRUST

Granta would be unable to fulfil its mission without the generosity of its donors. We gratefully acknowledge the following individuals and foundations:

Ford Foundation
British Council
Jerwood Foundation
Pulitzer Center
Amazon Literary Partnership
Sigrid Rausing
The Hans and Marit Rausing Charitable Trust
Anonymous
Bloomsbury Publishing Plc
SALT
Open Society
The Common Humanity Arts Trust
Jonathan and Ronnie Newhouse Fund
Hawthornden Foundation

We also thank the following readers, including those who wish to remain anonymous, for their kind support:

Anonymous
Alex Fardon
Jared Hameloth
Michael Isard

CONTRIBUTORS

Ikram Abdulkadir is a Swedish-Somali photographer whose published works include the photo book *Do You Remember the Ocean, Abaayo?*

Martin Aitken is a translator of Scandinavian literature, whose translations include work by Karl Ove Knausgård, Olga Ravn, Hanne Ørstavik and Helle Helle.

Mamma Andersson is a Swedish artist whose paintings draw inspiration from a wide-ranging blend of photography, theatre and art history. Her latest exhibition, *Oeuvres sur papier*, will be on view at David Zwirner Paris until the end of June 2026.

Kyrre Andreassen is a Norwegian author who has published multiple short story collections and novels, including *Furthermore, I Consider That Carthage Must Be Destroyed.*

Solvej Balle's books include *Lyrebird* and *According to the Law: Four Accounts of Mankind.* Six titles within her planned septology, *On the Calculation of Volume*, have been published in Danish so far, with translations under way in over thirty countries.

Charlotte Barslund translates books and plays from Norway, Denmark and Greenland. She is currently translating *The Forest and the River* by Karl Ove Knausgård.

Ingvild Burkey is a Norwegian author and translator. Her published works include two volumes of poetry, a novel, a collection of short prose and a book of stories. Among her translations into English are Karl Ove Knausgård's *Seasons Quartet.* She is currently at work on a novel.

Maja Daniels is a Swedish photography-based artist and film-maker whose work incorporates sociological methodology, sound, moving image and archive materials. Her books include *Elf Dalia* and *Gertrud.*

Jonas Eika is the author of *Lageret Huset Marie, Efter solen* (*After the Sun*) and *Åben* *himmel*, which will be published in English as *Open Heavens* by Granta Books and Riverhead Books in 2027. 'The Forest Kindergartners' is an excerpt from a novel in progress.

Jon Fosse is the 2023 Nobel Prize in Literature laureate. His latest novel, *Vaim Hotel*, will appear with Fitzcarraldo Editions in autumn 2026.

Stephen Gill's photographic practice spans over forty years and his works are held in private and public collections. Recently published bodies of work include *Night Procession*, *The Pillar*, *Please Notify the Sun* and *Magnificent Failure*.

Denise Rose Hansen is a Danish editor and writer. Her fiction has been published in *Granta* and *Ache*. Her novel *Blue Sunset* is forthcoming in 2026.

Sherilyn Hellberg is a writer and literary translator based in Copenhagen. Her work has appeared in the *New Yorker*, the *Paris Review* and *Frieze*. Her translation of Jonas Eika's *After the Sun* was published in 2021.

Helle Helle is the Danish author of multiple novels and two collections of short fiction. Her work has been translated into twenty-four languages and includes *Rødby-Puttgarden*, *Dette burde skrives I nutid* and *they*. Her most recent novel, *Hey Hafni*, was published in 2025.

Vigdis Hjorth is a Norwegian writer. Her novel, *Det gode mennesket i Sandvika* (*The Good Person of Sandvika*), was published in 2025. Her latest title in English translation is *Repetition*, published in 2026.

Eeva Kilpi is a Finnish poet and writer whose books include the novel *Tamara*, the poetry collection *Animalia*, and the trilogy of war memoirs about her evacuation from Karelia during WWII.

Karl Ove Knausgård is the author of the autobiographical novel cycle, *My Struggle*. His most recent novel to appear in English is *The School of Night*. His work is published in thirty-six languages.

CONTRIBUTORS

Aleksi Koponen is a translator from Finnish to English and an opera singer. His translation work includes the short story collection *Belgrade Noir* by Kati Hiekkapelto et al and *The Olive-Green Rucksack* by Jaana Johansson.

Larissa Kyzer is a writer and Icelandic–English literary translator. Her recent and forthcoming full-length translations include *The Mark* by Fríða Ísberg, *The Strongest Woman in the World* by Steinunn G. Helgadóttir, and *Sixty Kilos of Knockouts* by Hallgrímur Helgason.

Olivia Lasky translates literature from Norway, Sápmi, Denmark and Sweden. Recent work includes pieces by Karl Ove Knausgård and Laila Stien, with her translation of Thorvald Steen's *The Valet* forthcoming in 2026.

Sunna Dís Másdóttir is a poet and writer who also works as a translator, editor and teacher. She is part of the poetry collective Svikaskáld. Her first novel, *Kul*, was published in 2024, and her poetry collections include *Plómur* and *Postulín*.

Esja Alyssa Matich is a Reykjavík based poet-translator whose work spans contemporary and mid-century Icelandic literature. Her translations include Ásta Sigurðardóttir's *Nothing to Be Rescued* and Svava Jakobsdóttir's forthcoming *Twelve Women Under a Volcano*.

Lucy Moffatt has translated eighteen fiction and non-fiction books from Norwegian, most recently *Wolverine Tracks* by Dag O. Hessen.

Audun Mortensen is a Korean adopted Norwegian author of twelve books of fiction and poetry. He is currently a PhD candidate at the University of Oslo.

Asta Olivia Nordenhof is a poet and novelist. *Money to Burn*, published in 2020, and *The Devil Book*, published in 2023, are the first two novels in her planned septology.

Lars Norén was a Swedish playwright and author whose plays include *Natten är dagens mor*, *Kaos är granne med Gud*, *Personkrets 3:1* and *7:3*. The final volume of his *Diary of a Playwright* was published posthumously in 2022.

Patrick Phillips is the author of four poetry collections, including *Elegy for a Broken Machine*. His latest work of non-fiction, *The Kellogg Place: American Wealth in Black and White*, is forthcoming in 2027.

Sigrid Rausing is the publisher of *Granta* magazine and Granta Books. She is the author of *History, Memory and Identity in Post-Soviet Estonia*, *Everything Is Wonderful*, *Mayhem* and the co-author and translator of *And the Walls Became the World All Around*.

Olga Ravn is a Danish author. She has published eight books, three of them translated into English. Her latest novel, *The Wax Child* – translated by Martin Aitken – was published in 2025.

Jennifer Russell and **Sophia Hersi Smith** are translators based in Copenhagen. Their translations include *My Work* by Olga Ravn and *There Lives a Young Girl In Me Who Will Not Die* by Tove Ditlevsen.

Pirkko Saisio is a Finnish writer, actor and theatre director. She has written numerous novels, plays and scripts for film and television. *Suliko*, her most recent novel, was published in 2024.

Damion Searls translates the work of Jon Fosse and Victoria Kielland from Norwegian and is currently co-translating Jens Pauli Heinesen's *The Driftwood Man* from Faroese. He is the author of *The Philosophy of Translation*.

Sigbjørn Skåden is a Sámi writer from northern Norway. His most recent novel, the bilingual Sámi–Norwegian *Backwoods Fable* (*Láŋtdievvá / Planterhaug*), was published in 2025.

CONTRIBUTORS

Mia Spangenberg translates from Finnish, Swedish and German into English. Forthcoming translations include works for adults and children by Pirkko Saisio and Maija Hurme.

Inuuteq Storch is a Kalaallit photographer and visual artist who represented Denmark at the 60th Venice Biennale. Upcoming solo exhibitions include Kunsten, Denmark; Bonnefanten, Netherlands; and the Hasselblad Foundation, Sweden.

Ingela Strandberg is a Swedish poet whose books include *Nattmannen*, *Ingenstans mitt segel* and *När jag var snö*. Her most recent collection, *Under sjöarna*, is published in 2026.

Espen Stueland is the author of six poetry collections, a novel, as well as essays on law, climate change, culture and literature.

Malte Tellerup is the Danish author of four novels and a poetry collection focusing on local-oriented aesthetics, land struggle and regeneration (and handball). He is currently working on two novels.

Søren Ulrik Thomsen is a Danish essayist and poet whose books include *City Slang* and *St. Kongensgade 23*.

Caroline Waight is a literary translator working from Danish, German and Norwegian. Her translations include books by Ingvild Rishøi, Caroline Albertine Minor, Asta Olivia Nordenhof and Dorthe Nors.